In Good Hands

In Good Hands

In
Good
Hands

Investigating Death,
Mystery, and the Lessons
of Broken Trust in
One Family Day Care

DAVID HECHLER

Printed in the United States of America

ISBN 979-8-9882578-0-6: Paperback
ISBN 979-8-9882578-1-3: Hardcover
ISBN 979-8-9882578-2-0: Audiobook
ISBN 978-0-9968554-1-9: eBook

Website: davidhechler.com

Subjects: True Crime—Murder—Serial Killers | Family & Relationships—Abuse—Child Abuse | Psychology—Psychopathology—Personality Disorders

Cover design: Rob Ehle
Text design: Elliott Beard

Contents

Foreword   ix
BY NICHOLAS PILEGGI

Prologue   xiii

Dramatis Personae   xv

PART I

Learning to Investigate

1	The Day Care	3
2	Paths that Cross Will Cross Again	6
3	"You Said This Could Never Happen Again"	10
4	The Day After	14
5	What About the Day Care?	15
6	"How Did You Get Through It?"	17
7	Suspicion	19
8	The Other Case	21
9	The Investigator	28

Contents

<table>
<tr><td>10</td><td>The Road to Irmo</td><td>33</td></tr>
<tr><td>11</td><td>Josh</td><td>38</td></tr>
<tr><td>12</td><td>The Polygraph</td><td>41</td></tr>
<tr><td>13</td><td>Volunteer Investigator</td><td>45</td></tr>
<tr><td>14</td><td>Under Siege</td><td>47</td></tr>
<tr><td>15</td><td>The Second Polygraph</td><td>50</td></tr>
<tr><td>16</td><td>Pushback</td><td>54</td></tr>
<tr><td>17</td><td>N.A. Romance</td><td>56</td></tr>
<tr><td>18</td><td>The Colsons</td><td>60</td></tr>
<tr><td>19</td><td>In Good Hands</td><td>63</td></tr>
<tr><td>20</td><td>Complaints</td><td>65</td></tr>
<tr><td>21</td><td>The Salve of SIDS</td><td>68</td></tr>
<tr><td>22</td><td>Notes</td><td>71</td></tr>
<tr><td>23</td><td>Shut Down</td><td>74</td></tr>
<tr><td>24</td><td>A Cry from the Heart</td><td>76</td></tr>
<tr><td>25</td><td>Homing In</td><td>78</td></tr>
<tr><td>26</td><td>Grief</td><td>79</td></tr>
<tr><td>27</td><td>Gail</td><td>81</td></tr>
<tr><td>28</td><td>An Unexpected Reply</td><td>84</td></tr>
<tr><td>29</td><td>Small Steps</td><td>87</td></tr>
<tr><td>30</td><td>The Defense</td><td>91</td></tr>
<tr><td>31</td><td>Psychology</td><td>93</td></tr>
<tr><td>32</td><td>Examinations</td><td>99</td></tr>
<tr><td>33</td><td>Valentine</td><td>102</td></tr>
<tr><td>34</td><td>Roller Coaster</td><td>105</td></tr>
<tr><td>35</td><td>Last Letter</td><td>108</td></tr>
<tr><td>36</td><td>The Deputy Solicitor</td><td>109</td></tr>
<tr><td>37</td><td>The Meeting</td><td>114</td></tr>
<tr><td>38</td><td>Depositions</td><td>118</td></tr>
<tr><td>39</td><td>Experts</td><td>120</td></tr>
<tr><td>40</td><td>Coroners</td><td>122</td></tr>
</table>

Contents

41	Tears of Rage	124
42	The Politics of Prosecution	128
43	Arrested	131
44	The Defense Team	133
45	Ready or Not	137

PART II
Burdens of Proof

46	Playing the Angles	145
47	Opening Statements	148
48	Laying the Groundwork	150
49	Asher Maier	152
50	The Loyal Parent	156
51	Parade of Doctors	158
52	On the Defensive	163
53	Complications	167
54	Parents on the Stand	170
55	Missy Daniel	173
56	Fake SIDS	174
57	SLED on Trial	179
58	A Shaky Start	182
59	The Big Man	184
60	Expert for the Defense	191
61	"My Whole Family Is a Victim"	194
62	Normal	209
63	The Defense Rests	211
64	The Last Word	223
65	Closing Arguments	226
66	Deliberations	234
67	Verdict	242

68	Aftermath	247
69	Second Thoughts	252
70	Altered Lives	256
71	Not Over	264

PART III

In Whose Hands?

72	Visiting Day	277
73	Backstory	280
74	Who Is Gail Cutro?	284
75	What About Josh?	292
76	The Barfields and the Cutros	299
77	The Hallmans' Story	309
78	A Third Opinion	318
79	The Quiet One	323
80	Simple and Calm	333
81	Odd Logic	337
82	The Protector	342
83	Attention	349
84	A Theory	356
85	Denial	368
86	Thinking Like an Investigator	375
	Afterword	379
	Appendix: Interviews with Two Experts	383
	Notes on Sources	409
	Selected Bibliography	411
	Acknowledgments	413
	About the Author	415

Foreword

When two infants died in an Irmo, South Carolina, family day care within nine months, pathologists determined they were the victims of SIDS—sudden infant death syndrome. It seemed like a tragic coincidence, and it might have been dismissed as just that if not for the state police's newly formed Child Fatalities Department. This innovative unit, created two months before the second death, was designed to ensure that all fatalities of children under 18 were properly investigated. And it soon demonstrated why it was needed.

When the department's leader, Lt. Patsy Habben, began investigating, she discovered that the first death had never even been been looked into. And without an investigation that ruled out all other possibilities, it didn't meet the definition of SIDS. As she led the inquiry into the second death, she learned that between the two fatalities another baby who attended the day care had suffered a brain injury. He lived, but doctors found he'd been violently shaken. This alone meant that Child Fatalities was now leading a child abuse investigation.

Just like that, Habben found that her first big case now had three potential victims. And the unlikely suspects seemed to be Josh and Gail Cutro, the church-going couple who together ran the day care.

David Hechler's superb book takes us through the complex probe that ensued. The first death was never investigated because two counties were confused about jurisdiction. The case involving the shaking was complicated. The baby's mother was a recovering drug addict who had previously had a child removed from her care. And when the Cutros felt investigators were suspicious of *them*, they falsely told the day care parents that the mother had abused her other child. Further complicating matters, the shaking case drew the attention of the sheriff's department and social workers, but they came to opposite conclusions. The social workers thought the mother was responsible, while the police suspected it was one (or both) of the Cutros.

In Good Hands has enough twists and turns to make you wonder *what* to believe. Is this a tale about SIDS, a medical mystery that we still don't understand? Or is it about murder? And if these were murders, what could be the motive? In Irmo, where the Cutros had plenty of supporters, the notion that it was homicide just didn't compute. Members of the church the Cutros attended rallied around them, and so did the parents who continued to drop off their children—even after the second death. They couldn't fathom that these people could have harmed children. After all, the Cutros had three children of their own.

Rarely does a book take the reader along through the details and intricacies of such an investigation. Hechler talks to everyone: the investigators, the prosecutors, the defense lawyers, jurors, parents, psychologists, and, finally, Josh and Gail Cutro. I've been a fan of Hechler's for years and, once again, he not only includes all the information his readers need to weigh the evidence for themselves, he makes us feel we were there through the investigation and the trial that follows.

When the trial is finally over, Hechler doesn't end the book there. He goes back and does the work most writers don't. He tells us what we should know about these people that wasn't allowed into evidence in court. What did some parents see that led them to withdraw their children from the day care? Why did other parents defend the Cutros and only remove their children when a court shut the day care down? And what was *really* going on in that home? The answers may lead some readers to conclude that prosecutors went after the wrong person when they tried Gail Cutro, who had never been in trouble with the law, and not Josh, who had.

Finally, Hechler's book does something that's rare in journalism. Not content to simply point out the dangers, the author also focuses on potential solutions by explaining that home day cares, by far the most popular venues, are also virtually unregulated. No government agencies are monitoring the quality of care these children receive, so it's up to parents to protect their own. The last achievement of *In Good Hands* is that it informs parents how to help make their children safer.

Nicholas Pileggi
APRIL 2023

Prologue

Every week millions of children in the United States attend day care. How do parents know that their children are safe?

The dangers were underscored by a series of articles in the Minneapolis *Star Tribune* on day care safety that won a Pulitzer Prize in 2013. The reporters found that dozens of Minnesota children died in day care during the previous five years—nearly all of them in home-based settings. The newspaper also noted that state regulators weren't in a position to prevent these deaths. In fact, they weren't even aware that these numbers represented an alarming jump from previous years.

The key for parents is to recognize two things. The government is not monitoring day care. Parents have to undertake this job themselves. And second, parents are in a much better position to judge a day care after they select it than they were when they were choosing one. Many assume that the big task is interviewing caregivers and picking one. But afterward is when the real work should begin.

This book focuses on a true story about one day care that parents thought was exceptional. It was neat and clean, and the caregivers were a married, middle-class couple who were active in their church and had three kids of their own. The setting was a suburb outside of Columbia, South Carolina. The mothers who dropped off their children every morning were mostly in their early thirties. Many of them were college graduates, and they worked in a variety of fields. They all visited the day care before they chose it. Many of them had visited several others before they'd settled on this one.

There was nothing about the woman who ran it that alarmed them. On the contrary, she seemed sweet and dedicated, if a little reserved. Not the type of person you expect to stand trial for murder. But she did.

Many people in her community were convinced that the prosecutors who targeted her were completely off base. Among her strongest supporters were some of the parents who sent their children to her home—and stopped doing so only when the state shut it down.

The purpose of this book isn't merely to recount an intriguing mystery, even though it featured plot twists worthy of the best fiction. (In this respect, it may remind some readers of the popular podcast "Serial," which also brought to life an old murder case that had never been fully explored.) And the point is not merely to pass along a few tips on day care. It's to convince parents and grandparents that no one else will monitor the safety of their children, and to arm them with the knowledge to do the job themselves.

Finally, the Appendix at the end of this book features interviews with two experts who offer a wealth of practical advice. The second expert also notes that the lessons learned, and the skills acquired, from focusing on day care can pay huge dividends later in life, when you may be looking for a nursing home, or an assisted living facility, or a rehab center for your own parents.

Dramatis Personae

Extended Cutro Family
Gail Cutro
Josh Cutro
Joshua Cutro (son)
Kira Cutro (daughter)
Lara Cutro (daughter)
Pat Hallman (Gail's mother)
Harold Hallman (Gail's father)
Frances Barfield Cutro
    (Josh's mother)
Joe Cutro (Josh's father)

Families of Children
Lindy Colson
Gary Colson
Parker Colson (b.8/6/92; d.1/4/93)

Missy Daniel
Davis Daniel
Ashlan Daniel (b.4/22/93; d.9/9/93)

Catherine Maier
Chad Maier
Asher Maier (b.2/5/93;
    hospitalized 6/23/93)

Principal Criminal Investigators
Patsy Habben (SLED)
Richard Hunton (SLED)
Tim Stephenson (Irmo P.D.)
Jay Phillips (Lex. Sheriff's Dept)

Prosecutors
Johnny Gasser
Scarlett Wilson

Defense Lawyers
Wes Kirkland
Lisa McPherson
Thom Neal

Principal DSS Employees
Gary Kirkbride (Richland DSS)
Mary Landrum (Lex. DSS)
Daylene McDuffie (Lex. DSS)
Sherry Driggers (State Day Care Licensing)

SC Pathologists
Dr. James Reynolds
Dr. Beverly Daniel
Dr. Sandra Conradi

Out-of-State Defense Experts
Dr. John Smialek (MD)
Dr. John Pless (IN)

Out-of-State Prosecution Experts
Dr. Janice Ophoven (MN)
Dr. John Emery (England)
Dr. Enid Gilbert-Barness (FL)
Dr. Randall Alexander (Iowa)
Dr. Wilbur Smith (Iowa)

Additional Witnesses
Rob Brown
Renee Barefoot
Linda Bass
Rose Bozard
Ramona Bowers

Psychologists
Dr. Selman Watson (evaluated Josh and Gail)
Dr. Geoffrey McKee (evaluated Gail)

PART I

Learning to Investigate

Gail and Josh Cutro. Courtesy of *The State*, Columbia, South Carolina.

1

The Day Care

Missy Daniel had just arrived to pick up her daughter from day care in Irmo, South Carolina, when she saw the ambulance in her rearview mirror. She hated ambulances. She'd hated them for as long as she could remember. They made her nervous—the same way fire engines did. Like her mother, who checked her front door fifteen times to make sure it was locked before leaving the house, Missy was an inveterate worrier. She had no doubt that her little girl would follow suit.

But the ambulance rolled past the house from which Missy was about to fetch four-month-old Ashlan and continued down the block. Its pace was leisurely, Missy noted, as she breathed a little sigh of relief and parked the car.

An attractive woman with blue eyes and blonde hair, the twenty-seven-year-old mother let her mind drift as she walked toward the house. There was still plenty of time to go shopping. It was only 2:40—that was the beauty of her job. She worked only two hours a day, four days a week. All she did was answer the phones while her mother took a long lunch break from work. Missy didn't earn a whole lot more than she paid for day care, but she wasn't doing it primarily for the money. The new mother was doing it just to get out of the house and have some semblance of a normal life, if only for 8 hours a week.

Earlier on that day she would never forget, September 9, 1993, before dropping off her daughter at noon, Missy had taken Ashlan to the photography studio for her first portrait. The baby had looked adorable—fat cheeks glowing—but Missy had gone through a half-dozen outfits before she'd finally found one that still fit. The child ate like a horse; it was definitely time to go shopping.

Missy was abruptly shaken from her musings when a large man suddenly emerged from the house. It was Josh Cutro (pronounced KOO-trow), who shared child care duties with his wife, Gail Cutro. Even if Missy hadn't been the nervous type, she would have known from his pained expression that something was wrong. Josh began waving his arm, but Missy quickly realized he wasn't waving at her. He was looking past her, up the road.

Missy froze. "Is it Ashlan?" she asked, feeling a tightness in her throat. The ambulance had doubled back and was parking when he answered.

"Yeah."

Missy waited for the rest: Ashlan fell . . . she cut herself . . . she's unconscious. But there was only silence.

Josh began sobbing as he turned back toward the house. When Missy hurried to follow, he stopped her in her tracks.

"Don't come in here!" he barked before disappearing into the house. She stood there in shock for several moments, then she remembered the ambulance. Where were the paramedics? What were they doing?

She turned and watched in horror as they slowly removed equipment. What was taking so long? "Hurry!" she shrieked. "Get in there!" At last they walked past her into the house, and she collapsed on the lawn. A short time later Josh came back out. "There was nothing we could do," he said.

Within minutes Missy's mother arrived from work to embrace her hysterical child. When she understood that her daughter hadn't actually *seen* Ashlan, Sissy Rangely raced into the house, brushing aside resistance at the door. No force on earth was going to keep her from her first grandchild.

After she had confirmed the worst, Sissy Rangely took her daughter to her own house across the street. It was from there, the house in which Missy had endured her own sometimes turbulent childhood, that she had to call her husband, Davis. A secretary at South Carolina Electric and Gas, where he worked, paged him.

"Ashlan's dead! Ashlan's dead!" Missy screamed again and again.

"Where are you at?" Davis demanded. She told him and he dropped the phone, as if a surge of high voltage had just spiked through it. "Something's wrong with the baby," he told his boss, refusing to say—or believe—more. He found the colleague who had driven him to work.

Slumped in the passenger seat of the Ford van, the thirty-eight-year-old electrician tried not to think. The strength had left his powerful six-foot-five-inch frame, and the "Pancho Villa" moustache beneath his curly brown hair emphasized his downturned features. A man of few words under ordinary circumstances, he was silent during most of the half-hour trip. Inside he felt numb.

For Davis and Missy Daniel, the hours that followed were a blur. At some point they were aware that a group of people had arrived to comfort Josh and Gail Cutro. From across the street, the Daniels could see fifteen or twenty people surrounding the couple in their yard, commiserating. Then a group of them, including the Cutros, drifted over to pay Davis and Missy a visit.

Someone began talking about sudden infant death syndrome. They all seemed convinced that SIDS was the cause of Ashlan's death, and they wanted to help the Daniels work through their pain. A woman who introduced herself as Eve Powell, Gail's therapist, told Missy, "I want you to get on medication." She gave Missy a number to call for the tranquilizers, and suggested that Missy make an appointment to see her.

Later, Gail Cutro approached the couple. "This should never have happened to me again," Gail told them, "since it already happened to me once. I'm sorry."

To the Daniels, it was all unreal. How could the child who was almost never out of their sight, who had only been in day care eight hours a week for eight weeks, who had been quite literally the picture of health at the photographer's studio that very morning . . . now be dead? It wasn't possible. Yet, these people—these strangers—insisted not only that it was, but that they knew the cause.

Who were these people with all the answers? And why were they consoling the *Cutros* when the *Daniels* were the ones who had lost a baby?

The Daniels didn't say any of this. They were in shock, barely capable of speaking. It would take time for them to sort out the thoughts and feelings that coursed through them that day. But simmering beneath their confusion and despair, even then, was anger.

They were angry with themselves. They felt almost unbearable guilt that they had failed to protect what was most precious in their lives. And they were angry with the Cutros. How could they have let this happen?

2

Paths that Cross Will Cross Again

As Patsy Habben willed her body out of bed and into the shower, she was glad that she'd packed the car the night before. It was at 5:30 a.m., September 9, 1993, and at least she didn't have to lug out those big boxes.

All the materials South Carolina's forty-six coroners would need were neatly stacked in the three boxes that occupied the back seat of her gray Chevy Caprice. That was the only place they would fit. The trunk was stuffed with the supplies she always took with her: medical equipment, a floodlight, a saw and ax, rain gear, and emergency food and water in case she was assigned hurricane or tornado duty. For undercover work she carried Band-Aids to hide the prominent mole on her right cheek and several caps under which she could conceal her bright blonde hair. Her Remington .870 pump-action 12-gauge shotgun rested beside a large supply of ammunition. A Smith & Wesson .38 revolver was stashed in the glove compartment.

After her shower, Habben made coffee for her husband, Ken, and fed her eleven-year-old daughter and sixteen-month-old son. Her son's sitter lived just down the block. Once she arrived, Patsy and Ken squeezed into the front seat of Patsy's car with their daughter, and then dropped the child off at Grace Christian School.

Patsy and Ken Habben were both lieutenants at the South Carolina Law Enforcement Division. That was the somewhat odd name for the state police—a name that seemed designed solely to allow everyone to call it by its acronym, SLED. Patsy, who was thirty-nine, had worked with Ken in SLED's forensics lab for fifteen years, the last thirteen as his wife. Ken, who was forty-four, was head of toxicology while Patsy had been, until recently, in charge of the serology and DNA labs.

But three months earlier she'd begun a new assignment. A law had been passed mandating that SLED supervise the investigation of all sudden and unexpected deaths of children under eighteen. It was a progressive law in keeping with South Carolina's leading role in this field. (At the time, few states in the country undertook thorough, comprehensive child death investigations; and none had been focused on this issue longer, or had a better system in place, than South Carolina.) SLED administrators had responded to the state's new law by creating the Child Fatalities Department, which Patsy Habben had been asked to direct.

The task had proved even more daunting than she'd imagined. She'd done some research and couldn't find any states that had departments like it, so it wasn't simply a matter of collecting a few training manuals and putting together one of her own. It was more like inventing a discipline from whole cloth. And then teaching it not only to the three investigators who reported to her, but to the agencies around the state with which they had to work: from local police and sheriff's departments to pathologists and county coroners.

That was where the boxes in the back seat came in. Patsy Habben was on her way to the annual coroners' conference, where she would introduce herself and her agents to the coroners from the state's forty-six counties. It would be her department's first public appearance. She would distribute the three boxes of protocols she had just finished writing and explain that the new law required the coroners to fill out and return the forms each time a child died in their jurisdictions.

As head of toxicology, Ken was also going to the conference. Instead of driving the 10 miles to SLED headquarters, on the outskirts of Columbia, they would drive 110 miles to Charleston. Ken was at the wheel, and Patsy hadn't been this relaxed since she'd started the new job.

———

About 100 people attended the conference, including the coroners and assorted professionals who worked with them. Dressed in a conservative suit that concealed the Glock automatic strapped to her waist, Patsy Habben introduced her three investigators. Then she told the coroners what the new law required, and why they were crucial to its success.

She had a strong background in science, but she wasn't there to show it off. South Carolina didn't require its coroners to have medical training. At the time, in fact, they didn't even need a high school diploma. Some had prepared with years of training, a few were doctors, and about a third were funeral directors. Patsy Habben's protocol was designed to reach them all: simple, direct, no fancy medical terms. The point was to help them record information at death scenes, not perform emergency brain surgery.

When the conference broke for lunch, Ken and Patsy went to a café downstairs. Before they could order, a woman Patsy recognized from the conference asked to join them. Linda Bass was a nurse who specialized in bereavement support—particularly for parents whose children had died of SIDS. She worked at the Lexington County Medical Center, not far from where the Habbens lived. Bass was a perky woman of forty-three with a round face, clear blue eyes, and closely cropped brown hair flecked with silver. Until Habben's presentation, she'd never heard of the new child fatality law. Now that she had, she could barely contain her excitement.

Linda Bass felt that the law could be tremendously valuable in the diagnosis of SIDS cases. As she often had occasion to explain, sudden infant death syndrome was one of the great medical mysteries. Although it was only named in the 1960s, it was described as far back as the Old Testament. But modern medicine had learned little about its cause. In fact, the only way coroners could arrive at the diagnosis was by eliminating all other possibilities. They were justified in listing SIDS as the cause of death only when an apparently healthy child between one month and one year of age died suddenly and unexpectedly, and an autopsy, a medical history, and a thorough investigation revealed no other explanation. In 1993, it was the leading cause of death of babies under one, claiming around 6,000 victims a year in the United States alone.

But, as Bass knew, sometimes cases were called SIDS before all possibilities had been explored. In poor rural counties, where money for autopsies was scarce and pathologists qualified to perform them sometimes scarcer, a coroner might label a death SIDS without an autopsy. And local police did not relish questioning parents or delving into a child's medical history, so sometimes cases were not thoroughly investigated. Bass hoped that the new law would change all that.

She poured out her enthusiasm for the new Child Fatalities Department. She would do everything in her power to assist them. In turn, she hoped that Habben and her colleagues would tell parents of apparent SIDS victims about the services Bass offered. She ran the only support group for SIDS parents in the state. She also ran the only group for child-care providers who had experienced SIDS deaths. Glancing at her watch, Bass thanked Habben for listening and hurried back to the conference.

Patsy Habben was impressed. The woman seemed genuine in her desire to help, and she was certainly enthusiastic. The Child Fatalities Department needed all the friends it could get. Habben knew, even then, they would have little trouble making enemies.

Since Ken had driven on the trip out, Patsy took the wheel for the drive home. She hadn't been driving an hour when her pager beeped. It was SLED, and it was a "code one," which meant call immediately. She called headquarters, and that was how she learned that a baby had just died in a day care.

Habben directed the investigation while she drove. First she spoke with Irmo's police chief, who had just returned from the scene. He described the day care. The dead baby was four months old and was one of nine children under care. The day care owner's husband had attempted CPR, but when the emergency medical technicians took over, the child was dead. The chief had called the Richland County coroner's office, only to learn that the coroner couldn't go to the scene because he was at the conference that Habben had just left. His assistant said he couldn't go either. Two Irmo police officers were in the home now; what did Habben want them to do?

Patsy Habben fired off instructions. Take photographs of the residence. Collect the bedding on which the child had slept, the last bottle it had taken, and the trash. Secure them as evidence and drop them at SLED. She wanted the names, dates of birth, and Social Security numbers of the day care owner and all workers, and the name and date of birth of the baby. She also wanted an account of all activities at the day care that day, and a detailed statement from the last person who had seen the baby alive.

A few minutes later Patsy Habben was on the phone with one of the officers. The dead little girl was Ashlan Daniel, age four-and-a-half months. The day care was located at 1101 Chadford Road, and the Daniel baby was apparently the second child to die there. The officers had collected everything. There'd been only one hitch; the husband had insisted on speaking to his lawyer before relinquishing the trash. But in the end he did.

Habben had been scribbling notes in her Day-Timer. Once she reached home, there were more beeps and calls and hastily scratched notes. And there was dinner to cook, and a bath to give, and bedtime stories to read. So much for her "easy day."

Still, it hadn't been one of her harder days. Her new job was proving plenty challenging. This case sounded like routine SIDS. Except for one thing. That night, just before she went to sleep, something gnawed at the edge of her consciousness. The Irmo officer had said this was the second death at the day care.

3

"You Said This Could Never Happen Again"

When Linda Bass returned to the conference after her lunch with Patsy Habben, it was *her* turn to address the coroners. She wanted them to understand, above all, that parents of children who die of SIDS deserve compassionate investigations. If the coroners doubted this, they had only to listen to her clients.

One night a month Bass absorbed their pain. What she'd learned is that investigations often dragged on for week after anguishing week. The stress on the families was enormous. Inevitably, parents felt guilty, even after Bass had explained that no one is to blame for SIDS and no one can prevent it. Still, they blamed themselves—and, all too often, each other. Without support groups like the ones she ran, their feelings of depression and isolation often led to divorce.

Bass told the coroners that those who arrive at the death scene first are often the most important contacts. She emphasized the importance of sensitivity—particularly when speaking to families about autopsies. The need for one must be explained to the parents without a hint of accusation. She herself tells parents: "Nobody wants to know why this happened more than you. And the only way we're ever going to find that out is for the autopsy to be done."

There wasn't time during the hour Bass had been allotted to delve deeply into research, but she did note that a study found the annual number of SIDS deaths in South Carolina had ranged from seventy-seven to ninety-one. She wrapped up by distributing handouts that included her contact information.

———

It was about 5:30 by the time Bass got home. The blinking light on her answering machine signaled a half-dozen messages. The first was from Gail Cutro, and there was desperation in her voice.

"You said this could never happen again! Well, it's happened! What do we do now?!"

Bass knew immediately what she was talking about. Eight months earlier a baby had died in the Cutros' day care. That was how Bass and Gail had met. The infant's parents had brought Gail with them to Bass's support group. With Bass's encouragement, Gail had contacted other women who ran day care services where children had died of SIDS, and Bass had formed a separate support group for them. She had told Gail what she told the others: "SIDS rarely, if ever, happens twice in the same place. If you get bucked off a horse, the only way you can ride again is to get back on."

Now Gail Cutro had been thrown again. And Linda Bass was nearly as shaken as Gail. She, too, wondered how this could be.

The next message was also from Gail. She really needed to talk. Would Linda please call as soon as she returned? There were three more messages from Gail and one from Josh Cutro. Bass took a deep breath and dialed.

Josh answered; a moment later Gail picked up the extension. As they started to recount the day's events, both began to cry. Bass told them she'd be there as soon as she could.

A divorced mother with an eleven-year-old son, Bass first had to attend to other matters. After she and her son ate dinner, she called a friend and dropped him off. Then she drove to the other side of New Friarsgate, the Irmo subdivision where she and the Cutros both lived.

Josh and Gail Cutro were sitting in the living room of their three-bedroom home. It was still hot, and they were dressed in their customary shorts, sandals, and short-sleeved shirts. As usual, Gail, who was thirty-three, looked a little more ragged than Josh. Her hair, which was cut short, was shapeless. Josh, who was a year older than his wife, was much more fastidious about his appearance. His hair was also short, but always well groomed. His clothes always looked neat, and the strong scent of cologne filled the air around him.

About a half-dozen people were still there—Gail Cutro's mother, a few day care parents, members of the Cutros' church. Earlier, several day care parents had brought over food they'd prepared for the family. As the Cutros sat with their visitors, their large bodies seemed to sag under the weight of the day's events.

When Linda Bass arrived, Gail did most of the talking. Under ordinary circumstances, Josh was garrulous and emotional and dominated conversations. Gail was reserved, and it was often difficult to guess what she was feeling. On this occasion, however, she talked a great deal, which didn't surprise Bass. It was Gail, after all, with whom she had the relationship. Gail was the one who attended the monthly support-group meetings at which she bared her grief.

As tears welled in Gail's reddened eyes, Bass tried to answer her questions. Yes, statistically it *was* highly unlikely that a SIDS case could happen to her again. But not as unlikely for Gail, Bass now suggested, as it was for a family. "Families don't usually have more than two or three children, so the chances of its occurring again in the same family are almost nil. But because you're a baby-sitter, and in the course of your career you've taken care of as many babies as you have, while it still would be rare for a person to have this happen twice, I suppose it could."

Josh and Gail acted as though they were convinced that Ashlan Daniel had died of SIDS. Though Bass knew that a final determination would require an autopsy, toxicology tests, and an investigation, she, too, had little doubt.

"What happens to us now?" Gail asked. "And what are people going to think?"

There were two big differences between what they'd experienced after the first death, and what they could expect now—differences that the Cutros were just beginning to grasp. A second death was bound to arouse suspicion, even if there was no evidence of foul play. More important, when the first child had died, there hadn't *been* an investigation. The Child Fatalities Department hadn't existed. No police officers had come to their home. This time, three had stopped by on the first day.

Josh seemed disconcerted. Anxiety permeated his pale blue eyes. Bass thought he was feeling protective of Gail and was worried that people would presume they had done something to the baby.

She tried to be comforting and supportive. This was what crisis intervention was all about. But it was also about accepting her limits. She knew that she couldn't "fix" the Cutros' crisis. All she could hope to do was make it easier for them to deal with.

So Bass told them about *her* day. She told them that they should expect a thorough investigation—it was mandated by a new law—and she'd had lunch with the woman who would head it. Everything the Cutros had told her about the investigation so far corresponded to the procedures Patsy Habben had described in Charleston. And Bass had no problem with any of it. Even though they might feel accused, she told the Cutros, "there's nobody that's making accusations, because nobody knows what happened." On the other hand, she could understand the investigators' questions: "The logical thing is to think there's no way it can be SIDS, because lightning doesn't strike twice in the same place." They could expect a visit from Patsy Habben or one of her investigators, and another from the Department of Social Services, which, as the agency that regulated day care, would have to launch its own investigation.

Josh and Gail responded as they would so often in the coming weeks and months. Josh grew agitated and directed his anger at those he felt were persecuting him. He acted as though it was an affront that anyone would suspect them of harming a child. Hadn't they been caring for children for years? Didn't they have three of their own upstairs? Gail sobbed quietly and expressed concern not about her own circumstances, but about others she thought were also suffering. She told Bass about her brief encounter with Missy and Davis Daniel. She was worried about them. She vividly remembered Gary and Lindy Colson—the couple whose child had previously died in her home—immediately following *their* loss. Couldn't Bass do something for the Daniels, as she had for the Colsons?

It was so like Gail, Bass mused, to focus on others in greater need. Josh's reaction was certainly understandable; but Gail was able to put her own discomfort aside and empathize with the people most affected by this tragedy. It was confirmation of what Bass had long since concluded: Gail was a very special lady.

Bass picked up the phone and dialed Missy's mother, but the conversation didn't last long. Sissy Rangely explained that her daughter was in no shape to talk to anyone. Bass conveyed her condolences and said she'd call back the next day.

She'd been at the Cutros for about an hour. There wasn't much more to say. The Cutros would need time to heal from this new loss. It would be especially hard for Gail, who had only just begun to recover from the shock of the first death.

As Bass drove to her neighbor's to pick up her son, she thought about her strange day. The conference, the revelations about the new law, the lunch with Patsy Habben . . . and now this. In less than twelve hours she had not only heard a lecture about the new Child Fatalities Department, she was seeing it in action.

4

The Day After

Ashlan Daniel died on a Thursday. On Friday, the Cutro day care was open for business. Most of the parents dropped off their children. But Ramona Bowers didn't send Tate, who was six months old. She stayed home with him instead.

The day before had been the most harrowing day of her life. An elementary school teacher, Bowers was still at the school when Gail Cutro called to say that a baby had stopped breathing. Gail told her it wasn't Tate, but Bowers didn't believe her. School had let out, and she jumped in her car and sped to the Cutros' house, a half-mile away, with images of his lifeless body flashing in her head.

She ran in the house, but he wasn't in the small bed where she usually found him. Frantically rushing from room to room, she found Gail sitting in a chair in the kitchen, muttering that her therapist had said this couldn't happen again. Then Josh walked in, sobbing, with Tate in his arms.

Josh put his arms around Bowers, and then she was crying too, with relief, as they hugged with Tate between them. But all Bowers could think at that moment, as the big man squeezed her shoulders, was: "Don't squoosh my baby!"

Bowers hung around to see if there was anything she could do, and Gail asked her to call the other parents and tell them to pick up their children. She was too upset, Gail said. After Bowers had made the calls, she took Tate home, then returned several hours later with a meat tray and spent another hour with the distraught couple.

But when morning arrived, she wasn't ready to drop off her son. She just couldn't do it. She'd questioned Josh about his ability to carry on without a break. But Josh had been adamant. The parents wanted them to stay open—needed them to, he'd said. And Gail's mother was there. She'd volunteered to step in for as long as they needed.

Over the weekend, Bowers thought about it and overcame her qualms. "Tate's always been well cared for," she thought. Bowers and her husband attended the same church as the Cutros—they'd been in Sunday school class together. "You need to be supportive," Bowers told herself. So on Monday, Bowers dropped Tate off.

He was just fine.

5

What About the Day Care?

Like the parents who used the Cutro day care, Patsy Habben had to decide whether the children were safe. If they weren't, she would then have to figure out what she could do about that. But first she had to assess the situation, and she soon found herself trying to unravel a confusing jumble of information.

The first blitz came from Richland County Coroner Frank Barron. When Barron had returned from the conference in Charleston and learned what had happened, he'd immediately contacted his good friend Sissy Rangely, Missy Daniel's mother, and assured her that the death of her grandchild would be thoroughly investigated. The next morning he got right to work.

It wasn't only because he knew the dead child's family. Barron was a man who took his job seriously. Appointed to fill the vacant office of Richland County Coroner in 1978, he'd been elected at four-year intervals ever since. Though he was not a medical doctor (he made his living in real estate), he was an intelligent, inquisitive man who had attended countless trainings over the years to better prepare him to do a good job.

By the time he called Patsy Habben that morning, he'd done some checking on the Cutro day care. There had, indeed, been a previous death in that home, the coroner told Lt. Habben. The original records were in the Lexington County coroner's office instead of his in Richland County because of a mix-up in jurisdiction. Also, Ashlan Daniel's death might actually be the *third* in the Cutro day care. Two months earlier the Lexington County Sheriff's Department had called to tell him that they were looking at "another case" in that home. (Barron would later learn that this was a serious injury rather than a death, and, since coroners only investigate fatalities, he'd received no updates on the matter.)

Frank Baron thought it highly unlikely that these events had occurred at the Cutro day care by mere coincidence. It seemed much more likely that they were the result of foul play.

Suddenly Patsy Habben's investigation of a "garden variety" SIDS death was beginning to look like something very different. An autopsy of Ashlan Daniel was scheduled for later that day, Barron continued. Dr. Jim Reynolds, head of pathology at Richland Memorial Hospital, would handle it himself. Barron was sending his assistant to observe.

Just before he ended the call, Barron had one suggestion he wanted to leave with Habben. Try to get the Cutros to take lie-detector tests.

By the time she hung up, Habben's synapses were jumping. In a matter of minutes the workload on this case had tripled. She took a mental inventory of the investigation so far. The Irmo Police Department was investigating Ashlan Daniel's death and had completed what seemed to be a thorough examination of the death scene. An autopsy had been ordered. So far, so good. But what about these other two children?

Over the next few days, while she worked on the other cases the Child Fatalities Department was investigating, Habben chipped away at the day care case. She obtained copies of the coroner and autopsy reports on the first child who died in the Cutros' home. The little boy, Parker Colson, had been just shy of five months old on January 4, 1993. The Lexington coroner had said that the cause was SIDS, but another diagnosis had been typed in and crossed out. Habben could just make out the words: "Acute bronchopneumonia, bilateral."

The coroner had interviewed the child's pediatrician, who said Parker had been in good health, though he did have some nasal congestion for which the doctor had prescribed medication. The coroner had also interviewed the Cutros, who told him that that the child had seemed a little congested and had slept a bit longer than usual, but they hadn't noticed anything else out of the ordinary.

The only unusual finding was a positive lung culture, which was why the pathologist called it pneumonia. She hadn't been sure that this was a true pathogen, however, noting that it was "only mild to moderate," and had resolved to consult colleagues. A month later the pathologist filed a second report in which she discounted the lung culture and amended the cause of death to SIDS.

The coroner's investigation was the only one Habben had to work with. In the confusion about jurisdiction, the case had fallen between the cracks and the police had never looked into it. It was just the sort of glitch the Child Fatalities Department was created to prevent. But the department hadn't existed eight months earlier, when Parker Colson died. So Habben's would be the first investigation by law enforcement.

And the third case? That was still a mystery. Habben hadn't been able to learn anything.

What worried the investigator, and weighed on her, weren't the children who were already gone. It was the children they'd left behind. The day care hadn't closed for even one day after Ashlan Daniel's death—or Parker Colson's. If both were victims of SIDS, no one was to blame. The day care might be perfectly safe. But what if it wasn't—what if someone in that house was hurting children? That was the thought that made Habben feel she couldn't move fast enough.

6

"How Did You Get Through It?"

Lindy Colson was at work when a friend called to tell her that a fleet of cars had gathered at the Cutro house the day before. Lindy called Linda Bass to find out what happened, then she called Gail Cutro. After a brief conversation, she decided to drive over. Lindy figured that if *she* was this upset, Gail must be devastated.

The last time Lindy had driven this route was the day her son Parker died. Suddenly it didn't feel as though eight months had passed. But she was determined to put her own feelings aside. Gail needed her. Since the tragedy, they'd grown closer than ever. Among other things, they'd worked together to raise money for SIDS research.

When she arrived, Lindy Colson spent some time consoling Gail Cutro as best she could. Then she took a deep breath and crossed the street to talk to the Daniels. When she rang the bell, Sissy Rangeley opened the door. Lindy introduced herself and started to explain that she, too, had lost a baby to SIDS. Taking Lindy to be another emissary from the previous day's group, Rangeley cut her off.

"Well, we don't know *what* it was," she announced in a tone that precluded further discussion. Lindy didn't know what to say. After an awkward moment, she conveyed her condolences, then turned around and walked back toward the Cutros'. But before she'd made it all the way, Missy and Davis Daniel suddenly emerged from the house and followed.

Josh and Gail Cutro, who had been watching through their window, came out to greet Davis and Missy. Then they introduced them to Lindy, and the five of them sat on the porch steps.

"My son Parker died of SIDS here last January," Lindy told the Daniels.

Missy glanced at Davis, her brow furrowed in confusion. "But . . . but we thought it was Josh and Gail's *own* baby," she stammered.

There was an uncomfortable pause, which Lindy broke with small talk. The brief burst of animation faded from Missy's face, and Lindy could see that she was in shock. So was her husband. But Lindy knew that they needed to talk to someone who understood what they were going through, and she knew that the questions would come when they were ready. So she continued chatting until Missy finally managed to get the words out.

"How did you get through it?"

"You just have to take it hour by hour, minute by minute," Lindy told her.

There were so many things she could have said. She could have told Missy how isolated she and her husband Gary felt after Parker died—isolated from the world and from each other. How they merely "coexisted, like two roommates in a house with nothing but the house to come home to," as she would later put it. How for months they weren't really living so much as mimicking life. They ate dinner in front of the TV, but they couldn't watch any show in which a baby appeared. One particularly popular commercial featured cute little babies with wings who sat inside tires that floated in the clouds. "You think about that now and it's no big deal," Lindy would recall years later, but at the time it was a knife in the heart.

Or she could have told them that for months she and Gary had no desire to go out. And on the rare occasions when they did go out, the results usually made them wish they hadn't. Like the steakhouse they tried about a month after Parker died, where the laughter of the other diners felt like an assault. It got so loud in his head, Gary later complained, that it hurt his ears. Or the trip to the state fairgrounds about five months later, where Lindy noticed "everybody had babies out in strollers—and it like to kill us."

Yes, there was plenty she could have told the Daniels. But they would find out soon enough. She wasn't there to describe the living hell that awaited them. She was there to make them feel better, to help them "get through it."

So she kept it simple. She told them about Linda Bass's SIDS support group that she attended the third Thursday of every month. It helped her to sit and talk to people who knew exactly what she was feeling because they'd felt the same things. The next one was less than a week away. She would look for them there.

7

Suspicion

Missy and Davis Daniel were reeling from shock and were struggling to process what had happened. Their encounter with Lindy Colson had been another jolt. They were grateful for her advice, and the support group sounded worth a try, but they were astonished to learn that it was *her* baby who had died in the Cutro day care.

The Daniels had known that a baby had died there. The Cutros had said so themselves when Missy and Davis had interviewed them before enrolling Ashlan. Gail had said, "We had a baby die of SIDS," and then burst into tears. It was obviously an extremely emotional issue, and the Daniels did not ask questions. But it never occurred to them that the baby was not her own. "*We had a baby*," she'd said—not *one of the babies we cared for*. And her tears made it clear that this was a personal tragedy. Or so they'd inferred.

Other impressions were also discordant. The day after Ashlan died, Gail told the Daniels everything that had happened that day. She said she'd last checked on Ashlan half an hour before discovering her. But Missy reminded Davis that Gail had told them at the interview that she checked on the babies constantly. When Gail finished recounting all she could remember, she told Missy: "I'm just glad that I'm the one that found her, and that I could take this burden from you." Though Missy couldn't explain precisely why, something about this really bothered her.

What bothered the Daniels most of all, however, was what Gail had said about putting Ashlan down for a nap. She'd said the baby was sitting in her car seat, grew sleepy after a while, and Gail moved her to her portacrib for a nap. That did not sound at all like their child.

To say that Ashlan wasn't much of a napper would have been a gross understatement. She didn't take many and she didn't go easily. She fought sleep. Missy and Davis had to walk her around, or put her in the stroller, or drive her around the neighborhood. Sometimes they did all three. In four months, they couldn't recall a single instance when she'd gone down without a fuss. What was more, she'd already taken a nap that day—not long before Missy took her to the day care. Yet, Gail made it sound as though she'd drifted off without a peep.

———

A few days after their meeting with Lindy Colson, Missy and Davis Daniel were greeted by another visitor bearing information. This time it was the Richland coroner, Frank Barron, who stopped by in deference to his friendship with Missy's mother. But it wasn't merely a condolence call. Having done some investigating, and having shared his insights with Patsy Habben, the coroner felt he owed it to the parents—and to Missy's mother—to advise them as well.

Frank Barron put into words something that the Daniels up to then hadn't dared voice, even to themselves: the possibility of foul play. At this stage, it was almost beyond their capacity to comprehend. But Barron told them that the odds of two children dying of SIDS nine months apart at the same day care were astronomical. He wasn't sure what was going on, but his gut feeling said "there's something wrong here."

Something *wrong*? For the devastated couple, the phrase was too weak. There's something *wrong* when you must bury your infant, your first-born, before her life has even begun. There's something *terrifying* when you're told the killer was a mysterious disease that, without warning, strikes babies who appear to be perfectly healthy. There's something *unimaginable* when you're told that it could be murder, perhaps by the people you entrusted with her care.

Before the coroner left, he told the Daniels about the new law designed to ensure that the case would be thoroughly investigated. He gave them Patsy Habben's phone number and encouraged them to call her with questions. He believed that the Daniels could be important to the investigation.

8

The Other Case

Patsy Habben sat at the Formica conference table in the unadorned basement office that the Child Fatalities Department used for meetings and surveyed her guests. It was September 14, 1993—five days into her investigation—and ten cops and social workers were seated around the table along with coroner Frank Barron. All were players in this suddenly sprawling inquiry.

Habben had only been running the department for two months, but she knew this was no ordinary investigation. You don't usually find yourself examining three cases involving three distinct events (that occurred within months of each other) all rolled into one. That's why she'd called this meeting. She needed to hear from the investigators who had looked at the pieces.

There wouldn't have been so much miscommunication if it hadn't been for the crazy way the county line dividing Richland and Lexington zigzagged through Irmo. As a result, the Cutros and one set of parents who had lost a child lived in Richland, while the other set of parents lived in Lexington. To further confuse matters, the Cutros had originally registered their day care in Lexington even though it was located in Richland, and the paramedics who attempted to revive Parker Colson had mistakenly reported the death to the Lexington coroner's office. When administrators there recognized the error and forwarded the information to Frank Barron's office in Richland, each thought the other would notify law enforcement.

Much of the meeting focused on the other case—the one in which the child hadn't died but had sustained a serious head injury. This one had already been investigated—twice, it turned out. The Lexington County Sheriff's Department had looked into it, and so had the county's Department of Social Services (DSS). Further complicating matters, they'd reached very different conclusions. The two investigators had come to the meeting to review what they'd found.

The little boy was Asher Maier (pronounced mayor), and he, too, had been four months old when disaster struck. On June 23, 1993, following two days during which Asher wasn't feeling well, Gail Cutro called his mother at work and told her he needed to see a doctor. Catherine Maier fetched her son and drove him to the pediatrician, who, after a brief examination, instructed her to take Asher to the hospital emergency room just across the parking lot from his office.

Asher remained in the hospital for a week of tests and treatment. Two weeks after he was released, his mother noticed that his head seemed to be swollen. When she returned him to the hospital, doctors determined that the swelling had been caused by a build-up of fluids that could be fatal if not drained. They operated immediately, placing a shunt in his skull that allowed fluids to funnel into his abdominal cavity.

While the full impact of his injuries was not immediately clear, the cause appeared to be. The hospital staff confirmed what his pediatrician had feared from the first: Asher Maier had symptoms of shaken baby syndrome.

This diagnosis changed everything. Evidence of shaking is generally considered grounds to open a child abuse investigation. No matter what Habben learned about the other two cases, she now had a child abuse investigation on her hands. It was ironic that the victim was *this* child, the one who had lived. Under normal circumstances, this was a case that never would have landed in the Child Fatalities Department.

Lexington DSS got the call because Asher lived within its jurisdiction. Caseworker Daylene McDuffie and her supervisor explained to Habben and the others at the table that DSS regulations required them to complete their investigation within sixty days. They'd filed their report in August, just under the wire.

Their conclusion: Asher Maier had been abused and neglected. A week after they'd filed the report, when they requested that Asher's abuser be listed in the state child abuse registry, it was the first time they'd named the person they believed responsible. The abuser, they said, was Asher's mother, Catherine Maier.

In retrospect, it wasn't surprising—even to Catherine Maier—that she was a suspect. Her background alone made it almost inevitable. At twenty-four, she already possessed what some would call a "checkered past." She and her husband, Chad Maier, were both recovering drug abusers—they had met, in fact, at a Narcotics Anonymous meeting. They'd had a stormy relationship punctuated, Chad Maier claimed, by her "rage attacks." It ended when Chad left her two weeks before their first anniversary. Asher was injured a short time later.

It was Catherine's second try at marriage. Her first had ended in an acrimonious divorce. She'd accused her husband of beating her, but she'd also admitted that she'd hit him. Although she had initially retained custody of the daughter the marriage produced, when Catherine's occasional drug use escalated to addiction, her parents took in the child. Three years later, at the time she was being investigated, her daughter was still living with her parents.

Caseworker McDuffie explained to the group sitting around the big table how she'd reached her conclusions. She'd based her findings on statements from doctors, from Catherine Maier, and from the Cutros. Examinations of Asher at the hospital had determined that his injuries had been caused sometime during the seventy-two hours before he was admitted into the ER. By all accounts he was fine when Chad returned him to Catherine on Sunday, after a weekend visit. But the Cutros reported that he wasn't well Monday or Tuesday, and that they'd urged Catherine to take him to the doctor. Yet, the mother didn't seek medical attention until Wednesday. McDuffie therefore concluded that Catherine Maier had physically abused her son and then neglected him by waiting two days to seek treatment.

Detective Jay Phillips, the investigator for the Lexington County Sheriff's Department, saw things differently. He was also investigating for a different purpose. DSS is mandated to serve families in need by assessing the merits of allegations and devising a "treatment plan" for the family. Law enforcement was called in to determine whether a crime had committed—and if so, by whom. Jurisdiction was based on where the crime was committed, and Phillips got the call because Asher Maier was allegedly abused in his home in Lexington County.

The two investigators had very different takes on Catherine Maier. Daylene McDuffie had found the woman's behavior evasive. But not Phillips. As he would later testify in court, "She told me a lot of things that normally people don't want us to know. And she was very open about making sure we were aware of them at the beginning of the investigation." She volunteered, for example, that she was seeing a counselor for "stress and anger management."

Something else was rare about her statement. She didn't point the finger at other suspects. In fact, she quickly ruled out Chad: "She said, no, she didn't believe that he would ever do anything to injure the child. And that is unusual in a separation-type case," Phillips would testify. Nor did she hold herself entirely blameless. "You could tell she felt some responsibility her child was injured, which is natural," Phillips said. "With any parent whose child has been hurt, you always feel a certain amount of responsibility." But her desire to learn the truth was also clear, Phillips added. Maier "wanted us to find out what had happened to her child."

Detective Phillips conveyed his impressions to the group in the conference room. He also noted that Catherine Maier's account of her son's condition on Monday and Tuesday was quite different from the one that the Cutros had given to DSS. She agreed that Asher was out of sorts those days, but she and Gail Cutro had speculated that he might have a cold, or he might be teething, she'd said. Neither Gail nor Josh Cutro had ever suggested she take him to the doctor until Wednesday, when his condition was completely different than it had been the previous two days, she'd emphasized.

Why did the investigators form such different impressions of Catherine Maier? Daylene McDuffie's case notes suggest that her assessment was influenced from the start by what other people said about Catherine Maier. One of the first people the caseworker spoke with, even before she interviewed Catherine Maier herself, was Chad's father, Charles Maier. The elder Maier told McDuffie that he wanted Asher to stay with him and his wife. He also arranged to have a lengthy conversation with McDuffie the next day, during which he spoke about what he viewed as Catherine Maier's bad behavior.

Then, when the caseworker first spoke with Catherine, they weren't alone. Chad was present and, though he didn't directly accuse his ex of injuring Asher, McDuffie's case notes say that he did talk about her "howling fits of rage." He recounted some of the couple's arguments, including one episode in which Catherine tried to prevent him from taking Asher for a visit by grabbing the car seat in which Chad was carrying him.

These attacks on Catherine delivered a double blow. They seemed to influence McDuffie's thinking and, at the same time, put Catherine on the defensive, which McDuffie read as evidence that the woman was being evasive. The caseworker decided that Asher should not go home with his mother and suggested placing him instead with Chad's parents. Catherine objected, citing the history of bad feelings between her and Charles, who had opposed her relationship with his son from the start. But pressured by Chad and McDuffie, Catherine reluctantly agreed.

Another difference in the investigators' approaches was apparent from what they did *after* they'd questioned Catherine Maier. Detective Phillips continued examining all suspects. Caseworker McDuffie talked to more people, but she'd already decided who had injured Asher. She made this clear months later, when she admitted under oath that she never even considered the Cutros as possible suspects.

But she did arrange to talk to them. And that was of special interest to Phillips, who had also been eager to interview the couple but had found them uncooperative. Phillips and McDuffie had been sharing information, and when Phillips learned that the Cutros had agreed to speak with DSS, he suggested she arrange to meet at the sheriff's office. That way he could watch the interview on a television monitor in another room.

The Cutros had driven over one evening in late July. As they spoke with McDuffie, Phillips had observed from down the hall. And again the investigators saw things differently.

The Cutros' account of the days leading up to Asher's hospitalization rang true to McDuffie. They'd tried repeatedly to persuade Catherine to take Asher to the doctor, beginning on Monday, but for reasons they couldn't fathom she'd refused until Wednesday. McDuffie saw no reason to doubt their story.

Phillips, on the other hand, was quite skeptical. What he found most telling was not so much what the Cutros said as the way they said it. Josh Cutro appeared nervous. And even though Josh said repeatedly that he wasn't with Asher for much of Wednesday morning, he insisted on answering most of the questions—even those specifically directed at Gail. The whole performance struck Phillips as highly dubious.

Two investigations, two opposing views. Where did that leave Habben and the group? Barron, the coroner, told them that he was also suspicious of the Cutros. The numbers alone were damning: three events all while the infants were in their care, and all within just a few months. He believed that the odds ruled out coincidence, and he had ideas about where the investigation ought to go. As he had already told Habben, he wanted the Cutros polygraphed. If they balked, Barron thought that the parents of Ashlan Daniel might be able to convince them.

Habben appreciated the suggestions and intended to act on them. But it was the coroner's final point that was of most immediate concern. He wanted the day care shut until the investigation was complete. The safety of the children was paramount.

The trouble was that neither Barron nor Habben could order it closed. Only a judge could do that. And Habben knew that a judge wasn't going to be swayed by mere concerns or premonitions. It would take evidence demonstrating that children were in danger.

Habben turned to Gary Kirkbride, the Richland DSS investigator who had been assigned to check out the day care for safety violations. He'd been to the home the day before the meeting, Kirkbride said, and had noted that the Cutros were caring for eight children, all under age four. A ninth was due later in the day. This put the Cutros well over the number for which they were registered. A family day care in South Carolina—indeed, in virtually every state—was permitted to care for only six children, and this number included any of the caregiver's own who were under twelve. Since the Cutros' children were seven, ten, and fifteen, they were well over their limit. Furthermore, the Cutros were supposed to have their registration form, which specified the maximum number permitted, posted for all to see. When Kirkbride asked to see it, however, the Cutros claimed they couldn't find it.

Were these the sorts of violations that could shut them down? Not likely. A DSS official estimated that four-fifths of all family day-care homes weren't even registered; they simply ignored the law. The Cutros were in the small minority that had actually bothered to follow at least some of the rules. Even so, in South Carolina, as in most other states, registration didn't mean much. It was merely a "paper transaction." Family day care homes were not required to have a license, as the larger day care centers were. Unlike those centers, homes weren't inspected for safety, nor were employee backgrounds checked for criminal convictions. Gail Cutro applied, submitted three letters of reference, and received her registration. As for the numbers, the Cutros told Kirkbride that they thought they were entitled to care for twelve, since the two of them shared the duties.

They were wrong about the rules—there was no exception for two providers. But even this violation didn't seem likely to spur action. Legal proceedings against family day cares were virtually unheard of. The only time homes were shut down was when problems surfaced that couldn't be ignored, such as fires, flagrant safety violations, or abuse. In most instances, DSS responded to lesser problems not by seeking a court order to close a day care but by devising what in department jargon was called "a safety plan"—a list of actions recommended to correct the problem.

This was not to say that Gary Kirkbride and Richland DSS were treating the Cutro day care as a minor headache. Its response alone announced that it viewed the matter as urgent. Kirkbride had actually visited the Cutros *twice* the day before. In between, he had interviewed the three Cutro children in their schools. All had told him that they got along well with their parents, were disciplined with time-outs, and had little contact with the day care children, who were also disciplined with time-outs. Their guidance counselors confirmed that they were good students and well behaved.

Not only had Kirkbride moved with dispatch, he'd arrived at the home with an unusually forceful safety plan. In fact, he'd already attempted to do what coroner Barron had just suggested. He'd asked the Cutros to sign the safety plan and stop caring for children until the investigation was complete. The Cutros, however, had refused. They were "polite," Kirkbride said, but they simply wouldn't sign. Josh had done most of the talking, arguing that the day care provided an essential service to the children and their parents.

There was nothing Kirkbride could do. He wasn't even allowed to enter the day care without permission—which the Cutros had denied.

So that's where things stood. It had been a useful meeting. But it also left Habben feeling acutely aware of how much work was ahead, and how many questions were unanswered.

The work she could handle. What she couldn't abide was not knowing if the children in that day care were safe.

9

The Investigator

Patsy Rauton Habben had never intended to work in law enforcement. When she was growing up she wanted to be a pediatrician; SLED was supposed to be a way station. She had raced through Columbia College, a small all-girls' school on the north side of Columbia, in three years. She graduated with a major in biology, a heavy dose of chemistry—and a teaching certificate, in case her plans fell through. Then she'd taken a thirteen-month course in medical technology at Baptist Hospital downtown. The course was often used by students to help them get into medical school.

Next she'd worked for a year in the hospital's chemistry lab as she prepared to apply to med school. When a job opened at the SLED serology lab—the division of the forensics lab that tested body fluids—a colleague at the hospital suggested that she apply.

She wasn't sure she was interested, but she checked it out and was surprised by how much she liked what she found. She loved research and problem solving, and forensics appealed to her practical side. The research was never for its own sake. The aim was always to prove or disprove that a crime had occurred and, if it had, to help identify the criminal. She was impressed by the people in the lab, and they were surprised by the breadth of her knowledge.

But wanting the position was one thing; getting it was something else. In 1978, women at SLED worked in clerical jobs. To work in the lab you had to be a SLED *agent* with police training, a gun, a badge, and all the rest. Only one agent was a woman. And here was twenty-four-year-old Patsy Rauton. What experience did *she* have?

She knew how to shoot a gun—her father had taught her when she was a kid—but that was about it. Well, not quite. Back home in Johnston, a town of 3,000 located fifty-five miles west of Columbia, her father had also taught her about business. William Rauton owned a ranch, a farm, and a department store—and ran them all. Sometimes he brought Patsy to work to show her how to survive in a man's world.

By the time she applied for the SLED job, Patsy had learned a thing or two. Well before the administrators were ready to make a decision, she showed up at the lab every morning to let them know how interested she was. Then she used the "people" skills she'd acquired from her mother. Connecting with the agents came as naturally to her as the questions she asked them about their work. It wasn't long before she was hired.

It wasn't the kind of work, though, designed to thrill her mother. Especially since, unlike some of her colleagues, Patsy didn't mind going to crime scenes. She was soon traveling into dangerous neighborhoods at all hours, scouring them for evidence of behavior that was beyond repellent.

"I worried about it," June Rauton acknowledged, sitting in her living room with her daughter at her side. "I thought it was for a man to go out on these crime scenes. I was mortified. Her picture was in the newspaper one morning on this crime scene. And I thought, 'I am embarrassed to think that she would be out in the woods looking for . . . whatever!'" Habben remembered the article, in which she was quoted. "I said that I had found blood and semen, and Mama says, 'Oh my gosh, you said that word in the paper!' She went around to all of her friends' houses and pulled their newspapers out of their mailboxes."

"I did not," June Rauton laughed.

"You did, too."

Her father wasn't enthusiastic about her job, either, and he almost certainly could have dissuaded her from taking it. He chose not to, however, because he had even deeper reservations about a medical career. He knew the years of preparation required. He also knew how much his daughter loved children. "And I was thinking: wife, children, doctor? Somehow it didn't fit. And that was then, this is now. It's a different world today, and I would see it differently. But then I saw it that way, so I didn't encourage her." In hindsight, he kicked himself.

Despite her parents' concerns, Habben was hooked on forensics. She went to each scene determined to collect every bit of evidence, bring it back to the lab, and trace it to its source.

Her first crime scene was also the most gruesome. There were four murder victims with gunshot or stab wounds. Two men lay dead in the front yard. There was blood on every wall in the house; it dripped down and formed puddles by the baseboards. They found a little girl of about nine in a back bedroom. The fourth victim was a woman who had been cut in the house, as blood tests later revealed, then dragged into a car outside and repeatedly stabbed. Then she was thrown to the ground and run over with the car, which was left on top of her.

Patsy was particularly jolted by the little girl's death. "How awful to rob a child of the rest of her life." But her job brought her back to the task at hand. She couldn't imagine how they were going to collect and separate all the blood. In the end, it took six people twelve hours to complete the investigation.

The job took so long that after several hours the team left to get a bite to eat. In those days they didn't have special uniforms with "SLED" printed on the back; they dressed in jeans and sneakers, the rattier the better. While they were eating, local police arrived to secure the scene. When the agents returned in their beat-up old clothes and their unmarked car, the officers started to arrest them for entering a crime scene.

It wasn't just the clothes and the car that made them suspicious. It was the woman. By the end of Patsy's first year, five of the 146 SLED agents, or 3 percent, were women. Fifteen years later, at the time of the Cutro case, 36 of 282, or 13 percent, were women—but it still wasn't easy.

The obstacles Patsy bumped up against in this male-dominated world didn't surprise or deter her. What she really worried about was how constant contact with human depravity would affect her faith in God. Ultimately she found comfort in her belief that the dead bodies were only shells that had been discarded by the souls. She left it to God to dispense heavenly justice; her job was to advance the earthly kind. And the means wasn't prayer. It was science.

But the methods she inherited weren't all that scientific. There wasn't even an evidence collection kit to take to crime scenes. So she dug up some metal collecting cases and put one together. It was valuable preparation for her next project.

In the late 1970s and early 1980s, the women's movement helped to galvanize awareness that rape was a serious crime. Over time, "rape shield laws" were passed to deter defense attorneys from cross-examining victims about their sexual histories. On the law enforcement end, it was obvious to Habben that the bottleneck was a forensics problem: Too often they weren't getting evidence to analyze and take to court. She decided to construct a rape kit that could be used by medical staffs to gather and preserve evidence.

She spent the better part of 1982 researching and constructing a kit on her own time. When she was satisfied, she had it mass-produced. Then she traveled to every hospital emergency room in the state to distribute the kits, train the doctors and nurses, and—what was more important—convince them to use it. Cranking up the Southern belle charm that her mother had taught her, she would say, "Guys, y'all are great. And we are only as good as you are. If you don't collect the evidence for the lab, then we have nothing to take to court."

The kits cut the number of trials in half. The evidence was so strong that there were many more guilty pleas, and fewer victims were subjected to the trauma of testifying. Habben now understood why she belonged in the forensics lab: "You've got to be a woman to do this. Why would a man want to go into this and make a kit for women who have been raped? And if you didn't have a medical background—and I was the only one with a medical background in there—you wouldn't want to do it.

"Maybe that's why God sent me here, to make these kits for these victims," she thought. "Because nobody else really gives a rip." As if to underscore the last point, her superiors gave her a "below average" evaluation for the year because she had worked one case below the required number. She pointed out that she had produced the rape kit on her own time and had traveled the state to train the doctors. And had still been going to all the crime scenes when she wasn't traveling. Didn't all of that count for *anything*? Eventually, the powers-that-be relented—and gave her an "average."

The knowledge that the kit was making a difference was reward enough, but there was more. The FBI gathered rape kits from around the country to identify a model that could be replicated, and Habben's won. Soon, when she attended national conferences, she saw her kit being used by people from all over. "I made some company rich," she laughed.

Even this confirmation that she'd been way ahead of her time, and had set a national standard, didn't leave Habben resting on her laurels. She came to recognize that her kit had a serious limitation: It was geared to be used only with adults. Cases of child sexual abuse were still falling between the cracks. Doctors had not been trained in medical school to look for signs and symptoms. You couldn't talk to a child the way you talked to an adult rape victim, though plenty of doctors did, and the child certainly couldn't respond the way an adult could, though plenty of doctors expected them to. Habben realized that doctors needed a separate kit for kids (and the training that would go with it).

After further research, she realized that doctors were also missing evidence when children were beaten. They didn't always check for bruises on the scalp and under the hair. When a child came in with a fractured limb, they didn't always take full-body X-rays, to see if there were old fractures. Furthermore, she realized that doctors in some of the poor and rural areas didn't have cameras to document injuries. So she added a disposable 35mm camera to each kit. Then, once again, she made the rounds to every hospital, distributing, training, and proselytizing.

By 1987, Habben had worked her way up to lieutenant and head of the serology lab. She was proud of her achievement, but she was far from satisfied with the lab. It was an outbuilding behind SLED headquarters that lacked not only amenities but basic necessities. There was no ventilation, even though they were constantly handling dangerous chemicals. There wasn't even a back door in case of emergencies. The evidence was stored in a trailer, and Habben wondered what they'd do if a tornado hit.

It was time for a change. SLED Chief Robert Stewart was convinced and willing to take it up with the legislature. The question was, could they persuade the politicians to include a DNA lab in the package?

In the late 1980s, DNA matching was beginning to be recognized as an indispensable law-enforcement tool that had equal power to clear or convict a suspect. Stewart sent Habben to the FBI for DNA training, then dispatched her to help lobby the legislators. She went from meeting to meeting, telling the politicians about the "deplorable" conditions in the lab and why they desperately needed to upgrade. Then she took a legislative subcommittee on a tour of the current lab to see what she was talking about. Within ten days the legislature appropriated the funds.

Creating the DNA lab was the hardest task she'd ever undertaken. Not only did she build a department that hadn't existed, she helped design it literally from the ground up. She had to learn about everything from floor plans to electrical wiring. At the same time, she was still running the Serology Department. She had two labs, two staffs, two budgets.

It had stretched her to her limits, but by late 1991 the state's first DNA lab was housed in SLED's new five-story brick forensics building. Habben considered it her greatest achievement. It took a year of testing and fine-tuning before the DNA lab was ready for actual cases, but by 1993 she could at last heave a sigh of relief. Mission accomplished.

No sooner had she exhaled, however, than Chief Stewart called to talk to her about running the Child Fatalities Department. The timing felt terrible. It would have been nice to relax and enjoy the fruits of her labor. But she was also flattered by the offer—and intrigued by the challenge.

Taking on this new assignment would test Habben in many ways. Two stood out. She'd spent her entire career in a lab. Now she would head an investigative department—without ever having worked as an investigator. Yes, the lab work contributed evidence to investigations, and she'd had a little training working with investigators, but that wasn't the same thing as an investigator putting all the pieces together to solve a crime. Some people who respected her work in the lab questioned Habben's qualifications.

And heading this new department would place Habben in a highly public arena. This wasn't the quiet, dispassionate obscurity of the lab. She would be heading a high-profile department subject to high-profile attacks. And, as she would learn soon enough, it could get nasty.

10

The Road to Irmo

There had been no time to prepare. The legislation creating the Child Fatalities Department had only passed about two weeks before it was slated to launch. When Chief Stewart had asked if she was willing to head it, Habben had asked if she could have time to think. Sure, he'd told her—just let him know by the end of the day.

She was still trying to secure offices in the main SLED building when the phone rang in the DNA lab on July 2, 1993. It was the first call for the new department. So unprepared was she that when the man on the other end reported that a woman had thrown a baby off a bridge, Patsy Habben thought that it was a joke—a colleague pulling her leg.

And that's the way it went: overwhelmed from day one. The main reason wasn't that she had to scramble for office space—which she finally scrounged in SLED's basement—or figure out how to run a new department. It was the numbers.

Lt. Habben had not had a clue how many cases there would be when she took the job. It was all new—there was no data to guide them. The previous year 29 sudden and unexpected deaths of children under eighteen had been referred to the Child Fatality Advisory Committee, the statewide multidisciplinary team that reviewed them. Habben estimated that her department might have to deal with 100, because the committee could only *request* that coroners report cases, whereas the new law *required* them to. Chief Stewart insisted that there was no way she'd have more than 40.

They were both wrong. The first year she had 214, an average of more than one every two days.

It hadn't taken long to understand that she needed help. So she recruited Richard Hunton, whom she'd hired four years earlier to work in the serology lab. Hunton was five feet eight and trim, with short brown hair and a youthful appearance that made him look, even at age thirty-nine, more like an eagle scout than a cop. Unlike a stereotypical lab nerd, he was also personable, which was important for a position that required talking to lots of people.

Patsy Habben and Richard Hunton had a lot in common. Like his boss, Richard Hunton grew up aspiring to attend medical school. Unlike her, he actually went for one semester. But he quit when he realized that to succeed, he would have to sacrifice everything, including contact with his family and church.

Like Habben, he'd taken a job in a lab to prepare for med school. After he'd dropped out of school, he was quickly recruited by another lab. But he had his eye on SLED. The organization had a good reputation, and the lab was especially well regarded. So he put in an application, and, when Habben called, he jumped.

Habben had been impressed by his work: He was smart, methodical, and had a good eye for detail. She thought these attributes, along with his knowledge of medicine and forensics, would pay equal dividends in her new department. The choice raised eyebrows for the same reason her own selection had; Hunton had never worked as an investigator. There would be another learning curve.

But there was no time for a break-in period. Habben assigned him cases, and Hunton went out and investigated. One of his first was complicated and time-consuming. Two children had drowned in a beach resort near Charleston. They'd been with their father, who said it was an accident, but his account struck Hunton as suspicious. The scene was within view of a large Holiday Inn. Hunton decided to go door-to-door to interview everyone who might have seen something. It was too big a job for one man to accomplish before guests began leaving, so SLED brought in a retired federal agent to help.

Eventually, they gathered enough evidence to lead a grand jury to indict the father. For reasons Hunton never understood, the local prosecutor allowed the case to languish. Nonetheless, Hunton had learned the importance of interviewing a broad swath of witnesses, and he'd also come to appreciate the pivotal role of teamwork. He and his fellow investigator had worked well together. Hunton credits his partner with teaching him how to investigate.

As the number of cases continued to swell, Habben would hire two more investigators. And she would begin to feed more and more of the Cutro investigation in Irmo to Richard Hunton. She still devoted an enormous amount of time to it, but when she had to depart early from that first big meeting with all the agencies, Hunton took over for her. And when day care parents called Habben with questions, she referred them to Hunton. Learning curve or not, he was navigating the road to Irmo.

For the largest single task the investigation presented, however, Hunton and Habben worked in tandem. The pair took statements from at least one parent from every family that had ever used the Cutro day care. Over a period of about a year, they were to interview 25 parents who had used the service sometime between 1989 and 1993.

Their usual procedure was to travel to the family's home, where Habben asked the questions and Hunton wrote the parent's statement in neat block letters. The statements weren't verbatim—Hunton wasn't a stenographer—but they were quite detailed. Some ran six pages. Habben was careful to ask neutral questions, and Hunton copied down everything—the complimentary remarks about the Cutros along with the criticism. When they'd finished, the parent read the statement and was given an opportunity to make corrections before signing it.

The investigators were trying to learn everything they could about the Cutros and their day care. But the statements also said a lot about the 22 families that had used it. Collectively, these families formed a portrait of Irmo.

They were drawn to the town by the same opportunities that attracted the Cutros and young families everywhere: affordable housing and good schools. And between 1980 and 1990, they came in large numbers. During just that decade Irmo's population swelled from 6,300 to 11,300—a whopping 80 percent growth spurt.

Irmo owed its existence, and even its name, to the railroad. Located about ten miles west of the state capitol building in Columbia, the site had been chosen for development because it was the precise distance from Columbia that wood-burning locomotives could travel before they required refueling. It was incorporated in 1890, and the name was derived from the first two letters of the last names of two railroad-company men: C. J. Iredell and H. C. Moseley.

After the railroad, the next most important developmental milestone was probably the arrival of Interstate 26 in 1959. It ran from Charleston northwest through Columbia to Spartanburg and beyond and meant that Columbia was only a few minutes' drive from Irmo. And the addition a few years later of I-20, which went from Florence southwest past Columbia and on to Augusta, Georgia, added to the convenience of traveling around the area.

Still, population growth was slow to follow. As late as the 1970s only about 500 people lived in Irmo. It took a few years, the grinding of social forces, and the vision of Michael Mungo to bring about change.

Mungo was a developer who had learned from his studies at the University of South Carolina in Columbia that urban areas were decentralizing. That was the polite way of putting it. The reality was that the decline of inner cities, and especially their schools, was spurring more and more families to bolt for the suburbs—the so-called white flight. It was happening in South Carolina just as it was happening in the rest of the country. Mungo looked around Columbia, recognized the escape path to Irmo that I-26 presented, and seized the opportunity.

His tour de force was Friarsgate, where nearly all the parents who used the Cutro day care lived. The subdivision's three thousand homes—two-thirds of Irmo's housing stock—represented the largest residential area ever developed in the state. They were starter homes built to last, and School District Five quickly established a reputation as a vast improvement over some of the schools the young families had left behind. By the 1990s District Five's SAT scores were not only well above the state average—which wasn't saying much, since the state's scores often ranked last in the nation—but were also above the *national* average.

So it was no wonder that Mungo's homes looked good to a lot of people. And the prices weren't out of reach. Even in the mid to late 1990s they ranged from about $75,000 to $150,000. The higher end tended to be Old Friarsgate— just east of the railroad tracks that ran through the center of town—where the houses were a little larger. A lot of young couples were concentrated in New Friarsgate, west of the tracks, where the Cutros lived. Irmo's per capita personal income in 1990 was $14,700; but three-quarters of the female population sixteen or older were employed, bringing the median family income up to $44,300.

There were not many stay-at-home moms. That was why the Cutros never had to worry about customers. As the demographics suggested, and the stories the investigators were hearing confirmed, it could be a challenge for parents to find day care.

As Patsy Habben and Richard Hunton conducted their interviews, they wondered how the parents had found the Cutros. There turned out to be three paths. Some parents had called DSS to learn the names of registered day care homes. Others had called Yes, Inc., a child care resource and referral agency that charged $35.00 to provide a list of facilities. And many had heard about the Cutros through word of mouth—from a coworker who was using them, from another day care provider who was full, or from a member of the Cutros' church.

Most of the mothers, who were the children's primary caregivers, were in their early thirties. Many were college graduates, and they worked in a variety of fields. There were several nurses, a comptroller for a contractor, a technical writer, an accountant, a systems analyst for an insurance company, a teacher, a licensing engineer at a power plant, an operations manager for a mortgage company, and a stockbroker.

Virtually every mother drove to the Cutros' home and interviewed them, many accompanied by their husbands. There were two selling points that just about everyone found appealing. One was the price. It rose 20 percent during the first couple of years, but in 1993 it was still only $62.50 a week. Parents of infants supplied their own diapers, bottles, and port-a-cribs. Parents of toddlers could pay an extra $10.00 a week for breakfast and lunch.

The second factor that impressed the parents was the house. The three-bedroom center-hall Colonial was charming and spotless. Up the front steps was a well-shaded porch, where Gail lined up the children's diaper bags and car seats to facilitate the potentially hectic afternoon pickup. Entering the front door, the living room—where much of the day care activity occurred—was to the left. The salmon-colored walls formed a spacious rectangle in which an oriental rug was centered. Two wing chairs and a lamp were set back in an alcove on the right. One playpen was always stationed in front of the fireplace on the left to prevent the little ones from crawling in. The other playpens or port-a-cribs were strategically positioned out of the way along the perimeter. A couch near the front of the room faced the backyard, which was visible through a window. About halfway from the couch to the window, angled back toward the television set in the right corner, sat Josh's leather recliner.

The two other areas where children congregated were also attractive. The kitchen was roomy, its round table easily accommodating the toddlers' meals. And Josh often took the toddlers into the backyard, which featured a luxuriant lawn, a swing set, and a sandbox. The parents were invariably pleased by what they saw. "We were very impressed with the cleanliness of the Cutro home," was a typical comment in the statements Habben took. "And we also felt that everything was safe."

11

Josh

Patsy Habben was not having an easy time of it. Determining whether the day care was safe required answering two questions that were proving elusive: Who was Brenda Gail Cutro and who was Joseph Rubin Cutro (known to the world as Gail and Josh)?

In the interviews the parents sat for with Habben and Richard Hunton, they described Gail Cutro as shy and reserved. Many had a hard time getting a read on her themselves, so they weren't able to provide that much information. And there was another impediment the investigators faced: Josh Cutro. On the few occasions they were in contact with the couple, Josh took the lead. He was always in the foreground, dominating the conversation. Or, in the case of Gary Kirkbride, the Department of Social Services investigator who had sought entry into the home, turning them away.

Was Josh running interference to protect his wife from scrutiny? Or was this just a reflection of a domineering personality? It was hard to tell. There was certainly evidence that Josh's personality was as outsize as his physique. The parents readily confirmed it. Those who had used the day care from its earliest days had witnessed a clear demonstration.

When the day care first opened, Josh wasn't even involved. It was Gail's idea, and she started it herself. She may have been shy, but she wasn't too shy to start a business. And it was undoubtedly the most successful thing she'd ever done. But within six months, Josh decided to join her. And it wasn't his style to play a supporting role.

As the parents told Habben, the change was almost immediate. Josh was the one who answered the door, picked up the phone, and explained day care policies. Gail deferred to him. One mother who used the day care before and after he arrived said, "It was obvious that Josh was the 'man of the house.'"

Many parents noted that he connected more easily with them than his wife did. Though some parents praised Gail for her patience and attention to their children, others described her as not only shy but somewhat remote. "She did not talk to me very much when I picked up [my son]," one mother told Habben. "Josh came across as friendlier and was the one who made conversation."

Some of the parents also suggested that Josh interacted more easily with the children. The big man seemed to have a light touch with the little ones. "Josh Cutro is a very gentle person," one mother recalled. "The children loved him."

The perception that he was closer to the children may have had something to do with the division of labor. Josh cared for the toddlers, often taking them out to the fenced-in backyard. Gail watched the babies, prepared meals, and filled out "report cards" that described what the children did each day (for the babies, she recounted their moods and the food they consumed).

But the biggest difference Josh brought to the day care was that he turned it into more of a business—specifically, one with an eye on the bottom line. The Cutros told parents that, with two of them working, state regulations allowed them to double the number of children they cared for. Actually, they knew this was not the way the rules worked. The woman who first encouraged Gail to become a day care provider reminded her that this was a violation; they were still permitted only six. But that did not stop the couple from repeating the statement and taking in more children. At times they had more than double the legal limit.

Josh found other ways to enhance revenue. After he arrived, Gail began preparing dinners that the parents could purchase and take home. Parents could place orders when they dropped off their children in the morning, and that evening take home meals not only for the kids but also for themselves— all at very reasonable prices. Many parents told Habben they were happy to avail themselves of this service but were amazed that Gail found time to provide it.

There was one business policy Josh introduced that was not so popular. In fact, it so infuriated some parents that they withdrew their children. It concerned vacations. Families had always been free to take time off without charge. Josh changed that. And he did so without advance warning. The first word some parents received was a bill for the days when they were gone.

One family was particularly incensed. The father felt Josh had started acting "kind of like he was now the general manager or the CEO." The man and his wife pulled their son in response. The wife told Habben: "Once Josh became involved in the day care, it was like he wanted it run more like a business, and Josh treated Gail like the flunky who did all the dirty work. Money, not the children, seemed most important."

To many parents, the emphasis on money seemed to be an extension of Josh's background. He told them that he previously worked as a stockbroker. But he never did. Josh had actually worked as a freight broker. He connected companies that had products to ship with the trucking outfit that would give them the best price. If one or two parents had heard "stock broker" instead of "freight broker," this might be chalked up to a misunderstanding. But nearly all of them distinctly heard "stockbroker." One even remembered Josh saying, as an explanation for why he quit: "Wall Street isn't all that it's cracked up to be."

None of the parents discovered, or at least remarked upon, this discrepancy. But some did come to see another side of Josh's personality—the emotional and unpredictable side. Josh could erupt in anger one minute, and dissolve in tears the next. The father who was upset over the vacation charge recounted what happened when he called and told Josh he was removing his son. "Josh started crying, then he began cussing me," he told Habben. "I then went over to the Cutro home, where Josh came out the front door, again crying. He tried to talk me into letting my son stay."

It wasn't the most flattering picture of the man, but it wasn't the kind of information that would lead a judge to shut down the day care. It was something that Habben noted, and it added to her concern, but it didn't prove that children were in danger.

When Habben began probing Josh's past, she discovered more that troubled her. He'd had run-ins with the law. A quick search yielded skeletal records of three arrests: one for assault and destruction of property, one for shoplifting, and the third for damaging property.

On the surface these incidents raised more questions about the man, but the bare-bones printouts Habben obtained showed that they all occurred when he was quite young. He was 17 at the time of the first arrest, 18 the next time, and 25 when he was arrested the third time. If these were serious infractions, he certainly got off lightly. The first resulted in a misdemeanor conviction and a $100 fine. The other two didn't seem to result in any penalties at all. Were these evidence that he was a danger to children?

12

The Polygraph

Josh Cutro never seemed more animated than when he was angry. His voice rose. His eyes flashed. His entire body sprang to life.

In the days after Ashlan Daniel died, he was angry a lot. And most of his anger was directed at the investigators. Yes, he knew that there had to be an investigation. He said he had no problem with that. But how much investigating was required before you called it harassment? That's what he wanted to know.

Josh had been dealing with investigators even before Ashlan Daniel died. Since June the sheriff's department and Lexington DSS had been investigating the shaken-baby case. That experience alone had served up a cocktail of emotions. He claimed he'd felt sorry for Catherine when Asher was sick. When the child was taken to the hospital, he and Gail had visited Catherine there and expressed concern and sympathy. But all of a sudden they found themselves in the middle of a child abuse investigation. And they learned things about Catherine they'd never known. They'd had no idea, Josh said, that she was a drug addict, that she'd been married twice, and that a daughter from her first marriage had been removed from her custody.

Yet, the investigators seemed to be suggesting that the *Cutros* were responsible for Asher's condition. He claimed it made no sense. On the one hand, you had as a possible suspect a woman whose second marriage had just broken up, who had drug problems, and who had previously had her daughter taken away. On the other, you had Josh and Gail Cutro, who had been running a popular day care for years without complaint and had been caring for this child for less than three weeks. He couldn't understand, Josh said, why the police were focusing on *them*. His initial sympathy for Catherine gave way to anger, he explained, because she'd placed them in this situation.

Then Ashlan Daniel died. Her death brought back all the shock and grief they'd experienced eight months earlier, when Parker Colson passed away, Josh said. Only this time, while they were grieving, they also had to contend with the Irmo PD, the Child Fatalities Department, and Richland DSS. All at the same time, he pointed out. It was like those tag-team wrestling matches that Josh loved to watch, where the bad guy tags his partner but stays in the ring to gang up on the good guy. Only this wasn't fake wrestling on television; this was his life!

Now the Department of Social Services was talking about shutting the day care. Even though, Josh insisted, the people who had the most at stake— the parents themselves—had made it abundantly clear that they wanted the day care to remain open. Apparently DSS thought that Gail had done something to Ashlan. Josh wanted to know what evidence they had. No one had found any marks on her. There was no evidence of foul play, he said. No one had complained even once about the way Ashlan Daniel was treated during the three months she was in their care. All the authorities seemed to have was gossip.

Josh had heard the ugly rumors. One said that Gail had beaten the child. Another whispered that she'd smothered the baby with Saran Wrap. They made him so angry. He wished whoever was spreading them would come right out and accuse them, so he could respond. But of course no one did. That was the thing about rumors, he said: There was no way to fight them. So Josh did the only thing he could think of. He called the Irmo police department and demanded to know what evidence they had that either he or his wife had harmed Ashlan Daniel. Of course he got no answer.

———

While Josh Cutro railed against the investigators, one of them was trying to figure out how to convince him and his wife to take polygraphs. This was Richard Hunton's challenge. Patsy Habben had made him the lead investigator on the case, and they'd agreed that lie detector tests were a priority. They hoped the tests would help focus their investigation. But a suspect can't be forced to take one. It has to be voluntary, and that can be a hard sell.

Suspects may feel they have a lot to lose and not much to gain. In reality, however, they don't stand to lose as much as they may think. Polygraph results are rarely admissible as evidence in court because the test hasn't been proved sufficiently reliable. Its accuracy depends partly on the skill of the person administering it, and there have been plenty of false results.

Many investigators also view polygraphs as unreliable, but that doesn't mean they aren't valuable. For law enforcement, there's no real downside. Administering the test affords cops an opportunity to learn a lot about a suspect. How he responds to the test—or even the request that he take one—may say a lot. If the test finds that he's been deceptive, there may be a real opportunity to extract a confession right then and there, after telling him he failed. And if it shows he's been truthful, that doesn't mean investigators will or should give him a pass. But they may broaden their focus and take a close look at other potential suspects.

Richard Hunton called Josh Cutro and made his pitch. The investigators were examining all possibilities, Hunton told him, and since Josh had had a lot of contact with the children, he had to be considered. "It's not that we don't believe you," Hunton told him. "We just want to rule you out." The polygraph was an opportunity to "clear the air."

Hunton's message was perfectly targeted. Josh had been looking for some way to fight back, and this seemed to be a way he could climb into the ring with the whole investigation and pin it to the mat. Okay, he said. What did he have to do?

On the morning of September 16, a week after Ashlan Daniel died, Josh met Richard Hunton at SLED's forensics lab. Hunton walked Josh to the polygraph offices and left him in the waiting room while he continued to the office of polygraph examiner Robert Antonelli. Before they could administer the test, Hunton and Antonelli had to write the questions.

The theory behind the polygraph is that people get emotional when they lie. And rising emotion is accompanied by various physiological signs that the polygraph can measure, such as blood pressure, respiration, and skin conductivity. The suspect is asked a series of yes-or-no questions. Some are specifically about the events investigators are probing; these are known as the "test questions." Some are about other emotionally charged issues from the suspect's past—issues that could be expected to elicit a strong reaction. Still other questions contain no emotional content at all. When the examiner matches up the questions with the physiological changes the machine measures, he can sometimes determine whether the person has had reactions to the relevant questions that polygraphy says are indications of deception. (Critics have argued that some individuals are able to control their emotions sufficiently to beat the test, while others have faked results by trickery—such as putting a tack inside a shoe and pressing down on it while answering truthfully, so that reactions to these questions match up with the lies on the test questions.)

Hunton outlined the background of the case for Antonelli and explained what he wanted to know. With Antonelli's help, he wrote three questions about Ashlan's death. All the questions are important, but the test questions are especially so. Inartfully worded ones may destroy any chance of achieving credible results. Consider the question, "Do you feel bad about what you did?" An innocent person may truthfully answer yes, and a guilty person may truthfully answer no.

In addition to the test questions, Antonelli wanted ones that would explore Josh's general feelings about hurting people and getting into trouble, so the two men wrote several that asked whether he'd ever hurt a loved one, or done anything illegal. Finally they mixed in a couple of innocuous questions about Josh's address and where he was born. After an hour they were ready.

Antonelli led Josh down the hall to a small room with a couple of chairs and a desk that held the machine. Josh sat in the chair next to it, and the examiner strapped a cardio cuff around one of his biceps to monitor his blood pressure and pulse. Then he attached a small black electrode to Josh's fingertip to monitor changes in his electrodermal sensitivity, and twin black pneumograph tubes to monitor respiration of the lower abdomen and upper chest. Wires connected them all to the polygraph, which featured two dozen small knobs and a needle that scratched the test results on graph paper. When the subject's emotions rose, so did the line on the graph. (These days, it's all done on a laptop.)

There were ten questions in all. The test questions—the ones about Ashlan Daniel—were straightforward. "Did you intentionally do anything that resulted in Ashlan's death? Did you intentionally do anything that resulted in Ashlan's death while she was in your home? Are you withholding any information whatsoever about how Ashlan died?" Antonelli asked all ten questions three times. To each test question Josh answered "No."

Two hours later the examiner issued his final report. There was a big black X next to "NO DECEPTION INDICATED." Josh had passed.

13

Volunteer Investigator

Missy Daniel hated to be alone. And she'd never felt more alone than now. Her daughter had been dead for eleven days. At least her husband Davis got to go to work; Missy just sat in an empty house, alone with her grief.

Before Ashlan was born, Missy Daniel had been an insurance adjuster. She'd handled auto accidents, and a good deal of investigating was involved. She had to check out the condition of the cars, the various accounts of the accident, and the medical documentation. She was used to people lying. Her job was to figure out which ones were and then nail them.

The view of humanity that the job afforded wasn't a pleasant one, and the work was hard, but it was interesting and Missy was good at it. Now, as she sat in the empty house, she had a new case to focus on. Only this was a lot harder. She didn't have much to go on—just her thoughts and suspicions. But she'd never been more motivated to decide whether someone was lying.

She went over the Cutros' story again and again. A lot of what they said was plausible, but her gut told her that it wasn't true. Even forgetting the other death and the injury, and considering only what they'd said about Ashlan, it didn't add up. She decided to take coroner Frank Barron's advice and call the woman at the Child Fatalities Department.

"Has Gail taken a polygraph yet?" Missy asked after she got through to Patsy Habben. Missy knew that Frank Barron had been pushing hard for lie detector tests.

"Actually," Habben answered, "I'm not the investigating officer. Richard

Hunton is. I don't believe she's taken a polygraph, but since this is an ongoing investigation, I'm really not at liberty to answer yes or no."

"Well, can you tell me if the reason Gail hasn't taken the polygraph is because she's on medication or something?" Missy knew that Josh had passed his—he'd certainly told enough people—and she'd heard him use medication as an excuse to explain why Gail hadn't taken one.

"I really don't know if that has anything to do with it in this particular case, but I can tell you that we prefer that people not take drugs before a polygraph."

"Well, what about the autopsy samples? Have you finished testing them? Because I talked to Frank Barron, and he said in a case like this they ought to be back in less than a week. He said you talked about that at some conference he went to."

Habben told her that she'd check with Toxicology and get back to the coroner in the morning. She suggested that Missy call him for an update.

"When you do give Gail the polygraph, could you ask her one question? Could you ask her what time she put Ashlan down for a nap and how long afterwards she checked on her? Because EMS told me one thing she said, and Gail told me something else."

Habben knew that polygraphs didn't work this way, but there was no point in telling Missy that. Instead, she assured the bereaved mother that such inconsistencies were exactly the kinds of things her department was going to check. Then she asked: "Has anyone from the Irmo PD interviewed you or your husband yet?" Told that they hadn't, Habben said she'd have Richard Hunton call to set up an appointment.

After Missy hung up, she felt better than she had since Ashlan died. It may not have been much, but at least she'd contributed something to the investigation.

14

Under Siege

Josh was euphoric when he learned he'd passed the polygraph. But the feeling didn't last long. Richard Hunton seized the opportunity to propose the next step. All they needed to do now, he said, was test Gail.

Test *Gail*? Josh felt the anger in his gut returning. He thought *he* was the prime suspect. What did they need to test Gail for?

Hunton tried to lay the blame on the coroner, as Barron himself had suggested. He told Josh that Barron wanted both of them tested before closing his investigation. But that explanation didn't seem to impress Josh. A week later, Hunton was still waiting for him to call.

In the meantime, the investigator had plenty to keep him busy. He was running around interviewing parents as quickly as he could. The reason he hadn't met with Davis and Missy Daniel is that he was trying to be sensitive to their grief. After Missy's conversation with his boss, however, Hunton arranged to meet with her the next day.

Richard Hunton and Patsy Habben would take formal statements from Missy and Davis Daniel six weeks later, but Hunton's first meeting with Missy took an unexpected turn. They met in the Daniels' home, and Missy confided that she and her husband harbored suspicions about their daughter's death. Some of the things the Cutros were saying didn't make sense to her. Missy also mentioned that Gail had been calling once or twice a week to talk about Ashlan—and to complain about the constant intrusion of DSS and the police, which prevented her from properly grieving.

The telephone calls were the opening Hunton was looking for. Josh was adept at fielding and deflecting inquiries from the police intended for Gail. He always seemed to be the go-between, the shield between the authorities and his wife. But Josh couldn't block Missy if Gail was calling *her*.

Hunton remembered Frank Barron's suggestions during the big meeting in the Child Fatalities Department conference room. In addition to recommending that they administer polygraph tests to the Cutros, he'd also suggested that if the Cutros balked, the Daniels might be able to convince them. Missy had an open line. Hunton asked if she'd use it.

He didn't have to ask twice.

———

Gail Cutro said she was feeling beleaguered during this time. Nine days after Ashlan's death, Josh's sister Rose died in a car wreck. She was only 24. Gail said she was still raw from Ashlan's funeral when once again she donned her Sunday best for another one.

On top of this, there was now a new pressure: the polygraph. Josh was bragging about how easily he'd passed his. Now Missy had also raised the subject. Gail was beginning to feel surrounded.

She'd talked to her therapist about it, and much to Gail's relief, Eve Powell didn't think it was a good idea. Powell was the counselor who had been working with Gail since Parker Colson died. In Powell's opinion, Gail was in no shape to take a polygraph. She was emotionally spent from the succession of tragedies. And perhaps more important, Powell was convinced that Gail blamed herself for failing to protect the children who died—even though Gail understood on an intellectual level that SIDS can't be prevented.

Still, the pressure mounted. Missy was not only urging Gail to take the test, she'd begun calling. She mentioned that Frank Barron was pushing it in order to close his investigation. Josh called a prominent defense lawyer he'd spoken with to get his thoughts on the subject. Tell her not to take it, the lawyer said. Gail appreciated the advice, but it didn't stop Missy's phone calls. Gail wasn't sure what to do. All she could think of was to stop answering the phone.

———

"She's stopped taking my calls," Missy told Richard Hunton. She'd managed a few brief conversations with Josh instead, but when she tried to discuss the polygraph, all he wanted to talk about was the pressure Gail was under. Missy felt she'd hit a dead end.

Hunton recognized that the opportunity was slipping away. It was time to redouble their efforts, he said. So on the last Monday in September, Missy drove to the Cutros'. She could tell that Josh was angry. He spoke bitterly about the Child Fatalities Department, but Missy sensed that he was also angry with her. Gail, on the other hand, wanted to talk about Ashlan.

"Don't you hate it when you go to the grocery store and see other children or pregnant women?" Gail said. "Don't you want to avoid them?" Missy nodded—it was exactly how she felt.

"Do you ever look for her hairs and other things of hers and pick them up and smell them?" Gail asked. *She* did, Gail confided. She said it brought her comfort. Missy thought this odd, but she didn't say anything.

She asked if Gail was ready to take the polygraph. But Gail remained noncommittal. She just wasn't sure she could do it, she said, adding that her therapist was adamantly opposed.

When she left, Missy was more discouraged than ever. But Hunton felt they had one more card to play. A week later, Missy returned to the Cutros' house with Davis. Josh greeted them with an Arctic chill, but the Daniels didn't care. This was their chance. Gail was in the yard, and Missy walked straight up to her. She tried to sound supportive and, at the same time, needy.

"Do it for us, okay? SLED isn't going to stop investigating without that polygraph," she said. The one thing she was sure they both wanted was for the ordeal to end. "Let's get this over with," she implored. "Just tell the truth, and we'll be fine."

But Gail *wasn't* fine. She was torn by ambivalence. Her eyes welled with tears. She hemmed and hawed, and complained about the pressure. Then the dam gave way.

"All right, I'll take the test!" she spat. She paused a moment before adding: "And then I'll commit suicide!" She stormed into the house, muttering: "I have to call my therapist."

Davis and Josh had followed Missy into the yard and taken this in. Now the three of them stood in stunned silence. Missy and Davis weren't sure what Gail would do. Had she agreed, or was she accusing them of pushing her over the edge? Finally, Davis began to weep.

"Please, please," he begged Josh, sinking to his knees, "ask Gail to take the polygraph." He struggled to get the words out: "So we can put all this behind us." Josh looked down at the hulking figure of the former high school football star, his powerful frame wracked by sobs.

"Gail will take the polygraph," Josh said quietly. Then he turned and retreated into the house.

15

The Second Polygraph

Patsy Habben found herself in unexpected company the night of her thirteenth wedding anniversary. On the afternoon of October 4th, nearly a month after Ashlan Daniel died, Gail Cutro had agreed to take the polygraph. Now, at 10:00 p.m., Habben was ushering Gail and Josh—who insisted on coming along—into the same waiting room where Josh had been seated 18 days earlier. Chief polygraph examiner Johnny Hartley led Richard Hunton and Irmo detective Tim Stephenson into his office, where they filled him in on the case and helped him compose the questions he would use.

After they finished, Hartley brought Gail into his office. Just as Antonelli had done with her husband, Hartley had her sign a consent form, and then he explained how the test worked. Finally, he took her to an examining room, hooked her up to the polygraph, and began asking questions.

1) Were you born in the U.S.?

2) Do you intend to answer each question truthfully about Ashlan's death?

3) Is there anything else you're afraid I will ask you about?

4) Before your 30th birthday, do you remember ever hurting anyone?

5) Did you suffocate Ashlan?

6) Before your 30th birthday, do you remember ever thinking about anything serious?

7) Did you suffocate Ashlan on September 9?

8) Do you live in Irmo?

9) Before your 30th birthday, do you remember ever lying about anything serious?

10) Are you withholding any information about what caused Ashlan's death?

If she'd done nothing to harm Ashlan, then the examination ought to show that she was more concerned about some of the control questions than she was about the test questions—five, seven, and ten. If there was no significant difference between Gail's response to the control and test questions, then the test wasn't valid, and Hartley would check "INCONCLUSIVE."

Hartley ran through the questions three consecutive times, with a brief pause in between. When he was through, he had three charts. He detached them from the machine and examined them carefully. Then he looked up at Gail.

"You're lying," he said.

What surprised Hartley most was how calmly Gail reacted—or didn't react—to this accusation. Hartley had been sitting at the desk behind the machine. Now he came around front with a chart in his hand and sat on the edge—like a high school math teacher showing a student where she messed up.

"Gail," said the slim, handsome cop, "look at these charts. You don't have to be a polygraph examiner to read them. You can see clearly: every time the ink starts going up it shows a reaction. There's only one thing that can mean. You are lying about this. I mean, there's no other way around it. This is not something out of your unconscious. This is conscious. This is what you know when I asked you that question."

Gail shook her head. "I'm not lying. I didn't touch her. I never touched her." During their conversation, which lasted no more than ten minutes, Gail was wringing her hands, but otherwise she didn't look angry or upset. Toward the end Hartley raised his voice and injected more passion into his accusations. He was trying to elicit a confession or, failing that, at least some passion. If she was innocent, he would have expected righteous indignation. Instead, when Hartley bore down, Gail began trembling. She put her face in her hands and emitted small sobbing sounds, but she never actually cried.

It was over by midnight. Hartley wasn't getting anywhere, so he told her to sit tight and he stood up and left. He went to the conference room, where Josh Cutro was sitting at a long Formica table, drinking a Coke that Richard Hunton had brought him. Hartley joined the two men, and a moment later Habben and Stephenson came in. Hartley spread the polygraph on the table in front of Josh.

"She failed it." He pointed to the sharp peaks that corresponded to questions five, seven, and ten. "Failed it bad." Josh stared at the paper and silently shook his head. He seemed mildly surprised but neither shocked nor over-whelmed. He, too, was remarkably calm, almost matter-of-fact.

"Well," he said at last, still shaking his head, "Gail's therapist told her she shouldn't take the test because she felt so guilty about the death and all. I guess she was right. I guess Gail just felt so guilty that it came out on the test." The others were silent as they took in this statement.

Habben spoke first. "Well, Mr. Cutro, y'all both kept the children. Didn't *you* feel guilty when Ashlan died?"

He nodded. "Yes. Yes, I did."

"Then why did *you* pass the polygraph examination while your wife failed?"

Josh raised his eyebrows and shrugged his massive shoulders. "I don't know. But I know my wife. And Gail didn't have nothing to do with this."

A moment later Gail walked in. After sitting in the examination room for several minutes, she'd grown restless and tried the door. Finding it unlocked, she'd headed back toward the common room and then followed the voices down the hall. She walked over to Josh and grasped his arm, as if drawing strength from his physical presence.

Habben knew that Hartley wanted to talk to Josh a little longer, so she took Gail's arm and led her back out, suggesting that they get some water. Gail trembled and sobbed intermittently—still without tears—as Habben walked her down the hall. They sat in the common room, which was domi-nated by a ten-gallon fish tank on a bookcase to the left, and a twenty-gallon tank on a cabinet against the far wall.

In the notes she wrote about that night, Habben recounted the conversa-tion that followed—the only one she ever had with Gail Cutro:

I asked if she was on any kind of medication and she said she was on an antidepressant but had not had any today because of the test. I told her a person with emotional problems should not care for children especially more than DSS recommended. She agreed she had mental problems and that tomorrow her therapist would probably admit her to the hospital. I told her a rest would do her good and that she could close the daycare. She told me she could never close the daycare because those were her children and they needed her. . . . No one knew how they felt but her, not even their own parents. She stated she knew them better than their own parents be-cause she was the one who cared for them. I told her the children had done okay before they came to her daycare. She said she couldn't let go of their children. . . . At times her conversation was confusing because she has 3 children of her own and I had to keep asking her which children she was referring to—hers or the day care children. . . . Mrs. Cutro also stated that if she did hurt Ashlan that she would never see her children again. Once more I asked which children she was referring to and it was the daycare children. . . .

Then she noticed a small aquarium to the left of my chair. She had an agonized look on her face and said "Oh no!" I asked her what was wrong and she superficially cried and said, "that poor fish, he's all by himself. Please don't keep him in there by himself. Promise me you'll fix it." I told her I would ask the owner of the aquariums to put another fish in the tank the next day. With that she stared at the aquarium and shook her head.

Mrs. Cutro asked me if I thought she killed Ashlan and I told her yes according to the polygraph. I told her that she needed help and should not care for the children anymore until she received such help. . . . She said she and Josh always wanted twelve children. She said she was an only child and never wanted her children to grow up without a brother or sister. She had three children, two of which were on monitors as infants. We talked awhile about apnea and SIDS. She was well versed in this area also. After her third child was born the doctor told her she could not have more children because of her health.

Mrs. Cutro stated she wasn't feeling well and started to shake and moan. I told her I would get her some water and that we would walk around awhile. I braced Mrs. Cutro and we walked back and forth in the hallway. She said again that she knew she wasn't okay mentally.

Finally, everyone else joined us. Mr. Cutro asked Mrs. Cutro if she was okay? She said yes. He then asked her if she was really okay and said "you know what I mean?" She answered yes. They then left.

Habben would not understand the full implications of this conversation for months. It would take her almost as long to discover that some of Gail Cutro's statements, at least as Habben recorded them, were false.

———

Richard Hunton had promised the Daniels that as soon as he knew the results of the polygraph, he would drive over to their house and tell them—no matter what the hour. It was after 2:30 a.m. when he arrived. Missy Daniel would later describe this as the second worst night of her life.

16

Pushback

"I am concerned about the insensitive way your department is treating Josh and Gail Cutro." It was the day after the polygraph, and Gail's therapist had phoned Patsy Habben to give her an earful. It wasn't right, Eve Powell continued. The Cutros weren't guilty of anything.

Gail was in no condition to take a polygraph, Powell maintained. She was depressed after the first death, and she was just getting over it when Ashlan died. To add insult to injury, after the test someone had insinuated that Gail had a split personality. What qualified SLED, Powell demanded, to diagnose her patient?

The pushback had begun. During the days that followed, a number of parents called SLED to say that they supported the Cutros. Ramona Bowers, the teacher, told Habben how happy she was with the care her son was receiving. Then Bowers called Richard Hunton to say that the Cutros never kept more than eight children, and they provided better service than most day cares.

Jana Brown, a pediatric nurse who had two children in the day care, told Habben that she trusted the Cutros. Then she phoned Gary Kirkbride, the Richland DSS caseworker, and tried to talk him into dropping the investigation. A week later she asked Habben why it was taking so long.

Another phone call suggested that the Cutro case had already divided the community in unusual ways. Richland's assistant coroner told Habben that he was also concerned about the way the Cutros were being treated. He didn't think that the Daniels should have gone to their home to beg Gail to take the test. What made this criticism particularly surprising was that the idea of involving the Daniels had come from his boss, Frank Barron.

Habben was unfailingly polite, and recorded each contact in her meticulous notes, but her goal remained firm. As she'd told Gail after the polygraph, she was convinced that the day care should be closed. Despite Powell's insistence that Gail was merely depressed, Habben had seen enough to conclude that this was not a woman to whom parents should entrust children.

On that front, social workers continued visiting the home. The state Department of Social Services day care regulation unit had gotten involved, but its people hadn't been allowed in either. Josh always met them at the door and sent them away. His comments revealed the pressure he was feeling. He couldn't let them in, he explained once, because his family had been under so much stress. Another time he complained about the rumors that Gail killed babies with Saran Wrap.

Despite this opposition, the regulators were making progress. During one visit, a regulatory staffer hand-delivered a letter advising the Cutros that they were keeping more children than their registration allowed. A week later, when the staffer returned, Josh scrawled a note stating that the Cutros would close the day care in November.

But DSS wasn't waiting. Another letter delivered a few days later stated that the Cutros' registration was being withdrawn based on over-enrollment and threat of harm. All that was needed was a court order directing them to close.

Some of the parents shifted into overdrive. One mother told Hunton that the Cutros failed to sign the safety plan—the sheet that spelled out how they would comply with DSS rules—only because DSS said it was optional. Sharon Bell said she wasn't concerned that the Cutros were in willful violation of the law. "Knowing them," she said, "they wouldn't do anything below standard." And Ramona Bowers joined the chorus. She told Hunton that she would remove her son only if SLED "stood in front of the door and prevented me from going in."

A court date was set for October, when a judge would decide if the day care would be closed. Parents vowed to attend the hearing en masse.

17

N.A. Romance

Unlike the way the Cutros treated the Colsons after Parker died in January, and treated the Daniels after Ashlan died in September, the couple had quickly turned against Catherine Maier after Asher was injured in June. In mid-October, four months after Asher was hurt, Catherine Maier gave a statement to SLED laying out the events that led to her son's hospitalization. "I am in no way responsible," she said. "I also feel that my husband would not ever harm Asher. I feel that Asher was harmed while under Gail Cutro's care." This was the first time that his mother publicly suggested that Gail Cutro was involved.

But Catherine's husband gave a statement to SLED three days later, and he disagreed. "I feel that my wife Catherine is responsible," Chad said.

No machine would be asked to divine the truth. That job fell first to the Lexington County family court judge who was presiding over the Maiers' divorce. In a hearing also held in October, it would be up to him to decide who should be granted custody. Pending his decision, Asher remained in foster care.

Chad's lawyers had compiled an impressive sheaf of affidavits supporting their client's position. One statement filed in mid-August read, in part:

> Mrs. Maier was very angry and upset during the weeks of June 7 and June 14, 1993. She stated that she was very angry at Chad Maier for leaving her and Asher. She also vowed that Chad Maier would be sorry he ever met her. . . . Based on my observations of Mrs. Maier, I do not believe she has adequate coping skills. . . . My husband and I went to the hospital [the night Asher was admitted], and Mrs. Maier reported that the doctors suspected the baby had been shaken or dropped. Mrs. Maier was visibly upset and denied that she had done anything inappropriate to Asher.

It was signed "Gail Cutro."

Catherine Maier filed her own affidavit two weeks after Gail's. She had not yet decided who was responsible for Asher's injury. As she had done when interviewed by various investigators, she volunteered unflattering information about herself. She also proclaimed her innocence.

Chad's affidavit focused less on himself than on Catherine. After he spelled out how he planned to care for his son, he painted a scathing portrait of his wife:

> I met Catherine Maier in the recovery program. She is also a recovering addict; however, no one has seen Catherine at a recovery meeting in months. Catherine has an *extremely violent temper.* She has always complained of "uncontrollable fits of rage" and "hormonal imbalance caused by birth control pills." She has outrageously violent outbursts, but always apologizes later, and claims the outbursts are uncontrollable. Catherine uses extreme and gross profanity to me and in front of Asher ("fuck," "fuck you," "dickhead," "shit," "go to hell," etc.). On one occasion, I told Catherine that I was going to attend a meeting. She became so outraged and angry that she actually banged her own head against the wall several times. She showed up at the meeting and caused a terrible scene. She called me a "dickhead" in front of the members.

Catherine and Chad were not the only parties represented at the family court hearing in October. The judge had also appointed a guardian ad litem to represent Asher's interests. Laura Rogers, like the other representatives in the court's guardian ad litem program, was a volunteer who was not a lawyer. This was only her second case and would prove, by far, the most challenging that she would face during her six years in the program, she would later acknowledge.

Guardians ad litem received fifteen hours of training and were then assigned cases that required them to investigate the allegations, interview anyone with knowledge about the case, and forward recommendations to the court. By the date of the hearing, Rogers had interviewed Catherine and Chad, Chad's parents, Richard Hunton, and Lexington caseworker Daylene McDuffie. She had also observed each parent on a visit with Asher. She had been repeatedly rebuffed in her attempts to interview the Cutros, but was finally able to speak with them briefly by telephone on the morning of the hearing.

"When I first began my investigation, it appeared that Ms. Maier was the only person who could have hurt the baby," she wrote in her report, "however, further investigation has proved that this is not the case."

Her conclusion: "It is not obvious to this Guardian as to who injured Asher Maier. . . . Until the investigation into the Cutro in-home daycare has been completed by SLED and [the South Carolina Department of Social Services], this Guardian cannot make a recommendation."

———

It had all begun just 18 months before their divorce hearing, and from the start it was an unusual romance. After they met at the Narcotics Anonymous meeting, they gradually became friends. He was twenty and she was twenty-three. One night in April 1992, Chad was awarded a medallion signifying that he'd been clean for a year. Catherine took a white chip, acknowledging a relapse, and dissolved in tears. "What's the matter?" he asked. She'd had a glass of wine the night before. Although she was addicted to cocaine, N.A. considered the use of any drug, including alcohol, backsliding. Catherine would later disagree with this philosophy, but at the time she was devastated.

After the meeting they went out for a cup of coffee, and their friendship blossomed into something more. He was tall, boyishly handsome, and shy. She was brash, funny, and smart. "I think he saw me as some worldly woman," Catherine would say later, "which is a riot in retrospect"—though not to a twenty-year-old dating a divorced single mother. Maybe some of the magic that night derived from the role reversal. He was the one who was comforting and advising, and she was the one who felt incompetent and immature. Too often in the "real world" he was reminded of his immaturity, and she was reminded of her responsibilities.

Their first two months were lighthearted. Chad hadn't had a great deal of experience with women, and he felt as though he'd emerged from adolescence. Catherine's first husband had been ten years older than she, previously divorced, and no barrel of laughs. She felt as though she'd been freed from premature middle age.

But when she got pregnant just weeks after their first date, everything changed. His parents were convinced that Catherine had secretly planned it; she insisted that it was the last thing she wanted. Her daughter was living with her parents while she was getting clean. She was trying to focus on getting her child back. She wasn't looking for a husband, and she certainly wasn't looking for another child. She had no intention of pressuring Chad in any way, she insisted. She was ready to take full responsibility.

Chad talked to his father, who laid out his options. He decided to do the honorable thing. During an N.A. meeting, Chad asked Catherine to accompany him to the car.

"What is it?" she asked after they'd climbed in.

"We need to get a license," he said.

"A license?" she said. "A license for what?"

"To get married."

She didn't say anything right away. For once she held her tongue. "Whoo, romance!" she thought. "You old softy, you." She recalled the moment later with nostalgia, not bitterness—and an almost maternal affection. He wasn't trying to be unromantic, she decided, he just didn't know how to say it. "He later redid it and did it very well," she added.

They were married on June 26, 1992—two months after their coffee date. They moved in with his parents, and trouble moved with them. Catherine had had a stormy enough relationship with her own parents; she certainly wasn't looking for another go-round. Yet, Chad had a job, and she didn't. That left her alone a lot with his parents. Sometimes during her first trimester she spent all morning in bed, which fed his parents' fear that she was a freeloader. To them she was lazy, moody, and manipulative. Chad, who was in many ways dependent on his parents, was caught in the middle.

Finally, the Maiers boiled over, and Catherine was sent packing. Chad took off on a vacation with his buddies, leaving Catherine—jobless, homeless, and pregnant—to fend for herself. She quickly found an apartment and two jobs. By the time Chad returned, she was back on her feet. Chad wanted to make a clean start, and Catherine agreed, but their problems shadowed them. Catherine's life had long been a matter of one step forward, two steps back. Often it took a fiasco like her "honeymoon" at the Maiers to bring out the fighter who dwelled within. Chad was ambivalent about much in his life, and when pressure mounted, he had a tendency to bolt.

Things seemed a little better the following February, when Asher was born. They had been talking about getting Catherine's daughter Lauren back. Reuniting with her was something Catherine had been aiming for, and Chad, who got along well with the child, had expressed his full support. But when it was time to make a move, Chad had a change of heart. He was again feeling overwhelmed by responsibilities. And so he bailed out for the final time, two weeks before their first anniversary.

Chad's parents were much relieved. They'd tried, they said, but they never could abide this match. Their only concern about the impending divorce was how it would affect their access to Asher.

18

The Colsons

"Don't you know that my son was the first child who died at the Cutros' day care?" Lindy Colson asked Patsy Habben, her anger sizzling through the telephone line. "Aren't you interested in what I have to say?"

She knew that SLED agents were unterviewing parents as they investigated the day care. She'd also heard, to her disgust, that they seemed to be digging for dirt. She was doubly angry that no one had contacted her.

Habben assured Colson that she was very interested in talking to her. Could Lindy and her husband give statements right away?

———

With her shoulder-length blonde hair, blue eyes, and sturdy figure, Lindy Colson was the picture of wholesomeness. By nature strong, independent, and buoyant, her fortitude had been sorely tested by the loss of her son Parker. It had left her feeling much older than twenty-eight, and the ordeal was by no means over. There were new setbacks all the time. A big one was the death of Ashlan Daniel.

By the time Lindy Colson called Patsy Habben, it had been ten months since her son had died, and the equilibrium had returned to her marriage. Lindy and Gary Colson both worked for a graphics company that couldn't have been more supportive. When Parker died, the boss had told them to take as much time off as they needed—with pay. Lindy had come back after two weeks; she needed to be around people again. Gary also needed to get out of the house, but he wanted to be alone. He started going to work at odd hours, when no one was around. When he was finally ready to come back on a regular schedule, he told the boss he didn't want anyone treating him differently. The boss spread the word, and that's the way it was.

It helped that Lindy and Gary had both been married before—and had learned from those experiences. They supported one another, but they also coped on their own in different ways. To Lindy, Linda Bass's support group was crucial. The meetings made her feel that she wasn't alone, that others could understand and share her burden.

Gary's approach was different. At thirty-eight, he was a decade older than his wife and, unlike her, he hadn't grown up in Irmo, where Lindy had always felt safe. Gary was raised in Miami by parents who came from the Detroit area. His parents had always been wary of people, and Gary shared their caution. Lindy trusted her neighbors; Gary trusted few people. He had good friends in South Carolina, but when he had a serious problem, he called his sister, who was fourteen years older, or friends from Miami he'd known most of his life.

When Parker died, he immediately suspected the worst—and focused on the Cutros. "I'll kill them," he thought. He could never accept that his son died of natural causes. He never truly believed in the mysterious killer called SIDS. He needed answers. "When someone tells you that your son, who you waited thirty-eight years for, just goes to sleep and never wakes up, that's bullshit," he thought.

Gary went to the meetings with Lindy for a while, but really just to support her. It seemed to him that there was a competitive, "can-you-top-this" undercurrent to the group, and he was upset enough as it was. "Instead of you sitting by yourself wanting to blow your brains out," he would later put it, "you're in a room with ten other people that want to do the same thing." He was a very emotional person, but he kept a lot of it in.

When the Colsons gave their statements—on the same day that Lindy had called Lt. Habben—Lindy did more of the talking. It wasn't that Gary was the tall, silent type, like Davis Daniel. In fact, he was five foot six and could be an engaging conversationalist. He just didn't care to talk about the death of his firstborn. His feelings ran strong and deep, and he thought it best not to stir them unnecessarily. Besides, his wife had been the child's primary caregiver.

For Richard Hunton and Patsy Habben, Lindy's interview was the most challenging of all that they'd done—not because she was resistant or uncooperative, but because they knew she was pregnant. That was why they'd avoided calling her: They worried that asking about the most painful event of her life might jeopardize her pregnancy.

In the ten months since Parker's death, Lindy said, the Cutros had been "very supportive of us" and "we have been supportive of the Cutros." She went on:

> I don't believe that the Cutros had anything to do with Parker's death. . . . Both Josh and Gail Cutro came to the funeral home and also to the burial service for Parker. . . . Josh and Gail still go to the gravesite on a fairly regular basis. . . . The Cutros put a flower arrangement and a balloon arrangement on Parker's grave for his birthday. They recently left a Halloween gift on his grave and the Cutros have left other gifts there as well. Mrs. Cutro requested a set of Parker's footprints and a photograph of Parker. I gave both of these to Gail and she has them at her home. . . .

Just before the interview concluded, Lindy made her only reference to the baby growing inside her. "We had planned to take our coming child to the Cutros'," she said, "but after the death of the second child, we probably won't."

She also apologized for her abrasive manner on the phone earlier in the day. People were saying that SLED was on a witch hunt, and that had riled her. She knew that SIDS couldn't be prevented, and that Parker had "just gone to sleep." But she'd been pleasantly surprised to find the SLED agents polite and professional, and she felt much better about the investigation. Before she left, Lindy mentioned that her due date was in April. Habben wondered whether they could shield her from information that long.

A seedling of doubt had already been planted. Lindy had told Habben that she just wanted to know the truth, thinking that she already did. But the day after the interview she called back. She'd looked over her records and noticed a discrepancy. The coroner's report said that Gail found Parker. But Lindy distinctly remembered that Josh told her *he* had. Lindy wasn't sure if this was important, but she thought she ought to call. Habben thanked her and filed the information away. No, Habben mused, it might not be possible to shield Lindy Colson for very long.

19

In Good Hands

How do parents evaluate a day care? Dr. Julia Wrigley, a sociology professor at the City University of New York who has written extensively about child care, said economists have found that when people can't measure the quality of something directly, they focus on a proxy. She cited the example of large child care centers with beautiful lobbies. Parents are often convinced—consciously or unconsciously—that the standards of service inside are reflected in what they see when they enter the building. "The research shows there is no relationship between having a nice lobby and having well-paid, high-quality caregivers in your center," Dr. Wrigley said. "But the parents are going by what they can see, and they falsely assume there's some relationship."

In home day cares, a common proxy is cleanliness. The unstated (and in some cases unconscious) assumption is that someone who keeps her home neat and clean will look after children with the same efficiency. Dr. Wrigley has often heard parents voice this sentiment. "I know she's great," they'll say. "Her house is so spic and span, you can eat off the floor." Many parents who used the Cutro day care said something similar. They lavished their praise in nearly every statement Patsy Habben and Richard Hunton wrote down.

Some professionals who study child care have a different view of an immaculate home. Caregivers whose homes are pristine tend to be rigid, they say, and may be more likely to lash out when their ordered worlds are disrupted, as they inevitably are by the presence of children. There's no data on this, Dr. Wrigley noted, but it's a common anecdotal observation.

Whether a very clean day care is a good sign or a bad one, the point is this: It guarantees nothing. It's no greater assurance of quality service than a beautiful lobby. Impressions based on superficial observations are understandable, especially on first inspection, but they're inherently unreliable.

The challenge for parents is digging deeper, and a number of books purport to help. One of the most useful is *The Daycare Rating Book* by Josephine Santelli (Up Spirit Press, 2004). It explains the different child care options, lists the pros and cons of each, and includes questions parents should ask a provider. There are also checklists of what to look for. Santelli covers a wide range of issues, from qualifications, philosophy, and policies to safety. There's even a scoring system that allows a reader to rate a provider as unacceptable, average, above average, or excellent.

In the Cutro day care, virtually all the parents met with the Cutros before enrolling their children. Many went into the meeting predisposed to like the couple because of their active participation in their church, and nearly all came away duly impressed. Even years later, after they'd learned many things they'd never known, parents had a hard time picking out signs that they'd missed. When Ramona Bowers was asked to grade the day care using the form in Santelli's book (and based on the information she'd had at the time), she went through all the questions and ended up giving the day care the highest possible rating—excellent—even though she'd long since decided she should not have continued to use the day care after Ashlan died.

There's nothing particularly surprising about that. The Daniels, too, were at a loss to find something they'd missed. The information parents can obtain about a day care prior to enrolling a child is usually quite limited. Santelli herself implicitly acknowledges this. Her book doesn't end with the rating form. Unlike the authors of other books on this subject, she recognizes that the parent's job isn't over with the selection of a day care. In fact, it's just beginning.

Santelli's most important chapter is called "Keeping an Ongoing Review of Care." She talks about the need to be vigilant and to continue gathering information. One way to do this is to drop in unannounced. "I would like to stress that surprise or unscheduled visits are important not only to you but to the entire daycare system," she writes. "Due to lack of funds and the shortage of licensing agents, many daycare arrangements are not adequately monitored." Caregivers aren't always thrilled by the idea, but Santelli says parents can explain that the visits are necessary to make them feel comfortable. Providers who refuse to allow them "should be avoided," she advises.

One option for some parents is volunteering to spend time at the day care helping out. This often yields two important benefits: Parents can observe the operation regularly, and they can get to know other parents in the process. Other parents, Santelli notes, are a great source of information. This is especially true for the parents of infants. Their children can't verbalize what goes on inside the day care, while the children of other parents can.

The parents who used the Cutro day care had neither the time nor the opportunity to volunteer there. And with a few exceptions, they didn't share very much information. At least not before the Cutros were being investigated. Ironically, the day care parents communicated with each other more to rally around the Cutros when they were being investigated than they ever had before.

Still, the statements Habben took from the parents suggested just how much they might have learned had there been an open line of communication. Though many were quite satisfied with the quality of care, the feeling was by no means universal. And some of the parents who weren't happy raised serious questions about the operation.

20

Complaints

As Patsy Habben continued to interview parents who had used the day care, she found a pocket of disenchantment. Among the recent crop of families, it was a small contingent. When Ashlan Daniel died, eleven children were enrolled. The families of only two decided they needed to make a change.

One parent who pulled her child was Brenda Davidson. She'd begun using the day care in early 1992, but days before Ashlan died, she began splitting her son's time between the Cutros and a preschool program in a church nearby. A month after the death, Davidson made the switch full-time. But her statement to Habben made it clear that Davidson's decision was based not on what happened to Ashlan but on her own frequent clashes with the Cutros.

In her police report, Davidson described two main issues. She'd long complained about the amount of television her son Steven was watching at the day care, and she wasn't satisfied by what she saw as the Cutros' minimal efforts to curtail it. The couple also objected to her habit of dropping by unannounced to check on her son—even though this is something child care experts almost universally advise. The Cutros asked her to call in advance, which she did for a time. But when she resumed picking up her son without notice, she found the door locked and the curtains drawn, and she had to wait several minutes for someone to answer.

The second parent was Margaret Schuler Burke, who removed her 3-year-old son specifically because of Ashlan's death. "I felt like it wasn't a good emotional environment for J.T.," she told Habben. The Cutros were obviously very upset, explained Burke, a technical writer who had recently divorced, and "it seemed to take so long for the Cutros to heal from the first death, I didn't want J.T. to be exposed to this emotional experience again."

There was also something else that bothered her. Though Burke had been generally satisfied during the two and a half years she'd used the day care, she knew that the Cutros cared for quite a few kids, including two infants. They also prepared meals for the children, and additional food to sell to the parents. "I often wondered," Burke told Habben, "how the Cutros could properly care for seven to ten day care children, meet the needs of their own children, and still prepare meals for those that wanted them."

It's clear from the other parents' statements that Burke wasn't the only one who was troubled by this thought—or troubled by the emotional environment. Yet, neither these concerns, nor the two deaths and the injury, led the others to act.

The reasons varied. Some parents weren't even aware of all three events. Others, like Ramona Bowers, didn't feel it was fair to blame the Cutros for deaths that doctors were saying were no one's fault. Most felt sorry for the couple. After all, Josh and Gail had been the ones who had discovered the lifeless bodies and seemed so deeply moved—as if the children had been their own. Even the Colsons, despite the loss of their son Parker, had planned to send their next child to the Cutros' day care.

As for Asher Maier's injury, Josh and Gail had a ready defense when questions came up. They insisted that the child hadn't been well for two days before Catherine Maier took him to the doctor. Despite their own entreaties, the Cutros said, Catherine had refused to take him. It was only when Gail threatened to take the child herself that Catherine finally relented, Gail told the others.

Catherine Maier's version of the events was quite different. She agreed that she and Gail had been concerned about Asher the previous two days, and wondered whether he was teething. But she insisted that the first time Gail suggested she take Asher to the doctor was the day she did. After Asher was injured, however, Maier wasn't around to tell that to the other parents.

———

Dissatisfaction with the Cutros' day care actually ran much deeper than the minimal defections after Ashlan's death suggested. As Habben interviewed parents who had used the day care in earlier years, before Parker Colson and Ashlan Daniel died, she learned that seven families had been unhappy enough to remove their kids. This represented nearly a third of the 22 families that had used the day care, and it did not include families that moved or simply made other arrangements.

Some parents voiced specific complaints about the way their children were treated. One mother's confidence in the day care began to wane after her seven-month-old son came home with an injury for which the Cutros' explanation struck her as implausible. As she described it, he had a large red bruise on his back that seemed to be a handprint. When she demanded an explanation, the Cutors professed ignorance. Maybe he fell on a toy, they suggested.

Other parents complained about the caregivers' attitudes. Several echoed the common complaint that when Josh began working at the day care, the operation began to feel more like a business than a service. For others, however, there wasn't one big issue. There were lots of little things. Ultimately, these parents simply felt uneasy or uncomfortable leaving their children with the Cutros.

Michele Kelso pulled her daughter seven months before the first death. Nicole, who was five, was by far the oldest child there, yet the Cutros treated her the way they treated the younger ones. Until her mother complained, Nicole was made to wear a bib when she ate and to take a nap after lunch. Even more troubling to Kelso, who was a licensed practical nurse, was the locked door. Nicole usually stayed half-days, and when Kelso arrived to pick her up, she often had a long wait outside. This bothered her as much as it later did Brenda Davidson.

"When the Cutros answered the door," Kelso told Habben, "I had the feeling that something just wasn't quite right—kind of like they were preventing me from coming in, and then getting Nicole out the door as quickly as possible when they finally unlocked it." She found the experience unsettling. The "face" that the Cutros had put on when she interviewed them, Kelso told

Habben, summing up her dissatisfaction, didn't match the reality she found when her daughter enrolled.

Overall, the parents' statements revealed that plenty harbored at least some concerns. And the total number of families that removed their children as a result was nine out of 22, or 41 percent. Yet, paradoxically, fewer seemed to act on their misgivings *after* the deaths and the injury than *before*. Rather than frightening parents away, these events actually seemed to bind them to the day care.

The "emotional environment" that convinced Burke to leave after Ashlan died seemed to have a different effect on the other parents who were using the day care then. While Habben was grappling with questions about the children's safety, many parents were focused on the apparently devastated couple. Compassion seemed to trump hard-nosed analysis. The parents' decision to allow their children to stay may have been less a vote of confidence than an expression of sympathy.

21

The Salve of SIDS

The Daniels had been rooting for Gail to pass the polygraph exam. They desperately wanted to believe that Ashlan died of SIDS. It would have been an enormous comfort. If Ashlan died of SIDS, then no one was to blame, and no one could have prevented it. They hadn't chosen the wrong place or the wrong people. Their child had died peacefully in her sleep.

If Gail had passed the polygraph, maybe they could have believed that. There probably would have been lingering doubts. "How can she pass it," Missy Daniel couldn't help but wonder, "when I've sat here and heard all these different stories?" Still, as Davis Daniel later put it: "You don't want to believe that someone could hurt your child."

When Richard Hunton drove over with the polygraph results, the salve of

SIDS was gone. They still wanted to believe, and they were aware that polygraphs were imperfect, but there were too many reasons to doubt.

Without the exoneration of SIDS, they turned their judgment both outward, to the woman who failed the polygraph, and sharply inward. What could they have known? Was there something they didn't see? These were the questions that would haunt the couple for years.

"We investigated," Missy would later explain. "We checked Gail out thoroughly." They visited the home, interviewed Josh and Gail, called parents whose children were enrolled. They'd done everything they thought necessary.

"How do you know?" Missy asked, wishing the question weren't rhetorical.

She paused before she continued. "I hold the guilt," she said at last, "because I was the one who was able to stay home. And I wanted to get out and work. Because we needed the extra income. Always comes in handy. And my problem is I feel very selfish because that could have cost my child's life."

"We both made the decision," Davis countered. "I went to the same interviews." He searched for a minute to find the right words. "My guilt," he said, "is: How could I let this happen? What did I miss?"

The pain that was tearing them up inside was also taking a toll on their marriage. After their chance meeting with Lindy Colson the day after Ashlan died, they'd gone to Linda Bass's support group, as Colson had suggested. But Davis was taciturn by nature, and Missy had been raised by parents who insisted that family matters remain private. Not only was her family tight-lipped around outsiders, they didn't all speak to each other. Her family had been riven by her parents' extremely bitter divorce when Missy was still in grammar school. Missy's father and younger brother remained in Alabama, where Missy was born, while she and her mother moved to South Carolina. After the move, her parents had no contact.

Given this background, it was not exactly second nature for Missy to spill her guts to a "support group" of strangers. And then, after Gail failed the polygraph, and they no longer believed that their daughter died of SIDS, there didn't seem to be any point in going.

The Daniels looked elsewhere for help. Davis found a visit from the associate pastor of their church comforting, and Missy, who lost twenty pounds during the month after Ashlan died, leaving her five-foot-eight-inch frame a gaunt 120 pounds, visited a counselor several times. But by and large, they dealt with their loss alone.

There were times when it brought them closer together, but at other times it seemed to drive a wedge between them. Even before Ashlan died, and perhaps because of her own parents' divorce, Missy Daniel had had a hard time trusting people. She would get close and closer, and then she'd pull back—from friends, from relatives, even from Davis. After she was convinced that the people she'd entrusted with her daughter's care were responsible for Ashlan's death, Missy wondered how she could ever trust again.

Davis Daniel's family had been close when he was growing up and remained so. He and his sisters talked more often and grew closer in the wake of Ashlan's death. Sometimes he felt that closeness with Missy. She was the only person who could truly understand what he was feeling. And he needed that—someone to understand and share his sorrow. They both did.

But at other moments their loss seemed to underscore all the differences between them. At thirty-eight, Davis was eleven years older and had been married once before. He was the father of a sixteen-year-old daughter, whom he saw at least once or twice a month. At times these facts seemed inconsequential to his relationship with Missy, but at other times his past seemed to intrude. It bothered Missy that Davis cared so much about his daughter—as if this were a reflection on Missy's distant relationship with her own father. Davis didn't understand the dynamics very well. There was a great deal about her family that remained a mystery to him—a great deal that Missy wouldn't, or couldn't, explain.

The more immediate differences, however, were the obvious ones in their personalities. Davis was quiet and self-contained. He was used to being alone, and his natural inclination in the face of disaster was to withdraw into himself. Missy hated solitude under any circumstances. She needed to talk, and she needed her husband's support.

"I was leaning on him real bad," she recalled about that time. "I was leaning, wanting him to comfort me, and it was just pushing him away."

"You just look at each other and there's so much hurt," Davis explained. "And you don't know how to help."

So, like the Colsons, the Daniels grieved in their own ways. Often they did so side by side, rather than together. But for the Daniels it was more complicated. First, they had a harder time melding their differences. Davis struggled to communicate but inevitably began turning inward; Missy reached out and grew increasingly depressed. Second, they were wrestling with *two* cataclysmic shocks at once. They were struggling to cope with the loss of their child, as the Colsons were. But unlike the Colsons, they believed that she was the victim of murder.

They believed while fervently wishing they didn't. They struggled to assimilate the nightmare, and they staggered under the crushing guilt that came with it.

22

Notes

Where you had therapists, you had therapists' notes. And notes were good. You could learn a lot about a person from her therapists' notes.

These were Patsy Habben's thoughts as she struggled to learn more about Gail. They led her to visit one person whom she knew would have notes, and another she only suspected would.

Her first stop was the South Carolina Department of Mental Health, where she obtained a copy of Gail's file from her therapist, Eve Powell. That was the easy one. Habben had a premonition that her next stop would be harder.

She knew that Linda Bass had spoken to the Cutros the night Ashlan Daniel died and several times since. Bass, too, must have notes. But her situation was a little different. Habben remembered the talk they'd had over lunch at the coroners' conference. As diplomatic as Bass had been, she'd been talking about a well-known conflict that was usually described in quite *un*diplomatic terms: the clash between SIDS counselors and law-enforcement investigators. There was a lot of mistrust between the groups, and Habben wasn't expecting to be greeted with warmth. She hoped for a polite, professional encounter, but she prepared for a confrontation. She brought one of her female investigators as a witness rather than Richard Hunton, figuring that Bass might find two women less threatening. And she wore a wire to record the conversation.

There were good reasons for the mutual suspicion between the two camps. Sudden infant death syndrome hadn't even been named until 1969, and years later it remained as mysterious as ever. Many theories about its cause had been floated over the years, ranging from an enlarged thymus gland to a defective heart to an allergic reaction to cow's milk. Cases of SIDS were sometimes attributed to something else, such as pneumonia, because an autopsy revealed evidence of infection—though not enough of one to be fatal. But over time it was more often over-diagnosed. It was a convenient catchall used by some coroners and medical examiners as a kind of "dustbin diagnosis" in which to dump cases that were puzzling or troubling or politically unpalatable (as, say, when the authorities preferred to ignore the bruises on the body of a prominent family's child).

As SIDS began to be recognized as a legitimate cause of death—even though it was poorly understood—a movement was launched by parents of SIDS victims and sympathetic researchers to shield parents from accusation and suspicion. In the 1970s, cases in which the police had wrongly assumed that parents had murdered their children began to appear in the popular media as examples of investigation at its worst—insensitive, incompetent, and abusive.

Several years later came revelations of a trend the other way. Pathologists began to acknowledge that the diagnosis of SIDS sometimes concealed infanticide. In 1990, Gannett News Service ran a four-part series called "Getting Away with Murder," which won a Pulitzer Prize in 1991 for national reporting. "It is easy to kill a child and bury the secret," the first story began. "Throughout America, poorly trained coroners and shoddy death investigations are helping mothers and fathers get away with murder." Nearly one of every twelve deaths labeled SIDS, the reporters found, was not even autopsied.

This was the historical backdrop when Patsy Habben entered Linda Bass's office. It wasn't the first time the two had spoken about the case. Bass had called to volunteer information about the Cutros, with their knowledge and permission. Her goal then, she recalled later, was to "clear Gail" and to "help expedite things." In retrospect, she acknowledged, the gesture was naïve. "I guess with me not knowing any more than I knew about the legal system and how it works, you don't expedite something like this. It just is something that has to go its full course."

When the two women first met at that lunch in Charleston, Bass had been irrepressible. This time she was subdued. She smiled, but it was a tight, tense smile. When Habben asked to see her notes, Bass fumbled through her files. To Habben, she appeared nervous. Finally, Bass pulled out a page with an account of Ashlan's death and the notation "Story from Josh."

"Can I see the rest of this?" Habben asked after she'd read it.

"That's all there is."

"But Linda, it says 'over' on the bottom."

"The rest of it isn't relevant."

"Well, can I see it anyway?"

Bass told her that she'd have to talk to the hospital's lawyer if Habben wanted anything else. She hadn't minded sharing the one page, but Gail was her patient, and the hospital required her to maintain patient confidentiality.

The new child fatality law gave her department the right to subpoena all records, Habben replied. If Linda didn't want to turn over her notes, then they'd serve her with a subpoena.

"It's not that I don't want to," Bass protested. "There are hospital policies and procedures I have to follow." Asked later about this incident, Bass said that she didn't remember the entire conversation, but she remembered why she withheld the rest of her notes. The first page was purely factual, but the rest was "fairly sensitive stuff, and a lot of it was my opinion and really not so much fact."

Habben left without the additional notes. The next morning Richard Hunton returned with the promised subpoena, and Bass turned over two more pages. The notes read, in part:

> *9-16-93* Josh called—Had done polygraph→clean bill—Gail was suicidal this past Monday. . . .

> *9-21-93* I called Gail—talked [to] her re possibility of polygraph. She said she didn't think she could do it because her nerves were so bad. Said Eve had urged her not to because she probably could not withstand it & because of all the medication she is on—SLED had told me that the investigation would end if she came in & took the polygraph. I wonder about polygraphs—esp. if a person is self-blaming & feeling responsible for something they didn't do. I know she feels responsible—because she was responsible for the care of the baby and because the baby died while in her home. . . .

> *10-5-93* Talked [to] Gail. She took polygraph last night (?11pm) at urging of Daniels family. She failed it. She said they (officers) "got in my face" & told her she suffocated the baby [with] saran wrap—they said a part of her "split off" & that's why she doesn't remember doing it. I feel sick

inside. This is not a murderer. She's been in child care 14 yrs. With an unblemished record until this year. Parker *couldn't* have been suffocated. He still had a heartrate when Josh started CPR. Suffocation would have been reversible; SIDS isn't. And Asher would have been dead if Gail hadn't noticed that he wasn't acting right; his mother was a known abuser (but not known by Gail at the time). Ashland died with Gail & other children in the room. SIDS babies die with no warning or sound. To accuse Gail of suffocation doesn't make sense. There's no reason or motive.

23

Shut Down

In South Carolina, day care providers were required to report deaths or serious injuries to DSS, as Josh had done after Parker Colson died. But according to DSS records, no one reported Asher Maier's injury or Ashlan Daniel's death. After 1993, partly as a result of the Cutro case, procedures were introduced to facilitate better communication between the DSS child protective workers and the organization's Day Care Licensing division. But at the time, even though Lexington DSS investigated the shaking of Asher Maier, the state licensing people knew nothing about it.

Once they did, and once Patsy Habben got up to speed on how the system worked, she soon recognized the key role of that department. Habben knew that she'd have to go to court to close the day care. The licensing agency was her ticket, and the hearing in mid-October was the show.

———

The parents weren't the only ones who spoke up for the Cutros as the date approached. Additional endorsements came from professionals. Linda Bass told DSS's Gary Kirkbride that Gail was in one of her SIDS support groups and was "the reason it started up." A former family day care provider named Pat Reid wrote to the state DSS. Reid was active in the South Carolina Home Child Care Association and also administered a U. S. Department of Agriculture Child Care Food Program. In that capacity she'd inspected many homes, and she was greatly impressed with the Cutros, she wrote.

A number of the parents were eagerly awaiting the hearing. They worked the phones to ensure they'd have a good turnout. Several hoped to have a chance to testify to show their support.

When the big night finally arrived, about ten of them showed up. More wanted to, but it wasn't easy for working mothers with young children to get away. Ramona Bowers was there. So was Jana Brown. And Pat Reid showed up. All had much they wanted to say.

But they never got the chance. To their surprise, the confrontation they expected never materialized. None of the things they'd pictured and prepped for happened. There was no passionate testimony, no public debate. Instead there were meetings behind closed doors, and a short time later a settlement was announced.

The parents weren't the only ones who were surprised by this development. Sherry Driggers, the diminutive director of Day Care Licensing, arrived for the hearing expecting a battle. She'd been led to believe that the Cutros and their lawyer were prepared for combat and was relieved when the couple offered little resistance.

There were good reasons. Intellectually, the Cutros had already accepted the inevitable—as the note Josh had given caseworkers promising they'd close in November had suggested. Emotionally, they were looking for something to make the closing palatable. That was what the Cutros and their lawyer, Thom Neal, seemed to be seeking as they talked about settling.

After some back and forth, Driggers offered them a temporary injunction. They wouldn't be shut down permanently by the court order. They would be enjoined from operating until SLED completed its investigation. If and when they were cleared, the Cutros would be free to reopen—provided, of course, that they complied with the enrollment requirements. They took it. And why not? Under the circumstances, this was a pretty sweet deal for them.

After all the eager anticipation, the air was suddenly out of the balloon. When it was over, the Cutros seemed to be in better spirits than the parents. They didn't appear devastated. The deal struck their lawyer as eminently reasonable. He expected that the investigation would, in fact, clear his clients, and that they would then be free to restart their business. And the Cutros agreed. So after all the build-up, the settlement was quick and easy.

It was the last piece of the Cutro case that was.

24

A Cry from the Heart

Missy Daniel sat down to compose the letter she'd wanted to write ever since the polygraph. She'd wanted to get Ashlan's car seat back—she felt that she was finally capable of dealing with it. Then she thought about the phone conversation she'd had with Josh Cutro just the week before.

"If this is any help to you," Josh had said, referring to the day he'd tried to revive her daughter, "she was still warm." Just thinking about that remark made her queasy. She thought about all the other things Josh and Gail had said: how they blamed the EMS people for responding so slowly, how Gail was glad she could "take this burden" from Missy.

She picked up her pen and started writing.

10-30-93

Gail,

I am writing to you because you must hear my feelings for what has happened to my daughter.

I'm unsure as to what has happened to Ashlan Melissa. She was a precious gift from God to Davis & I and her life was taken for no reason. Ashlan was a person, a human, a future ahead of her, our future. God's child. I put all my trust in you or she would never have been left. This is the reason I quit my job so this would not happen, nothing would happen to such a precious child who was so loved & wanted.

In my heart I can't believe this is a SIDS case. She is against all the odds of this. I don't like how we have been pushed to believe this, pushed into a support group, the community thinking this. Turned against EMS. You telling us they didn't do anything. Well when you called 911 you said she was dead! This bothers me. Why tell me that she was warm? Why did you say you had done CPR till the ambulance arrived when infact nothing was done? I'm very disturbed of the story you have told me that she was tired you laid her down & she went to sleep w/out rocking or strolling her. Never! Also she will never go into a playpen let alone go to sleep by herself. I know my daughter. She was a extremly healthy & happy child. Do you at all realize how this makes me feel to live w/out my child but to wonder how she died? It is terrible, you have never experienced losing a child of your own.

Remember when Davis & I first came to interview you in May. I was very specific in making sure CPR was known & also about watching her & checking her & you told me you would check her constantly. You told me you had a previous SIDS in your home. Just because this was discussed there is noway this would happen. She has never had any problem w/breathing, sickness etc. Also I'm w/her 22 hours a day and the 2 hrs. she was left she died?? Why was her formula poured out? Why won't you cooperate w/the police, SLED etc. & you have an attorney. If your not guilty why all this? Why was the test failed? Can't you remember what happened? What happened Thursday September 9th, 1993?

Put yourself in our place & wonder if we were keeping your child. Wouldn't you want us to cooperate? Yes! Would you just let this go? No. Would you just sit back? No. We can't & refuse to any longer.

I'am a Christian & I believe in God & the only peace I have is knowing that Ashlan Melissa is happy w/God & can never be hurt ever.

I want the truth! If the truth doesn't come now it will be known on judgement day. For God know's all!

All I want is for this to never of happened & Ashlan returned to us for we love her, miss & need her.

Missy

25

Homing In

Penetrating the Cutros' private world wasn't easy, and Patsy Habben had only Richard Hunton working on it full-time. But she also had help from outside her department. Two people in particular were adding pieces to the portrait.

Irmo police officer Tim Stephenson, who had been the first cop on the scene the day that Ashlan Daniel died, was a big contributor. Stephenson lived just around the corner from the Cutros, and his proximity proved valuable. In the mornings he drove by to see who was around. If the house was empty, and the Cutros had left their garbage out for collection, he returned home, got in his pickup truck and grabbed the bags himself. Or, if the garbage truck was already in the area, he let the sanitation men do the dirty work and met them around the corner. Either way it was legal as long as the garbage was by the curb, where the courts have deemed it fair game. He drove the bags to SLED, where he and Richard Hunton would take them out to the parking lot and sift through the detritus, looking for anything that might prove useful.

One thing the trash told them was that the Cutros had financial problems. Hunton recalled "numerous bills from a number of agencies." Over time they saw a pattern. "There would just be a lot of them overdue by months and months." Then came the letters from collection agencies.

One time Hunton found an application for a food program the Cutros had filled out. They were claiming an income of something like $10,000, Hunton remembered. But when he multiplied the number of children by the amount their parents paid, he figured they had to be making at least $30,000 to $40,000 a year.

Stephenson's surveillance wasn't limited to garbage collection. Sometimes he parked near the house and spent a few hours watching who was coming and going and listening to conversations. His listening device was a scanner that picked up the Cutros' conversations on their cordless phone. The technique was later outlawed, but at the time it, too, was legal, and Stephenson recorded many conversations.

Initially, Missy Daniel had been another active contributor. During the first several weeks she'd been able to report to Habben regularly about her telephone conversations with Gail. But then their communication grew strained. She knew that Gail was visiting Ashlan's grave. This alone was disturbing to Missy, but then Gail began leaving behind not just the usual flowers but knickknacks like cards and toys.

There was something about this—turning grief into a kind of fetish—that Missy found unbearable. She asked Gail to stop, and that led to a rift between them. Gail complied, but she seemed offended and treated Missy coolly. Then came the polygraph followed by Missy's letter, and communication stopped altogether.

For Missy, this was even worse. She'd vented her anger, but what had that accomplished? She needed to feel that she was doing something to advance the investigation. And now she just felt impotent. She wished that she could patch things up with Gail and continue to ply her for information. But she didn't know how.

26

Grief

Unlike Missy Daniel, Lindy Colson did not find Gail's demonstrations of sorrow off-putting. Quite the contrary; their mutual grief over Parker's death had forged a bond between them.

They'd both joined one of Linda Bass's support groups, and they'd worked to raise money for research on SIDS. Their first project had been Red Nose Day back in April. This was a nationwide fundraiser organized by the National SIDS Alliance. Lindy and Gail had set up a table at a mall on the designated day and sold red noses to publicize the cause. (For those who didn't want to wear them, a badge was available.)

Gail had also helped Gary and Lindy organize a fundraiser of their own. In July they'd hosted a softball game, and the three of them along with Linda

Bass even appeared on television news the night before the game to talk it up.

It was really a way for Gary to get involved. He'd never been comfortable with the support group. When he thought about doing something to honor Parker, the first thing that came to mind was baseball. He'd played at the University of Miami, and more than anything he'd looked forward to playing with his son.

As welcome as Gail's expressions of grief may have been to Lindy Colson, they were not uniformly embraced by the day care parents. After Parker died, Gail asked Lindy for imprints of his feet. She'd framed these and displayed them in her home, along with a photograph of Parker, as a memorial. She'd also talked to the children regularly about Parker, urging them to remember him. All of this made some parents uncomfortable.

Several parents mentioned this in their police statements. Brenda Davidson later elaborated in court, where she testified that Gail was "obsessed" with Parker Colson's death. "It wasn't a once-a-month mentioning of Parker," Davidson testified. "It was almost a daily mentioning of Parker. She told me she would talk to the children about remembering" him.

That was where Davidson drew the line. "I told her that I had a small problem with that," she said, "because I didn't want my two-year-old son—actually less than two-year-old son—to be talked to about death, because I didn't think it was something he needed to know about." Margaret Schuler Burke had a similar reaction. She removed her son from the day care after the second death so that he wouldn't be exposed to that emotional environment.

Ramona Bowers, on the other hand, continued to bring Tate to support Gail in her hour of need. It would be years before she regretted that thinking. Parents sometimes find it hard to separate their own feelings from the needs of their children—and to ensure that their children's safety comes first. It can be difficult and inconvenient and require uncomfortable introspection.

Dr. Julia Wrigley, the sociologist, has found that changing day cares grows more difficult over time. If parents encounter egregious problems during the first week, she said, they may quickly pull the child. But inertia soon sets in. "People have a desire to be trusting," she noted. They want to believe that the caregiver really cares. "In a way," Dr. Wrigley said, "you're *manifesting* trust in the hope that it will help *generate* trust." The mother and the day care provider often become "quasi-friends," she added. "They feel a liking for each other. They chit chat. So whatever doubts the mother might feel are often held at bay by the social interaction, which makes it harder for them to distance themselves."

For that reason it's often easier for parents to take a hard look at a day care when they're shopping for one than when they're already in the relationship. Even though a parent using a day care has access to a wealth of information not available at the time she signed on, she may not feel comfortable looking for faults. If the provider is viewed as a friend, the instinct may be to support rather than judge her.

For some parents, Dr. Wrigley observed, removing a child from day care "is the most traumatic thing that's ever happened to them." A mother may feel particularly uncomfortable firing someone she has come to view as more of a friend than an employee. And then there are the practical considerations. Severing the relationship means finding someone else. And that means interviewing more people, checking more references, and taking time off work. "It's too exhausting for people," said Dr. Wrigley. So parents often rationalize the easier path and stick with what they've got.

Beyond Dr. Wrigley's observations, it can be hard to know the right thing to do. There are so many questions parents may ask themselves. Suppose a day care provider is a little short-tempered, but good-hearted—and her home is located right on your way to work. Is that okay? What if she's quirky or forgetful. Should that be a deal-breaker?

What if something unfortunate happened in her house, but it wasn't her fault? Should she be blamed for something she couldn't control?

27

Gail

The parents' impressions of Gail Cutro were generally positive. "I was always impressed with Gail's patience," said one. "Also, I noticed that the day care was always very organized. The Cutros kept the children on a good, regular schedule." Gail was described by most parents as reserved or remote, even shy—especially when her husband was around. But they found her pleasant enough, although some noted that she always looked tired.

There was no mystery about that. In addition to running the day care, Gail cooked for her family, cooked for the day care children and their families, cleaned the house, and shuttled the girls to their Southern Strutt dance classes—and young Joshua to karate. And she still found time for church. She not only accompanied Josh to outreach on Tuesday nights and prayer meetings on Wednesday nights, but also baby-sat children during Sunday's second service.

Somehow, she also found time for the activity she seemed to love the most: crafts. Her handiwork was on display everywhere in the house. She sewed lovely needlepoint scenes—Charleston cityscapes were her specialty—which she mounted and hung in wooden frames. She painted a Charleston Victorian house on a piece of wood, screwed cup hooks into the bottom to hang car keys, and mounted it on the wall near the door that led to the carport.

People were always praising her work. After a while, it seemed only logical to try to profit from her talent, so Gail started a side business. She worked whenever she could, plying her sewing machine on the kitchen table or tinkering in the workshop they'd installed in the shed. Then she brought what she'd made to local crafts fairs, sometimes accompanied by her mother or a friend. She kept her prices low, and most of it sold quickly. The business probably would have been more lucrative had she lowered her standards, but she insisted on quality materials and took pride in her work.

How did she do it all? Josh later explained that it wasn't as hard as it looked. They kept the house clean and safe by laying blankets and sheets on the floors and furniture before the kids arrived. At day's end they just folded them up, and the place was good as new. The toys were stored in a huge garbage can that was dumped out in the morning and filled in the afternoon. From an early age the kids were taught to pick up after themselves. (This was more Josh's doing than Gail's—he was the neat freak.) As for the meals, Gail was already cooking for her own family of five. It wasn't much harder, Josh explained, to cook the same meal for other families as well. And it made her feel good to help working mothers who spent little enough time with their children as it was. The last thing these women wanted to do when they got home was spend an hour or two over a hot stove.

As Josh described her, this kind of thing was typical of his wife. Asked what he liked best about Gail, Josh said: "She never puts herself first. Always, you know, ready to do, to please me. And she's always at home, always way ahead. She's not the type of person you have to say, 'Could you do this for me?' She's already done it."

———

All that changed abruptly when the day care closed. The Cutros had to scramble for anything they could get. Josh took a job at a Burger King. Gail eventually began cleaning homes.

But before Gail began doing so, she continued to care for one child in her home, despite the court order barring her from the day care business. Many parents had been upset when the day care was forced to close, but none more than the "Hogans" because they were caught in the biggest bind. (Their names have been changed to protect their daughter's privacy.) Not only were "Gloria" and "Sam" Hogan going through a divorce, they were both hospitalized. As Gloria later explained, she was suffering from mental and emotional problems and Sam was battling cancer. They needed round-the-clock care for their daughter "Rachel," who was almost 3 at the time. They wanted someone the child knew—and someone who wouldn't charge an exorbitant fee. They pleaded with Gail to help them out and were extremely grateful when she agreed.

At the time, the Cutros attempted to conceal Rachel's presence in their home. But ultimately they had to acknowledge it. In retrospect, Josh Cutro was bitter about the whole business because Gloria Hogan first denied the arrangement in her SLED statement, then returned and told the truth. "You know," Josh said about the Hogans, "we went out of our way with those people. They kept coming and begging us to watch Rachel when we shouldn't have, and didn't want to. But they made us feel like, you know, we were just throwing them to the wolves."

Gail was not the kind of person to throw the Hogans or anyone else to the wolves. She never had been good at saying "no"—not even to her own kids. Josh was the disciplinarian in the family. Gail's mother recalled a time when her daughter was having so much trouble dealing with her young children that she telephoned asking for help. "Sometime whenever they'd be real, real, real bad," Pat Hallman said, her daughter would get her on the phone and plead, "Mama, when you come I want you to spank 'em." To which Hallman replied: "Gail, what kind of grandmother do you think the kids are going to think I am if every time I come over there you want me to spank them?" Her daughter's resigned response was: "Well, Mama, I can't do it."

Most of the day care parents thought the Cutro children were well behaved, though some found it odd that the children called their father "Dad" but their mother "Gail." One mother saw something else: "I also noticed that the Cutro children were pretty rowdy, unruly, and disrespectful to their mother."

This woman added a curious coda at the end of her SLED statement: "Once, when I noticed [my daughter] pulling another child's hair at the day care, I popped her lightly on the back of her hand. Gail became angry and said, 'You don't have to hit her. Just move her away.'" The mother was taken aback: "I didn't understand why she overreacted to this minor situation."

This comment was noteworthy because it seemed to be the only instance when a parent described Gail as "angry." Many had seen Josh's temper, but they'd never seen Gail's. Equally unusual was the image of Gail confronting a parent—or anyone else. Josh was no stranger to confrontation; Gail usually withdrew long before it reached that stage.

The incident was all the more remarkable for the source of Gail's anger. She was angry with the mother for using corporal punishment—in its mildest form. Yet, it wouldn't be long before Gail Cutro, who was upset with a mother who had "popped" her daughter's hand, would herself stand accused of snuffing out a child's life.

28

An Unexpected Reply

After Missy Daniel sent Gail Cutro her angry letter, she heard nothing from Gail for weeks. Then, in early December, a letter arrived. There was no name or return address on the envelope. It was postmarked December 2nd, though the date on the letter was three weeks earlier. It was written in a neat script on four sheets of yellow legal paper. As Missy began reading, she saw immediately that whatever she'd expected, this wasn't it. Here's what it said, just as it was written:

11-8-93

Dear Missy,

I don't know if you remember meeting me. I am Gail's mom.

Please don't be angry with Gail for letting me read your letter. It broke my heart to feel so much pain from you. The loss & the why's will always be with you. Our children are truly gifts from God.

From the time Gail was 2½ and I told her that God had planted a baby seed in my stomach & she would have a baby sister or brother, she has wanted to be a mother. A Sunday school teacher once asked her class what they wanted to be when they grew up & Gail told her she just wanted to be a mommy.

She was always more of a mother to Barry, than a sister. When she was a teenager learning to cook, she was always baking cookies for him. She worried over him when he was sick. Later she told me when she was real small that she really thought that Barry was her baby. She always wanted five or six children, but after Lara was born, the doctor told her she should not have any more.

Once when I worked & left them at a day care, the lady whipped Barry (I didn't take them back) & Gail said when she grew up & had children she would never leave them in a day care.

After Gail was told not to have any more children & Lara got older, she thought about keeping little ones that she could love & care for. When their mothers had to work. She told me one day, I feel so empty without a baby in my arms. I really feel like a second mother to my babies, it's sad to see them leave on Friday's.

When you visited in Gail's home to see if she would keep Ashlan, you had to feel this special love or I don't think you would have ever left your little one there.

Barry has two precious little girls, the oldest was born on Gail's birthday & is so special to her. The second one Kaitlin looks like Gail & Barry when they were babies. Gail thinks she looks just like Barry & her heart just melts every time she looks at her. One day I was at Gail's house & I met your little Ashlan. I told her, oh Gail this baby looks like you when you were a baby. Gail said mama look at her real close, don't she look like Kaitlin. She felt the same with your little Ashlan, as she did Kaitlin.

Gail don't keep children, because it's a job she does it because she loves them. I have never heard her raise her voice even at her own children.

What happen to Barry left a scar on Gail & she wanted to try to give these children a home, with lots & lots of love, homemade cookies & taking time to read to them.

After Gail lost Parker, she read everything she could get her hands on about Sids. She could not believe that a healthy baby could lay down for it's nap & go into such a deep sleep. This was very hard for her to accept. If it had not been for the support group & finding out that this had happen to other sitters. I don't think she would have been able to go own keeping children. There have been eight sid death's in her neighborhood in 2 years. She said she would not ever keep another infant. When she would go to church, grocery shopping, etc. if she saw a baby sleeping she wanted to check them & be sure they were still breathing.

I was really surprise when she started keeping Tate & Ashlan, but I knew she was healing & that with some one that loves babies so much, that it would help her. She did check on them often when they were sleeping.

She was told that this would be very rare for this to happen to her again. I prayed & prayed all the way over to her house that every thing would be alright. I did not think she could go through this again.

Being the mother I am that loves her daughter dearly. I told Gail, oh why could this not have happen a little earlier or later at her home & not yours. (Please forgive me for thinking this) She looked at me, & said, oh mama that would have been so hard on Missy, to have found Ashlan like that, it is devastating to lose a child, but to find your own baby, would have been so hard to bear.

I pray that this nightmare will soon be over my daughter has been treated like a criminal. She had had to give up a job she loves, but the pain she feels that you might think that she could hurt your baby is almost too much for her to bear.

Maybe soon (& I do pray for all of us that it will be soon) when this investigation is over. The two of you can talk & she can answer some of your why's. Right now everyone tells her not to talk with you. She really does want to.

Please believe me Missy, my heart just breaks for you & Davis on losing your little bundle of joy & I try to understand why this happen.

My prayers are with you.

Gail's mom
Patricia Hallman
"NANA" to all the little ones that Gail kept.

P.S. Missy, "Jesus Christ" will give us strength to go through each day, with out him we could not make it.

After she read the letter, Missy called Patsy Habben with the news. Habben wanted a copy, and Missy promised to make one and send it right over. In the meantime, she read aloud several passages while Habben scribbled notes. To the SLED agent the letter provided a valuable opportunity to learn about Gail's family of origin. It also underscored how little the investigators knew about her. Apparently she had a brother; yet, Habben remembered that on the night of the polygraph, Gail had told her she was an only child.

Habben added to her long list of things to do: "check with Vital Statistics."

29

Small Steps

The day care was closed, and the temporary injunction meant that Patsy Habben could investigate without worrying about the safety of the children. That was the important thing—or so she'd thought. But it wasn't long before she needed to reassess.

The consensual agreement Day Care Licensing had reached with the Cutros gave SLED no leverage. Once the investigation was complete, the temporary injunction would be lifted, and the Cutros could be back in business. On the other hand, if DSS Licensing managed to obtain a *permanent* injunction, the Cutros would have to petition the court to have it lifted, and they could be required to provide information to convince the court to do so. DSS could ask them to undergo psychological evaluations, and it could require them to answer questions of direct relevance to the criminal investigation.

But Habben hadn't known any of this at the time of the court hearing, and no one from DSS had told her. She didn't know much about the work of DSS, and they didn't know much more about hers. Yet each needed the other in order to function most effectively. That was one of the reasons the Child

Fatalities Department had been created in the first place: to facilitate just these kinds of interdisciplinary efforts.

What Habben needed was a group from DSS that could help her create and execute a strategy going forward. She asked the DSS commissioner for help, and received in return a hand-picked team. The result was that DSS continued its investigation of the Cutros' operation and Habben did the same, but now they began coordinating their efforts. After the day care was closed, for example, DSS made unannounced visits to see if there were still children there.

By then, Habben had additional sources of information, and these proved their value when DSS found no evidence that the Cutros were still caring for children. Tim Stephenson, the Irmo police officer who continued to conduct surveillance, thought that they were still caring for one. So Habben arranged to have DSS investigator Gary Kirkbride pay a visit. He arrived to find the Cutros at home, but with the shades drawn. When he asked to be admitted, he was again turned away.

But Habben had established a new surveillance outpost. She'd convinced Missy's mother, Sissy Rangeley, to allow cops to install a video camera in her home across the street. That's how they gathered evidence that proved Stephenson was right. Periodically the Cutros took a child out of the house and later brought her back, doing their best to hide her from view. The child, Habben would later learn, was Rachel Hogan.

Habben thought it was a clear violation of the injunction. But, here again, she didn't understand all the rules. A DSS lawyer advised her that caring for one child wasn't the same thing as running a day care. After all, no registration was required to baby-sit a single child. Habben acknowledged the point, but still wondered if this wasn't different. The Cutros, after all, had agreed to close the day care. Yet this child, who had been enrolled there, had never stopped attending—and was now staying overnight as well. Weren't they flouting their agreement?

It was a tricky situation. If the child was in danger, they had to find a way to remove her. But if she *wasn't* at risk, investigators didn't want to let the Cutros know that they were under surveillance. Habben opted to finesse the situation. She asked the DSS lawyer to call the Cutros' lawyer and confirm that they were not to keep children, hoping that he would see that his clients complied.

Meanwhile, DSS continued its own digging. The primary investigator was Kirkbride, who, it turned out, had previously investigated a complaint about the day care. The complaint had been lodged in February 1991, nearly two years before Parker Colson died. It was initiated by a mother whose child had come home one day with what she thought was a large bruise in the shape of a handprint. The mother was certain it hadn't been there before she'd dropped him off. The Cutros were at a loss to explain, and Gail suggested it could have happened in the child's own home rather than hers. The mother was not happy with this response, and decided to take her son to the doctor. The pediatrician saw a bruise, but he did not see a handprint. He didn't know the cause, but he didn't believe it was from contact with a toy, which the Cutros also suggested, so he reported the injury to DSS.

By the time Kirkbride saw the child, all that was left was a small red mark. The Cutros' explanation didn't strike Kirkbride as outlandish. It was also possible, he thought, that an older child had hit the youngster. There was no way to know how or where it had happened, so Kirkbride labeled the complaint "unfounded"—meaning there was insufficient evidence to justify a "finding" of abuse—and he closed the case. According to the mother's SLED statement, she continued to be uncomfortable with the Cutros, who began telling her that her son's pediatrician was a "quack" and she should find another. But she didn't remove her son from the day care until November 1991, nine months after the bruise.

In 1993, Kirkbride's investigation wasn't focused on any specific allegations, but on the risk of harm to all the children in their care. When he was finished, he produced a seven-page report that "indicated" a finding against the Cutros based on the danger that children in their care would be abused or neglected. The last paragraph of Kirkbride's report recommended that Gail's registration be withdrawn permanently based on "deception." Among the examples he cited: The Cutros had told one parent that they were each registered to care for six children, when only Gail was registered. Gail had falsely told another parent that she was licensed as a Group Home, which would have entitled her to care for twelve children. And Gail had failed to abide by the registration form she'd signed, which clearly stated that she could care for only six children, and any of her own children under age twelve would count in that number.

Although there was not yet a court order granting a permanent injunction, Patsy Habben believed that they now had leverage with which to press the Cutros to submit to depositions and psychological evaluations.

Satisfied, for the moment, with their hammerlock on the day care, Habben focused on the quagmire surrounding Asher Maier, the baby who had lived. There was a new development in the dispute over Asher's condition in the days before he was hospitalized.

The quarrel was between Catherine Maier's account and Gail Cutro's. Lexington caseworker Daylene McDuffie had decided that Catherine had abused the child on Monday, when Gail first remarked on his discomfort, and had neglected Asher by withholding medical treatment until she brought him to the doctor on Wednesday. McDuffie's conclusions were based in part on the Cutros' contention that they had tried to persuade Catherine to take Asher to the doctor on Monday and Tuesday. Catherine said that never happened.

Searching for evidence that might corroborate one account or the other, the investigators thought of the "report cards" that Gail gave parents at the end of each day. Patsy Habben and Richard Hunton had heard many parents attest to their accuracy in describing children's conditions. If Catherine still had the ones she'd received from Gail on those days, they might prove valuable. So Tim Stephenson gave her a call.

Catherine was almost certain that she had them. In fact, she'd already looked; but for some reason she couldn't find them. For months her life, which was always somewhat chaotic, had been in utter disarray. First Chad had left. Then she'd spent a week shuttling back and forth between work and the hospital. There was a second round of hospital visits when Asher had surgery. Then, once it became apparent that Chad wasn't coming back, she'd had to move into a smaller place.

She'd thrown out a lot when she'd packed, but she was almost positive that she'd saved the report cards because she was already aware of their potential importance. Besides, she was a "pack rat." She hoarded all kinds of things. It wouldn't have been like her to throw them away. But WHERE WERE THEY? She'd torn her house apart. She'd even looked behind her washer and drier and gone through everything she had in storage.

One Sunday in early winter she decided to clean out her car. Turning to the unholy mess in the trunk, which she'd saved for last, she decided that there was nothing to do but take everything out. She dug in, grabbing great armfuls of clothes and papers and depositing them on the lawn. She paused for a moment when she came upon her daughter's Barbie notebook. She picked it up and began distractedly flipping through the pages, and—there were the missing report cards!

On Monday and Tuesday—the days Gail later claimed Asher should have seen a doctor—the report cards said he had eaten and napped. His diaper had been changed five times each day. There was one place on the report cards where Gail gave an overall assessment of the child's mood. Under "Today I was," the word that Gail checked on each form those days was "happy."

At last, Catherine thought: confirmation! She quickly called Tim Stephenson, who drove right over to have a look. When he saw them, Stephenson seemed almost as excited as Catherine Maier.

Later, at Child Fatalities, Tim Stephenson and Patsy Habben stared at the two pieces of paper titled "Small Talk" that were illustrated with drawings of a dog, a cat, a chick, and a mouse. They looked like anything *but* evidence in a murder investigation. Yet, there was so little physical evidence so far, that these forms struck Habben as two of the most important documents she had.

They seemed especially significant when compared to another document Stephenson had brought with him. It was the affidavit that Gail Cutro had filed in the Maier divorce. In it she'd sworn that Asher was "quiet and lethargic" those days, and that he "fussed when I tried to feed him a bottle and refused solid foods."

30

The Defense

Thom Neal was organized, conservative, and sensible. Though he was only thirty-four when he began representing the Cutros, his wife told him that he was born middle-aged. His strength as a lawyer was analysis, but he said he wouldn't have represented the Cutros if he hadn't had a gut feeling about them.

Before he'd gone into private practice, Neal had worked for the prosecutor—

known in South Carolina as the solicitor—in the division that represents the Department of Social Services. During his two years there, he'd handled lots of child abuse cases. In the five years of private practice that followed, he was often appointed by the family court to represent adults accused of child abuse. He considered it a professional necessity to take those cases, but when someone walked into his office, that was another matter.

"I've got to believe in the case," said Neal, whose neatly combed hair was graying at the temples, "because I've been in child protection too long." He didn't assume that people accused of child abuse were innocent. He had to believe in them, or he declined to represent them. And he believed in the Cutros.

At this stage the case struck Neal as unusual and interesting, but not particularly big. He didn't even mention it to his wife, Betsy. As far as civil litigation, in his mind the worst had already happened: the day care had been closed. The sword hanging over the Cutros' heads was the possibility of criminal indictments. If that happened, it would be a big case all right. But it wouldn't be his.

Neal didn't take criminal cases and, if it came to that, he already knew who would represent the Cutros. It would be his friend, Wes Kirkland. Josh Cutro had once consulted Kirkland's father, Henry, when Josh was sued by former employers who claimed he'd stolen their client list (a dispute that was ultimately settled). When the day care investigation heated up, Josh contacted Kirkland again, only to learn that Henry was semi-retired. His son was available, but Wes specialized in criminal matters. So Josh was referred to Thom Neal with the understanding that, if criminal charges were filed, Wes Kirkland would handle that end.

Even if it seemed like a relatively small case to Thom Neal, that didn't mean it wasn't challenging. So many investigations were going in so many directions that it seemed to Neal as though DSS and law enforcement were trying to find something—anything—to throw at the Cutros. This was in spite of the fact that the parents who used the day care thought it was great. Yes, Neal conceded, the state had a reasonable basis for concern. The Cutros themselves had recognized that and had voluntarily closed the day care. But all of a sudden that wasn't enough. The state wanted to make the injunction permanent. To Neal it was like saying: "Now that we've shut down your business, we're going to seize your home—just to be safe."

That didn't sit well with Thom Neal. After DSS slapped his clients with its new findings, Neal's focus was clear. The Cutros were ready to take on the bureaucracy, and so was he.

———

At the turn of the year, the DSS case turned a corner. Where progress had seemed to crawl for so long, there was finally decisive action. The Cutros and DSS agreed to "discovery," which meant that each side would supply the other with information necessary for litigation. Among the documents they would exchange were statements witnesses gave to DSS; medical and mental-health records; and DSS case notes. Day Care Licensing would depose the Cutros. Though Sherry Driggers believed that they were entitled to interview only Gail, they would try for both. Richland County DSS would order full psychological evaluations, again hoping for Gail *and* Josh.

Two crucial issues were resolved in January 1994. Laura Rogers, Asher Maier's guardian ad litem, reported that she now believed one or both of the Cutros, not Catherine Maier, had most likely abused Asher. And Daylene McDuffie and her agency, Lexington DSS, which had handled the original investigation of Asher's injury and had initially found Catherine Maier responsible, agreed to send the case to Richland DSS, which should have had jurisdiction from the start.

31

———

Psychology

David Caldwell was a large man with deep lines on his forehead and a grizzled beard starting to go gray. In late 1993 he was thirty-nine and looked like he'd once played offensive tackle somewhere and would just as soon break every bone in your hand as shake it. In reality, he'd never been a football player, was exceedingly polite, and had gone to work for SLED out of a love not for violence but chemistry.

During his first ten years as a SLED agent he worked in the forensics lab.

He figured he'd testified in court three or four hundred times. What he liked best was following the case from the crime scene to the victims to the perpetrators. He liked to learn all he could from each stage.

At the end of ten years, then-Chief Pete Strom asked him if he wanted to study psychology at the FBI Academy in Quantico, Virginia. SLED needed a psychologist, and the chief figured it was easier to train cops in psychology than to train psychologists in criminal investigation.

Chemistry to psychology was not a well-worn career path. It wasn't something he'd planned or requested, Caldwell explained in his self-effacing, plain-folks manner. It evolved naturally from his work in the lab.

He illustrated what he meant with an old police story. A detective arrives at a crime scene, looks around, and says, "I've seen this sort of thing before. Is John Smith out of prison? This looks exactly like something he would do."

"No," comes the answer. "John's still in prison."

"Well," says the detective, "it's somebody just like him."

Caldwell explains: "You can't go to hundreds and hundreds of crime scenes—if you're paying attention—without starting to pick up on who's doing what and why. So, while I was in crime scenes, I guess I developed a penchant for going in and saying, 'This is an inside job, obviously. Clearly, the husband did it, for the following reasons.' Or, 'This would be a stranger. We're going to have trouble finding him.' So, if I've now connected chemistry to a forensics lab to crime scenes to the prediction of human personality as a result of the behavior demonstrated at crime scenes, then you take that person and send him to the FBI for a more formal study of it."

Off he went for a fifty-week course in human depravity. Officially, he studied psychological profiling and criminal-personality profiling. He lived at the academy, attended lectures, including a psychiatry class at the University of Virginia, and read "a pickup truck load of literature."

"One of the primary goals," he said, "was to learn to predict personality characteristics and to be able to paint a description of an unknown offender as their friends or associates might see them—so that we might narrow down the focus of the investigation to more quickly resolve the crime."

When he returned to SLED, he wasn't a psychologist in the common use of the word. He didn't treat people, or test them, or testify about them in court. He was a "behaviorist." In essence, he was a consultant, a resource for law enforcement. He was asked for advice in finding criminals. Or he might suggest an effective strategy for interviewing a particular suspect, victim, or witness. And he himself did a good deal of interviewing.

"I know a lot about people," he said. "I know a lot about violent crime. I know a little bit about predicting what people might be like. But I don't pretend to know a lot about the deep-seated etiologies of all these mental disorders and illnesses."

Perhaps thinking of Hannibal Lecter from the popular book and film *The Silence of the Lambs* (which also highlighted the work of the FBI Academy), he went on: "My single biggest advantage in investigations, if I have one, is having the opportunity to see so many things. In a small town, in the entire lifetime of every cop in that town, they've never been to a crime where someone was murdered and their body parts were eaten. It's ghastly, and it's mind-boggling. And when it comes time to talk to this guy, they don't know where to begin. It doesn't make them bad cops. It's just that they've never encountered such a thing before.

"At the FBI Academy, I bathed in bizarre human behavior for a year and studied these people. So that, when you have a cannibal in South Carolina, then I've got a starting point. And I can say, 'Well, this is not the first one of these I've seen.'"

Patsy Habben and Richard Hunton were seeing things that they had never seen before. They believed that Gail Cutro was a viable suspect in a murder investigation, but there were many things about her that they didn't understand. Why was she visiting the children's graves? Why was she leaving presents and mementos? Why had she asked Missy Daniel for Ashlan's photograph? And what was she doing with a set of Parker Colson's footprints? They weren't sure whether these were all normal expressions of grief (or, perhaps, eccentric but harmless forms of it), or behavior that signified something much deeper. Patsy Habben decided it was time to talk to David Caldwell.

When he was consulting on a case, the first thing Caldwell liked to do was review all the documents. Habben gave him copies of the statements they'd taken, the polygraph results, the notes of Eve Powell and Linda Bass, Pat Hallman's letter, records on Asher Maier, Parker Colson's autopsy report, and the report on Ashlan Daniel that she'd just received. It said that the cause of Ashlan's death was "undetermined—presumed Sudden Infant Death Syndrome."

So far, as Ashlan Daniel's autopsy report underscored, the hard science was mostly absent or ambiguous. What about the "soft science"—what could psychology tell them? Although much of Caldwell's training involved profiling—predicting the likely characteristics of unknown perpetrators—he could also work up "personality assessments" of people. These weren't limited to suspects. His analysis of peripheral players could also be helpful to investigators, and Habben regularly picked his brain for insights.

But Caldwell was not merely a passive font of information. During the Cutro investigation he did much more than answer investigators' questions. He helped devise strategies to gather evidence, and he worked with the investigators to put them in practice. One of his prime partners in this endeavor turned out to be Missy Daniel.

———

When Caldwell met her, Missy Daniel was stuck. She'd been talking to Gail, gathering what she believed to be useful information, and then she'd written that letter. Now she was at an impasse. She wished she could find a way to connect with Gail again in order to help advance the investigation, but she didn't know where to start.

Caldwell came up with an answer. After reviewing the material that Habben had provided, it struck him that Missy was going to need help and that the person she should ask was Linda Bass. Although Caldwell had never met Bass, Habben had described her, and he'd read her notes on the Cutros. He'd also listened to the recording of Habben's visit to Bass's office. Caldwell figured that she was the perfect go-between. Gail Cutro was in her support group, and it was obvious that they were close. Bass's job was to promote healing. Given an opportunity to facilitate the reconciliation of a mother and a sitter whose relationship had shattered over what Bass believed to be a SIDS death, he predicted she would jump at the chance.

After Caldwell and Missy talked it over, and worked out the best way to pitch her request, Missy called Bass. "I need to talk to Gail," she said. It was time the two of them came together to heal. At least that's what *she* wanted, Missy explained, but she wasn't sure about Gail. What did Bass think?

Bass thought it was a great idea. She believed it would be really beneficial for Gail, and she offered to talk to her about it. She called back a few days later and assured Missy that Gail was eager to talk. But first Gail had to check with her therapist; she was having a "bad day." Bass said she'd wait a few days and try again.

That was how Missy's partnership with Caldwell began. At times she was his pupil, at times his teacher. She provided information, and he figured out how they could use it. It was almost as though he were directing a play in which she was the star. But it was more: It was a play based on her life, and they were collaborating on the script.

Missy felt no compunction about what she was doing. She'd had no qualms about pleading with Gail to take the polygraph. Her mission was to find out what happened. She owed it to Ashlan. If that meant playing a role to encourage Gail to reveal her true self, then Missy would do it. Because the deck had always been stacked against Ashlan.

That was one of the reasons child homicides were so challenging to investigate. Patsy Habben was convinced that they were the hardest of all. When adults are murdered, they may put up a fight and extract some evidence from the killer that can be collected at the death scene—strands of hair, fibers of clothing, drops of blood. If the victim scratched the perpetrator while fighting for her life, there will likely be bits of skin under her fingernails.

When the victim is a child, sometimes the hardest job for investigators is determining whether a homicide has occurred. Small children may not be capable of fighting back. There is often no murder weapon, since an adult can easily kill a child with bare hands. Or the murder weapon may be something as innocuous-looking as a pillow. Without evidence of a struggle, the presumption may be that the death resulted from natural causes, and there may be only a cursory examination of the death scene—or none at all.

An adult victim can also leave behind other kinds of clues. She may confide to friends that she's afraid of someone, or may document a pattern of victimization. Comparatively few child victims, on the other hand, complain directly to friends or authority figures. Even those who are subjected to chronic abuse almost invariably blame themselves. They may hint at their distress indirectly, but these cries for help may be misunderstood, or no one may be listening. Some victims can't complain for the simple reason that they're too young to speak.

And this, of course, was the case with Ashlan Daniel. Victim or not, she couldn't speak for herself. So Missy felt that her efforts, and whatever methods they required, were completely justified. But that didn't mean that prying information from Gail was going to be easy. Not after Missy had sent her that letter. Missy had never discussed the letter with Gail, but you didn't have to be a psychologist to guess how it was received. Missy had written out of anger and frustration and had expressed herself as honestly as she knew how. *Too* honestly to come back now as a friend—unless she could convince Gail that the letter reflected a stage of her grief that she had since left behind.

This was Caldwell's underlying idea. Not that Missy would address the issue explicitly. Caldwell was hoping, rather, that Gail would read this in Missy's behavior. After all, Gail knew something about grief. She'd experienced it, and she'd spent a lot of time talking about it in her support group. He thought she was intelligent enough to put it all together. And if she couldn't by herself, Linda Bass was there to explain it. That was why Bass was the perfect intermediary.

Missy began attending SIDS support group meetings. She'd gone to one, then stopped. Now she resumed, and it yielded some quick results. Through Bass, Missy and Gail agreed to exchange letters. Caldwell had advised that they would be less threatening to Gail than a meeting, and less emotionally demanding on Missy.

The first one was especially difficult to compose because it required some sort of apology for the earlier letter, but it also had to offer more. There had to be the suggestion of a bond between them. Missy and Caldwell studied the letter she'd received from Gail's mother, Pat Hallman. Then they discussed Gail's relationship with Lindy Colson. Caldwell thought it might serve as a model, and it was this line of thinking that led to his boldest stroke.

Caldwell asked Missy if she was willing to send Gail some memento of her daughter, similar to Parker Colson's footprints. Clearly Gail wanted one. Missy's reaction was immediate and visceral: The idea repulsed her. But they kept talking and arrived at a compromise. Ashlan had grown so quickly that there were gowns she'd outgrown before she'd had a chance to wear them. Missy would send Gail one of these.

The letter they wrote was very much a joint effort. Caldwell wrote it, with Missy's help, and then Missy copied it by hand.

1/13/94

Dear Gail,

I'm sorry it took me so long to get these words to you. Earlier, I was so distraught and inappropriate. I hope you can find it in your heart to forgive me. I've now recognized you are a victim as I am, probably even more so, because this unfortunate accident happened in your home. I know you loved Ashlan and Ashlan loved you, and I wanted you to have the enclosed item in hopes it will be of some comfort.

I really look forward to being able to sit down and talk with you, and or cry with you so that we can begin to recover. Please call me.

Yours in Christ,
Missy

32

Examinations

Catherine Maier had good days and bad days—just like everybody, only more so. She was smart, high-strung, sharp-tongued, and funny. She was also unpredictable. She was five feet, six inches tall, and her weight had bounced between 130 and 210. On a good day her brown eyes sparkled, her brown hair shone, and she was witty and vivacious. On a bad day she looked pasty and depressed and wasn't much interested in talking. The day she came to SLED in late January was a pretty good one. She seemed confident, co-operative, and in good humor. And she'd clearly learned lessons from all the investigating she'd been through; she was accompanied by her lawyer.

Patsy Habben had invited her for several reasons. She wanted to give David Caldwell a chance to talk to Maier. And Habben wanted to have a good look herself. Also, there was a test they needed to run. After Maier had dug those report cards out of her car trunk, Habben had given copies to Lexington DSS. And before the agency withdrew from the investigation, the supervisor had shown them to Gail Cutro. "That's not my handwriting," was Gail's response. So Habben called in SLED's handwriting expert, who needed Catherine Maier to come in and produce samples of her writing. After she'd done that, Maier met with Caldwell (while Patsy Habben, Richard Hunton, and Catherine's lawyer sat in).

During an hour's conversation, Caldwell was impressed by Catherine's apparent candor. She acknowledged the many mistakes she'd made in her life and accepted responsibility for them. By the same token, she did not seek to blame Asher's injury on all potential suspects. She never intimated, for example, that her estranged husband Chad might be responsible, despite their bitter custody battle.

Habben was particularly interested in her comments on the Cutros. At first they'd seemed supportive, Catherine said. During Asher's first night in the hospital, they brought her food and a gift for the baby. They hugged her and cried. They returned the next night with more food. After they learned that there was a DSS investigation, however, they never came back.

While Habben and company were busy assessing Catherine Maier, the scrutiny was mutual. And Catherine, too, was impressed. For the first time since That Day, she felt the people who were inquiring were listening. It was a welcome change from the way she felt she'd been treated by Lexington DSS. Daylene McDuffie's investigation had been swayed from the outset, Catherine believed, by comments from Chad and his father.

––––––

Catherine Maier may have preferred talking to the people at SLED, but at that point Lexington DSS wasn't yet through with Catherine Maier. Lexington had agreed to allow Richland to determine who had hurt Asher, but Lexington was still monitoring Catherine's supervised visits with him and was still a party to the family court case that would determine custody. Three weeks after her day at SLED, a Lexington DSS lawyer had an appointment to depose her.

Maier was confident when she sat down in the Lexington DSS conference room, accompanied again by her lawyer. The SLED documents expert had confirmed that the handwriting on the report cards was, indeed, Gail's, and Catherine saw the deposition as another opportunity to set the record straight. While she wasn't exactly looking forward to it, she knew that it was a test she had to take if she hoped to get her son back.

DSS lawyer Paula McDonald began the examination by probing Catherine's recollection of the events leading up to Asher's hospitalization. The questioning was gentle at first, but then McDonald challenged Catherine with Gail's version, gleaned from her affidavit and the statements she'd given Daylene McDuffie and guardian ad litem Laura Rogers. Catherine seemed unfazed.

About halfway through, Catherine demonstrated how confident she felt by agreeing to continue without her lawyer present. He had to meet a client in Richland family court. He asked that they take a break and resume when he returned, but Catherine insisted that it wasn't necessary. It seemed like a risky move for someone who was supposed to have a volatile temper.

In answer to McDonald's questions, she explained that Gail's "lies" and "inconsistencies" were the main factors that had convinced her that Gail had injured her son. Why would Gail have injured Asher? "I don't think she's right mentally," Maier responded.

The questions grew sharper. McDonald asked about the "rage attacks" that Catherine had ascribed to her birth-control pills. They were "mood swings," not "rage attacks," Catherine countered, and she'd only brought them to her doctor's attention under pressure from her husband and father-in-law.

The topic of Catherine's temper continued to dominate the second half of the session, particularly after Chad's lawyer, Rochelle Williamson, began asking the questions. Had Catherine hit her head against the wall in anger? How many times? Did she call Chad a "dickhead" at an N.A. meeting? Wasn't this evidence of a violent temper? Hadn't she acknowledged attacking her first husband? "A name is hardly violent," Catherine answered, and Chad used as much profanity as she. Her first husband regularly attacked *her*, Catherine charged, and that could be confirmed by police reports. When she hit him, she was defending herself—and *she* was the one who had filed for divorce.

"Do you think you're an angry person?"

"No. I think I'm a very happy person."

What about the time she was assaulted when she was a child? Wasn't she angry about that?

"I've dealt with that through therapy. I don't think it makes me an angry person by any means. If I can sit across the table from people who accuse me of horrendous things and not get riled, I think it's obvious that I'm not an angry person."

Williamson asked about another alleged assault she'd suffered.

"I think this is a little ugly," Catherine shot back, adding that *she* would never ask *Williamson* that kind of question.

"I'm dealing with issues of anger," Williamson explained, but she let the question go and returned to the rage attacks. "So if Doctor Odoms wrote then that the patient is having rage attacks—"

"That's his interpretation."

"—Those aren't your words, those are his words?"

"Mine were 'mood swings.'"

"Okay."

"I mean Chad and I both had angry times, but—"

"Did you shake Asher?"

"No, I did not."

"Did you hurt Asher—"

"No."

"—Monday?"

"In any way, shape, or form, no."

The deposition ended moments later. It had lasted three and a half hours. Chad and Gail and their lawyers now had a document that pinned down Catherine under oath. They could use it in court to attack her. But if any of them had expected Catherine Maier to crumple under the pressure of a hostile examination, they must have been sorely disappointed.

33

Valentine

Shortly before Valentine's Day, Missy Daniel and David Caldwell collaborated on another letter. By now they'd honed a strategy. They'd understood from Linda Bass that the first letter and gift had been very well received, so they would include another gift with the new letter. But this time Caldwell wanted to go a step further: He wanted to bring Ashlan into the conversation, and speak of her as if she were conscious and aware of their actions.

He was laying the foundation for the ultimate goal: a meeting at the grave. Caldwell was convinced that Gail was going there to communicate with her victim. If Missy showed that she wanted to participate, he hoped that eventually she could meet Gail at Ashlan's grave and coax her to say what happened.

Missy began with a reference to a cherub Gail had placed on Ashlan's grave, and referred to a Cupid pin she'd enclosed with the letter.

Dear Gail,

Ashlan appreciated the gift. The "I Love You" on the bottom has disappeared as all things eventually do in life. All the recent rain has washed it away. It was thoughtful of you and I'm feeling much better now. She's okay, I'm okay and I hope you are okay.

Ashlan wanted me to give this to you at the holiday season but I just wasn't ready. I know how you love cherubs. I bought two of these at Christmas, one for you, and one for me, but as I said, I just wasn't ready. Valentine's Day is coming soon and Ashlan reminded me to give it to you. Even though it is a Christmas pin, I think it looks appropriate for Valentine's Day, also.

I still look forward to talking to you or hearing from you. Please call me.

Yours in Christ

Missy

———

In truth, Missy was not okay. To the world she appeared to be "holding up," but she was all too aware it was subterfuge. She was playing a role with Gail, and she was acting with all her friends as well. She had to pretend that Ashlan had died of SIDS. She had to appear to be comforted by their words of solace. She was dissembling every time she went to one of Linda Bass's SIDS support meetings. With Patsy Habben and Richard Hunton she had to be strong to advance the investigation, but she didn't *feel* strong. So she wasn't herself with anyone.

Missy Daniel desperately needed to grieve, but she couldn't. She had to put grief on hold. She was too busy right now. And the truth was that she preferred to be distracted. Her misery was too much to bear. And it was about to get worse.

———

Davis Daniel couldn't take it any more. He felt like he was on an endless highway of pain. There was no escaping and no forgetting, because every time he looked up, there was Missy: a portrait of agony.

So he left.

"I don't say it was the right thing to do," he explained. "I just felt like it was something I needed to do. I'm a quiet person. I just needed to be by myself. If I wanted to come home and sit and turn the lights off and be in the dark, then that's what I did. If I wanted to talk, I stayed with friends and talked with friends. A lot of it was alone time."

Missy was sure that the marriage was over. "When he left," she said, recalling that day in February years later, "I couldn't believe it. He just came home one night—no warning, no talking about it, no nothing—and said he was going. Packed his stuff and left. And of course, I asked him not to, because I needed him."

She paused and shook her head. "I think I had a lot to do with it," she went on, "because I just kept leaning on him. I was hurting so bad I didn't know what to do. And I leaned on him, and I'm sure it pushed him away."

She would cry and want to talk about the things she couldn't say to anyone else, but he couldn't deal with it. She didn't know that, since he never explained it. He'd just sit there, quiet, and Missy would talk and talk.

Suddenly there was no one to talk to. "I was devastated. It was like, why live? This is not worth it." But she was hurting so badly already that she almost didn't feel the difference—as though she'd already exceeded her tolerance for pain, and the needle on the meter could go no higher. So she compartmentalized and stored it, as she had so much of her grief: "That was coming later. I just couldn't deal with him right then."

What she couldn't ignore, though, was the void. "For me, the worst thing—even to this day—is being alone. I can't stand to be alone." She filled the emptiness, or tried to, with the trappings of fun. "I went wild. I went out with my friends. I partied a lot. Continuously, consecutively. It was just awful."

She was running so that she didn't have to think and, more important, feel. After a couple of months she began seeing a counselor. She needed to talk, and there was no one else to talk to. She was placed on medication, though she continued drinking. Why should she care about the risks of mixing the two? She wanted to die anyway.

Ironically, during this period Missy had for a time adopted a lifestyle that resembled the one for which many people looked down on Catherine Maier. Yet, even though Catherine had sought help and seemed to have pulled her life together, she would remain the target, while Missy would endure no such criticism. Some of that may have had to do with their backgrounds and personalities. But as far as their roles in the Cutro case, there was one clear distinction: Missy could never be blamed for her daughter's death.

Even during her lowest times, Missy continued investigating. Sometimes that seemed to be all she had. She didn't have as much time—after Davis left, she had to get a full-time job to support herself—but she continued to provide Habben with valuable information. She called to tell her about the glass vase and flowers Gail had left for Ashlan on Valentine's Day.

But that wasn't the main reason she'd called. She wanted to report the long conversation she'd taped with Linda Bass. According to Bass, someone had left a note reading "Death to You" on the Cutros' nine-year-old daughter's desk at school. The child came home hysterical, saying that she never wanted to go back. A teacher actually suggested that the child might have placed the note there herself—for attention. "This is the same kind of thing that has happened to Gail," Bass told Missy.

Bass then repeated some of the accusations about SLED's behavior that Habben had already heard from Gail's therapist, Eve Powell. After Gail's polygraph, Bass told Missy, someone from SLED accused Gail of suffocating Ashlan with the Saran Wrap they found in her trash. And most infuriating to Bass was the suggestion that maybe a part of Gail had "split off," and she didn't remember what she'd done. This led Gail to wonder whether it was possible.

"Where she is with this," Bass continued, "is like, 'If *they* believe I did it, could I be crazy enough that I really—Is it possible that that could happen?'" Eve Powell had assured Gail that she didn't have multiple personality disorder and wasn't crazy; she was depressed. But real damage had been done. The whole series of events had played havoc with Gail's therapy, Bass said. Eve Powell was livid. And so was Bass.

34

Roller Coaster

Patsy Habben found that working with the various divisions of the Department of Social Services was an emotional roller coaster. While there were clear benefits to her own investigation, it was not always an easy alliance. What happened in March was a perfect example.

From her perspective, the news that month was mostly very positive. Lexington DSS finally backed off its finding against Catherine Maier. At the hearing to determine custody of Asher, all parties agreed to a consent order that included a statement that Asher was likely abused "by an unknown perpetrator." And that seemed to end Lexington's involvement.

Richland DSS, which had basically taken over the investigation, was getting close to reaching its own conclusions about Asher Maier's injury. The key question was when it had occurred, which would help determine where it had happened and who was responsible. There was no dispute that Asher's symptoms were clear the day he was taken to the hospital, but how much time had elapsed between the moment he was injured and the onset of his symptoms?

What they had so far was based on the examination of an ophthalmologist, and it was a pretty wide window. The ophthalmologist had been consulted because one of the ways doctors decide whether a baby has been shaken is by determining if there are retinal hemorrhages—bleeding in the eyes—that violent shaking causes. The ophthalmologist who had examined Asher had documented bleeding, and had estimated that the baby was shaken sometime during the seventy-two hours before he was admitted to the hospital. That meant that he could have been injured while in the care of Catherine, the Cutros, or even Chad, who had him for a visit over the weekend.

Could they pinpoint the most likely time? Habben contacted Dr. Susan Breeland, a local child abuse expert who headed Columbia's Abuse Recovery Center, and asked her to examine the medical records. After Breeland had pored through them, she told Habben that it was her opinion that Asher must have exhibited signs of serious injury not *hours* after he was hurt, but within *minutes*.

For the Richland DSS staff, this seemed to be the breakthrough they were looking for. Almost immediately after they learned of Breeland's analysis, they concluded that it was more likely than not that Asher was abused by Josh and Gail Cutro. The department's "Determination Fact Sheet," dated March 11, 1994, listed three supporting facts:

1) Asher Maier has been diagnosed as having Shaken Baby Syndrome.

2) Asher Maier did not exhibit symptoms of these injuries until Wednesday, June 23, 1993.

3) Child's clinical condition/status at the time he saw his pediatrician and was admitted to the hospital indicated injury occurred while in the Cutros' care on Wednesday, June 23, 1993.

This development did *not* mean that the Cutros had been found guilty of a criminal offense. It did not even mean they would necessarily be prosecuted. Before a decision was made about that, Habben had to complete her own investigation. And even then, the final decision would not be hers; it would be up to a prosecutor. But it did seem to ensure that the Cutro day care would not be reopening any time soon.

Habben also welcomed progress on another front. A judge had ordered DSS to depose the Cutros. Yet, this news came with another reminder of how frustrating it could be working with DSS. Though Habben was only just learning of this in March, the judge had actually issued his order three months earlier. But no one at DSS had bothered to do anything about it—or even mention the fact to Habben.

Timing can be crucial in an investigation. Investigators want to interview suspects multiple times, beginning as soon after the event as possible. They want to talk to witnesses when memories are freshest, and before the various parties can compare notes or mull over what might "sound good." Then they want to see if the stories remain consistent.

There was one more disconnect with DSS. After Richland completed its fact sheet, the department mailed the results to the Cutros and their lawyer. Habben agreed with the opinion, but it killed her that DSS was spelling it all out to the Cutros. As she put it in her notes: "There goes our entire case in a letter!!!"

It was a clash of cultures—and required procedures. Police investigators are trained to learn as much as they can from all sources and to reveal nothing in return. Social workers are trained to provide services. When there's a finding of abuse, they share that information with the perpetrator because, for one thing, everyone listed in the child abuse registry has a right to appeal. Still, for Habben it was like sitting in the passenger seat of a car while the driver steers directly into oncoming traffic.

It wasn't an easy alliance to maintain, but the potential benefits were undeniable. If it weren't for Richland DSS, Habben would have no chance of obtaining depositions of Josh and Gail, or their psychological evaluations. And what cop or prosecutor wouldn't give her eyeteeth for these? But it was frustrating. The only obstacle that was still preventing those depositions from taking place was a DSS lawyer, who still hadn't turned over discovery materials to the Cutros that had been requested weeks earlier.

35

Last Letter

As she struggled to hold herself together, Missy Daniel soldiered on. She was hoping to meet with Gail. Linda Bass agreed that it would be healing for both women, but the Cutros' lawyer advised against contact with anyone connected to the investigation. In the meantime, Bass wanted Missy to know that Gail was equally anxious to meet.

Gathering that the letters had been well received, Missy and Caldwell wrote one more. This one included more of Missy's real life than the others. Like the second one, it was undated; it was sent in early April.

Dear Gail,

I'm having a bad day. Some days are good—this one is not. Not only do I miss Ashlan, but I can't always talk to Davis. Men see things so differently than women. I would love to talk to you since we have shared a common pain. Linda told me that you were going to write. I'm so glad because I need you to, and I know that you will. I am very much looking forward to it and for us to talk. I have been back to the grave and I feel so good there. At the grave it seems so very peaceful.

I have redecorated the house a little and rearranged some of the furniture. I have finally put Ashlan's things away. I am also, looking for a job. I feel both of these things are self healing. The job will help me keep my mind off little Ashlan. Also, Davis and I need the money because I haven't really had a full time job since Ashlan was born.

I know I'm boring you to death with all of this. I just needed to talk. Call me soon. Hope you are doing okay.

Yours in Christ,
Missy

36

The Deputy Solicitor

Patsy Habben and Richard Hunton had spent nearly seven months investigating. They'd worked with cops and caseworkers and citizen volunteers, and had gathered what they believed was enough evidence to bring charges against the Cutros. But the prosecutor's office would have to decide that.

Coroner Frank Barron had recommended that Habben take her case to Johnny Gasser, deputy solicitor of the Fifth Judicial Circuit. He was a prosecutor who could handle this kind of case, Baron had said. So on April 4, 1994, Habben and Hunton drove across the Congaree River to the Richland County Judicial Center-—the same building where a judge had closed the Cutro day care five months earlier.

When the SLED agents walked into his spacious third-floor office, with its big wall of windows that looked down on Main Street, Gasser knew almost nothing about the Cutro case. All he knew was that his boss, Solicitor Dick Harpootlian, had told him the previous Friday that he was meeting with a couple of agents about "some dead babies."

The meeting lasted two and a half hours. Most of it was Habben and Hunton telling him, step by step, what they'd done. Gasser was a good listener, but he radiated energy no matter what he was doing. There was a restless, distracted quality about him, like the kid who could never sit still at school. His eyes wandered, he fidgeted in his chair, he ran his hand through his thinning brown hair. Sometimes his head suddenly dipped toward his right shoulder, as if he had just emerged from a swimming pool and was trying to shake water out of his ear—a nervous habit. But all the while he was paying careful attention, as his occasional questions revealed.

At five feet seven and 155 pounds, Gasser was built like a wrestler, though the sports he had favored growing up were football, basketball, and baseball. He was a Maryland boy who had come to Columbia to attend the University of South Carolina and liked it well enough to stay for law school. At thirty-one, he'd been working in the solicitor's office for nearly nine years, clerking for the first two while still in law school. After graduating, he had started as one of about twenty-five assistant solicitors and after only six years had worked his way up to deputy, the number two job in the office. He tried cases and also handled many of the office's administrative duties.

Gasser's wife, Sandy, had also clerked in the solicitor's office. Five years his junior, she'd recognized when their dating turned serious that they couldn't continue to work in the same office. She took a job with defense lawyer Jack Swerling (with whom Josh Cutro later consulted) before she and Gasser married in 1992. On the day Gasser met with the SLED agents, Sandy was seven and a half months pregnant with their first child.

When the agents had finished recounting the events, Gasser was far from convinced that they had a case. "I told them flat-out I was skeptical," he recalled. "I think any fair prosecutor would be skeptical—should be skeptical when you're dealing with a case where there's no murder weapon, there's no eyewitness, there's no confession." Also, he acknowledged, "I was unfamiliar with child death prosecution." But he knew enough about trying homicide cases to spot weaknesses. "If we don't have experts telling us that these were homicides, that these children did not die of SIDS, that these children did not die a natural death—of pneumonia, what have you—without that," he told Habben and Hunton, "you don't have a case."

The challenge was clear. "You need to convince me," he told the agents. "You convince me, and I'll convince my boss to go after indictments, and I'll do everything in my power to convince a jury. But first you need to convince me."

Far from being put off by Gasser's attitude, Patsy Habben welcomed it. She believed a prosecutor *ought* to approach a new case with skepticism. "The very worst thing you can do is put an innocent person in jail"—that's what Habben had been taught. Until Gasser was completely convinced that Gail Cutro was guilty, he had no business proceeding.

They were an odd couple, these two who were to spend so many hours together in the months to come. The tall, blonde police lieutenant loomed several inches over the short, compact, almost swarthy lawyer. One exuded calm, the other restless energy; but they were both intense and focused. And by the meeting's end, each came away impressed: Gasser by the job the investigators had done and also by Habben's phenomenal memory; Habben by Gasser's clear analysis and direct response.

Before they parted, Gasser agreed to prepare questions that could be forwarded to the DSS lawyer who would presumably depose the Cutros later that month. While Gasser researched the forensics issues, Habben would begin searching for experts they might consult and, ultimately, call as witnesses. They agreed to meet again in a month.

For Richard Hunton it was all a new experience. He liked Gasser's self-confidence. He liked the Phi Beta Kappa certificate on his wall. Hunton felt like he was in the big leagues now. "During the investigation, I mean, you're making progress," he explained later. "You're getting the information you need. But it's still not like when you walk up to the plate. It's just a different atmosphere."

———

Gasser had his work cut out for him. He had no medical background. He'd learned a lot about medical evidence in prosecuting cases over the years, but he didn't know much about child homicides. And he knew virtually nothing about SIDS or shaken baby syndrome.

As he read, he was surprised to learn that many people thought a substantial number of cases diagnosed as SIDS were actually murders. The conservative estimates ranged from 2 percent to 8 percent or higher. Too often these cases seemed to fall between the cracks—especially in instances where parents had killed their own. Under these circumstances, who was demanding justice for the child? "No one," argued child advocates. They offered a solution that was gaining wide currency: Child Death Review Teams.

These were local and statewide multidisciplinary committees that reviewed child fatalities to recommend changes that might improve investigations and prevent deaths. Where they succeeded, more homicides were identified and prosecuted. And that seemed to be the case in South Carolina. The new Child Fatalities Department was working closely with the South Carolina Child Fatality Advisory Committee. Though the latter was only formed in 1993 by the same legislation that established SLED's Child Fatalities Department, the advisory group was a new incarnation of South Carolina's Child Fatalities Review Committee, which was first formed in 1985, making it one of if not the oldest statewide team in the country.

In this climate, prosecutors nationwide seemed to have greater interest in these cases. In some instances investigations were opened—or reopened—involving deaths from years earlier that had never been properly investigated.

Just two weeks before Gasser's meeting with Habben, a woman in upstate New York had been indicted for killing five of her children—the last of whom had died twenty-three years earlier. It was widely reported that Waneta Hoyt's children were all diagnosed as SIDS victims, though it wasn't true of all five. It would be a year before Hoyt was tried and convicted, but her signed confession had been made public five days before Gasser first heard about Gail Cutro. One reason the case attracted so much interest was that the Hoyt family had been held up as evidence for the theories that infant apnea can trigger SIDS, and that both apnea and SIDS can run in families.

The Hoyt case wasn't the first or only instance in which infanticide was prosecuted decades after the fact. Barry Siegel's *A Death in White Bear Lake* chronicles the conviction of a woman who had killed her adopted son twenty-two years earlier. Another case well known to people who studied child homicide involved another New York state woman whose nine children died between 1967 and 1985, most of them diagnosed as SIDS victims. Two decades after the first death, Marybeth Tinning was convicted of killing one of them.

As Gasser absorbed these developments, he was encouraged by the trend—and also appalled by the historical context. "My God," he reflected later, "you think about all the people that have literally gotten away with murder—and of the worst kind, killing your own."

Every now and then, when he came up for air, he thought of two experiences that had helped shape his perspective. A close friend from college had lost a baby to SIDS. Gasser had attended the funeral, and he'd watched as his friend "threw himself into the SIDS network," raising money and meeting parents of victims. Thinking of his friend gave Gasser a personal perspective on the danger of a false allegation. "The most frightening experience in life would be to lose a child. And I had to make sure that we weren't wrongly prosecuting or persecuting a mother of three children of her own."

The second experience was a case that haunted him. Dr. Michael Durfee, a California child psychiatrist who founded the first Child Death Review Team in Los Angeles County in 1978, and later crossed the country urging others to follow suit, said in a speech he gave once that these review teams are formed by people who carry "ghosts" in their heads. The ghosts, he explained, are child homicide victims whose deaths so infuriate people in the child-protection system that they feel compelled to act.

The case Gasser couldn't forget involved a two-year-old girl who died in the care of her mother's common-law husband. The autopsy revealed a massive subdural hematoma—blood between the brain and skull. The mother was a prostitute and had been absent for thirty-six hours. The man's story was that the child had been eating grits when she fell off a kitchen chair and hit her head. This claim in itself was implausible, but the autopsy revealed seventy-seven bruises and seven ribs that had been broken at different times.

When the Cutro case came along, South Carolina had a "homicide by child abuse" law that allowed prosecutors to present evidence that a murder was the result of a series of assaults over days, weeks, or even months, rather than one attack. But the law hadn't existed in 1992, when Gasser worked on the little girl's case. At first that hadn't been a problem because the pathologist who performed the autopsy disputed the man's account. But as the case neared trial, the pathologist began backpedaling.

"I was a young prosecutor," Gasser said. "I didn't even think about going over his head. There are specific experts that deal just in child death. I didn't know that. I was ignorant as to how to prosecute these types of cases. If I would have known what I know now after reading all this material, I would have gone and gotten outside experts to review the autopsy reports—even if it meant delaying the trial."

Another problem was that no photographs had been taken of the child at the autopsy and no X-rays had been retained. Why? "Because it wasn't their standard procedure," Gasser said. At the time, he was also unaware that evidence can be obtained from a disinterred body. After discussing the case with his supervisor, Gasser decided the best he could do was try to get a plea. The man pled to involuntary manslaughter and unlawful neglect of a child and got ten years, four of them suspended. He was imprisoned for two and a half years—about as long as the girl had lived.

Gasser was glad the killer was held criminally responsible, "but if I would have known many of the things I know now, I could have created a very strong case for murder."

That little girl was Johnny Gasser's ghost.

37

The Meeting

Patsy Habben and David Caldwell were discussing dates that Missy Daniel could propose for the meeting at Ashlan's grave. April 21 would be Gail's thirty-fourth birthday. April 22 would have been Ashlan's first. Mother's Day was also coming up. One of these might appeal to Gail.

Then came the break they'd been working for. On Friday, April 8, Missy called, breathless. Gail's mother, Pat Hallman, had just phoned her at work. She and Gail could meet with her! Today!! In twenty-five minutes!!!

Missy raced to SLED, where a wire was concealed under her clothing, then she sped to the appointed location—the parking lot of the Winn Dixie supermarket in Irmo. By the time she got there, the SLED surveillance vehicle was in place to record what the wire picked up.

It was an emotional half hour that began and ended with hugging and handholding. In the beginning and near the end, Hallman did much of the talking—sometimes speaking for Gail, sometimes interrupting her.

Missy thanked Gail for meeting and assured her that she didn't blame her for anything. Gail's voice was shaky at first, but she seemed to gain confidence. She felt she was always being watched by SLED, she confided. She talked about how slowly the investigation was progressing. "I don't think they understand it," Gail said in a dreamy voice, speaking of the investigators.

Suddenly she continued in a staccato burst: "*I* don't understand it. *I* want answers. *I* want to know. I want to stop waking up every morning and feeling so responsible."

"I don't hold you responsible," said Missy.

"I do," replied Gail.

Later, when Missy mentioned how much she liked talking to Ashlan, Gail volunteered that when she was on vacation in Atlanta, she got up on the roof of the highest hotel she could find to be closer to heaven and to Parker Colson. "I felt like the closer I got to him, the better I would be able to talk with him."

She was no longer comfortable in the presence of babies, she continued. "I've gotten to where I can't look at them. Because every baby I see looks like they have died. I don't think I'll ever get through this. I'm scared to death of them. Anytime I see a baby in a little car seat, I cannot look at them, because when I look at them, I see them not breathing. I see them dying."

At one point she sounded as though she felt cursed. "I feel like if this happened again, there's something wrong with me. I am just some kind of a . . . a terrible person. Why would something so horrible happen to me?"

When Missy asked Gail to remind her exactly what happened that day, Gail said: "I . . . I really—I just don't remember what happened. I . . . I . . . I freaked. I lost it. I couldn't believe—it was . . . it was like it was happening to somebody else." Hallman interrupted at this point, reminding Gail that she'd dialed 911 and had also called her. Gail said she didn't remember placing either call.

"When she called me," Hallman told Missy, "at first I didn't hear anything, and I said, 'Hello.' And I didn't hear anything. And I [repeated], 'Hello?' And she says, 'Mama. I've got a baby not breathing. I need you.'" For some reason Hallman laughed at this point before adding: "And so I came on over. And I prayed all the way over."

Pat Hallman dominated the conversation as the meeting wound down. She complained that the police were hounding Gail for continuing to care for children. They hadn't told anyone about this meeting, Hallman said, knowing that the lawyers and others wouldn't approve. Apparently, not even Josh knew.

"Nobody can tell me not to do or say anything," Hallman added with another laugh. "Gail will tell you this: I'm very psychic. I don't know if you've ever met anyone that was or not. But I've seen dead people and angels. And sometimes I know when there's going to be a death. I feel like that's a gift from God that I have. And I think about you every day. And I think about Lindy [Colson]. And I pray for y'all. And I told Gail, I said, 'I just got this feeling that y'all got to see each other.'"

Just before they parted, Gail told Missy, "I feel like I let you down."

"Why have you let me down?" asked Missy, as Gail began to sob. "I trusted you and I don't—you didn't take her, either. God took her. You didn't hurt her. Or I never would have trust—I mean, do you know what I'm saying?"

"But just to know there's people out there that think I did," said Gail.

Before they parted, they talked about meeting again. The Hallmans were living in Pelion, about thirty miles away. Pat would be back in Irmo for a doctor's appointment in a week, and they tentatively agreed they might meet then.

———

Habben and Caldwell said they thought it had gone well. Even if the meeting had produced no evidence that could be used against Gail, it left them feeling more convinced than ever of her guilt—despite her protestations of innocence. They hadn't expected a confession. Even if Hallman hadn't been there, they wouldn't have expected one. They'd always believed it would take more than a single encounter. But Hallman was definitely the wild card. Her involvement had been a surprise, and had limited Missy's ability to engage Gail directly. Hallman reinforced her daughter's self-protective instinct, which the investigators believed was at war with the other instinct Gail had demonstrated: her need to place herself at the center of an emotional vortex.

If Gail were ever to confess, it seemed highly unlikely that she would do so in the presence of her mother. It wasn't just the embarrassment. Her mother seemed almost physically incapable of allowing it. She let her daughter go only so far before she jumped in and took over the conversation. It was the same sort of thing Josh did when an investigator questioned Gail in his presence. When Pat Hallman took over, it was almost impossible for anyone to break in. Gail couldn't confess if she couldn't get a word in edgewise.

When they focused on what did happen at the meeting rather than what didn't, they saw real payoffs. Gail's vivid description of ascending to the hotel roof in Atlanta to speak with Parker Colson confirmed that she did, in fact, speak to the dead children. Most important, the meeting seemed to have accomplished the primary goal: allowing Missy to establish a new bond with Gail. After one or two more, who knows, Missy might be able to arrange a one-on-one at Ashlan's grave, where anything was possible.

At least that was the way the investigators viewed it. But Missy had a very different reaction. Hers was visceral. She wasn't sure she could keep going. This had been one of the most emotionally draining experiences of her life. She had a hard time picturing even one more meeting.

She and Habben spoke on the phone two days later. Habben needed to know if Missy was willing to meet again. If she was, SLED needed time to prepare for Hallman's return visit. It was decision time again. Missy took a deep breath. Okay, she said, she'd do it. At midweek she met with Caldwell. They wrote a letter from Ashlan to Gail and scripted what Missy would say at the next meeting. They also planned for the one at Ashlan's grave.

The next night brought a setback. Missy called Pat Hallman to confirm plans for the next day, but Pat was noncommittal. She wasn't sure how she would feel after the test scheduled during her doctor's appointment. She would call Missy if she felt up to it. What troubled Missy most was her suddenly cold tone.

The meeting didn't happen. It was several days before Hallman called to apologize. She hadn't felt well after the test, she explained. She was also afraid that she had some bad news: Gail couldn't talk to Missy any more.

That was the way it ended. Missy's immediate reaction was relief. She told Caldwell that even if she could somehow change Gail's mind, she didn't think she could meet at the grave. She already felt like a basket case. Her daughter's birthday was four days away; her husband was gone; she felt like she was hanging by a thread.

Now that it was over, Missy had one request. She wanted to tell Gail how she really felt. Caldwell agreed. Two days later, the day before Gail's birthday, SLED ran surveillance at 1101 Chadford Road. When Gail returned home, Missy was alerted. A few minutes later she phoned and got the answering machine.

As she spoke into the machine, she didn't shout or even raise her voice. She broke down momentarily when she spoke of missing Ashlan, but she quickly recovered. She believed that she had suffered the ultimate betrayal and she hoped that Gail felt betrayed now, too. She hoped that whatever pain Gail might feel was one one-thousandth of what she lived with every day:

Gail, hey, this is Missy. I just wanted you to know that all those letters that I sent you were a joke. I didn't mean any of those kind words I've said, and I *hate* you for what you've done to Ashlan. I know you killed my daughter, and I know that you're going to jail. I've seen all the evidence that SLED has, and they're going to send you to jail for a long time and you deserve it. You'll never know how much I miss Ashlan. And I *hate* you for destroying my life. For killing Ashlan. God knows what you've done. I can't wait until you go to jail, and I *hate* you.

38

Depositions

When the Cutros were deposed by Richland DSS at the end of April, the circumstances were unusual and, from Patsy Habben and Johnny Gasser's perspective, less than ideal. Josh and Gail were deposed separately, but each was present for the other's deposition. The prosecution team would have preferred to have them separated, but they didn't have enough leverage to insist on it. DSS had a temporary injunction—though the department probably had enough to upgrade it to permanent. And the Cutros hoped to reopen their day care at some point. That was the extent of the power DSS had over them. If the Cutros were pressed too hard, they could simply walk.

Still, the upside of a deposition could be substantial. It was a sworn statement, not an interview, and a court reporter would record every word. Josh wouldn't be allowed to interrupt to answer for Gail, as he had done before. DSS lawyer Virginia Batson would ask the questions, with Thom Neal present to protect his clients' rights. And the ground rules were a prosecutor's dream. The rules of evidence in a criminal case did not pertain, so Batson could ask virtually anything she wanted—or anything Habben and Gasser suggested—including questions about Gail's mental-health history or even her failed polygraph.

Each deposition lasted about two hours. The Cutros were asked to describe their families, work histories, significant traumatic events. They were asked how they disciplined the day care children and their own. And, of course, there were detailed questions about Parker Colson, Asher Maier, and Ashlan Daniel.

Their answers threw their personalities into sharp relief. Gail's responses were clipped to the point of grudging. Through much of her testimony she answered with a simple "yes" or "no," rarely volunteering explanations. It was hard to make progress. Josh, on the other hand, was even harder to slow down. One was the horse that had to be begged to pull the cart; the other was a runaway.

Some of the most interesting moments in Gail's deposition came near the end, when she began responding in a slightly more expansive fashion. One example occurred when Batson asked: "Do you believe that you could be a responsible person to provide child day care for other people's children now?"

"I don't think that I can ever do it again," Gail responded.

"Why do you feel that way?"

"Because I'm afraid of kids, I'm afraid that they'll get hurt, I'm afraid of putting a baby down to go to sleep."

What was most remarkable about this answer was the follow-up question it raised (but went unasked): If Gail Cutro didn't want to run a day care, why did she and her husband fight so hard to keep theirs open, and why were they fighting now for the right to open it again?

Batson's next query was a tricky one that Gail handled with remarkable aplomb, demonstrating her strength as a witness. "Mrs. Cutro," Batson began, "looking at the convergence of the deaths of two young children and the serious injury to a third child and all of them having been in your day care, all within a period of nine months, do you have a reasonable explanation other than some fault or wrongdoing on your part for how this happens to three children in your home?"

Gail seized on a series of car accidents her family had experienced, one of which took the life of her sister-in-law. "How can you explain things happening to you like that?" Gail said. "How can you explain us being in an accident and a couple of weeks later my husband's brother was in an accident, his sister was in an accident, all within three different locales? How can you explain his mother having to go through three accidents within a month and losing a child?"

Josh revealed much about his own style when he was asked the simplest of questions: "What's your job?" He'd been working at Burger King since the day care closed, but throughout the deposition he seemed intent on burnishing his image. "As a quality assurance manager with Hinton, Incorporated," he responded

"And what is Hinton, Incorporated?"

"They're a company based out of Texas that last year came and has purchased a chain of fast food restaurants and they're also building new restaurants in South Carolina."

"What's the chain?"

"Burger King."

At times Josh showed an utter disregard for the truth. He denied, for example, that he'd ever been arrested, even though the arrests were easy to prove and were for minor offenses in the distant past. He also talked about his "close" relationship with his parents. A few years later, under different circumstances, he would readily admit that he was neglected throughout his childhood by both. He seemed unwilling to concede anything that might cast him in a less-than-sterling light.

But given an opportunity to present himself as he wished, he was off and running. And no opening was too small. He gave a typically expansive answer to the question of whether he'd taken a polygraph in the case of Asher Maier: "Yes, I did," he replied, even though in reality he was only polygraphed on the death of Ashlan Daniel. "And they did a very thorough polygraph," he continued. "And this is from the words of Richard Hunton at SLED, he told me right after the polygraph that it came back absolutely clear, there was no ifs, ands, or buts about it. That he had never seen one any more perfect than mine."

"Now this polygraph was taken in connection with which child?" Batson asked.

"In connection with everything. I mean they were very thorough from the time I was born up until that day in the questions that they submitted to me to answer. And if I—I mean, if I had hurt a butterfly they would have known about it."

39

Experts

The prosecutor had been clear: The case would depend on the experts. Patsy Habben had been searching, but they hadn't been easy to find. Sure, there were thousands who could testify in a murder trial, but this wouldn't be your ordinary murder trial. They needed experts who knew a lot about murder, *and* knew a lot about SIDS, *and* could distinguish between the two. Where was she going to find ones like that?

There was no Google to perform a search. The Internet was in its infancy. Habben searched the old-fashioned way: She combed the medical literature. She was looking for experts who not only understood the science, but would also make good witnesses in court. The two qualifications didn't always go together.

That was how she happened to be reading an article published in a British journal that jolted her awake right from the title. It was called "Three Crib Deaths, a Babyminder and Probable Infanticide." "Crib death" was the British expression for SIDS.

The article was based on a Wisconsin case that resulted in two murder convictions and, at least on the surface, bore a startling resemblance to what Habben thought she was dealing with. Habben had found almost nothing about day care workers or babysitters in the literature, but this one sounded remarkably like Gail Cutro. She was thirty-five, married with two children, and she cared for babies in her home. SIDS had become a big part of her life: she actively supported research, counseled bereaved parents, and even lectured on the subject.

What was more, the article was almost a blueprint of how to put together a case. The police conducted a thorough investigation, locating important witnesses. They exhumed the bodies of the dead babies, and the authors of this article had reexamined them and obtained medical evidence. A statistician calculated the long odds of three children—aged fourteen months, nine months, and six months—dying of SIDS in the care of one sitter. And a thorough investigation revealed, in the authors' words, "that this woman was not in a normal stable mental state and had not been so for several years."

It wasn't long before Habben had the name of the babysitter, Sandra Pankow, and the investigating agency, the Appleton City Police Department. As for the authors, they were all pathologists—one from England, two from the United States. The statistician was also an American. When Habben called the lieutenant who had headed the investigation, he told her that the statistical and medical evidence were the keys to winning the case.

Habben had a feeling that she'd stumbled on a gold mine.

40

Coroners

The Cutros were not the only ones wondering how long the investigation would last. Linda Bass was also concerned. She'd been shocked when she'd learned what Missy Daniel had done to Gail. In a sense, Missy had befriended Bass as well. She'd thought they'd established a level of trust.

Bass felt sorry for Gail. When she learned that Gail was cleaning houses to make ends meet, Bass hired her and recommended her to a friend. She knew how hard it was for the Cutros, financially and otherwise.

Bass also feared for her own program. None of the hopes she'd voiced about working with Child Fatalities had materialized. The emphasis these days seemed to be on investigation period, and there didn't seem to be much room for compassion. There was still no mechanism even to inform parents of SIDS victims that a support group was available. She couldn't see the harm if the police told parents about her program—or at least notified her about possible SIDS deaths while they investigated.

Then the Columbia newspaper, *The State*, ran a series of investigative articles that seemed to confirm Bass's worst fears. It was called "Burying our Mistakes," and on four consecutive days near the end of May the paper trumpeted the failures of the coroner system. It enumerated myriad perceived failings: no qualifications were required to be elected coroner; budgets, especially in rural counties, were minuscule; some coroners were poorly trained. Later stories focused on solutions, including SLED's Child Fatalities Department.

A one-sentence summary was printed in a box: "Many coroners did such a poor job of investigating child deaths that the state passed a law giving SLED the authority to make sure that coroners didn't let killers go free."

"Between 1990 and 1992," the paper reported, "coroners certified the deaths of 21 babies as cases of sudden infant death syndrome without ordering autopsies."

Patsy Habben, who was quoted extensively, decried the ease with which adults brutalized children, sometimes using SIDS as a cover. "Ill-trained coroners might continue to bury their mistakes in cases involving adults," read a passage near the end, "but 'not children anymore,' Habben says."

Missy Daniel called to congratulate Patsy. But Bass wasn't the only person who begged to disagree. One group of readers was definitely not throwing bouquets. The coroners were irate, and none more than Aiken County's Sue Townsend, the newly elected president of the South Carolina Coroners' Association.

Sue Townsend's background bore an uncanny resemblance to Patsy Habben's. Nine years older than the SLED agent, Townsend also began her career in SLED's forensics lab. She left in 1978, the year Habben arrived. After she and her husband moved back to her hometown of Aiken, she took a job at the sheriff's department as a crime-lab technician, moved over to investigations, and worked her way up to lieutenant and then captain of training. When the coroner's job opened up in 1982, and the governor offered to appoint her, she jumped at the chance. She'd been one of only two female graduates from a class of fifty-two at the police academy, and she was the state's first female coroner. She remained the only one for ten years, and for the first eight was secretary-treasurer of the Coroners' Association.

Sue Townsend and Patsy Habben were pioneers in related, male-dominated professions. They should have been on the same team, Townsend said, but instead of reaching out to the coroners, Habben immediately put them on the defensive.

"Where Patsy and some of us differ a little bit is that she was an expert in serology," Townsend said, acknowledging Habben's rape kits that were adopted by the FBI. "She's very smart in her field of serology, but she was not a field investigator. And when the Child Fatalities Department was set up, it was like overnight she became the expert investigator, telling everybody what to do. And that is something you earn, you can't demand."

Her other complaint was that SLED had always been an "assisting agency." That was the expectation Townsend and many of her colleagues had for Child Fatalities. But in her view, it didn't work out that way.

"It is very, very difficult when you have a SLED team that wants to come in and knock on doors and investigate, when we have said, and the doctor has said, that this is a natural death. It's no fun, to the families that have lost children, to have state police looking at them and experiencing what the Cutros experienced. When you have nothing there, and you've done everything right, I resent the hell out of that. I really do."

Townsend wasn't quite finished. "Now, if I've got a baby case, and I've got a problem with it," she continued, "and I'm stuck in the mud—oh, God, could Patsy be an awesome asset to me, there for the asking. Okay? But don't come looking over my shoulder and beating down the doors of some of my best citizens, with your big badge, your pink suit, and your 9 mm, when they've just lost their baby."

41

Tears of Rage

Missy Daniel wanted to talk to Lindy Colson. After Gail told her about speaking to Parker from an Atlanta rooftop, Missy was curious to know what Gail had told Lindy. But Lindy had just given birth to a baby girl in April, and Habben asked Missy to hold off. She might have a chance to talk to Lindy soon, Habben advised—possibly in the solicitor's office.

It was a strange situation. Missy knew that Lindy had . . . what? Disliked her? Mistrusted her? She wasn't sure. But Missy had gone one way, and Lindy another.

Lindy's way had brought her closer and closer to Gail. She and Gail had done SIDS work together—Red Nose Day, the softball game. Lindy knew nothing about Missy's work with SLED, but she knew that Missy had attended support meetings only sporadically, and that she'd been suspicious of Gail. So there was a distance between them.

But there was also a bond. They were the two mothers whose children had died at the Cutros' day care. And now, for the same reason that Lindy had visited Missy the day after Ashlan died to try to help her learn to cope, Missy wanted to talk to Lindy; only this time their roles were reversed. Missy had been living with the investigation since September. She was even a participant. But Lindy knew nothing of this. To Lindy it was all going to be new. She'd probably never even considered the possibility that her son had been murdered. Missy could see that she was going to need help.

———

Patsy Habben was more concerned with the investigation than with the coroners. She'd known that she was going to take some hits. It was predictable, even without the newspaper article. It was a replay of what she now knew had happened in Wisconsin. The Pankow case was the blueprint for what they were likely to experience in South Carolina. Various investigators had pointed fingers at each other for "missing" something. Outside experts had come in and second-guessed the local pathologists. And Wisconsin also had coroners who—surprise, surprise—were angry when their findings were questioned. The only difference was the timing. In Wisconsin, the controversy emerged during the trial. In South Carolina, the newspaper series accelerated the process. Their controversy had already begun, and they hadn't even decided to seek an indictment.

But Habben was much too busy to worry about it. She was on the phone with the prosecutor all the time now. Every day Johnny Gasser seemed a little more integrated into the investigation. At the latest meeting, he was starting to put it all together. And he was challenging them. Okay, he'd said, I want you to tell me why the following scenario could not have occurred. Catherine Maier wakes up between 4:00 and 5:00 a.m. on June 23 and Asher's screaming. She's dead tired, she still can't figure out what's wrong with him, and her life is falling apart. She just can't take it any more, so she picks him up and shakes him until he finally stops screaming. Why couldn't that have happened? (Maybe it was a little easier for Gasser to imagine a child's cries, now that he had a baby of his own. His daughter was thirteen days old the day he ran this theory past Habben.)

And then, while they were sitting in Gasser's office—where Habben spent more and more time these days—Solicitor Harpootlian would wander in and ask for an update. Gasser would tell him something—Habben could see that Gasser was convinced that Gail was guilty, even if he wasn't sure he could prove it—and Harpootlian would listen for a second, shake his head, and, in that typical barroom language of his, say, "You ain't got dick." And Gasser and Habben would both be scrambling for a comeback. But Habben knew what Harpootlian was doing. It was the same thing Gasser did. He was the coach preparing his team for the Big Game. He was telling them: "You're not ready yet, guys. You gotta work harder, do more drills."

———

By June 30 the prosecution team had been in touch with experts who had reviewed the autopsy reports and the slides—the tissue samples that had been preserved from the autopsies. The experts were telling them that Ashlan Daniel and Parker Colson looked like murder victims. It was not definitive, though.

They might find more evidence if they reexamined the bodies. That was the opinion of their experts. And, of course, that was what had happened in the Pankow case. When they asked Dr. Enid Gilbert-Barness, a pediatric pathologist in Tampa who had done the "second autopsy" in that case, if she would be willing to do so again, she agreed.

In Gasser's view, it was not a hard call. If there was a chance that they might find evidence that would clarify the question of guilt—one way or the other—they had a duty to do it. That was why they'd called a meeting on the last afternoon of June.

It was in Harpootlian's big office, next to Gasser's, and all but the solicitor were sitting around his long mahogany conference table. Normally they would have been bathed in light from the wall of windows that looked out on Main Street, but today the curtains were drawn, creating a somber, almost funereal, atmosphere. Harpootlian stood at the head of the table. On his left were Missy and Davis Daniel, who had seen each other earlier in the afternoon for the first time in four months. Davis had told Missy that he wanted to come home. He felt that they needed each other now more than ever. The Daniels had a pretty good idea of why they were in the office. To their left sat Gary and Lindy Colson, who weren't at all sure.

Patsy Habben was sitting next to Lindy, near the end. On the other side of the table were Catherine Maier and Nancy Moody, who was the office's victim/witness support person. This would be one of those days when she more than earned her salary. Richard Hunton and Johnny Gasser flanked Harpootlian, who would later describe this meeting as "the worst experience of my twenty-two years practicing law."

Harpootlian's professional style was detached. He didn't get overly emotional about cases, and he believed that this manner made him a more effective advocate. But this meeting was unlike any he had ever attended. He was about to tell a roomful of strangers why he wanted to dig up their babies, and the normally glib solicitor, the master of the sound bite on the evening news, was, for once, tongue-tied.

"We now need to be able to get the forensic evidence to tie this sort of circumstantial case together," he remembered saying. "And without this forensic evidence, we won't have a case, and it's going to require us to re-autopsy the kids."

He was fumbling along, he said, recalling the meeting years later, "feeling like a funeral director, using every euphemism I could think of, and everybody was sort of saying, 'What do you mean?' And I said, 'Well, we're going to have to disinter them and re-autopsy them.' And one of them, I think it was the tall guy—Davis—went, 'You mean cut them open?' And I said 'Yeah.'"

A collective wail enveloped the room. Gary Colson began crying and pounding his fist on the table again and again as he repeated, "I *knew* it! I *knew* it! I *knew* it!" From the moment he'd learned that his son was dead, something had told him it wasn't from natural causes. He had done his best to contain his anger, for the sake of his wife, but this moment unleashed eighteen months of anguish.

Patsy Habben and Johnny Gasser looked at each other, trying to keep their emotions in check. Habben glanced over at Hunton, but too late. He was already crying. When she scanned the room again, they all were. Including her.

"It scared Catherine Maier to death," Habben recalled, "because I think she knew that Asher could have been dead. It was something that she'd felt all along but couldn't prove."

Harpootlian continued, even after his voice broke, explaining why this was so important. Then Habben, who was the only one in the room who had exhumed bodies, helped everyone regain their composure by explaining the procedure they needed to follow. She asked each couple to make a list of everything they remembered placing in the coffin so that they could positively identify the body and establish a chain of custody.

Gary Colson pulled Gasser aside. "Look," he said, "I trust everything that you're doing, but I want you to know that my baseball glove and my University of Miami baseball cap are in that coffin. I know that you're going to do everything possible, but it's important to me that those things stay in the coffin." Tears welled as he told Gasser that this meant everything to him. For Gasser, this was the moment when it really hit home just what he was putting these people through.

"I'll never forget that," Gasser said, recalling the moment. "I've known the man for an hour and a half. I've just looked at this man and said, 'I'm digging up your son—after he'd been buried for eighteen months—and taking him down to somebody. You don't know me. And people you don't know are going to be driving your son down I-95 in a refrigeration truck to some hospital in Tampa, Florida, where people that you don't know are going to be analyzing whatever's left of your son.

"They all had a lot of questions, but I don't know whether I could have—" Gasser paused in mid-thought. "I guess they just had tremendous trust in us. And I will always appreciate that."

42

The Politics of Prosecution

The decision to exhume the bodies had not been an easy one. It was far from clear that another autopsy would yield evidence the prosecution could use. And Gasser felt he had pretty strong evidence without it. But this was going to be a difficult case to try, and he wanted to secure every bit of medical evidence available.

Those were Gasser's calculations. But he didn't make the decision alone. He had to talk it over with Dick Harpootlian. Ultimately the decision to disinter the bodies and to prosecute the Cutros was up to the solicitor. And the factors that Harpootlian might take into account were not limited to how the potential evidence might play in court.

The forty-five-year-old prosecutor was in a somewhat fluid situation. Harpootlian was going to leave office. He was, in fact, in the middle of an election campaign that was about to shift into high gear: He wanted to be South Carolina's attorney general, a statewide office that mainly handled civil litigation rather than the regional criminal caseloads of the solicitors. That also meant there was a contest to see who would replace him. As it happened, Johnny Gasser was close to both contestants, and each had already made it clear that they wanted him to remain as deputy solicitor. So Harpootlian didn't seem to have that much at stake in the Cutro case, win or lose. And the path seemed clear for Gasser to try it, regardless of what happened.

But it wasn't quite that simple.

If the case didn't go to trial before the end of the year, then the new solicitor would have to decide whether to prosecute a case that was already proving controversial before any charges had been filed. Just because the new solicitor wanted to retain Gasser as his deputy didn't mean he'd agree with Gasser's opinion about this case. Even if he did, Gasser was sure politics would intrude.

"This was a major press case," Gasser explained. "Whoever got elected, I'd understand from a political point of view they'd need to be a part of this case. It doesn't look great if they're elected and one of the biggest cases in the Midlands in several years—they're not a part of.

"But I also knew," Gasser went on, "that it took me several weeks first of all to be convinced of her guilt. And it took the investigators several months to compile the case and come to me, and it took me several months to educate myself and be in a position to directly examine and cross-examine the best experts in the country. And I'll be honest with you, I didn't have time to babysit the new district attorney."

Harpootlian had his own tallying to do. First, there was the matter of bringing in outside experts. In the vast majority of cases in which a pathologist testifies in a criminal case, it's the local pathologist testifying for the state. They perform the autopsies, and when a murder case goes to trial, they are often the state's best witnesses. Prosecutors depend on having a good, solid relationship with local pathologists. When a prosecutor hires experts from out of state and pays them to come in and, in a sense, second-guess local pathologists, that's not likely to be appreciated.

Moreover, there were two local pathologists in this case. The one who autopsied Parker Colson was inexperienced and that was one reason she needed to consult before amending her initial report. The second one, who did Ashlan Daniel, was Dr. James Reynolds, who headed Richland Memorial Hospital's Pathology Department. *And* his daughter was a lawyer in the Solicitor's Office. He was also a friend and a political supporter of none other than . . . Dick Harpootlian.

"I mean, he was one of my big supporters in the A.G.'s race," Harpootlian said. "Raised money for me, had a reception for me. In the old days, somebody might have just said, 'Well, shit, we're not going to embarrass Jim. Just move fucking on.' But that ain't even an issue anymore."

Harpootlian said it wasn't a close call. "Here's the deal: You've got two dead kids, one kid with some brain damage, and this woman is still around kids." He knew what he had to do. "But once I understood that if we were right, it was going to put some people who had been very kind to me—personal friends of mine—in an embarrassing position," he added, "I wanted to make sure that before we did, we had a reasonable likelihood of conviction." And that meant gathering all the evidence they could get.

But the first thing they wanted to do was find a resolution to the conflict with Dr. Reynolds. The prosecution team eventually decided that the best thing to do, and the right thing to do, was to confide their concerns and see if he was willing to help. Patsy Habben called and told him that Dr. Enid Gilbert-Barness suggested removing and examining the eyes. Habben asked if Dr. Reynolds wanted the opportunity. She emphasized that they had confidence in his abilities—in fact, she asked if he would reexamine both children. They weren't asking out of disrespect, she said. They just wanted to do all they could to secure every bit of relevant evidence.

Dr. Reynolds, however, was not convinced this was necessary or desirable: "My response to her was, and I think rightfully so, 'I think we ought to have a very good reason for doing all of this. And I'd like to talk to whoever suggested that we do that.'" They discussed a conference call with Dr. Gilbert-Barness, but it was apparently difficult to arrange. He said he explained during their next conversation that he had serious reservations about removing the eyes. "There's something very sacred, to some people, about the eyes," he explained. "And also there's a lot of controversy about: What does it really mean if you take the eyes out and look at them, and there are subretinal hemorrhages?"

Dr. Reynolds said he never absolutely refused, although he did allow that he was "disinclined." He was leaving for vacation over the July 4th weekend, and he left a phone number at which he could be reached. Habben remembered a firm refusal. In any case, Jim Reynolds did not reexamine any bodies. That task fell to Enid Gilbert-Barness. It wasn't the smooth solution the prosecutor had sought, but it would have to do.

———

Law enforcement by the book says you never tip-off the suspect. Gail Cutro obviously knew she was under investigation. How much more she knew, they couldn't be sure (though Missy Daniel had certainly given her something to think about in that phone message). Still, this was a delicate moment in the investigation. They were about to go after what was potentially the most important evidence. There was a good possibility they would seek indictments immediately thereafter. And if they did arrest the Cutros, they might well have an opportunity to interrogate them and to search their home. But if the couple got wind of any of these plans, they might destroy incriminating evidence.

The problem was that Gail Cutro was known to visit the graves. Suppose she dropped by? Once she saw their condition, she would know the law was closing in. What could they do?

They would perform the job as quickly and efficiently as possible and, to further minimize the opportunity for discovery, in the dark. They would start on Friday night, July 8th, using backhoes at each cemetery to speed the task. Then, they would drive straight to Tampa, where Gilbert-Barness would be ready the moment they arrived. The instant she finished they would be off again. By Sunday morning the graves would be in the precise condition they'd been in Friday afternoon. That was part of the agreement they'd struck with the parents: Everything would be back in time for church.

This became Sandy Gasser's most vivid memory of the whole case. She remembered listening fascinated as her husband described the plan when he came home from work one night. For the first time the expression "under cloak of darkness" came alive in her mind—it wasn't just a phrase from some cheap novel.

43

Arrested

An arrest is often the best chance that law enforcement has to interrogate someone accused of a crime. So far, the only real interrogation of Gail Cutro had been the one conducted by Johnny Hartley on the night she failed the polygraph. But even then, she knew that Josh was just around the corner. Every other time she'd been questioned, Josh had been beside her and had sometimes answered *for* her. SLED psychologist David Caldwell was convinced that under those circumstances, they had no chance at a confession. But under the right conditions, it might be a different story.

It all depended on the arrest. Gasser was seeking to indict both Gail and Josh. If they were arrested together, Caldwell figured that Josh would tell her to keep her mouth shut and that would be that. If Caldwell was going to have a shot, he thought that the couple had to be arrested separately as soon after the indictment as possible. And that's how they planned it.

Everything was ready on July 13, 1994, the day Gasser presented the case to the grand jury. They weren't worried about an indictment. All Gasser needed to do was show evidence of "probable cause," or reasonable grounds for suspicion. Richard Hunton was there to testify and to make a telephone call. The bench warrants were ready to go as soon as the grand jury voted.

Hunton called the Irmo P.D. in midafternoon. The grand jury had voted to indict, he told the dispatcher. Eleven investigators were already in their vehicles on that rainy afternoon, some staking out the Burger King where Josh was working, some waiting at 1101 Chadford Road, and some following Gail, who was running errands in her Ford Aerostar with two children in tow. Habben, who was supervising the operation, was riding with victim advocate Nancy Moody, whose role was to provide care for the children.

Everything was proceeding as planned. But where was the call from the dispatcher? They kept looking at their watches, wondering what could be taking so long. As the minutes turned into hours, the cops following Gail found themselves passing near their colleagues staking out the Burger King. They all sat there watching as Gail picked up Josh from work. Then the cops all followed as the couple seemed to drive around with no discernible purpose.

What was going on? Finally, Nancy Moody's cell phone bleated. It was Gasser. He'd just gotten a call from a newspaper reporter seeking comment on the indictment and arrest! It turned out that the police dispatcher had simply failed to relay Hunton's message. The newspaper had known that the case was coming down, and after the indictments were handed up, the reporter called the prosecutor. Then he called the Cutros' lawyer for *his* comments. Thom Neal had obviously notified the Cutros.

So much for best laid plans. There was nothing to do but bring them in. By this time the Cutros were driving toward the Irmo police station, where David Caldwell was waiting. That seemed as good a place as any to pull them over. They were handcuffed virtually in front of the station and ushered into separate rooms.

David Caldwell introduced himself to Gail Cutro, and they had a very brief conversation. Gail's end of the conversation was that she wanted to see her lawyer.

Three months later, David Caldwell had another chance to interrogate a woman suspected of killing children. Susan Smith was the South Carolina woman who eventually admitted drowning her two small sons by rolling her car into a lake. (Before she confessed, she made national headlines when she reported that her children had been abducted at gunpoint by a Black man.)

Though Union County Sheriff Howard Wells would reap most of the acclaim for coaxing Smith's confession, insiders like Johnny Gasser would nod their heads knowingly and talk about Caldwell and fellow SLED agent Pete Logan, who worked with Smith for days until she was ready to talk to Wells. It was consummate SLED, the "assisting agency." They did their work behind the scenes and let the locals step forward for the photographers.

Gasser and company had been hoping for that kind of result when they'd planned the arrest. What happened was a lesson in humility. In a complex exercise, a lot could go wrong—and an arrest was nothing compared to a trial.

44

The Defense Team

Thom Neal was furious. Normally mild-mannered with an upturned mouth that always looked on the verge of smiling, his face was now contorted in rage. It wasn't just that his clients had been arrested that bothered him—it was the way the police had done it. They'd followed around a churchgoing, middle-class couple—who posed no risk of flight—just so they could arrest them *in front of the police station?* And then handcuff these "dangerous criminals" in front of their own children?! How callous can you get?

Neal wasn't a criminal defense lawyer, but he knew that this wasn't the way it was done. Usually people who have been indicted under these circumstances are permitted to surrender with a modicum of dignity. His first concern had been for the children. As soon as he'd learned of the indictments from the reporter who'd phoned him, Neal called Josh and Gail and urged them to make arrangements for their kids.

Next he'd tried to reach Wes Kirkland, who had agreed to handle any criminal charges. Kirkland was out when he'd called, but Neal knew where he could find him later. Kirkland's sister Leslie was hosting a fund-raiser for the Republican candidates she supported for solicitor and lieutenant governor. Though her family had been lifelong Democrats, the candidate for solicitor was a family friend. Also, the Kirklands had never gotten along with Dick Harpootlian, and he was supporting the *other* guy. Even though Leslie knew that Thom Neal generally steered clear of "political stuff," she had given him a hard sell about coming. He hadn't made up his mind, but the arrest did it for him.

As he was parking his car near Leslie's house, he noticed that Lisa McPherson was just emerging from the car in front of him. Though Columbia was a city of 120,000, in many ways it was a small town—and never more than at these professional mixers. Lisa McPherson was also a lawyer, and as they walked to the house and chatted, Thom Neal suddenly asked her, "What are you doing tomorrow, first thing in the morning?" He was thinking about the bond hearing. He figured that Wes Kirkland would represent Gail, but there was also Josh to think about.

The party was lively. People wandered through the big house and out to the capacious deck and yard, where caterers had barbecued half a pig. But the two lawyers were in a different world. McPherson listened, rapt, to the strange story of the day care, the deaths, and now these indictments. When Wes Kirkland finally arrived, he quickly joined them.

Thirty minutes later their plans for the bond hearing were set. Kirkland would represent Gail, and McPherson would take Josh. They were only committing to the bond hearing, however. They were undecided about representing the Cutros going forward. As for Neal, he would make sure that his clients were well represented; then he would bow out.

———

The bond hearing was a revelation. Neither Wes Kirkland nor Lisa McPherson had gotten the sense from the discussion the night before—nor from the lead article in the newspaper that morning—that this was a "big case." Kirkland's first inkling was the fact that Dick Harpootlian was there. The solicitor didn't show up for just any old case. And then, when Kirkland saw his presentation, that was when he knew.

"They had charts and everything," Kirkland recalled. "This was the *bond* hearing, and he was ready for the *trial.*" The prosecutors laid out the chronology of events and a sampling of evidence. Then they mentioned the exhumed bodies, Kirkland remembered, "and I was going, 'Oh, God!'"

Gail was charged with one count of murder and one count of homicide by child abuse for each of the deaths. For the baby who lived, she was charged with assault and battery with intent to kill, aggravated assault, and neglect. Josh was charged with one count of unlawful neglect of a child. The judge set bond at $200,000 for Gail and $50,000 for Josh.

The Hallmans came up with the money to bail out Gail, but no one bailed out Josh right away. That night, even though Josh wasn't his client, Kirkland stopped by the jail. He knew that they had a TV, and he figured that by now things might be uncomfortable for Josh, whose case was getting a lot of air time. He was right—he found a deeply shaken man. "I mean, he was pitiful down there," Kirkland said. He was "teary-eyed, angry, and scared." Josh remembered it differently. Yes, he'd been threatened, and he was nervous because he was outnumbered. But if he was going down, he was going down swinging, he later maintained. The two agreed on one point: Josh was much relieved when Kirkland arranged for a private cell.

It didn't take long for Kirkland to decide that he would continue to represent Gail. It was the highest-profile case he'd ever handled. His client was a well-spoken woman who had quite a few supporters in the community. And the more he learned about the case, the more interesting it sounded. He might even have a real shot at winning.

His one big concern was the amount of work. There were a lot of issues to research. Could he handle them all alone? The clincher came when Thom Neal told him that he wouldn't have to. Neal had changed his mind. "By the time the criminal indictments came down," Neal said, "I felt so strongly about the case that I couldn't just discard it." The two would work together.

———

Kirkland and Gasser were a contrast in styles. Whereas the compact prosecutor was hard-charging all the way—worked hard, played hard, liked to knock back a few beers—Kirkland was laid back. A lanky five feet ten with a thin face and curly brown hair that he wore swept back, he was diligent and wanted to succeed, but he tried to stay on an even keel. He'd been a decent student at school, but he'd never been driven the way Gasser was. Away from the courtroom, Wes Kirkland took it easy. "In his personal life, he hates controversy," noted his wife, Kim.

Professionally, there was a big difference in experience. Johnny Gasser had tried sixty-four murder cases. Of the fifty that had resulted in jury verdicts (the others were mistrials or pleas during trial), thirty-seven defendants were convicted of murder, ten more were convicted of manslaughter, and only three were acquitted. Wes Kirkland, who was thirty-five, had been practicing law for about seven years and had only handled two murder trials. On paper, it didn't look like an even match. But Kirkland had gone up against Gasser in one of those trials, and he'd come away with a victory.

Lisa McPherson's role wasn't immediately clear. Josh would be tried separately, after Gail, and the case against him looked like an afterthought—or an attempt to pressure him to testify against his wife. As McPherson spent time with the couple, however, she felt herself drawn to their plight. Here were two people who cared about kids at a time when there was a real need for child care, and first the state shuts them down, then it accuses Gail of heinous crimes. McPherson just couldn't see it.

It was not as though she was a naïve young lawyer, fresh out of school. She was thirty-four, and though there was a wholesome softness in her round face framed by short blonde hair, and she often came across as disarmingly sweet, there was a tougher side underneath. She'd spent six and a half years in the Lexington County solicitor's office prosecuting a wide range of cases, including a heavy dose of child abuse. But her gut feeling about this case was different. The more time she spent with Gail, and the more she talked to Kirkland and Neal about the evidence, the more disturbed she grew.

Nine months earlier she'd left the solicitor's office to go out on her own. She'd tried a couple of murder cases. She'd also handled personal-injury and matrimonial cases, but criminal defense was what she liked most. And this case looked like a real opportunity to build that practice—if she could help defend Gail as well as Josh.

The first question: Was there a conflict of interest? Were Josh's interests aligned with Gail's? Over time, and in consultation with the couple, the lawyers decided that they were. McPherson could represent both. The trickier issue was one of territory. There was a natural fit between Kirkland, the "fact man" at ease in front of a jury, and Neal, who was good on the law and more comfortable researching briefs. What was left for McPherson?

She would prepare Josh to testify. It was also clear to McPherson that there would be advantages in having a female lawyer question some of the witnesses, but she wasn't sure how Kirkland felt about this. It was *his* case, and she didn't want to shoulder her way in. "I didn't have a huge role," she remembered. "And I kept thinking, 'God, I'd really love to be involved, but I don't want to step on their toes.'" It was like waiting to be asked to the prom.

She didn't have to wait long. Kirkland was overloaded. There were far too many witnesses for him to handle, and the medical research by itself was overwhelming. Once Kirkland started asking for McPherson's help, the melding began.

45

Ready or Not

Prosecutors always have a head start. They develop their cases before the defense ever gets involved. The balance is discovery, which requires each side to turn over information about its case to the other. This gives the defense a chance to catch up.

That's the good thing about discovery for the defense. But if there's a great deal of evidence, because the case involves three alleged victims, and defense lawyers have to wade through a mountain of documents, praying that they don't miss one that could come back to haunt them, and they also need a crash course in forensic pathology, then discovery can be overwhelming.

"It was such an unusual type of case," Wes Kirkland said. "We had a lot of medical research, had to talk to doctors. It was hard putting together. We were scrambling." By the end of August the documents were pouring in, and from October to December Kirkland spent virtually all of his time just going through them.

Like Gasser, Kirkland thought that the medical evidence was the key. The prosecution's case would probably rest largely on the testimony of Dr. Enid Gilbert-Barness, so Kirkland immediately began searching for experts who disagreed with her findings. He quickly lined up two who were respected in the field and told him that Gilbert-Barness didn't know what she was talking about.

What Kirkland worried about most as the trial approached was all that medical terminology. He was having a hard time getting comfortable with it. It sort of felt like being a student again, and he hadn't loved that feeling the first time around. So he did two things. First, he watched Dr. Reynolds perform an autopsy. It was the first one he'd seen, and it wasn't easy, but he learned a lot. Then he flew to Baltimore and visited his star expert.

Dr. John Smialek was Maryland's chief medical examiner. Kirkland felt a little intimidated as he waited to be admitted into his office. Glancing around, he noticed a wall of photographs of the medical examiners who had preceded the current resident. As he scanned the images, he thought he recognized the one in the middle. He moved closer. It was the actor Jack Klugman in his TV role as the medical examiner Quincy. "These people have a sense of humor," he noted with surprise and relief.

At fifty-one, Dr. Smialek (pronounced SMY-aleck) was a handsome man with longish hair graying at the temples, an easy charm, and a soothing voice. His office was near Camden Yards, the Baltimore Orioles' much-praised stadium that had opened two years earlier, and he suggested they stroll the neighborhood and get a bite to eat. They had a leisurely lunch, which Kirkland was enjoying until it struck him that he might be imposing on the doctor's time. He started to apologize but then caught himself. "It's not like your patients are going anywhere," he said.

Dr. Smialek, as much as anyone, helped Kirkland prepare for trial. He helped with the science, but he also loosened the lawyer up with his calm presence and sense of humor. Dr. Smialek assured Kirkland that he would be fine and agreed to sit at the defense table to help him through some of the early medical testimony.

But just as Kirkland seemed to be getting a handle, Gasser filed a motion that added another twist. It said that the prosecution would introduce evidence on something called Munchausen syndrome by proxy. The term refers to a pattern of behavior by a caregiver who repeatedly brings an injured child to doctors for treatment. But in these cases, the caregiver is secretly inflicting the injuries out of a desire to have a close relationship with doctors or other authority figures. The term has also been used to describe the psychological condition of the caregiver who does this. (Since 2014, the official term for this psychiatric disorder has been factitious disorder imposed on another.)

Gasser intended to show that Gail Cutro was injuring children in order to get attention.

Kirkland shook his head. It meant more articles to read, new experts to find, and more dollars to squeeze from the Hallmans. He'd have to move to delay the trial.

———

Gasser had put a lot of thought into the choice of a prosecutor to assist him. He wanted a young lawyer who was smart, good on research and in court, and willing to work ungodly hours. Gasser liked to make lists. He'd made one reviewing the kind of person he was looking for and another listing who was available. One name came up no matter how he sliced it: Scarlett Wilson.

Wilson, twenty-six, was an attractive woman who wore her brown hair pulled off her face, emphasizing her large blue eyes. Though she'd been in the office for barely a year and was just two years out of law school, she'd made an immediate impression. She grabbed cases and tried them, never complaining about how petty most of them were. "She tried more cases in the limited time that she was here than some of the lawyers that had been here three or four years," Gasser recalled.

One of the first things Gasser asked her to do was research and write a brief on Munchausen syndrome by proxy. He also wanted her to focus on Asher Maier and shaken baby syndrome, and to construct an hour-by-hour timeline of the day Asher was hospitalized that spelled out why the evidence pointed toward Gail Cutro and away from Catherine Maier.

With the addition of Scarlett Wilson, the prosecution team was complete. But it wasn't just the two lawyers. Patsy Habben and Richard Hunton remained key players who worked closely with them up to and during the trial. Though Gasser was in charge, all four were involved in discussions and decisions. In fact, some of their meetings grew quite animated—and loud. At peak volume, the voices were rarely Hunton's or Wilson's.

When Gasser and Habben went at it—and it wasn't a rarity—it was passion, not anger, that elevated their voices. The case had become an obsession for both of them. With his excitable personality, Gasser spoke loudly no matter what he was talking about. Habben's voice was usually much softer; but once Gasser made it clear that he wanted to know what she *really* thought, she matched him decibel for decibel. A favorite topic for high-fidelity discussion was overkill. Once they'd lined up experts, Gasser wanted to check out additional experts and their opinions of the evidence. Then he wanted experts' opinions of the other experts. Habben wondered where it would end. The irony was that some of her agents at Child Fatalities wondered the same things about her.

"Put it this way," Gasser said, chuckling at the memory of those days and nights, "thank God Richard Hunton and Scarlett Wilson calmed us down." He credits Hunton's tolerance for the group's chemistry. "I don't think I ever did anything as stressful as this, and we spent a lot of time together, the four of us. Richard is a deacon in his church and he is very, very religious. He doesn't smoke and he doesn't drink and he doesn't swear. But he's not one of these people that condemn you for doing the same. I come from a family of four boys, plus where I'm from, cussin' ain't nothing to me, and some of the women I work with, it doesn't bother them, either. I think about all the outbursts I had, and he never made a comment, never let it bother him."

Wilson blended seamlessly, but her involvement did create one problem for her in the office. One of her closest friends was Leiza Reynolds, an assistant solicitor and daughter of Dr. Jim Reynolds. As the trial approached, it was apparent that Leiza took issue with some of their evidence. Dr. Enid Gilbert-Barness claimed to have found a subdural hematoma—a blood clot on the brain—in her reexamination of Ashlan Daniel. The unavoidable implication was that her father had "missed it." Dr. Reynolds resented this suggestion, and he'd told the team that in his opinion their "new evidence" was bogus. If asked about it on the stand, he would have to say so. And if they continued on the course they'd charted, he told them, they were going to embarrass themselves.

Wilson could handle the situation professionally, but the personal side was trickier. It was hard to know what she and Leiza should and shouldn't talk about. After a few uncomfortable weeks, they agreed that they wouldn't discuss the case. And that solved the problem. Leiza was no longer torn by conflicting loyalties, and Scarlett had her friend back. But there was one chance encounter some weeks later, after she'd been working long and hard to prepare, that Wilson would never forget.

"Obviously we're in a small place," she began, referring to the sometimes insular world of Columbia. Two months before the trial, Wilson visited Leiza, who was staying with her parents because her foot had just been operated on. As Wilson was about to leave, Jim Reynolds walked up and said, "Scarlett, I need to talk with you."

"I felt like I'd been caught drinking or something," Wilson recalled, "and

I was getting ready to get a lecture." Reynolds put his arm around her, led her into the kitchen, sat her down in front of the sink, and gave her an impromptu lesson in pathology. The sink, he explained, was the inside of the skull. "When you remove the brain, if the subdural is on top of the brain, then you see it immediately." He picked up a tomato from the counter and placed it in the drain. "If it's underneath the brain," he continued, "you're going to see it down there. It would be that obvious," he said, pointing to the tomato. "You can't miss it."

Having survived the long hours, the Munchausen brief, and the lecture from Jim Reynolds, Scarlett Wilson had one more rite of passage. Shortly before the trial began, she learned that she would be the one standing in the courtroom questioning experts about Asher Maier. Gasser had told her early on that Asher was "her baby." But she thought that she was preparing everything for *Gasser* to do. She'd done similar things for senior lawyers plenty of times, but this time she would get in on the action herself.

The 1994 trial of Gail Cutro (from left, Wes Kirkland, Thom Neal, Lisa McPherson, Patsy Habben, Scarlett Wilson, Johnny Gasser; Gail and Josh Cutro in background). Courtesy of *The State*, Columbia, South Carolina.

46

—

Playing the Angles

The Richland County Judicial Center, where Gail Cutro was tried, is a large concrete-and-glass structure built in the late 1970s. The most unusual aspect is its shape: a long rectangle with a canted front, as though a wedge had been sliced off like a piece of pie. The limestone exterior also features a traditional touch: There are five massive columns along the path to the entrance. Asked about these, the architect, Robert Kennedy, smiled and said, "That's our little nod toward Southern architecture, I guess."

When the new courthouse was being planned, there were not many older buildings to "refer to," as architects say. The block that was cleared to build the courthouse was unvarnished urban decay: A row of shops and stores, some of them abandoned and crumbling, created an unsightly "gap-toothed" effect. It was a phenomenon well known in cities around the country, and it had a lot to do with the kind of "white flight" that led to the tremendous growth of Lexington County and Irmo.

Fifteen years after the courthouse was built, Richland County's demographics were still different from Lexington's, as every prosecutor was acutely aware. Lexington County was 93 percent white, compared to Richland County's 63 percent. Richland drew more people from other parts of the country, courtesy of the University of South Carolina and Fort Jackson, the largest army training base in the country. The result was a much more heterogeneous population.

The bottom line was that Lexington and its jury pool tended to be much more conservative and sympathetic to prosecutors. "You know, the joke around here," Gasser said, "is that being a prosecutor in Lexington County is like shooting fish in a barrel."

The quirk of the county line running through Irmo, and the fluke of the

Cutros' location just inside Richland County, had played havoc at times with the investigation. Now it might give Gail Cutro a jury that was, at a minimum, more inclined to hear a defendant out.

The Judicial Center looked even more modern inside than out. The building's unusual shape had painted the architects into some strange corners. Courtroom 2A, where Gail Cutro was tried, had six walls, no two the same length. It was all odd angles, as though designed by Picasso. The effect was softened by the size of the room, which featured a fifteen-foot ceiling and two galleries: one behind the prosecution and defense tables, as in traditional courtrooms, and a second, to the left and several steps up, that formed a larger mezzanine.

From the smaller gallery the center of vision was not, as is usual in courtrooms, the judge's bench—though this one, made of travertine marble, was vast. Instead, it was the witness stand, which was between the jury box on the left and the judge's bench on the right. The prosecution was seated to the left, the defense to the right, and behind them was a long bench on which individuals involved in a trial could sit. The Daniels, the Colsons, and Catherine Maier stationed themselves behind the solicitor's table, and Josh Cutro, when he wasn't sitting at the defense table with Gail, sat behind her.

Judge Duane Shuler's first order of business on Monday, December 5, 1994, was wading through the pretrial motions. A tall, broad-backed man of forty-six, Shuler had a reputation as a fair judge who kept trials moving. His plain-spoken, unpretentious style was underscored when he took up one of his first orders of business: Munchausen syndrome by proxy. Johnny Gasser had told the defense that he would not introduce any testimony on the issue; he repeated this vow to Judge Shuler, who quipped: "So that's good news for me. I couldn't pronounce it until I got here today."

Gasser and Wilson had recognized two problems in pursuing this line of testimony. In a case already top-heavy with experts, how many more could a jury stand? And even if the defense wasn't granted the delay that Kirkland had said he needed to prepare for it, the additional testimony almost certainly would have added another week to the trial. That would have pushed it into Christmas, which would have required rescheduling in January, which would have meant a new solicitor—precisely what Gasser was seeking to avoid. Moreover, they'd realized that they could introduce motive at least as effectively by using common-sense explanations rather than experts and psychological jargon.

Even though the jury never heard the word "Munchausen," the prosecution seemed to reap some benefit in the court of public opinion just from having filed the motion about it. Before they changed their minds, the prosecutors had tipped the press that they were planning to introduce this exotic-sounding subject, and a spate of articles had reported that this would be the first such testimony in a South Carolina court. The articles raised questions about Gail Cutro's mental health and put the Cutro team on the defensive. Many people who remembered few details about this trial would later recall, incorrectly, that it had something to do with "Munchausen."

One final motion would result in the most important ruling the judge would make. The defense had asked him to sever the charges so that Gail would be tried on one case at a time. Though Gasser had not conceded the point, he knew that South Carolina law favored his opponents. He regarded that law as archaic—he would not have had such a hard time in most other states, he said. Still, had he fought the motion and won, he might have obtained a conviction that was later reversed on appeal. He had what he thought was a better plan. There was a precedent that should permit him, he argued, to try Gail Cutro for killing one child but introduce evidence concerning all three. The circumstances were similar for all three, Gasser argued, and the proof for one child would tend to prove the others. That was why the jury needed to consider them all.

Shuler gave each side something that they wanted. He would allow evidence on all three children, but if Gasser didn't tie them all together when he presented the state's case, as he had promised to do, the judge would declare a mistrial. Gail could be retried, but they'd be back at square one. Having given the state this crucial victory, Shuler severed the cases so that the jury had the burden of deciding only one. Gail Cutro would be tried only for the murder of Ashlan Daniel.

Jury selection in South Carolina is generally rapid, but it was particularly swift because, although they didn't know it, both sides were shopping for the same kind of juror. They both believed that the strength of their case was the medical evidence, and they wanted intelligent individuals who would concentrate closely on complicated information over a long period of time. Each side was happy when two nurses were selected, along with two people who worked in hospitals. Two others had worked in day care. The jurors ranged in age from twenty-eight to sixty; half were female, one-fourth were Black.

47

Opening Statements

Right off the bat, Johnny Gasser hit the jury with the motive. Gail Cutro killed these children out of "an innate desire for sympathy and attention." He went through the chronology of events, from Parker Colson to Ashlan Daniel. He described what was necessary to diagnose SIDS and explained why the label didn't apply to these children. Then he told them why Gail Cutro killed and injured the children and what proof they would hear to support his contention.

To understand, he told them, you had to go back to 1991, well before children died in the Cutros' day care. That was the year a child named Elizabeth Lightfoot died of SIDS at a day care just down the street from the Cutros'. The child's family, the day care operator, and the Cutros were all acquainted, and all belonged to Riverland Hills Baptist Church. Within the church community, there was a tremendous outpouring of sympathy for both the Lightfoot family and the day care provider.

This event had a profound effect on Gail Cutro, Gasser argued. Just how profound only became apparent when a woman named Renee Barefoot contacted the authorities after Gail Cutro was arrested. What they learned from this witness provided a window into the mind of Gail Cutro. And the jury would hear from Renee Barefoot. When she testified, the jury would hear evidence that the defendant was obsessed with SIDS long before children died in her care, and that Gail Cutro craved the attention that had been showered on the Lightfoot family, and their day care provider, after Elizabeth Lightfoot died.

"You will hear evidence of fixation," Gasser said. Ultimately, Gail Cutro's need for sympathy and attention led her to talk a great deal about SIDS. "But that wasn't enough," Gasser told them. "That did not satisfy her," the prosecutor said as he walked to a diagram that displayed the names of the alleged victims, "until *this* and *this* and *this*," he said, pointing to the three children's names.

He paused to let the jury take this in. Then the prosecutor talked about the medical evidence that would be so important to his case. He taught them a new term: *petechial hemorrhages*, small broken blood vessels. The jury would hear it a lot. When petechial hemorrhages were found in the brain, they were evidence of unnatural death. And they were found, Gasser said, in Parker's brain and in Ashlan's brain. The jury would hear about this from two doctors, one of whom was the leading expert in the country and the other the leading expert in the world.

He told them that his case was based on circumstantial evidence. They would need to look at all the pieces to discern the full picture. And when they did, there was only one conclusion: Gail Cutro killed Ashlan Daniel.

———

Wes Kirkland immediately attacked SLED. Yes, he acknowledged, these deaths were unusual. But SLED's focus was not on conducting a thorough investigation. It wanted to enhance its own reputation. The new Child Fatalities Department was investigating its first major case and was eager to prove itself. The investigators found something unusual, concluded that it was homicide, and then scurried around trying to figure out how to prove it. They only began a serious investigation after the indictment. And they were still scrambling, desperately searching for evidence.

"It's a case, ladies and gentlemen, just like a runaway train. When they indicted Mrs. Cutro, they got all the press and the attention, and there was no turning back."

Kirkland hammered at the absence of evidence, reminding the jury that his client didn't have to prove anything. Then he reviewed some of the items seized from Gail's home. There were Stephen King novels. *This* was supposed to be incriminating evidence.

The state was intent on twisting his client into something she wasn't. "Mrs. Cutro is a normal woman," he said. The state was attempting to take pieces of her life out of context and transform them into something bizarre. "But every bit of that has a natural and normal explanation."

He moved on to the medical evidence, trying to raise doubts about the objectivity and competence of the state's experts. Then he introduced his own, dwelling on Dr. Smialek's impressive qualifications.

He asked the jurors why, if Gail Cutro was so intent on killing children, she didn't kill the one who had lived. Why, instead, did she call the mother and tell her to take him to a doctor? The real culprit responsible for this injury was not Gail Cutro but the mother herself, "Ms. Catherine Maier," he said, pointing an accusing finger. "And the evidence will show," he went on, "that she had every opportunity to have shaken that child. Every opportunity. And that she changed her story multiple times."

Like Gasser, Kirkland concluded with an exhortation on circumstantial evidence. But he suggested a different way of viewing it. "Look at it as a house of cards," he said. "If one of those cards is knocked out, the entire house falls."

48

Laying the Groundwork

Lindy Colson cried when she described the day her son died. It was the kind of testimony that made the defense lawyers wonder whether they even had a chance.

She was at work when Josh called and told her that Parker wasn't breathing. She arrived just as the ambulance was pulling out and jumped in to ride with her son. Her husband met her at the hospital, and they were ushered into a room.

"When the doctor walked in I just knew they were going to tell us he was okay," she gasped through her tears.

Gasser took her gently through the circuitous path by which the pathologist arrived at a diagnosis of SIDS, with a detour through bronchopneumonia. Then he took out a chart and asked her whether she had matched any of the risk factors for SIDS when she was pregnant: Had she smoked? Was Parker a low-birth-weight baby? She answered "no" to all but two: he died in a winter month, and he generally slept on his stomach.

Gasser asked her at length about one of her answers. She was certain that Parker hadn't been congested the morning he died. When he *was* congested, she always put him in his car seat for naps. The first time she heard that someone had said Parker was congested the day he died was during the investigation, when she was told that Gail Cutro had said so.

Lindy recounted her efforts to raise money for SIDS research, and her contact with Gail during this time, including their joint appearance on television. She talked about Gail's visits to Parker's grave and her requests for an article of Parker's clothing, photographs of the child, and an imprint of his feet. And it didn't end there. Gasser asked if she'd known that Gail had requested and received a copy of her son's autopsy report. She hadn't known about it until Gasser himself told her several months earlier, she replied.

——

Defense lawyer Lisa McPherson began her cross-examination by asking Lindy to repeat some of the favorable things she'd said about Gail on direct, like the clean house she kept and the report cards she filled out. McPherson established that Josh seemed to be a full participant at the day care and that the Cutro children, who also helped out on occasion, seemed to be normal kids who did not appear to have been abused or neglected.

She seemed to catch Lindy slightly off-guard by asking whether it was fair to say that Gail was a loving, sensitive, caring person and whether she behaved that way with Lindy and with the children. Somewhat reluctantly, it seemed, Lindy answered both questions affirmatively.

"Did she appear to be somebody that very easily bonded to children and loved them?"

"Yes."

At Parker's visitation and funeral, the couple had appeared grief-stricken, particularly Gail. When Lindy began attending SIDS support-group meetings, she invited Gail to join her. Through this group Gail met Linda Bass and a woman named Suzanne Pope, and McPherson seized the opportunity to mention that Pope also ran a day care and that a child had died of SIDS there, too.

"So," said McPherson, "Gail Cutro is not the only person that you met during this time who actually had a child die in her care?"

Finally, the lawyer drew a comparison between Lindy and Gail. No one was suggesting that *Lindy* was "fixated on death," yet wasn't *she* also raising money for SIDS, attending support-group meetings, and receiving a SIDS newsletter?

——

Gasser used his examination of Dr. Beverly Daniel, the pathologist who performed Parker Colson's autopsy, to give the jury a fast introduction to the science of pathology. The complexities and controversies would come later; at this stage the jurors needed a grounding.

After Dr. Daniel (no relation to Missy and Davis Daniel) explained what a pathologist was, Gasser quickly moved to what he viewed as the strongest evidence that emerged from Parker's autopsy. Using the term he had taught the jury during his opening statement, Gasser got Dr. Daniel to agree that in SIDS cases petechial hemorrhages were commonly found in the chest, between the diaphragm and the neck. In Parker Colson she had found none there, either "grossly"—visible to the naked eye—or microscopically. Had she found any of these pinpoint hemorrhages in any other organs? Yes: in the brain. These she observed both grossly and microscopically. It was the first time Dr. Daniel ever recalled seeing them with her naked eye.

After discussing the difficulty of distinguishing between SIDS and suffocation, she said that she believed that Parker's death was in some ways consistent, in other ways inconsistent, with SIDS. It was also consistent with "forced asphyxiation," that is, suffocation.

On cross, Wes Kirkland went over the negative findings—the kind of evidence that one would expect to find had Parker been suffocated but that Dr. Daniel did *not* find. He pointed out that she consulted one of the foremost SIDS experts in the world and, petechial hemorrhages notwithstanding, the expert didn't hesitate to diagnose SIDS.

49

———

Asher Maier

The first unusual thing Catherine Maier remembered when she picked up Asher on Monday afternoon, June 21, was that Gail was sitting on the porch with him in heat "that was almost one hundred degrees." Usually Asher would be inside, where it was cooler, she told the jury.

When Maier approached, Gail was rocking Asher in her arms. "Has he ever acted this way before?" she asked. Asher appeared exhausted. Catherine thought he might be suffering from the heat. After all, Gail's report card said he'd had a good day.

Gasser asked her to tell the jury what she did next. Maier took him with her to her Narcotics Anonymous meeting, where he slept. Afterward, she took him to a friend's house, where she and the friend speculated about what might be bothering him. Then they took him in his stroller to the mall, where they saw a movie, and Maier went home. Asher slept most of this time.

On Tuesday morning, Maier told the jury, she asked Gail to call her at work if Asher seemed uncomfortable. She heard nothing, so she called at noon to check. Gail said that Asher seemed fine. Catherine picked him up without incident, received another report card that said he'd done well, and went to another N.A. meeting. Asher seemed a little cranky that evening, but there was nothing that raised her concern.

On Wednesday, June 23, Asher awakened at about 5:00 a.m. and drained a bottle. Mother and child then slept a little longer before Maier arose to get ready for work. She dropped Asher off as usual. Everything seemed normal until 10:30 that morning, when Gail called.

"She sounded frantic and said that Asher wasn't feeling good. And she couldn't console him, and he wasn't—he wouldn't eat and he wouldn't sleep and he just kept crying."

"Do you know of your own personal knowledge whether or not somebody had instructed Gail to call you?" Gasser asked.

"I believe Josh had asked her to call me."

She called her pediatrician, explained the situation to her supervisor, and hurried to pick up her son. When she arrived, the Cutros were waiting.

"I wasn't even out of my car yet and Gail and Josh were both coming out of the door on the carport with Asher in his car seat, moving rather quickly, coming towards me."

"So did you even have to go inside the Cutro home to pick up your son?"

"No, sir, I did not."

"Did you have to place your son in the car seat?"

"No, sir. He was already in the car seat."

"So he was just handed off to you by the Cutros in his car seat?"

"He was shoved at me like a hot potato in his car seat, yes, sir."

In the car he cried off and on and fell asleep. In the examining room she was asked to remove him from the car seat, and when she did so, she found that he was limp. Following a brief examination, she was instructed to carry him across the parking lot to the hospital emergency room. At that point she'd been told only that something was wrong with his brain.

Asher spent seven days in the hospital, Maier said, and she cared for him the whole time. Josh and Gail visited the first two evenings but didn't return after that. When the medical staff asked Catherine if Asher had fallen or suffered some injury, she scoured her memory in vain for some explanation. When she was told that her child had been shaken, she was shocked. It was incomprehensible; there must be another explanation.

———

Wes Kirkland began his attack with his first question. "Ms. Maier," he said, "would you please tell the jury how much you love your children?" When she answered that she loved them both a great deal, he accused her of being a hypocrite. She "loved" her two children, he repeated sarcastically, but had custody of neither. Through his questions Kirkland established that she was "close" to her mother, but acknowledged unspecified conflicts between them. She considered herself "a family person," yet her first marriage ended in a messy divorce. And she hadn't bothered to attend hearings at which her daughter's custody was at stake.

Though the picture that was emerging wasn't pretty, Catherine Maier never lost her composure. She was able to parry some of these thrusts, and at other times her candor was disarming. In response to the charge about the custody hearing, she said, "No, sir, I did not appear at that hearing. And the reason being, my father and I had discussed it. I had agreed to my parents' having custody of my daughter because I thought it was a safe and proper place for her to be at the time. My father made it clear that there was no need for me to be there, it was just a matter of doing some paperwork and that it was unnecessary."

"So you agreed with your father that it was safer for them to have your child than for you to have your child?"

"I agreed, Mr. Kirkland, that at the time that Lauren was better suited staying with them, yes, sir. I was not going to expose my child to my drug addiction."

Kirkland asked about the "rage attacks" she complained about to her gynecologist, and he made much more headway with this subject than the DSS lawyer had during Catherine's deposition. Maier agreed that she was having both mood swings and rage attacks, which she attributed to her birth-control pills. Kirkland effectively linked three events: Chad Maier's departure, Catherine Maier's complaint of rage attacks, and her decision not to seek psychological counseling, even though her gynecologist had at least mentioned it. All three occurred within three weeks of Asher's injury.

Kirkland reminded her about a conversation she'd had with Daylene McDuffie, the Lexington DSS caseworker. Catherine had admitted she'd briefly jogged with Asher in her arms the evening before he was hospitalized. Kirkland suggested that she'd changed her story, implying that she'd caused Asher's injury. But Catherine said she'd asked a doctor about this, and the doctor had assured her that it wasn't possible that Asher's injury had been caused by a short jog.

Kirkland pointed out that she'd missed a scheduled visit with Asher, possibly more than one. Near the end of his questioning, he laid out her motive to lie. Referring to her children, he asked: "You don't have custody of either of them?"

"Not currently. As soon as this trial is over, I intend to pursue custody of my son."

"Because this trial has a bearing on whether or not you get custody, doesn't it?"

"No, sir, it does not."

"If Mrs. Cutro was not charged with the shaking of your baby, you may be charged; isn't that correct?"

"No, sir, that's not correct."

"There are only two people that were investigated in this matter, weren't there? You and Mrs. Cutro?"

"That's my understanding."

"She's on trial today, right?"

"She's on trial for shaking my son, yes, sir."

"And you don't have your baby?"

"He is temporarily with his grandparents."

"That's by court order, isn't it?"

"That's by agreed upon decision that his father and I made."

When it was Gasser's turn to ask questions again, he handed Maier a document she had typed and given Gail Cutro when her son began day care. He asked her to read it to the jury. There was a list of people to call in an emergency with their phone numbers, a description of Asher's feeding habits, and a list of some of his favorite foods.

While Catherine was reading the list of foods, she began to cry and asked if she could have a minute to gather herself. She'd just withstood a furious attack on her character without so much as flinching, and now a list of baby foods brought tears. In that moment, any doubts raised by Kirkland's insinuation that she didn't care about her children seemed to dissolve.

In retrospect, Kirkland's strongest moment had probably been the fusillade with which he'd begun. Maier had appeared staggered. But he hadn't been able to follow it effectively. He had leaped from one subject to the next, as though he was so excited to be cross-examining a witness with so many vulnerabilities that he was determined to hit every one. He had landed a lot of blows, but after a while he'd seemed arm-weary, without much power in his punch.

"I didn't really know the best way to handle her," Kirkland candidly acknowledged years later, "and it may have backfired."

After she'd finished testifying, Catherine Maier and her lawyer were having dinner at a Greek restaurant near the courthouse when who should walk in but Wes Kirkland. The lawyer was once again the affable fellow the world generally saw when he was not in court, and he stopped at their table to pay his respects.

"You're pretty tough," he told Catherine, adding that he might come by the men's department of the clothing store where she was working at the time.

"You might want to let me cool down first," Maier shot back, "or I'll stitch you up so high you'll be singing soprano."

50

The Loyal Parent

Of all the day care parents, nurse Jana Brown and her husband Rob were among the Cutros' most loyal supporters. It wouldn't be surprising for the *defense* to call them as witnesses, but Johnny Gasser had a good reason to call Rob Brown himself. Brown had observed Asher on the morning the child was hospitalized.

Before Gasser asked him about that, the prosecutor wanted to establish Brown's allegiance to Gail Cutro. He also wanted the jury to understand that Brown had frequent contact with the Cutros. It was Rob Brown, not his wife, who usually dropped off and picked up their two children. He was employed nearby as an auto mechanic and occasionally stopped in when he was test-driving a car. Brown claimed to know the Cutros well and considered them close friends.

"In fact," Gasser encouraged, "you would to this day be willing to allow Gail to care for your children as you sit here today?"

"Yeah, I would let her take care of my newborn kid that's on the way. . . . Gail is a loving woman."

Having established which side Brown was on, Gasser wanted to extract two important points. First, he wanted Brown to repeat what he'd told SLED: Gail's report cards were accurate. This could help prove that Asher had not been shaken on Monday or Tuesday, days when the report cards said he'd been fine. Second, Gasser wanted Brown to confirm that on Wednesday, the day Asher was hospitalized, he was not seriously ill when he arrived at the Cutros'.

But Brown threw up a roadblock. Were the report cards accurate? Did they inform parents when children were sick? They *seemed* accurate, Brown hedged. His wife was really the one who paid attention, since she was a nurse. Furthermore, he added, the Cutros sometimes telephoned when children were sick and didn't bother to write it down.

Gasser asked to approach the bench, and the jury and witness were removed from the court. The prosecutor riffled through his papers and pulled out Brown's SLED statement, taken the previous April. He explained to Judge Shuler that the parents SLED interviewed consistently spoke of the accuracy of the report cards, and Brown was no exception. Gasser had gone over this very issue with Brown in his office the week before, as others who were present could attest. Now, for the first time, Brown was saying something different. Shuler accepted that Brown had "surprised" Gasser and declared him a hostile witness, which meant that the prosecutor could now challenge his own witness as though he were cross-examining.

When the witness and jury returned, Gasser reminded Brown of their conversation the previous week. Brown appeared to be chastened, and with a little prodding he acknowledged that the report cards accurately reported his children's health.

Next came questions about the crucial morning. When Brown dropped off his children, Gail answered the door with Asher in her arms, Brown remembered. How did Asher look? Tired and ill, Brown said, as though he didn't feel well. Brown offered to demonstrate, using a doll. In response to Gasser's questions, he acknowledged that Asher had turned around and looked at him when Brown approached. Asher had been able to move his head and focus his eyes, according to Brown's testimony. But he didn't smile the way he usually did, Brown added.

"Mr. Brown, was he moving his head on his own when you patted him on the back?"

"Yeah."

The importance of Brown's testimony to Gasser was that it established a contrast between Asher's condition when he arrived at the Cutros', and the condition his mother and doctors found him in a few hours later. And it came from someone who was leaning over backwards to help the defense.

51

Parade of Doctors

The case was built on the medical testimony, and with three alleged victims there was no way around it: Lots of experts were going to testify. They dominated the early part of the trial.

Johnny Gasser let Scarlett Wilson conduct the direct examination of the two who offered evidence about Asher's injury. It was the young lawyer's first active role in the trial and a sobering transition from observer to participant. During a break in the testimony, she'd turned to Patsy Habben, who sat beside her at the prosecution table, and said: "A year ago I was trying a girl for running a red light."

Her first witness was the chief resident of Richland Memorial's pediatric ward. When Asher was diagnosed with shaken baby syndrome, the doctor testified, he was limp and unable to support his head. He was able to take nourishment only through an IV. Yet, he wasn't dehydrated—even though dehydration in a baby his age occurs within hours. Symptoms of this severity would show up within minutes of a violent shaking, the resident added. All this seemed to confirm that his mother had fed him that morning, which seemed to corroborate her story, since she wouldn't have been able to feed him had he been in the condition he was in when he was admitted.

Wilson reviewed Rob Brown's testimony for the doctor. Assuming Asher had been able to focus his eyes and turn his head when Brown observed him, the doctor testified, then he was injured sometime between 7:30 a.m., when his mother dropped him at the Cutros', and 11:30 a.m., when he arrived at his pediatrician's office.

The second witness was Dr. Susan Breeland, a pediatrician who was known to SLED and the solicitor's office as a local child abuse expert. After Dr. Breeland had explained shaken baby syndrome in layman's terms, Wilson asked her to demonstrate with a doll the force required to induce the injury. Dr. Breeland picked up the doll and shook it long and hard, finally slamming its head on the edge of the witness stand. It was a powerful moment that dramatized an important prosecution contention: Asher Maier's injury was not an accident; it was an act of violence.

Gasser questioned the key experts, and the one who presented the trickiest challenges was Dr. Jim Reynolds, Richland's chief pathologist who had performed the autopsy on Ashlan Daniel and had given Scarlett Wilson that impromptu lecture on subdural hematomas in the kitchen of his home. The pathologist was called to talk about Ashlan Daniel, and he seemed intent on treating the situation as professionally as possible. Gasser wanted to give the witness a graceful way out by establishing the difficulty of distinguishing among SIDS, forced asphyxiation, and accidental asphyxiation. Dr. Reynolds agreed that at times it was simply impossible to do. He acknowledged that the medical background of the child and the background of the caregiver were "exceedingly important" in establishing a cause of death. And he admitted that he'd never before seen a SIDS case with gross petechial hemorrhages in the brain.

Were his findings consistent with SIDS? They were. How about forced asphyxiation? That, too.

"Now," said Gasser, "are petechial hemorrhages in the brain more likely found in forced asphyxiation cases or sudden infant death syndrome cases?"

"Statistically, I think one would have to acknowledge they are more frequently seen in forced asphyxiation." He testified that he did not know what caused the death of Ashlan Daniel.

When it was Wes Kirkland's turn, the defense attorney wanted to emphasize what Dr. Reynolds had *not* found. He went into exhaustive detail, seemingly intent on covering every part of the body where no trauma was found—and Reynolds had found no trauma at all. The most important negative finding was the absence of a subdural hematoma. Kirkland made sure the jurors knew that Reynolds had performed his autopsy with a policeman and a representative of the coroner's office present.

Kirkland asked Dr. Reynolds how he reconciled his finding that there was no subdural hematoma when he examined Ashlan's body with the report of Dr. Enid Gilbert-Barness, who had found one when she'd reexamined the body. What the doctor from Tampa had seen, Dr. Reynolds asserted, was not something that contributed to the baby's death. It was a postmortem artifact—that is, a condition that occurred after Ashlan had died. Dr. Reynolds added that he'd shared his conclusions with two of his colleagues, whom he called the state's best forensic pathologists—specialists with specific training in the uses of pathology in court—and they had agreed with him.

It was an important moment for the defense. If Kirkland was going to raise reasonable doubt in the minds of the jurors, this was his fundamental point of attack.

Gasser wasn't about to let the jury ruminate on this last point. He quickly returned to the podium for redirect, and he asked Dr. Reynolds if he knew of a single instance from anywhere in the world where a pathologist had found a SIDS case with grossly observed petechial hemorrhages in the brain. Reynolds didn't. How often did pathologists at Richland Memorial do autopsies on exhumed bodies? "I don't remember doing one," he said. Were Dr. Reynolds's findings more consistent with SIDS or forced asphyxiation? The doctor acknowledged that they were more consistent with forced asphyxiation.

———

Dr. Janice Ophoven (pronounced OP-hoe-ven), who had flown in from Minnesota, was Gasser's first outside expert. He'd chosen her because she was a forensic pediatric pathologist (one of fewer than ten in the country), had no ties to the state's other outside experts, and she was good at reducing esoteric information to a level that anyone could understand.

Gasser quickly got to the point. "Let's just cut to the chase right here, Dr. Ophoven. Did these children die naturally or were they murdered?"

"I have an opinion that they did not die naturally."

Dr. Ophoven cited the importance of the petechial hemorrhages in the brain. She'd performed more than a thousand autopsies of infants during her eighteen years of practice and had never seen them grossly in a SIDS case. Nor had she read of anyone else having done so. In her opinion, the two children died of child abuse.

Gasser had her show the jury a blown-up photograph of the subdural hematoma that Dr. Gilbert-Barness had found in Parker Colson. The bleeding, she explained, had clotted into the dura, the thick white membrane that serves as a protective covering between the brain and skull. She could tell that it wasn't postmortem artifact because it adhered to the dura. If it could have been washed away, then it could have been blood that happened to pool in that space during or after the autopsy. But clotting could only have occurred while the child was alive.

Dr. Ophoven noted the importance of three procedures critical in differentiating SIDS from homicide. All three are important components of a good autopsy, she said, and they were *not* performed during the original autopsies. First, the eyes were not removed and examined. By the time Dr. Gilbert-Barness removed them, they were too badly decomposed to be of use. Second, no photographs were taken of the body during the autopsy, so no one could go back and look for evidence of the subdural hematoma Dr. Gilbert-Barness had found in each child. Finally, neither of the original pathologists had "stripped"—that is, removed—the duras of these infants. Dr. Gilbert-Barness had done so, and it was on the duras themselves that she had uncovered the key evidence.

The subdural hematoma was most likely caused by shaking, she said, and the petechial hemorrhages were more likely linked to asphyxia. Scans of Asher Maier's brain had revealed an accumulation of fluid in the subdural space that was similar to that of the children who died.

Gasser asked about a paradox in her findings: There seemed to be more evidence of trauma in Asher Maier than in the two children who died. Dr. Ophoven explained that when a child is shaken with sufficient force, the child can die almost instantly. When that happens, the heart stops pumping—and there may not be the accumulation of blood in the brain that you find in a child who lives and whose heart continues to beat.

Finally, Gasser introduced what he hoped would prove the clincher. He had asked Dr. Ophoven to review the autopsy reports of all South Carolina children who had died in 1993 and 1994 with SIDS as the listed cause of death. There were 102. Gasser had an exhibit that he showed the jury. It was a chart that showed an outline of South Carolina with each county marked. For each SIDS death with *no* gross or microscopic evidence of petechial hemorrhages in the brain, he had placed a blue dot in the county where it occurred; for each *with* evidence of those hemorrhages, he had placed a red dot. One hundred blue dots were sprinkled throughout the state; two red dots were planted side by side in the center, where Richland County was located.

"Tell the jury the names of the two infants with the two red dots reflected on this exhibit?"

"Parker Colson and Ashlan Daniel."

———

The defense was stunned. And it wasn't just the chart that rocked the lawyers back on their heels. They'd prepared a defense against the charge that Gail had asphyxiated Ashlan. That's what the indictment said. Yet now the state seemed to be saying that all three children had been *shaken.*

In the face of this new challenge, the lawyers were doubly glad to have the stabilizing influence of Dr. John Smialek, the Maryland pathologist who had helped Kirkland prepare and had just entered the building. Facing the onslaught of the state's experts, Kirkland was grateful to have a defense expert on hand for a quick consultation.

After a ten-minute break, Kirkland stepped up to the lectern and briefly probed for a link he could exploit between Dr. Ophoven and Dr. Gilbert-Barness. When he couldn't find one, he changed direction. He pointed out that Dr. Ophoven was criticizing not only the mistakes of the local experts, but also their whole methodology.

While the Minnesota pathologist had avoided criticizing the locals when the prosecutor questioned her, Kirkland was determined to force her hand. He tried to get her to say that her counterparts had "missed" a hematoma. Even though she would say only that they hadn't "documented" it, he'd made his point.

Next, he asked if it would be possible simultaneously to shake and asphyxiate a twenty-pound baby. "I think that would be difficult," Ophoven allowed. Then he asked if there was evidence of edema, or swelling, in the children's brains, which, Dr. Ophoven agreed, often results from asphyxia. She acknowledged that there wasn't.

Gasser had anticipated that the defense would try to appeal to local pride. And he recognized the potency of the "us versus them" battle line. So on redirect, he tried to defuse the issue immediately. His first question was: "Have you ever made a mistake in all your years as a physician?"

"Oh, yes."

"Have you ever met a doctor that's never made a mistake?"

"No."

This wasn't the first time she'd seen a subdural hematoma missed, Dr. Ophoven added. Nor was it an extremely rare occurrence. Removing the dura, she asserted, can help avoid such mistakes. Gasser had her clarify one additional matter: shaking *can* cause asphyxiation, she said.

Just before Dr. Ophoven was excused, Kirkland, who had been thrown for a loop by what he thought of as the prosecution's changing theories, inadvertently gave the witness a chance to tie them together in explaining how the babies were injured. When Kirkland questioned her one last time, Dr. Ophoven explained that the hematomas were evidence of trauma, but they didn't kill the children. Asphyxiation caused by shaking did.

52

On the Defensive

Even before she took the stand, the jury had heard plenty about Dr. Enid Gilbert-Barness—enough to know that she was a key part of the prosecution's case. So far the defense had not scored heavily in attacking the state's experts. If Gail Cutro was going to have a chance at an acquittal, her lawyers were going to have to do better challenging this one.

Originally from Australia, Dr. Gilbert-Barness had been practicing medicine for forty-four years, forty of them as a pediatric pathologist. And over the years she had developed strong opinions about the way things should be done.

For instance, she fully endorsed the procedures Ophoven had mentioned. If anything, she was even more adamant. Though she insisted that there was nothing wrong with the methods of the pathologists who autopsied Parker Colson and Ashlan Daniel, she advocated removing and examining the eyes, stripping the dura, and photographing the body.

The heart of her testimony was her description of how she'd found the subdural hematomas in the two babies, and why she believed that such injuries were sometimes missed. The key, in her view, was stripping the dura, placing it in a fixative, and examining it several hours later. When it is not stripped, or when it is examined immediately, injuries may be concealed by the natural flow and pooling of blood during the autopsy. After she'd stripped the duras of Parker Colson and Ashlan Daniel, she'd also found bruises on their craniums—hemorrhaging of the skull itself—which she called "uncontroverted evidence of trauma."

She added that she thought that the children were "almost certainly" shaken and that there was "no doubt whatsoever" in her mind that they died of trauma caused by an intentional act.

Wes Kirkland's cross-examination was his best of the trial so far. He was much more confident, patient, and focused than he'd been when examining the previous experts. He began with questions about controls. Dr. John Emery, with whom Dr. Gilbert-Barness had consulted (and who would follow her on the witness stand), had suggested that she compare her findings with a random selection of other cases. Kirkland got her to agree that controls made for good science. Then he pointed out that she had only done six reexaminations in her entire career—not many for comparison. While Gilbert-Barness was able to fend him off, she grew increasingly irritated with Kirkland's line of questions.

He shifted to a study he had first raised with Dr. Reynolds. A SIDS expert had found petechial hemorrhages in the brains of 16 percent of the SIDS cases she'd studied. On direct examination, however, Gilbert-Barness had pointed out that the hemorrhages were only observed microscopically, and, since the study was old, the data included many cases that, had they been thoroughly investigated, undoubtedly would have proved to be something other than SIDS.

Kirkland challenged this conclusion. How did she know? Did she go back and look at them? No, she admitted, seeming a little flustered.

"Doctor . . . isn't it true that good science says you don't look at a problem from one end and, without doing the proper research and investigation, jump over here to the other end, from 'A' to 'C,' without doing the work in between? Isn't that good science?"

"No, I don't agree with you because I think you do have to formulate an opinion. On those cases, there's no way. I can't go back and look at them. They're not available."

"Would you admit—"

"So it's a ridiculous argument. The facts are the facts. And I am here to tell you what I believe are the facts."

"Doctor, you don't know the facts on those 16 percent, do you?"

"I do not, but I suspect in reference to what we know now that the incidence of SIDS is dropped—it's plummeted from just a few little things that we're doing to prevent sudden infant death."

"Doctor—"

"And, therefore, I think you must jump to some conclusions. There's incontrovertible evidence in the statement I've just made."

"Doctor, if you're jumping to a conclusion, that constitutes incontrovertible evidence, doesn't it? Jumping to a conclusion?"

"Not necessarily."

"There is no evidence when you're jumping to a conclusion, is there?"

"Well, I think we can argue this and we can bore the jury to the nth degree, but what is, is. And all I can tell you is that I believe that that 16 percent in which microscopic petechial hemorrhages were found, in view of the fact that more than half of what we've been calling SIDS isn't SIDS, that it's very likely that many of those cases were not true sudden infant death syndrome."

"And that's based—I think you've stated this, that you may be jumping to a conclusion?"

"That is based on my opinion, yes."

"And in this case here you jumped to the conclusion that we had hematomas in these babies; is that correct?"

"I haven't jumped to any conclusions in what I saw when I opened the skull of these babies," the pathologist retorted. "It's there. You can't jump to a conclusion in that."

It was Wes Kirkland at his best. He had succeeded in putting one of the state's most important expert witnesses on the defensive. He'd managed to cast her in a light in which she may have sounded a little too sure of herself. She did have answers, but the battle was joined.

Dr. John Emery, who was nearly eighty, had been practicing medicine even longer than Dr. Gilbert-Barness. He was a small man who—with his bow tie, wispy white hair, and gray Van Dyke—looked every bit the professor. He was well known for his many articles on SIDS, among other subjects, and age had not diminished his passion for forensic pediatric pathology.

He and Gilbert-Barness had been friends for many years and were coauthors on the article about the Pankow case in Wisconsin—the one that seemed to have parallels with the Cutro case and through which Patsy Habben had discovered them. Dr. Gilbert-Barness had brought Dr. Emery into the case when she'd asked him to look at some of the evidence. Dr. Emery had wanted to be sure that what appeared to be petechial hemorrhages weren't artifacts created by a quirk in the autopsy procedures of the two hospitals, so he had asked Gilbert-Barness to have each hospital supply three randomly selected control samples of infant brain tissue. He had also suggested that she test control samples from other sections of the duras to be sure that the subdural hematomas weren't artifacts as well.

"If one is called in as an expert witness," he explained from the stand, "you've got to make sure that your observations are valid. And I was just validating my observations."

He and Gasser got off to an awkward start. They were like two experienced dancers out on the floor together for the first time: They each knew how to dance, but they hadn't figured out how to do it together. Gasser would pose a question and find himself slightly thrown by the response. For instance, he asked how many books Emery had written on unexpected child death. None, actually. After a pause, Gasser asked how many *chapters* of books he'd written, which brought the desired response of "several." Later, when Gasser asked him a question about SIDS, Dr. Emery answered:

"You're asking a question which implies that there is a condition called sudden infant death syndrome. What exists is a large number of babies who die unexpectedly. To say that they all die from a particular syndrome is going to a conclusion which I am not certain that I believe."

After a while it got better, but Gasser still didn't have a great feeling about it. Dr. Emery wasn't being arrogant or prickly, but Gasser didn't know what he was going to say. After several minutes, Gasser retreated to the prosecution table and asked Scarlett Wilson what she thought. She didn't think it was going that well, either, so Gasser resolved to keep it short and move on.

Dr. Emery testified that the petechial hemorrhages were the key medical finding. Their location in and around the medulla, the part of the brain that controls breathing, led him to believe the children died of reflex apnea—that is, that their breathing mechanisms shut down. The most likely scenario, he said, was that the children were shaken. But in some respects their injuries seemed to be the result of suffocation. He thought that they were likely shaken *and* smothered.

If Gasser had doubts about the effectiveness of the pathologist's testimony, Wes Kirkland had none. He'd been watching the jurors during Emery's performance, and they were obviously taken with the man. Emery knew how to look at them, and he talked in that venerable British accent. As he warmed to his subject, his eyes even twinkled. Despite the grim topic, several jurors who had been listening intently actually smiled. How the hell did you cross-examine that?

Kirkland tried, but not for long. He wasn't going to win points by attacking the jury's darling. He could only hope that the points he'd scored in his cross of Dr. Gilbert-Barness were enough.

53

Complications

The prosecution's next two experts turned out to be more important to the defense than they were to the state. Drs. Randy Alexander and Wilbur Smith were nationally recognized child-abuse experts from the University of Iowa.

Dr. Alexander was a pediatrician, Dr. Smith a radiologist, and they often functioned as a team, coauthoring papers and lecturing together at conferences. One subject they'd written about extensively was shaken baby syndrome.

Scarlett Wilson, who questioned most of the experts who testified about Asher Maier's injury, examined these two. She started with Dr. Alexander, who seconded Dr. Breeland's testimony about the time frame of Asher's injury.

It would have occurred a very short time before the symptoms his pediatrician and the doctors in the hospital observed, he said. This was the testimony the state expected from him, building on and solidifying previous testimony.

But it wasn't long before Dr. Alexander began telling the jury things they hadn't heard before—which seemed to complicate the state's case. For example, Asher Maier had been shaken not once but at least twice, Dr. Alexander testified. He and Dr. Smith were able to identify the previous shaking by reviewing the CT scans and the MRIs performed at Richland Memorial Hospital.

While this information may have surprised many in court, it hadn't shocked Dr. Alexander. He and Dr. Smith had discovered that this sort of thing was quite common, he said. When they examined diagnosed cases of shaking for evidence of prior episodes, they found it about 70 percent of the time.

The potential problem for the state was that this changed its carefully calculated timeline. The first shaking would have been about two weeks prior to the second, Dr. Alexander noted. Although it might have been milder than the second, it would have been severe enough for any caretaker to notice, he testified. Though Asher had started at the Cutros' more than two weeks before the second shaking, the jury might conclude that this information implicated not Gail Cutro but Catherine Maier.

The second problem for the state was potentially even more serious. Comparing the effects of accumulated blood and swelling in shaking victims, Dr. Alexander said: "The brain swelling in many respects is the more significant finding. They're really both significant, but the brain swelling is the part that causes you the symptoms, and in the extreme cases it causes death."

As soon as the statement was out of the doctor's mouth, Scarlett Wilson realized it was a problem. The prosecution's experts had found little evidence of edema in the brains of the two children who died. Wes Kirkland now had a new line of attack—and from one of the state's own experts!

On cross-examination, Kirkland tried to turn the first shaking into the severe one and make the second shaking disappear. Wasn't it possible that the first shaking caused the injury, and that the second set of symptoms occurred when the child was jostled in a fashion that would have been innocuous absent the original injury? This was precisely the strategy famed Innocence Project lawyer Barry Scheck would adopt three years later in defending Louise Woodward, the English au pair who was convicted of shaking to death a

Boston baby and whose case became a cause célèbre. But Dr. Alexander rejected the suggestion that jostling a child who has been shaken produces the effect of a second shaking.

Kirkland settled for nailing down the edema issue. "Doctor, one last question. In all your studies of shaken baby syndrome, in all those cases where children have died, there's been swelling of the brain?"

"That's correct."

After Scarlett Wilson's very brief redirect examination, Wes Kirkland had one more question on recross: Could that first shaking have been, say, *three* weeks before the second—which would have put it *before* Asher began day care on June 7? Dr. Alexander didn't answer the question. He deferred to his colleague, the radiologist, who was better qualified to address it, he said.

That lead-in had the state sweating when Dr. Wilbur Smith took the stand. The drama built as he explained how he dated injuries. Finally, he delivered the date everyone in the courtroom was waiting for. In his opinion, Asher Maier was first shaken on about June 9 or 10, give or take a day or two. That shaking, he testified, was not severe enough to guarantee that, in the hours that followed, a caregiver or even a physician would have recognized that Asher had been injured. The only thing that *would* have been clear, Dr. Smith said, was that the child was unhappy.

Near the end of Dr. Smith's testimony, Scarlett Wilson asked him about Asher's prognosis. He could only give a general answer, Smith said. There would almost certainly be some permanent neurologic damage. It was hard for him to predict what effect this would have on the child's functioning. "I can say this," Dr. Smith added. "Asher will never be what Asher would have been had the shaking not taken place."

These two prosecution experts, brought in to solidify the shaken baby case, had, instead, introduced information that seemed to have the opposite effect. Scarlett Wilson's inexperience may have shown through here, along with Gasser's failure to oversee her work. It seemed clear that there had been several unwelcome surprises for the prosecution, and that the state's lawyers had not devoted sufficient pretrial prep time with their experts.

Wes Kirkland had quickly seized the opportunity and turned the testimony to his advantage. It was not the last time he would do so.

54

Parents on the Stand

Eighteen parents who had used the Cutro day care testified during the trial. Most appeared only briefly to make or support a point. The questions they addressed, however, were crucial. Did they trust the Cutros? Did they find that the report cards were accurate? Were they happy about the care their children received? In answering these and other questions, the parents presented the jurors—and the public at large—with a rare opportunity to examine the workings of a family day care, and the thinking of the parents who used it.

Eleven parents were called by the state. In addition to the Colsons, the Daniels, Catherine Maier, and Rob Brown, the other five had pulled their children before the day care was closed. And that seemed to be the main reason they were called. Four of them testified only briefly. The rules of evidence did not permit them to go into detail about events that were not part of the trial, and they were not allowed to give their general opinions about the Cutros' behavior and motives. But the prosecution wanted the jury to understand that a number of parents had been dissatisfied enough to make a change.

The first parent from this group who was called was Brenda Davidson, and she was the one who testified at length. The day after Asher was taken to the hospital, she said, the Cutros volunteered the information that Catherine Maier had shaken her son. Davidson had never met Catherine, but based on the picture the Cutros had sketched, she imagined "a druggie on the street, thin with long stringy hair." Of course, the jurors had already seen and heard a very different Catherine Maier on the stand.

Davidson also happened to be a notary public, and she had notarized a sworn affidavit that Gail Cutro filed in the Maier's divorce. It was Gail's version of the events that led up to Asher's hospitalization, and after Gasser had Davidson identify the document, he took the opportunity to read it to the jury. Gail said that she and her husband took care of six children (not the 12 she'd told some parents they were entitled to), and that she'd been in the day care business for 14 years (not the four that SLED had concluded). She went on to assert that, during the two weeks prior to Asher's injury, Catherine had been angry about the breakup of her marriage. Gail was so concerned about Asher's condition on the day before he was hospitalized, she said, that she called Linda Bass to discuss what she should do, "including attempting to get Mrs. Maier to take him to the doctor." Asher had refused solid foods that entire week, she added.

Gasser also asked Davidson to describe Gail's behavior after Parker Colson died. Gail was "obsessed" with his death and talked about him all the time in the months that followed, Davidson testified. "It wasn't a once-a-month mentioning of Parker," Davidson said. "It was almost a daily mentioning of Parker or about Lindy and Mr. Colson. And every month she observed Parker's death after that. She told me she would talk to the children about Parker and about remembering Parker. And I told her that I had a small problem with that, because I didn't want my two-year-old son to be talked to about death, because I didn't think it was something he needed to know about."

Later in the trial, when it was their turn, the defense called seven parents who had used the day care. The first was Renee Perry, who testified the longest. Under the questioning of Lisa McPherson, Perry insisted that she and other parents encouraged the Cutros to keep the day care open the day after Parker Colson died—not only to keep life as "normal" as possible for the children, but because it would be good for Gail.

Even before an investigation had been conducted to determine the cause of death, Perry knew in her heart that Gail was blameless. "The first time I met Gail I would not have left my child with her if I didn't trust her," she testified. "I wouldn't have taken my children back the next day if I didn't continue to trust her. And I would take my children there today if she were still open."

The other parents were also supportive. Especially Jana Brown, who spoke with the authority of a pediatric nurse—and even wore her uniform in court. Brown said that she was known to "rave" about the Cutros. "I was always pleased," she testified. "I never had anything negative." Nor was this a result of willful blindness, she continued. "It's not that I didn't look. I mean, I felt like I was, you know, inquisitive." She did acknowledge, however, that her husband Rob was almost always the one who picked up and dropped off their children.

The defense spent a good deal of time trying to chip away at the accuracy of the report cards. Jana Brown testified that they were accurate, as far as they went, but were not a complete record of a child's day. Under Lisa McPherson's questioning, she testified that Gail sometimes phoned with important health information. But on cross-examination, she was forced to back away from that assertion. Gasser introduced into evidence eight report cards that Jana Brown had given SLED, and in responses to his questions, she agreed that these samples did, indeed, include detailed information about her children's health.

The next witness was Ramona Bowers, who was able to explain why members of Riverland Hills Baptist Church showed up at the Cutro home on the day that Ashlan died. At the suggestion of her husband, Bob, who was a deacon at the church, Ramona had called over there to let them know what had happened. It wasn't something that Gail asked for or initiated, Bowers emphasized. She never saw Gail grieving in an inappropriate way—that day or later—she said.

Bowers was also asked about the information on the report cards. Like Brown before her, she testified that Gail sometimes called when her son was sick rather than convey the information on a report card. This line of testimony was important to the defense because what Gail had written on Asher's cards the week he was injured seemed to contradict her later statements, including the affidavit she'd submitted in the Maiers' divorce. The defense was doing its best to bolster Gail's contention that she conveyed her concerns about Asher's health in person and over the phone.

Nearly all of the parents called by the defense were asked whether they'd seen Gail make a "spectacle" of herself, or otherwise seek attention. In asking these questions, of course, McPherson was eliciting testimony from witnesses in a position to deny what the prosecution contended was Gail's motive for murder—her desire for sympathy and attention.

Yet, in many ways, their testimony revealed what Ramona Bowers herself would come to realize only years later: The parents were, indeed, influenced by sympathy. Whether or not Gail had committed a crime, and, if she had, was acting for this reason, sympathy was clearly part of the equation in the aftermath. In fact, Renee Perry made this point explicitly when she explained why she and most of the other parents brought their children back to the day care the day after Parker died. "The parents know that Gail really gets a lot of strength from the children," she'd testified. "I mean, she has a real gift with children, and we thought it would be good for her to be around the children."

Though the testimony from these parents did not pack the drama of some other witnesses, and did not amount to a key moment in the murder trial, it contained significant evidence about the risks children face in day care. One risk is that parents often fail to communicate with each other. Brenda Davidson, for instance, knew nothing about Catherine Maier. Ironically, it was only the deaths and SLED's effort to shut the day care that brought many of these parents into contact with one another. Had they shared more information earlier, they might have had a clearer sense of what was going on.

A second risk is that a parent's judgment may be clouded by emotion—in this case, by an attachment to the caregiver. The parents who went to bat for Gail by testifying for the defense had also supported her when they decided to bring their children back after Parker Colson died. And they'd done so even before a cause of death could be established.

There was also a stark irony in some of their testimony. In a murder trial, the burden of proof rests with prosecutors, who must prove beyond a reasonable doubt that the defendant is guilty of the crime as charged. There is no such burden when a parent hires an individual to provide a service. If the parent is dissatisfied, she can simply find someone else. It may be a matter of personal taste, or a gut instinct. There doesn't even have to be a reason.

Yet, some parents acted as though they had an obligation to continue to employ the Cutro day care even when bad things happened there. *Especially* when bad things happened there. They somehow owed it to Gail Cutro to show that they trusted and supported her—unless there was clear evidence that she'd done something wrong. It was as if there was a burden of proof that was just as exacting as the one the prosecution faced in the murder trial, but this one was carried by the parents. If the circumstances were ambiguous, the benefit of the doubt went not to them or their children. It went to the Cutros.

55

Missy Daniel

Missy Daniel was six months pregnant when she testified. After the wrenching meeting in the solicitor's office in June, she and Davis had gone to Charleston for a weekend getaway. It had been a wonderful reprieve. But even then, during that time that seemed like pure romance after all those bleak months, in the back of her mind she knew it would never be the same.

That's what Linda Bass had always said. And even though Missy Daniel did not put much stock in Linda Bass's advice, about this the nurse was right. It *would* never be the same. *She* would never be the same. Bass used to say things like, "You're not the same, but you don't have to be worse. You're just different." It would have been so nice if Missy Daniel could have believed that. But she could not and did not. She was worse. She would always be worse.

She could take pride in the trial. She had worked hard to make it happen— beginning when it was anything but a certainty. And she'd thought often about this day—about getting up on the stand and finishing what she'd started more than a year earlier. But the experience itself brought her no peace.

She couldn't mention the polygraph exam, which wasn't admissible, and she wasn't asked about her role in the investigation. She testified about her early suspicions and the information she had shared with SLED. She went through the day her daughter died, and she recounted Gail's requests for a memento.

There was only one part of her testimony that allowed her to convey a small shred of her contempt for the woman she believed had murdered her daughter. She told the jury about sending Gail the gown that Ashlan had never worn, and about Gail saying that she "smelled" Ashlan every time she picked it up. That was the image of Gail that she wanted the jury to see and remember.

56

Fake SIDS

In his opening statement, Johnny Gasser had promised to produce evidence that would offer a window into the mind of Gail Cutro. Now, as he neared the end of his case, the time had finally come. He believed this evidence would pierce the mask that had misled so many parents. And it would demonstrate that Gail Cutro was focused on SIDS well before Parker Colson died—if, that is, the jury believed it.

The full story required the testimony of several witnesses. The first was the father of a child who had died of SIDS. His name was Buckley Lightfoot, and he testified about the sad day in October 1991 when Elizabeth Lightfoot died in a home day care run by a woman named Suzanne Pope. The Lightfoots and Pope were members of Riverland Hills Baptist Church, and after Elizabeth died, they received tremendous support from the church community.

Though Lightfoot knew who the Cutros were, they weren't his friends. As far as he knew, his daughter had never had contact with them. Gasser showed him a bulletin announcing Elizabeth's funeral that was found in the Cutro home. He had not given it to the Cutros, Lightfoot said, and he didn't know if they attended the funeral.

The defense hardly seemed rocked by this testimony. The situation itself seemed to help them. The prosecution was acknowledging, after all, that babies in the Cutros' neighborhood do die of SIDS in day care. In her effective cross-examination, Lisa McPherson found ways to counter some of the prosecutor's insinuations, and to use Buckley Lightfoot's testimony to her client's advantage. Gail may not have been friends with the family, but McPherson established that the Lightfoots and the Cutros had friends in common—and had attended the same Sunday school class. The unstated implication: Maybe it wasn't odd for Gail to attend the funeral. Also, Lightfoot confirmed that Suzanne Pope was grief-stricken after his daughter died and was wracked by feelings of guilt. She even required several days of hospitalization. Again, the implication was clear: Maybe Gail's reaction to Parker Colson's death and to Ashlan Daniel's death was normal—even typical.

Then Renee Barefoot took the stand. She was the woman whose testimony Gasser had previewed—almost hyped—in his opening statement. She was a pretty woman of twenty-nine, slender with long red hair. Gasser's questions took her back to the spring of 1992, shortly after her son was born. As she was planning her return to work at a car dealership, she was looking for day care. She also happened to be looking for a church to join, and she was considering Riverland Hills.

Through the church's outreach program, Renee Barefoot met with a retired schoolteacher named Rose Bozard. When Barefoot mentioned that she was looking for child care, Bozard quickly recommended fellow church member Gail Cutro. Rose Bozard spoke highly of the woman, but she wanted Barefoot to know that there'd been a death in the Cutro home. "She told me that Gail had lost a baby that she was taking care of in her home earlier that year," the witness testified, "and that it was due to sudden infant death syndrome." But this was months before Parker Colson died.

Renee Barefoot knew that no one can prevent SIDS, and the death did not deter her from making an appointment to visit the home. She dropped by during the afternoon to observe how the children were cared for. Gail showed her around and answered her questions about the facilities and routines. Josh was in the backyard with some of the older children during their entire conversation, so she never met him.

Gasser was finally ready to ask about what he had come to call a case of "feigned SIDS." He glanced over at the jury. "Now, did *you* bring up the incident of the previous child dying?"

"No, I did not," Barefoot said.

"Why didn't you bring it up?"

"Well, I already knew it, of course, from Rose Bozard. And just let me say, I was not going to hold something like that against her, because sudden infant death syndrome can happen anywhere at any time."

Barefoot recounted the details of the conversation that followed. "We were sitting on the couch, and she had given me a sheet of rules, regulations, guidelines, and she was the one that brought it up to me. She told me that she was taking care of a baby and it died of SIDS."

"Tell me exactly—if you remember, tell me how she told you."

"Well, she said that she had laid the baby down for a nap. And when she went to check on it or wake it up, it was dead."

"And what home was she talking about?"

"She was talking about in her home. She said, 'I put the baby down. I went to check on it. And when I did, it was dead.'"

"What was her demeanor like, in May of 1992?"

"Well, it obviously bothered her," Barefoot said. In recounting the supposed death, Gail became very emotional. "I truly felt sorry for her, and I told her that, you know, 'I'm sorry. That could happen at any time.' And she shouldn't feel guilty about it or anything like that."

That evening, when Renee Barefoot discussed the visit with her husband, they decided not to send their son to the Cutro day care. Her husband was uncomfortable with a home where a child had died and, Renee Barefoot added, there was "something about her I just did not like."

"Let me just ask you this," said Gasser. "Are you positive, are you absolutely sure that no mention was made of any other day care? In other words,

Renee—look at this jury—are you sure she's talking about a baby dying in her home when you visited her in May of 1992?"

"I'm positive it was in her home and it was in 1992."

The Barefoots found child care elsewhere, so they had no further contact with Gail Cutro. After meeting with Bozard several more times, Renee and her husband decided not to join the church, so they had no further contact with Bozard, either. The next time Renee Barefoot heard anything about Gail Cutro was in July 1994, when Gail was arrested. Renee was at work in the accounting department of a car dealership when she found out.

"There's a coworker sits beside me. She read an article in the paper that said that there were two deaths and a baby that had brain damage and it was in '93. She was reading this to me. And I asked her to go back and tell me what year that was.

"So she went back and she read it—the year again, and it was '93. And I immediately, you know, told her that I knew of a death in '92 that Gail had told me herself."

Barefoot called the newspaper and asked to speak to the reporter. "I asked him if there was any way there was an error in the year." He said he was pretty sure he had the dates right, but he would check. When Barefoot called him back, he said he'd confirmed the dates. "Well, I talked to her in '92," Barefoot told him, "and she told me that she had a baby die in her home of SIDS. What do I need to do?"

The reporter called SLED, and Patsy Habben and Richard Hunton contacted Renee Barefoot. "That's how it all began," she said.

Gasser asked Barefoot if she knew the Colsons or the Daniels or Catherine Maier. No, she said. She was seeing them for the first time in the courtroom that day. The first time she heard that no baby had died in the Cutro home in 1992 was when she met with Gasser in his office the previous month. It was during that meeting that he told her that he was going to call her to testify.

Gasser turned over the witness to Wes Kirkland, but the defense lawyer spent no more than a minute or two cross-examining her. One problem Kirkland had was that Barefoot had a lot to corroborate her testimony. Gasser had lined up several witnesses who were about to testify, and he'd already introduced relevant documents such as Barefoot's employment records and her son's birth certificate to further bolster her account.

Even though Gasser had named this witness in his opening statement and had more than hinted that she held the key to understanding Gail Cutro's motive for killing Ashlan Daniel, the defense seemed ill-prepared to deal with her.

Next up was Rose Bozard. Under questioning by Johnny Gasser, the retired teacher testified that she'd come to know the Cutros during Tuesday night outreach at their church. "I was pleased to be their friend," she said. "I recommended Gail Cutro because I felt she was a super person, a good environment for children to be in. And I still feel that way."

Although this comment appeared to be a boost for the defense, it was probably even more valuable to the state because it suggested that Rose Bozard had no motive to lie. But there were a couple of weaknesses in her direct testimony that the defense might have been able to exploit. First, she'd said nothing about SIDS, nor had she mentioned the syndrome in her SLED statement. She testified only that she'd heard that there was a death in the Cutros' home. She didn't know precisely how she learned about it; she thought it was in church, but she wasn't sure whether she'd read about it in a church bulletin or simply heard an announcement. Also, she remembered telling Renee Barefoot about it when she visited the young woman's home in August—but Barefoot had visited Gail Cutro in May.

Wes Kirkland's cross-examination was one of the "small town" moments that ran through the case: Kirkland had been one of Bozard's math students. It probably had nothing to do with how things went on cross, but by Kirkland's own account, math was his worst subject. Kirkland was able to establish that Bozard had never actually spoken to Gail about the supposed death; she'd merely expressed her sympathy in passing. This provided a possible opening: What exactly *did* Bozard remember hearing? Was the announcement—whether written or oral—simply about a death in the home? How could she be sure it was a SIDS death? Rather than pursue these questions, however, Kirkland assumed that it *was* SIDS, and he, not Bozard, was the first one to utter that word. And he never picked up on the contradiction between Renee Barefoot's testimony that she interviewed Gail before she went back to work in June and Rose Bozard's memory that she first recommended Gail in August.

Renee Barefoot's husband, Keith Barefoot, followed Bozard on the stand. He hadn't accompanied Renee to the Cutros', but he'd been present when Bozard recommended Gail and told them about the death. Keith Barefoot also recalled his conversation with Renee after her meeting with Gail. His wife was "rather upset," he testified. "She said that Mrs. Cutro had acted like she was almost having a nervous breakdown. . . ."

But he, too, had left a little room for the defense. Keith Barefoot had told the jury that Rose Bozard had been "counseling" Gail, but Bozard had testified that she had never even had a conversation with Gail about the situation. Kirkland left it alone. The defense's approach to Renee Barefoot and the witnesses who corroborated her story seemed to be: Let's get them off the stand as quickly as possible and hope that the jury forgets all about it.

What made Renee Barefoot's testimony important—and possibly pivotal—was that this was a circumstantial case with no confession and no eyewitnesses. Renee Barefoot didn't change that: She was not an eyewitness to any crime. But Gasser hoped that the jury would believe that, when Gail Cutro made a play for Barefoot's sympathy, the new mother had been an eyewitness to a state of mind.

In essence—if Gasser was right—what Gail did that day was a dress rehearsal for murder.

57

SLED on Trial

The prosecution's case was nearly complete. Among Gasser's last witnesses were Richard Hunton and Patsy Habben. He knew that the defense would try everything it could to discredit the investigation and the investigators. Kirkland had all but promised as much in his opening statement, when he likened SLED's handling of the investigation to "a runaway train." No surprise there. Who else could the defense attack? Lindy Colson? Missy Daniel? Attacking the mothers of dead babies would only offend jurors, not persuade them. Basically, Gail's lawyers had three available targets: Catherine Maier, the experts, and the police. Gasser figured that the best way to counter the attack on SLED was to put SLED on the stand and let the jurors judge for themselves.

Richard Hunton went first. Gasser asked about his background in forensics and about his earliest days in the Child Fatalities Department. He wanted the jury to understand that, despite what Kirkland had said in his opening, Cutro wasn't Hunton's, or the Child Fatality Department's, first big case. Then he had Hunton spell out for the jury the strategies he pursued and the evidence they yielded.

Hunton's testimony was almost like a final summation of the state's case. It gave Gasser a chance to introduce into evidence some of the material the cops had seized from the home, and Hunton could explain what the investigators made of it. This was particularly important in a case that might turn on what the jury concluded about Gail's state of mind. Gasser also hoped that Richard Hunton's testimony would raise doubts about the Cutros' credibility—doubts that would resurface if and when Gail or Josh took the stand.

One of the items investigators had seized was Gail's 1993 Monthly Planner. Though it had looked innocuous at first glance, Hunton found significance in the fact that after Parker died on Monday, January 4, on each successive Monday throughout the year Gail had marked the weekly anniversary with the number of weeks that had elapsed since the event. Where the calendar book was found also seemed important, he said: The planner was in the Cutros' kitchen, as were photographs of Ashlan Daniel's grave, a copy of Parker Colson's autopsy report, and a folder that contained Elizabeth Lightfoot's funeral bulletin, Parker Colson's obituary, and photographs of Parker's grave. The gown that Missy had sent Gail was in a china cabinet in the dining room. By contrast, Hunton pointed out, pamphlets and fact sheets on SIDS and grieving were found in an envelope buried at the bottom of a closet.

Hunton was able to underscore the point when he was cross-examined by Kirkland. The defense lawyer asked why Hunton seized a number of horror books by authors such as Stephen King and Dean Koontz. What was suspicious about bestsellers available in any bookstore? The books seemed significant, Hunton replied, because they were found in the master bedroom, next to Gail's side of the bed, at a time when she was supposedly grieving. "And what really didn't make sense to us was here was the grief material that she supposedly needed to overcome the grieving process and get this behind her and that type thing—that was up under a bunch of other stuff hidden away in a closet. But, yet, readily obvious and apparent were the books by her bed which dealt with death, killing, horror, murder, that type thing."

Kirkland asked if Hunton knew that the Cutros had been redecorating their home at the time of the search, which necessitated depositing some of their possessions in the closet. Hunton said that he didn't.

After Hunton, Gasser didn't need Patsy Habben to review the evidence. The main reason he called her was to demonstrate that the state had nothing to hide. Her name had come up during the trial and would come up again. If she failed to testify, the jury might wonder why. So he put her on for a short direct examination.

Gasser quickly took her through her accomplishments at SLED. Then he let her respond to a question he knew would be coming from Kirkland. During his cross-examination of Hunton, Kirkland had implied that SLED shopped for experts who would tell them what they wanted to hear. Before Kirkland had an opportunity to challenge her, Habben told the jury that it wasn't her decision whom to hire; it was the solicitor's. Then Gasser turned her over to his adversary.

Kirkland fenced with Habben before he attacked. "Your testimony today is you are objective in your investigation?"

"I am very objective in my investigation, yes, sir."

"Lieutenant Habben, you will admit this is a very big case for your division; isn't that correct?"

"My answer to that would be any case—any investigation that leads us to believe that it could be a homicide is a major investigation . . ."

"This is the only case where you've hired many out-of-state experts, isn't it?"

"This is the first time that we've had to go outside the state, because we didn't have those experts in our state to call. . . . We don't have a forensic pediatric pathologist nor a pediatric pathologist. . . ."

"So is it your testimony that there are no doctors in this state that are competent to testify for you all in this trial?"

"Let me say this, Mr. Kirkland. I feel like Dr. Reynolds and Dr. Daniel did a good autopsy. They found the petechial hemorrhages on these children grossly that indicated that there was something there. So they did a good job. I think that we have good pathologists here in this state." But when Dr. Emery suggested that they should consider exhuming the bodies, Patsy Habben continued, they needed to find an expert competent to conduct the examinations. They had no idea what the results would be, she said. All they were trying to do was "find someone who doesn't lean too much one way or the other, and just straight down the road that will give us the answer." And that's what they did, Habben asserted.

Kirkland continued to dwell on the purported snubbing of the locals. It was hard to guess how this tactic would go over with the jury, but with the limited hand he held, Kirkland was playing it for all it was worth.

After Habben, the state rested. The prosecution's case had taken six and a half days. Judge Shuler had allowed Gasser to introduce evidence involving all three children. He had vowed, however, that he would declare a mistrial if he wasn't satisfied that Gasser had tied the three cases together. At this point he proclaimed himself satisfied. It didn't mean, of course, that she'd be found guilty; it only meant that the case could go forward.

58

A Shaky Start

The first defense witness was Sandra Jeter, and a little bit of everything went wrong. Jeter worked at the state's Department of Health and Environmental Control. Part of her job, she said, was to function as a SIDS information coordinator. Lisa McPherson called her to talk about the grief caregivers feel after a SIDS death, and she asked Jeter to talk about a report that had been prepared by an epidemiologist on SIDS clustering in the Cutros' neighborhood. Gasser objected: Where was the report? Jeter hadn't brought it, and she didn't remember the specifics.

McPherson then asked Jeter to tell the jury about her work on "the progressive nature of shaken baby." But she hadn't done any studies—she'd only done some reading. Jeter had told McPherson that her research had shown that parents were the ones who typically shook children, and that they did so when frustrated and under stress.

On cross, Gasser asked whether it would be stressful for someone to take care of fourteen kids. Yes, Jeter allowed. Picking up on Jeter's earlier work as a member of South Carolina's Child Fatalities Review Committee, during which she'd spoken with Gail Cutro after Parker Colson's death, Gasser asked: "I believe you indicated that when Gail Cutro called you over the phone, she appeared sincere and genuine over the loss of this particular child?"

"Yes."

"But you would agree, based on your experience and with your Child Review Committee, that a caregiver or an adult or parent might appear to be upset over the loss of a child, maybe even appear to give another story as to what happened to the child in a way to mask or obscure or deceive either the public officials or their friends or family members or churchgoers? It could happen?"

"Of the cases that I reviewed, I did not have any direct contact. But, yes, it could happen."

When it was Lisa McPherson's turn again, she steered the examination in a surprising direction: "Of course, it's difficult to imagine, but Susan Smith is now charged with the drowning of her two children, right?"

"Yes."

"So it happens?"

"Exactly."

"Probably more than people even realize?"

"It does happen, yes."

"Now, Mr. Gasser asked you whether or not you ever had a caregiver who will mask their story. Have you ever had a parent, for instance, who would be charged with shaking a baby who may say, 'Well, yesterday I jogged with the child. Could that have possibly done it?' You do have parents who try to mask their own misconduct with that sort of thing, don't you?"

"Yes."

"And you have parents who blame other people, maybe a baby-sitter or somebody else who had access to the child?"

"Yes."

"To throw attention from themselves?"

The prosecutors would have risked a mistrial if they been the first to utter the name of Susan Smith—the South Carolina mother who drowned her two young children by letting her car roll into a reservoir—in an effort to link her to Gail Cutro. But McPherson made the connection for them. Asked about this strategy years later, McPherson said that she was sure everyone in the courtroom was thinking about Smith after Gasser finished his cross-examination. She decided that it was better to tackle it head-on, especially since the Smith case involved not a baby-sitter but a mother. So she'd tried to redirect what she thought Gasser had already hinted at in his questions by acknowledging the Smith case, and then telling the jury in so many words that the more appropriate link here was between Smith and Catherine Maier.

Perhaps McPherson was right. The Smith case had received enormous publicity, and jurors may well have made the connection. There was some risk in taking the bait: Smith had not yet been convicted, and the last thing the defense wanted the jury to do was assume that a woman accused must be guilty. But in this instance, Smith had already confessed before Cutro's trial began. And McPherson did find a way to turn it at least partly to her advantage.

Over all, it was not a great way to start. But this was not a truly important witness. The defense had to hope it all went better when the key ones appeared—which would be soon enough.

59

The Big Man

Josh Cutro could have declined to testify in order to avoid incriminating himself. After all, he had been charged with a crime in connection with Asher Maier's injury and the charge still stood. But Josh did the opposite. He testified at length, and he tried to make the case all about him.

He was dressed in a well-tailored suit and a tasteful tie, but nothing else about his performance was understated. When McPherson asked him to tell the jury about himself, Josh immediately focused on his church. He portrayed himself as a pious man who sometimes skipped meals to race to the next church-sponsored event.

Turning to the day care, Josh contradicted previous testimony by parents who'd said that Gail took care of the infants and Josh cared for the toddlers. He denied any such division of labor. He was actively involved in all child care, he said. Asked about the report cards, Josh asserted that they were important and accurate—a real service to the parents. He added, however, that the amounts of food noted were what was "offered" the child, not necessarily what was consumed.

He was more than ninety minutes into his direct examination before McPherson asked about any of the charges. Josh insisted that Parker Colson had a stuffy nose on the day he died, and that Gail never even touched him that day. She was out running errands. By the time she came back, lunch was over, and Parker was napping. Gail noticed something strange about the baby's breathing, but Josh told her that she was overreacting. A few minutes later Josh discovered him lifeless in his crib.

"That entire day," Josh reiterated, "Gail had not interacted with Parker. She had not touched him. She did not hold him. She did not feed him. She did not have any contact with Parker that day. And that is why it has been so upsetting for her. It's because she was busy doing other things on that Monday, and she didn't have her usual contact with Parker."

McPherson asked about some of Gail's behavior that previous witnesses had characterized as obsessive. "Now, did you know that Gail was going and visiting Parker's grave?" she asked.

"Yes. I—I went and—and I didn't—I didn't tell Gail. There was lots of times that I would go and visit Parker's grave by myself and there was times I would go with Gail and visit Parker's grave. There's—there's been a lot of emphasis put on the pictures of these graves. Gail didn't take those pictures."

"Who took them?"

"I took those pictures."

If McPherson was worried that some of her client's testimony might strike jurors as "over the top," she didn't show it. Quite the contrary: She encouraged Josh to discuss other ways he and Gail expressed their grief. She asked if he was aware that Gail had asked Lindy if she could keep some of Parker's clothes.

"Yeah. We—she—she had told me—and—and I could understand the comfort she was getting from it. And, here again, I—I've never told Gail, but I too, whenever I was in the closet where Parker's car seat, before it was given back to Lindy and all, I would make contact with that car seat and smell the car seat."

"Would you touch it?"

"Yes."

"What did it make you feel like to do that?"

"It made me feel close to Parker."

They moved on to Asher Maier, the child Josh was charged with neglecting for failing to provide immediate medical assistance. Josh recounted the baby's weak condition on June 23, the day he was admitted to the hospital. Then he testified about the Cutros' visit to the hospital later that evening.

Catherine had already heard that her son had been shaken, Josh said, and she began explaining that she would never hurt him—she would sooner bang her head against the wall. "She then told us that she had a daughter that she had lost custody of due to abuse—is her words, not mine. And that she had a drug problem. At this point after she said the stuff about the banging the head, I was like, 'Come on, Gail, it's time to leave.'"

Finally, he talked about Ashlan Daniel. Gail was gone much of the day Ashlan died, taking their son to the orthodontist. Again, Josh was the sole caregiver. "Gail did not even touch Ashlan that day. Gail had not touched Parker the day that he died. Gail was not the primary caregiver on those two occasions. I was the one that was responsible for their care. I was the one that was supposed to be watching these kids, taking care of them, making sure that they're safe and sound. I was the one, not Gail."

Josh was on the stand for about three and a half hours on direct examination. It was after 6:00 P.M. when Johnny Gasser strode to the lectern, but the judge was determined to press on.

Holding a copy of the deposition Gail had given to DSS, Gasser reminded Josh that Gail had testified under oath, three months before she was indicted for murder, that on the day that Parker died she fed him, clothed him, diapered him, and played with him. And here was Josh testifying for the first time that she had never even touched the child. Josh had been present at Gail's deposition, and when he was deposed right after her, he'd said no such thing. How could he explain this?

Josh pointed out that he had not been permitted to correct Gail or interrupt in any way during her deposition. Moreover, he added, it was sometimes hard to remember because the events were both distant and still very upsetting. Neither answer explained, of course, why the jury should trust him now that his wife was on trial for murder, rather than believe her own words from a time before she was even charged.

"I wanted to state that I am not perfect," Josh continued. "I have made mistakes. I have done things that I have regretted and asked forgiveness from my Lord about. I have told lies before. I am not perfect. But given this situation, the sincerity of it and all involved in it, what I am telling you up here on this stand is the absolute truth, irregardless of anything else that has happened. What is coming out of my mouth now is the absolute truth. And I've swore on the Holy Bible, which is the words that I read on a daily basis, the words that I try to live by."

Gasser pointed out previous testimony and evidence that contradicted his account. Yet Josh maintained that he was telling the truth. Gasser moved in. It would be up to the jury to decide who was telling the truth, who were the credible witnesses, wouldn't it? Josh agreed. Did he remember an earlier witness testifying that he and Gail were known in the community for their honesty? He did. Did he remember a parent who had testified earlier that day complaining that the SLED agents had asked her whether the Cutros had ever lost any children of their own? Yes, he remembered.

"Okay. Now, you have three children, correct?"

"That's correct."

"And you've never lost any children before—you, yourselves?"

"That's correct."

"And you've had no foster children or adopted children?"

"You know, I already know what you're getting to."

"Well, let me ask you this, let me ask the question. If SLED had a reason to believe that at one point in time you had more than three children, then in 1993, it was a fair question for them to ask parents if you'd ever lost a child. That's fair, is that not right?"

"That's fair."

"And you know that SLED had a reason to believe that you had more than three children, correct?"

"That's right."

"Because they had some tax returns of yours, correct?"

"That's correct."

"Where you'd indicated you had five children?"

"That's correct."

"But in fact, you only had three children?"

"That is also correct."

"Now, can you explain to us please why you—you're the one that brought up the fact you had lied before?"

"Uh-huh."

"And, of course, your lawyer brought out the fact of truthfulness in the community. Can you explain to us why in 1989 you filed a tax return and you indicated you had five children living in your house for twelve months?"

"I did something that a lot of people do; and that's put down extra dependents."

"So the person 'Johnny Cutro' and 'Saul Cutro' according to you in 1989 were under the age of two years and were your two sons, those people don't exist, do they?"

"That's correct."

There was no loud crash as Josh fell from the pedestal he'd been trying to construct. But the admission was devastating. After all those words about piety and the Bible and serving his Church, he suddenly had no choice but to own up to filing false tax returns.

But if Josh felt humiliated or chagrined or even just chastised, he didn't show it. He did what he always seemed to do when he was under attack: he attacked back. First, he pointed out that Gail had nothing to do with the preparation of their tax returns. Then, when Gasser was talking about all the people who had come to court—some unwillingly—to testify truthfully about what they had seen and heard, Josh broke in.

"Did you check *their* tax records?"

"Mr. Cutro," said Judge Shuler, without waiting for an objection, "you can't ask questions. He asks the questions."

"Yes, your honor," said the temporarily chastened witness.

Gasser continued: "You've testified to certain very important points that the state's witnesses last week and this week have testified about completely different than you, do you understand that, because you were in the courtroom?"

"Uh huh."

"So the jury's going to have to weigh your believability against those witnesses, correct?"

Josh nodded.

"And there's a lot at stake here for you and your family and your wife?"

"Yeah."

"Now, you lied about something that's as trivial as the number of children that you have on a federal income tax return?"

"That's right," said Josh, lunging at this opening. "And I'm glad you made that point. It is trivial. It shouldn't even be brought up, because this is a serious matter. We're talking about murder. We're talking about sending away a woman that has done nothing wrong, that has not even touched these two children, a woman that has three children of her own at home and they're wanting to send her away, life in prison, and there's not even evidence of any wrongdoing being done, that—I mean, and—and I have pointed out to people time and time again, I was the one taking care of these children, not Gail. I was the one there. If anything had been done wrong to them or if anyone had the opportunity to do something to these children, it was certainly not Gail. It was me."

Later Gasser returned to Parker Colson's car seat. "You indicated that with Parker sometimes you would smell his car seat and—"

"No," said Josh. "I said I would touch his car seat."

"You didn't say you would smell his car seat?"

"Did I say that?"

"Well, let me—well, would you?"

"I—I think I would not stick my nose into it, but get close to an object like that, you can smell it. You don't have to put your nose, your face in the object."

"You could smell Parker—Parker Colson on the car seat months after he died?"

"Well, not necessarily Parker, but of his substance."

A few minutes later Gasser asked his last question.

"Everything you just testified to, as you said during several of your comments both on direct and cross-examination, it's your testimony to this jury is 100 percent the truth?"

"Everything that I have said to my recollection of the events, some of which are stronger in my mind than others, is absolutely true. I can sit here and tell you that my wife, Gail, did not in any way with any of these children, harm them, or do anything to them that would cause them any injury whatsoever. She did nothing wrong. She has done nothing wrong. She is an innocent woman, and she should not be on trial. If anyone should be on trial today, given these circumstances, these events and all, it should be me. It's only because Gail sought help from a therapist. Gail was seeking to find out what happened, that the attack focused on her. I did not have that. I did not go, so I was—I was not the weak person. I did not succumb to help from others and all. I turned to the Lord and gathered strength from the Lord."

"Thank you, Mr. Cutro," said Gasser, returning to his chair. He didn't mind that Josh Cutro had turned his questions into opportunities to lecture the jury. It would have been almost impossible to rein him in, and Gasser didn't feel the need to. He had confidence that the jury had seen that Josh Cutro's testimony was a transparent attempt to save his wife. And coupled with his admission that he'd lied on his tax returns, Gasser believed that the big man's credibility had been damaged beyond repair.

Whether McPherson agreed or not, she apparently had nothing to add. She declined to ask further questions. It was 7:40 p.m., the end of a long and difficult first day for the defense.

———

Was it a mistake to put Josh on the stand? Some of the risks had been predictable. As he had demonstrated many times before, once he started talking he was hard to stop. But there were also potential rewards.

In one way or another, he would point the finger at himself. He'd been doing that for longer than a year, and sure enough he did it on the stand. And that could have helped his wife. There were people who knew Josh well who suspected that he had injured those children. Even if most of the jurors discounted this possibility, there was always the chance that one or two who did not believe that Ashlan Daniel had died of natural causes would have a hard time believing that Gail was the more likely culprit than Josh. And they might latch onto his testimony as reasonable doubt. That's all you need for a hung jury.

But the tax returns were a blow to the entire defense—including the lawyers. It was most certainly a surprise to them. There had been so much material to go through that Wes Kirkland had simply missed those phantom kids. Asked later what the single worst moment of the trial was for them, Thom Neal, Wes Kirkland, and Lisa McPherson were unanimous. At the moment Josh was forced to admit that he'd lied, each had an overwhelming desire to slide under the defense table and disappear.

He'd hurt not only his own credibility, but also theirs. And that was not a plus for Gail. But the defense would go on. And there was one good thing about Josh's testimony: It happened on the first day of Gail's defense. There was a lot more testimony to come, and it was all bound to be better.

60

Expert for the Defense

The defense lawyers pinned their hopes for a second-day comeback on John Smialek. His credentials were, indeed, impressive. He was not only Maryland's chief medical examiner, he'd also published widely—including articles on SIDS, shaken baby syndrome, and death-scene investigation. He had been qualified as an expert in some twenty states, and had lectured at the FBI Academy on infant death investigation and on asphyxiation. He had also performed about a hundred exhumation autopsies. On the stand he was calm, articulate, and self-assured.

Earlier in the trial Smialek had sat at the defense table for two and a half days to assist as Wes Kirkland struggled through the state's medical testimony. Kirkland had seemed to gain confidence as the trial progressed, and he credited Smialek for that. Now, the student examined the teacher.

After reviewing all the materials the pathologist had examined, Kirkland asked if he had an opinion as to how Ashlan and Parker died. Smialek told the jury that both died of SIDS. He could find no evidence of any trauma, nor did he agree with previous witnesses who suggested that performing an autopsy on a child was different from performing one on an adult. A hematoma was a hematoma. "If there's a blood clot there, you would see it. I would see it. It's not a great mystery. It's a simple fundamental fact that a physician is trained to observe. . . . To say that a trained, experienced pathologist would miss that to me is incomprehensible." Furthermore, what Enid Gilbert-Barness saw in the dura was just normal discoloration that you would expect to see, since that portion of the dura is normally engorged with blood.

Kirkland asked about the absence of edema, or swelling of the brain. Bleeding and edema were linked in brain injuries, Smialek explained. When force sufficient to cause injury was applied to the head, you always saw edema. Furthermore, most shaken-baby cases with which he was personally familiar also involved impact: the child was shaken and then slammed against a hard surface. Such an action usually produced external trauma, such as skull fractures. He testified that research suggested shaking alone, without impact, will not produce a fatality.

As for petechial hemorrhages, Smialek dismissed them as irrelevant because they were postmortem artifacts: "There were no petechial hemorrhages in terms of evidence that hemorrhages had occurred while either of these children were alive. What was present was evidence of blood that had escaped from the blood vessel when the autopsy examination was done." Had they been hemorrhages resulting from trauma, there would have been swelling.

Near the end of his testimony on direct, Smialek explained that babies who are shaken don't die suddenly; they die as a result of the swelling that accompanies the bleeding. Asher Maier was a case in point: his injury grew progressively worse until the swelling could only be halted by a shunt.

When it was his turn, Gasser got Smialek to back off rather quickly from his statement that shaking alone, without impact, does not cause death. Smialek had covered himself by talking about cases with which he was "personally familiar," but now he was willing to concede the point. He held firm, however, that you had to have edema. Smialek may have cut short his quarrel over impact when he recognized the direction of Gasser's questions. The prosecutor pulled out one of the pathologist's own articles and quoted Smialek to Smialek.

As the two men continued to joust, Gasser's cross-examination bogged down badly. But, finally, he spied an opening. Smialek agreed that a diagnosis of SIDS required a negative investigation, so Gasser peppered him with questions. What if there were inconsistent statements by the caregiver? That would require further investigation, Smialek conceded.

"And were you provided with any evidence or testimony or statements that Gail Cutro fabricated a death in her home a year before the first child ever died?"

"No."

"Would you think that was important?"

It would have to be investigated, Smialek said.

Gasser turned to the Asher Maier case. Piece by piece he described the evidence to Smialek, asking whether each additional fact would change his opinion. It was incredibly slow going, but they finally seemed on the verge of agreeing. Then, at the last minute, Smialek wouldn't budge—even when Gasser framed his question as a hypothetical. "Say for the sake of argument, if it was a fact that Gail Cutro shook [Asher], you couldn't come in here as a forensic pathologist and say that these two babies died of SIDS, could you?"

"Well—"

"That takes these two deaths out of the category of SIDS by your own definition, correct?"

"I wouldn't want to assume that. And I wouldn't want to tell you what conclusion I would reach based on an assumption."

"So you won't answer my question?"

"I don't think I can."

Finally the judge jumped in. Though the defense lawyers didn't appreciate it, he had done so before during the trial and it was well within his discretion.

"How about this, Solicitor?" Shuler interjected, turning to address the witness. "*If* you determine that Asher Maier was shaken by the defendant, *if* that was your determination, if that was your final analysis and your determination—I know it's not. But he's asking you if it was, then would that change your opinion as to the SIDS deaths?"

"I believe it would."

"And I understand that's not your opinion. I'm not suggesting that it is."

"And I'm not suggesting that it is either," said the relieved solicitor.

It was a hard-fought concession that Gasser and the judge had extracted. And an important one from a formidable, and sometimes intractable, witness. After this exchange Gasser and Smialek seemed to communicate more easily, as if they'd both surmounted some obstacle. There was even a moment of humor, although it was unlikely that many of those present got the joke. The deputy solicitor, who was born and raised in Maryland, landed an artful little dig at his home state in a way that associated it with Yankee impatience. Reminding Smialek that on direct examination he had testified about an infant he had autopsied in Baltimore two days earlier, Gasser asked: "And you've already had a diagnosis of SIDS in this case?"

"That's correct."

"How many investigators do you all have in Maryland to be able to work on any one particular case like that?"

"There is one person who is designated to work under my supervision and carry out those types of examinations and investigations."

"You all have had an opportunity to review the entire clinical history of that particular child, take statements from the caregivers, interview the pediatrician and the emergency people, all within forty-eight hours?"

"That's correct."

"You all work fast in Maryland?"

"Well, we do what we have to do."

It was more than a private joke. It was a matter to which Gasser planned to return later in the trial.

When it was Kirkland's turn again, he went right to work. "Dr. Smialek, you heard Mr. Gasser ask you a good bit about red flags?"

"Yes."

"And you can testify that there were red flags in this case?"

"Absolutely."

"When you have red flags and you do your investigation, you then go to see whether or not the autopsy results confirm these red flags, turn out to be more than red flags, don't you?"

"That's correct."

"And upon your review of all the medical evidence after knowing about the red flags, is your diagnosis still these are SIDS deaths?"

"That's correct."

The defense's second day was done. It had been a lot better than the first, no question about that. On balance, Kirkland had to feel good. Smialek had given them a much-needed boost.

61

"My Whole Family Is a Victim"

As Lisa McPherson walked to the lectern with her notes the next morning, she prayed that Gail's testimony, unlike her husband's, would bring no surprises. She only wanted the jury to see the same Gail Cutro that she had seen every day. And, in truth, the Gail Cutro on the witness stand made a good impression. She was dressed in a navy-style dress, blue with silver buttons down the front and white piping on the shoulders. Her hair was nicely shaped and her make-up just right. She'd lost a lot of weight since the day she was arrested. She hadn't looked this good in years.

"Gail," McPherson began as the defendant settled herself, "the jury's heard an awful lot about you this week. So it's not really necessary for you to introduce yourself more than that. Tell the jury what you would like them to know about your life, about the kind of person that you are."

"I'm a normal person. I have a normal life. We do things like any other family. We're involved in a lot of different things in our community. My children are involved in after-school activities. Sometimes I feel like I run a taxi service, running children back and forth."

"And can you tell the jury how you feel about the day care not being a part of your life any more?"

"I miss all of my children."

"Gail, you say 'my children.' You refer to them like a schoolteacher would. I mean, it's not uncommon for you to refer to them as 'my children' or 'our children?'"

"No, it's not."

When McPherson asked her about the day that Parker Colson died, Gail repeated many of the things Josh had said two days earlier. She'd gone out to run errands—to the bank to make deposits, to the craft store to pick up supplies and look for a birthday present for Lara. It was the usual Monday routine: Josh would take care of the children, and she would be back later, maybe after lunch. McPherson took her through the death and then the funeral. She felt guilty most of all, Gail explained, because she felt that it had been her responsibility to return Parker to his mother.

Sometimes McPherson's questions, and Gail's answers, tried so hard to portray Gail as "normal" that they came across as forced and stilted. Typically in such instances, McPherson asked leading questions—Gasser only objected if he thought that they were hurting his case—and Gail answered in clipped sentences, not bothering to explain. One example was their discussion of the books that SLED had seized from Gail's bedroom and that Hunton had described during his testimony.

"And how about your son, Joshua? Does he read any Stephen King? Being a fifteen- or sixteen-year-old, does he read that sort of thing?"

"Yes, he does."

"Are any of those books Joshua's?"

"Yes, they are."

"What kind of books do you read? I mean, are you normal or abnormal?"

"I'm very normal. I read all types of books."

"So if the jury were to believe that you only read these books, what would you tell them?"

"I do not read just those types of books. I have read them in the past. I enjoy Stephen King movies. But I have a lot of craft material, because I'm always busy with my hands."

The books did not seem very important in the scheme of things. SLED may have overreached in seizing them in the first place. But Gail's testimony seemed, at best, odd. She wasn't actually denying that she'd read the books. But she was claiming that some belonged to her son—even though they were found next to her bed.

Gail sounded more comfortable when she was talking about her hunger to understand why Parker died, and the counseling she received from Linda Bass. "And what was Linda Bass encouraging you to do throughout this counseling process?" asked McPherson.

"Stop blaming myself."

"How many times has she told you that?"

"Dozens."

"And what did she also encourage you to do in terms of getting information from the SIDS Alliance or any source possible?"

"She encouraged me to read anything I found that might help me to come to grips with blaming myself and to understand that nobody—not even the doctors—could have stopped what happened." That was why she obtained Parker's autopsy report, which Bass thought might convince her "that there was nothing I could have missed. I felt like if he was sick enough to die, I should have seen something."

Gail added that she didn't remember putting any of the literature Bass gave her in her closet, but she'd read and assimilated it anyway, so she didn't need to keep it handy. Besides that, they were redecorating the house.

McPherson tried to neutralize prior statements she anticipated Gasser would use during cross-examination by giving Gail a chance to respond in advance. What about the statement in Gail's deposition that she'd fed Parker, played with him, changed his diaper, and dressed him? What she meant, Gail explained, was that Parker had engaged in those activities in day care that day. On that particular occasion, almost all were performed by Josh.

Turning to the shaken baby case, McPherson asked Gail about the affidavit she signed that became part of Catherine and Chad Maier's custody dispute over Asher. Gail denied that it was an effort to incriminate Catherine. After Asher was hospitalized, she and Josh tried to remain neutral. "We tried to pull away from the situation, because I didn't want to get caught between Catherine and Chad."

Finally, McPherson asked about the day that Ashlan Daniel died, and Gail described discovering the lifeless body.

"When I go to her crib, I notice right away when I lean over to turn her over—I'm getting ready for her to get mad at me for waking her up. And I go—go to reach down to get her, and I notice something's not right. Something's definitely wrong, but I don't want to admit it."

"What do you mean, you don't want to admit it?"

"I don't want to believe it."

"Gail, after Parker died, were you afraid to take other infants?"

"Yes."

"And Asher was the first infant you all took after Parker, wasn't he?"

"Yes."

"Did you want to take Asher?"

"No."

"Who encouraged you to take Asher?"

"My husband."

"Why?"

"He thought it would be good for me."

"And did Linda Bass ever talk to you about getting back on the horse, that sort of thing?"

"Yes."

"And had you ever talked with people about the fact that [since] this had happened once to you, a SIDS death, it wouldn't happen again?"

"Yes."

"And based on those conversations, what did you believe?"

"I felt that it wouldn't happen again. There was no way it could happen again. I felt comfortable with the fact that I could put a baby down to sleep and they would wake up."

"Now, when you looked at Ashlan's crib, you said you knew something was wrong. But why? What did you see that told you something was wrong?"

"She looked very light and I didn't see any movement whatsoever. And I hit up against the crib to bend over to wake her up. And around her mouth was blue."

"Did you touch her at that point?"

"No, I did not. If I touched her, it would make it real."

"It would what?"

"It would have made it real."

"And what did you do then?"

"I went to get Josh."

"Josh wasn't there."

"But in my mind I didn't know that. In my mind the first thing I would do would be to get Josh."

"So what did you do?"

"I went to the back door to get him. I knew that he would be coming back. And when I went and opened the door, he was coming up the driveway."

"What were you saying or doing or feeling?"

"I was in shock. I didn't—I still was not accepting it. I didn't accept it until I heard Josh scream."

Josh moved Ashlan to the dining-room table and began administering CPR. He told Gail to dial 911, and she placed the call the defense had played for the jury earlier that morning.

Now McPherson wanted to give Gail a chance to address the prosecutor's theory about motive. "Gail, I want you to tell this jury whether or not you have been happy with any of the attention that you have gotten because of these two deaths?"

"Happy?" Gail sounded incredulous. "I would trade my life for it to have never happened."

"Will you tell them in any way whether or not you've gotten any benefit from the deaths of these two babies?"

"No."

"Will you tell the jury whether you have sought out attention from TV or counseling? Why did you go on TV?"

"Lindy asked me."

"Gail, throughout all of this what is the most painful thing for you?"

"The most painful thing right now? Having parents of children that have died in my home think I've done something to them that I haven't."

Later McPherson brought up the person the prosecution viewed as the single most important witness in establishing Gail's motive: Renee Barefoot.

The conversation Barefoot had described portrayed Gail as quite different from the "normal" woman she claimed to be, and on cross-examination the defense had done nothing to discredit Barefoot's testimony.

"Okay, do you deny to the jury that she ever came there?" McPherson asked, referring to Barefoot's visit to Gail's home.

"Oh, no."

"Did a lot of parents—you talked to a lot of parents?"

"I've interviewed a lot of parents."

"Now, you heard her testimony that when she saw the article in the paper about you, that essentially for the first time she recalled the conversation that she had with you in your living room, right?"

"Yes."

"Did you have any contact with her—do you know of any reason why for two years she would ever have had to even think back on that conversation?"

"No."

"What can you tell the jury about whether or not you ever told her that you, yourself, had a child die while in your care of SIDS?"

"I don't remember a conversation of that nature."

The lawyer tried another tack. "Do you know whether or not Renee Barefoot, based on her conversation with Ms. Bozard, had any understanding prior to her being to your house that you had had a SIDS death there?"

Gail seemed confused by the question. "Did she hear that from Ms. Bozard?"

"Do you know?"

"I have no idea."

McPherson moved on. Barefoot still seemed to be a problem for the defense, but McPherson had other things to worry about. First and foremost, her client was not very expressive on the stand. Gail displayed no passion or emotion. This lack of affect was particularly troubling, since Gail was claiming that she'd been as devastated by the deaths as the children's own parents; yet, her demeanor betrayed nothing like the emotion displayed by those parents. After the trial, Gail's lawyers would argue that she had come across as emotionally "flat" because she was spending her nights in jail, where she was under great stress and wasn't able to sleep.

As the direct examination went on, however, the problem went beyond a lack of emotion. Even while answering her own lawyer's questions, Gail began to get testy. The longer she was on the stand, the less she sounded like the normal, perky suburban mom who chauffeured her kids all over town. She began to respond to McPherson with a defensiveness that at times bordered on hostility and made the friendliest questions sound like cross-examination. A judge who observed from the gallery said that she came across as "crabby."

Near the end of her examination, McPherson brought up Elizabeth Lightfoot's funeral, and Gail seemed to flinch.

"Now, I'm going to ask you about a few specific things that have come up. Do you remember when Elizabeth Lightfoot died?"

"Yes."

"And you attended the funeral?"

"As did lots of people."

"You all were all in the same church together?"

"Well, I didn't know everyone there, no."

"But you and the Lightfoots—"

"Yes."

"—you all were in the same Sunday school class?"

"Yes, we were."

"And did you save the program from Elizabeth's funeral, right?"

"I save the program from every funeral I go to that has one. I think it's disrespectful to throw them away."

McPherson ended the direct examination by giving Gail a chance to make a final profession of innocence: "Gail, I want you to look at this jury and tell them whether or not you did anything to cause Parker Colson to never wake up from his nap."

"I did nothing to cause his death."

"I want you to tell them whether you did anything at all to cause Ashlan to not wake up."

"No, I did not."

"And if there were anything that you could have done to prevent their deaths, tell this jury whether or not you would have done it."

"I would have done anything."

It had not been a sparkling performance. McPherson was never able to elicit for the jury the warm, loving, maternal woman she seemed to be trying to present. But Gail had held up fairly well, and she had already responded to some of the prosecutor's strongest evidence. Her lawyers hoped that would blunt his cross-examination.

The challenge for Gasser was whether he could summon forth a very different side of the defendant. He started with some basics. He asked Gail if it was true that Asher Maier was shaken on June 23, 1993. She conceded that he was. This admission was surprising, since the defense had expended a good deal of energy suggesting that the child had been in poor health for several days, during which his condition progressively deteriorated.

Gasser did not dwell on this concession, however. He turned to the documents, referring first to Gail's affidavit in the Maier divorce. He reminded her—and the jury—that at the time she signed this statement she knew both that there was an ongoing investigation of Catherine Maier and that she herself was also under scrutiny. Yet, she'd sworn in the document that she was caring for six children. Gasser asked why she'd lied. Gail hemmed and hawed.

"That's a lie, isn't it?" Gasser repeated.

"It was not a fact, no," Gail finally admitted.

"So it was not the truth?"

"No, it wasn't the whole truth."

"And this is a court affidavit, a sworn statement from you in August of 1993 when the focus of the investigation was on Catherine Maier?"

"That's correct."

"And isn't it a fact the reason why you lied was because you didn't want any government agency focusing in on you?"

"No, it's not."

"Then tell the jury why you lied."

"I had no reason to lie."

"So you don't know why you lied?"

"No, I don't."

This exchange set the tone. It was thrust and parry, parry and thrust. Nothing came easily. Every admission and concession Gasser extracted was hard-earned. At times it seemed as though Gail viewed admitting anything as tantamount to admitting everything. She had testified that Parker Colson was congested. Gasser remembered that she'd told the EMS technicians the same thing; hadn't she? No, she didn't remember that. Well, she'd told the deputy coroner, then. No, she hadn't spoken to him. All right, she told Dr. Selman Watson, didn't she? Gasser asked, without identifying for the jury the psychologist who had evaluated Josh and Gail during the DSS investigation. Bingo! This time she agreed.

And when Parker was congested, Gasser continued, she and Josh always put him in his car seat for naps, didn't they? No, countered Gail. They did so when Lindy asked them to. So even though they knew that this was the method Lindy preferred, they ignored that and put him to sleep in his crib? No again. "He was not congested until after he went to sleep."

Gasser suggested that Gail knew that a child who was congested ran a greater risk of dying from SIDS. She hadn't known that before the trial, Gail replied. And she'd never told the Colsons that Parker was congested that day because it was clear that they had a hard time talking about his death, and she didn't wish to inflict additional pain.

Gasser turned to her deposition and her contact with the two children on the last days of their lives. He had blown up copies of the pertinent testimony, and he placed them on the easel so that the jury could follow along. He reviewed her testimony on direct that she'd had no contact with the children. But when she'd been asked the same question concerning Parker during her deposition, she'd given a different answer. Now Gasser wanted to hear her defend what she'd told McPherson earlier in the day.

"I took it as me or Josh. And I knew what activities he had that day."

"So when they asked you what activities did you have that day, when they asked you that in reference to Parker Colson, you took it as you and Josh; that's your testimony?"

"Yes."

"When they asked you that a few minutes before that, you took it as just you?"

"Yes, I did."

"Any reason why?"

"Maybe because of the tone of her voice, the questions before that—I don't know. That's how I took it."

"So when you were asked what your activities were with Ashlan Daniel, you told under oath what your activities were—"

"—I had no activities."

"Okay."

"And the question on Parker Colson," she continued, "it did not say, 'I played with him' or 'fed him' or 'changed his diaper.' These were the things that were done with him that day."

"Does the question say, 'Tell us please what you and Josh did with him that day?' Does it say that?"

"No, it doesn't. But me and Josh were partners. And anything we do, we do together."

"In fact, Josh was deposed the same day as you, correct?"

"Yes, he was."

"He was asked the same questions, correct?"

"I suppose he was."

"So the jury understands, when you were asked this, this wasn't a combined answer by you and Josh?"

"No. We gave separate depositions."

"Okay. So when they asked you what activities did you have with him that day, you answered, 'playing, feeding, diaper changes, that sort of thing'; that's what your answer was three months before you were ever indicted, correct?"

"Yes, it was."

"And isn't it a fact, Mrs. Cutro, that one of the first things this jury has to decide when they go back in that jury room is whether or not you had access, physical access, to these two babies? You understand that, don't you?"

"Yes, it is."

"And now after you've been indicted, after you've been shown this particular deposition that was taken three months before you were indicted, you're telling this jury you had no contact with Parker Colson?"

"No, I did not."

"'Did he sleep any?'" Gasser asked, reading from the deposition. "Your response was?"

"'Yes.'"

"'What kind of play did he engage in?' Your response was?"

"'Just, you know, little face things. My husband played with him more that day than I was able to.'"

"Okay. Did you say, 'My husband played with him that day. I did not?'"

"No. But you can play with a child without having physical contact with him, too."

"So when you answered, 'My husband played with him more that day than I was able to,' you're saying that that doesn't mean that you actually played with him, just Josh played with him a little bit more?"

"I never held him that day."

"'Did he eat or take a bottle?' What was your answer?"

"'My husband fed him that day, I didn't.'"

"So you were specific about you not feeding him, correct?"

"That's right, because that's one of the things that has bothered me the past two years."

"So you are very specific when you're giving your testimony—you're very specific that you didn't feed him, but you're not specific about whether or not you touched him at all, whether or not you played with him at all?"

"Because I was preparing his meal when he died."

Gasser moved on to the Asher Maier case. "Now, let's get right to the heart of the matter here," he began as he introduced the report cards that he had made a cornerstone of his case. "Tell the jury on 6/21, when you were sitting down to prepare accurate reflections of Asher Maier's condition on that day, like you do every single day with every single child, when you checked off what his mood was, you tell this jury what you checked off."

Gail looked over the report cards the prosecutor had handed her. "I can't say that I did check this off."

"Are you saying they are forged?"

"I'm not saying that they were forged, no."

"What is checked off on that day?"

"I can tell you what is checked off, but I cannot tell you that I checked it off. 'Happy.'"

"Tell this jury when you sat down on June the 21st, two days before Asher Maier was ever even shaken, when you sat down to tell his mother what food he took in and what bottles he drank, tell them what you put down."

"What food he ate?"

"What food he ate."

"'Cereal and fruit; cereal, fruit, and carrots; and his milk.' The next day 'cereal and peaches; cereal, peaches, and sweet potatoes.'"

"So he ate all of that food, and you indicated that on June 21st and June 22nd, when you were filling out those forms, correct?"

"These are the foods that were offered to him. It does not say how much food he ate. It has how many ounces of milk he took, but it does not indicate he ate a whole jar, a half a jar, or a quarter of a jar."

"Let me ask you this, Mrs. Cutro, we've been at this now for—this is our ninth day. You've seen six or seven or eight parents called by both sides to come in and talk about the report cards?"

"Yes, I have."

"Other than you and your husband, Josh, tell this jury how many of those people have testified that what's on the report cards deals with what food was offered, other than you and Josh?"

"No one."

"So after you gave your affidavit in August of 1993, after you gave your deposition in April of 1994, after you were indicted for two counts of murder in 1994, before you ever knew that Catherine Maier would have saved those report cards, you had never indicated to anyone that this was just offered food, did you?"

"No. But I voiced it to the parents if the child didn't eat that good that day, especially if they were a good eater."

"Isn't it a fact, Mrs. Cutro, that you and your husband, Josh, have to come in here and testify that it was food that was offered because of the medical evidence that's been presented in this case—"

"We have to? No. We're here to tell the truth."

"And you're telling the truth?"

"Yes, I am."

"That now these report cards only reflect food that was offered?"

"I would say the majority of the time it was food ate in great consumption. If I had a problem with the child during the day with their appetite, their parents knew it. If not during the day, when they come to pick them up."

"Well, explain this to me. You're telling the jury on 6/21 you offered him cereal and he didn't take it, so then you offered him fruit and he didn't take it?"

"I didn't say he didn't take it. He showed no interest in it."

"And then at 12:00 you offered him cereal, fruit, and carrots, and you're saying you offered three different foods; that's what you're saying now, he didn't take it?"

"Trying to get him to eat something, yes."

Gasser was satisfied that he'd covered the most important evidence in all three cases and had, in the process, damaged Gail's credibility. Her cross-examination hadn't been nearly as dramatic as Josh's, but he felt that it had been effective. He'd been surprised by Gail's fortitude and resilience, however. And she was smart, too—he gave her that. He wanted to hammer home a few more points and then finish with evidence supporting his theory of motive.

He turned to the children's clothes that Gail had kept and other evidence that he believed helped establish her state of mind. He had to negotiate a delicate balance in these questions. To jurors who were not convinced that Gail was guilty (and he had to assume that they were all in this camp), he might appear to be mocking her grief. If he came across as a bully, the jury might see her in a sympathetic light, and he might lose the moral high ground he had sought to stake out: the polite prosecutor who, throughout the trial, had sought to be decent and fair. At least, that's the way he hoped he had come across, and he certainly didn't want to blow it now.

"Do you recall requesting of Lindy Colson to keep Parker's clothes?" he began.

"I don't remember requesting it. I remember talking to her about his clothes, and she told me that I could keep that, his jacket."

"And the rest of the clothes in that bag?"

"I found those later. What she requested back, I gave her."

"And you requested photographs of Parker, and she gave you them, as well, correct?"

"The photographs I have of Parker were given to me before his death."

"You requested photographs of Ashlan?"

"I asked for some and never received them."

"And you requested something of hers, correct?"

"I don't remember the specifics of that, no."

"You don't remember asking Missy for a piece of clothing or something from Ashlan Daniel?"

"No, I don't."

"You just don't remember it, or you deny it?"

"I don't remember it."

"Missy sent you state's exhibit 40 [Ashlan's gown], did she not?"

"Yes, she did."

"And isn't it a fact that you would tell her and other people that you could at times smell Parker's clothing whenever you were feeling bad and grieving, you could go up and smell Parker's clothing and smell Parker?"

"That's what he smelled like, yes."

"At times when you were upset or grieving and thinking about Parker, you would go and smell his clothes?"

"Yes, I did."

"And you would tell people how it made you feel good, too, after Ashlan died that you could take this yellow gown and smell it and you could smell Ashlan; that made you feel better?"

"I don't remember telling anyone that, no."

"So you sat in the courtroom here when Missy Daniel testified, correct?"

"Yes, I did."

"And so isn't it a fact that [that was] the first time that you were ever made aware that this wasn't Ashlan Daniel's?"

"I never even thought it was."

"So you requested something from Ashlan Daniel. Missy Daniel sends you something, saying it's her daughter's gown. And it's your testimony that you never thought it was hers?"

"Ashlan wore beautiful clothes. I never saw Ashlan in anything like that at all."

"You deny telling this woman right here [indicating Missy], after you received this gown, that at times when you thought about Ashlan Daniel, you would go to the gown and smell—you could smell her?"

"I remember her—I remember thanking her for that and it did smell like Ashlan. It did. But it come from Ashlan's home."

"So is that—I know you don't deny it. You're admitting you would smell this and you would smell Ashlan?"

"I may have told her, but I don't recall telling anyone else that."

"Do you remember telling Missy Daniel—do you remember meeting with her in a grocery store in April of this year?"

"Yes, I do."

"Do you remember telling her how the time that you were in Atlanta, you went to the tallest building in Atlanta to be closer to Parker? Do you remember telling her that?"

"I did that on one occasion."

"You went to the tallest building in Atlanta?"

"No, not the tallest building. I went to the highest floor of our hotel."

"So you could be closer to Parker because you knew he was in heaven?"

"Yes, I did. It was on a—I think it was his three-month death anniversary."

"And you kept track of his—a weekly track of his death anniversary, as well, correct?"

"Yes, I did."

"And I believe that's in state's exhibit number 41 [the Daily Planner]?"

"Yes, it is."

Gasser asked her about the photographs of Ashlan's grave. She denied even knowing that they existed, even though they were found in her kitchen. Then he returned to the Daily Planner, which he'd handed her to refresh her memory. Other deaths were noted in the planner, and several funerals were mentioned, as well. Gail and Josh had testified that it wasn't unusual for them to take photographs of graves. Gasser wanted to know why, then, photographs of only two graves were found in their home: Parker's and Ashlan's.

"We were very close to the children," Gail answered.

Gasser was not going to end without taking the opportunity to highlight Renee Barefoot's testimony again. Gail did not deny that she had met with Barefoot; nor did she deny that they'd had the conversation Barefoot had recounted. Her only explanation was: "I had no reason to tell her that. That was not the truth, and I don't remember telling her that. That's what I'm saying."

What was ironic about Gail Cutro's testimony was that in some ways she seemed more natural, more herself, on cross-examination than she did on direct. It was as though her demeanor was so defensive and guarded from the start that she could only appear natural under attack. With McPherson, that defensiveness appeared out of place, as though she'd come to a beach party wearing a bulletproof vest. At its worst, her direct testimony had a mawkish sentimentality that sounded forced. On the other hand, at times during cross-examination she demonstrated more strength and composure than many people had given her credit for.

At the end of her three and a half hours on the stand, Gasser gave Gail a platform for self-serving statements. "Mrs. Cutro, you deny killing Ashlan Daniel?"

"Yes, I do."

"You deny shaking Asher Maier?"

"Yes, I do."

"And you deny killing Parker Colson?"

"Yes, I do."

"And you feel that you've been violated?"

"Yes, I do."

"And you are a victim?"

"I am a victim," she said. "My whole family is a victim."

As he returned to the prosecution table, Gasser shook his head because he thought he'd blown it—he'd given her too much. But it was a ringing line that seemed to sum up her testimony just right.

62

Normal

The defense was fighting a two-pronged war. The first prong was the attack on the prosecution's medical evidence. The second was the battle over what constituted normal behavior. Johnny Gasser had spent a lot of time focusing on what he suggested was abnormal. Now Lisa McPherson called the defense's best witness to deflect this attack: Linda Bass.

What made Bass particularly important for the defense was that she could talk not only about what was normal in the grieving process, she could also tell the jury what she'd advised Gail to do. Between the two, she covered a lot of ground. The question the jury would have to answer was whether Bass was there to go to bat for the woman she'd counseled and befriended, or to express her professional opinions as objectively as she could.

Bass's style of testifying was quite a contrast to Gail's. Whereas Gail could be as grudging with her answers as a teenager facing parental rebuke, McPherson hardly had to ask a question to get Bass going. When she inquired how Bass knew that Gail was devastated following Parker's death, Bass's response saved McPherson the trouble of asking a half-dozen questions.

"I know she visited the cemetery a lot," Bass began. "And part of that was probably due to me, because in my experience working with families that had lost infants, there are a lot of things that you can tell people to do. And it used to be a number of years ago that people thought you were crazy if you suggested such things to people. But it's been documented over and over again in literature that relates to death and dying and people coping with bereavement that there are a lot of things that help people. And the normalcy of it is really widely varied.

"It's very hard to say in the first year after anybody died that anything that anybody experiences or does is real abnormal. I told her that it would probably be real helpful to her if she had some mementos of the babies that had died. I did give her—or had told her that it would maybe be a real nice thing if she had an article of clothing for the baby—you know, that the babies had had or if she wanted to keep something like a picture or if she had footprints. I know I made footprints copies for the babies that had died. I didn't get that opportunity with Ashlan, but with Parker I made several copies of footprints."

Bass didn't specifically remember suggesting that Gail obtain a copy of Parker's autopsy report but allowed that she "may have." It was also quite common for bereaved parents to take photographs of the grave site and even the coffin, she said.

"Now, Ms. Bass," McPherson inquired, "in all the time that you have met with Gail and spent time with her, tell the jury how anxious she ever seemed to have any focus directed on her or any attention, how much of a spectacle she ever wanted to make of herself over these deaths?"

"I never saw any of that. I never saw that she wanted to be in the center of any kind of attention. She was a person that was dealing with her own internal pain."

When it was his turn, Gasser saw no point in arguing with the witness. Instead, he used his cross-examination to review the improbability of these events happening by coincidence. He began by placing an exhibit on his easel that showed the names and ages of the children the Cutros were caring for on the days of Parker Colson's death, Ashlan Daniel's death, and Asher Maier's injury. Then he had Bass confirm that 90 percent of SIDS deaths occur in children six months of age or younger.

"It's been previously testified to by Josh Cutro that these fourteen children were either full-time or part-time being cared for on the day Parker Colson died," Gasser said. "I just wanted to give you that background information. Now, on January 4, the day Parker died, how many children there are in the high 90 percent category of risk of SIDS, under the age of six months?"

"Parker."

"Parker Colson?"

"Right. He's at the—at highest risk. She also had two seven-month-olds there who were at lower risk, but still at risk."

"So the one child of the fourteen that were at the highest risk category under the age of six months was Parker Colson?"

"Yes."

"And he's dead now?"

"Right."

"And in June of 1993, on the day Asher Maier was injured, of the thirteen children that were being cared for part-time or full-time, how many of these children were in the highest risk category of under six months?"

"Okay. Ashlan Daniel and Asher Maier."

"And Ashlan Daniel is dead now, right?"

"That's right."

"And Asher Maier has suffered a brain injury?"

"That's true."

"And on September the 9th, when Ashlan Daniel died, of the twelve children that were being cared for, tell us how many were in the highest 90 percent, under six months?"

"Ashlan. And then there was Tate, who would still be at risk. He wouldn't have been in the highest risk, but still at risk."

"So the only person of the twelve that Gail Cutro was caring for on September the 9th, 1993, in the highest risk was Ashlan Daniel, correct?"

"That's true."

"And she's now dead?"

"That's true."

"Ms. Bass, you don't think Gail Cutro did anything to these children, do you?"

"I don't."

"She's just got, quite frankly, the worst luck in the world?"

"Probably."

63

The Defense Rests

On a very long last day, the defense finished with three experts—two locals and an out-of-town professor. Wes Kirkland was determined to punch holes in the medical evidence, and, as he took his best shots, the wounded pride of the local practitioners took center stage.

The first witness was making a repeat appearance. Dr. James Reynolds, Richland Memorial's chief pathologist, decided he had more to say after *The State* newspaper reported the testimony of other prosecution witnesses who contradicted his findings and seemed to disparage his training. Though Dr. Reynolds had never testified for the defense, and never expected to do so again, he was so incensed that he called the defense lawyers and volunteered to return.

Early in his testimony a dispute arose that afforded observers (but not the jury) an insight into Judge Shuler's view of the case. Wes Kirkland had brought to court a model of a head that he hoped would allow Dr. Reynolds to show the jury how hard it would be to miss a subdural hematoma. The skull could be opened to reveal a large red blob. Johnny Gasser objected in advance, and the judge sent the jury out to discuss the issue with the lawyers.

Judge Shuler agreed that it would be misleading for Reynolds to say, "This is what I would have seen, if it had been there." On the other hand, the judge agreed with the defense that this was a key issue in the trial. In fact, for the judge, whether the jury believed there was a subdural hematoma was "the whole case."

Gasser said it was a shame that they were using models when they had the actual duras—with the purported hematomas—that Dr. Enid Gilbert-Barness had removed from the children's skulls. He had tried to introduce them into evidence earlier, but the judge had kept them out. He had done so reluctantly, Judge Shuler now confessed. He, too, thought that they were important pieces of evidence, but the defense had objected.

"Our only problem was the shock factor," Kirkland explained. Judge Shuler said he understood—that was why he'd ruled as he had. But he'd been reluctant because, though there were blown-up photographs of the duras in evidence, a depiction was not the same as the thing itself. "I mean, if I were on the jury," Judge Shuler said, "to be honest with you, it would help me to look at that." For him, the judge continued, the whole two-week trial came down to "how this physician or how the other physician interpreted what they saw." And presenting the actual things the experts were looking at "can't do anything but help the jury."

The defense team huddled for a private conference, then told the judge that they would withdraw their objection. Judge Shuler made the duras exhibits of the court and, bringing the jury back, explained that both sides now agreed that they ought to be part of the evidence.

A few minutes later, Wes Kirkland handed Dr. Reynolds the bag containing the dura of Ashlan Daniel and asked him to tell the jury what it was. Floating in the heat-sealed polyurethane bag filled with a preservative, the dura looked like an infant-sized bathing cap, but thinner and more pliable. It was grayish white and semitranslucent, and though it looked fragile, it couldn't be sectioned without a scalpel.

"Well, I haven't seen this before," Dr. Reynolds said, scrutinizing it intently. It was surprising and poignant that Dr. Reynolds had never even seen this piece of evidence that had been the source of so much controversy and, for him, anguish.

"Do you see any hematoma?" asked Kirkland.

"Well, I see some dark color here, which could be clot. I wouldn't try to interpret this right now unless I had histologic studies and a lot of other things . . ."

"How does the appearance of the dura at the time of the autopsy compare with what we see here?"

"It has no comparison whatsoever. It was clean, shiny, and without hematoma or any defect."

"So none of what we see here, as far as the dark coloration, was there when you did the autopsy?"

"No, sir, it was not."

Gasser did not cross-examine the witness for long. He asked Dr. Reynolds to confirm that a good deal of the work during his autopsies was performed by his assistant. Then he asked if, based on the fact that in twenty-three years' experience Reynolds had never before seen petechial hemorrhages grossly in a SIDS case, this wasn't more likely a homicide than a SIDS death. Reynolds objected to the word "homicide," but he agreed that it was more likely some sort of asphyxial death, whether accidental or intentional, than SIDS.

Next up was Dr. Sandra Conradi, Charleston's medical examiner. Dr. Conradi, like Dr. Reynolds, almost always testified for the state. Unlike Dr. Reynolds, however, she was a forensic pathologist, and she considered child abuse and sudden infant death syndrome to be her specialties. An affable woman of fifty-seven with curly gray hair and large, thick glasses, Dr. Conradi came across as more down to earth and approachable than the defense's main pathology expert, Dr. Smialek.

Kirkland asked her to explain how she'd come to testify in the case. She had first been consulted by the prosecution two months before the trial, and some of the facts they had presented then had made Dr. Conradi highly suspicious of Gail Cutro. Her suspicion was further aroused by the description of Gail Cutro visiting the graves frequently and acting in what sounded like a peculiar fashion. After she reviewed all the information, however, she had told Johnny Gasser that she did not believe that the two children had died as a result of shaking.

She did not know what to make of the petechial hemorrhages in the brain, but she had told the prosecutors that she would research the subject. After she did, she concluded that they were insignificant. She placed much greater confidence in the original autopsies than in the subsequent examinations, and she attributed the later findings to postmortem artifacts.

Like Dr. Reynolds, Dr. Conradi had decided to testify after reading an article about the trial in *The State* newspaper. In reporting Dr. Janice Ophoven's testimony, the article "was very inflammatory towards South Carolina pathologists," Dr. Conradi testified, "and I was afraid that it was going to leave a bad impression among the pathologists of South Carolina because of this case." It left her feeling "obligated to testify," she added.

Kirkland handed her the duras. They appeared completely normal, she said—only slightly stained by blood with which they must have come in contact after the initial autopsies.

On cross-examination, Gasser challenged several of Dr. Conradi's statements. When he'd met with her two months before the trial, hadn't she immediately said that she'd never seen petechial hemorrhages in the brain in a SIDS case? And didn't she say that this was a red flag and that she would remove the eyes under these circumstances? She acknowledged that she'd said it was unusual but didn't recall using the term "red flag." She would, indeed, have removed the eyes, but she did so much more readily than other pathologists, she said, and that was no reflection on them.

Gasser reminded her of what he viewed as the true source of their disagreement at their meeting: "When we left your office on October the 17th, it wasn't the cause of death that you were concerned about, homicide, it was the mechanism of death that you had a disagreement about with the two doctors; is that not correct?"

"Can you be more specific? What do you mean by mechanisms of death?"

"In other words, after you observed all the evidence in this particular case, it wasn't the fact that you weren't convinced it was a homicide, it was the mechanism of death. You thought it was more of an asphyxial, suffocation-type death, and the other doctors thought it was a shaking-type death?"

"Well, as I recall indicating to you, I was very suspicious that the death— they may be homicides, both cases may be homicides, the Colson and the Daniel case. But that I did not think they were shaken."

A moment later she added: "And I really couldn't rule out SIDS, either, in either one." This addendum was surprising, since, by definition, she would *have* to rule out SIDS if she couldn't rule out homicide, since SIDS is a diagnosis of exclusion (meaning all other possibilities must first be ruled out).

Gasser asked Dr. Conradi when she was first contacted by the defense. It was right around the time the trial began, she said. She felt obliged to clear the contact with the state first, and Gasser pointed out that SLED and his office had told her that she was perfectly free to speak to the defense.

"You know very well," Gasser continued, "that at times for strategic purposes the prosecutors and defense lawyers and civil lawyers . . . they retain experts for the sole purpose of keeping them away from the other side. You're aware of that strategy, are you not?"

"That does happen, yes, sir."

"And the fact of the matter was, we told you—it was told to you that we had absolutely no problem with you talking to the defense?"

"Yes, that's correct."

Moreover, the pathologist acknowledged that after she met with the defense, they did not hire her. "Isn't it a fact that after meeting with the state, indicating you had a difference of opinion about the mechanism of death in this case, meeting with the defense attorneys in the case, them not hiring you or retaining you, the trial started, the newspaper started covering the trial, that article came out. After that article came out, that's when you decided that you wanted to testify in this case?"

"Yes, sir."

"And the reason why you decided to testify," Gasser continued, "was not based on any medical evidence, it was based upon personal and political [considerations], was it not?"

"I'm not sure what you mean by that."

"I mean, you met with the defense and they did not retain you two weeks before the trial, correct?"

"That's right."

"And then the article in the newspaper comes out—whether it's true or not, the article in the newspaper comes out that questions some of the methods used by South Carolina pathologists, and you all of a sudden decided you wanted to come testify?"

"I thought that by testifying I could perhaps clear the name of the South Carolina pathologists, both of whom I know and both of whom I trust to do an accurate and truthful autopsy report and autopsy in general, and to more or less rehabilitate the reputation of South Carolina pathologists whom I trust, yes, sir."

"And are you aware that all the pathologists and investigators that have testified in this case have spoken highly of the pathologists before this jury?"

"I find that hard to believe if one of us missed a subdural hemorrhage. I find that very hard to believe."

"So you're saying that it's impossible for a South Carolina pathologist to miss a subdural hematoma?"

"A pathologist that misses a subdural hematoma is not a qualified forensic pathologist, no, sir."

"So a qualified, competent pathologist in this state or in this country has never missed a subdural hematoma?"

"You said that, sir, I didn't say that. I wouldn't agree with that."

"Well, *are* you saying that?"

"No, sir."

"So they can be missed by a competent, qualified pathologist?"

"I don't think a competent, qualified forensic pathologist should miss a subdural hemorrhage; that is one of the things that we're trained to look for, one of the primary things we're trained to look for. And if we miss it, in my opinion, you are not a qualified forensic pathologist. . . ."

Gasser came back to their October meeting, reminding her of her first reaction to a key piece of evidence. "[W]hen the slide of the dura of Ashlan Daniel was shown on your wall, isn't it true that the first response you had was, 'Jeez, I can see why Dr. Reynolds has been unable to dissuade Enid that this is a subdural hematoma'?"

"Yes, I may have said that, yes."

"Because this to you looks like a subdural hematoma?"

"It does, it looks like it, yes."

"And in your direct examination you had indicated that at the meeting it was your opinion that this was very likely an artifact?"

"Yes."

"That's a quote from your direct examination today?"

"Yes, sir."

"So you based your opinion that this was—even though it looked like a subdural hematoma, not on anything medically?"

"It does look like a subdural hematoma. But as I mentioned earlier, I trusted the first autopsy more than I trust the re-autopsy. The best way to examine a child is in the fresh state by a competent pathologist; and that's what was done in this case."

"So on October the 17th, when we met with you and you looked at this photograph and you indicated that looks like a subdural hematoma but it's probably an artifact, you weren't basing it on any test that you run or analysis that you've done on the dura, it was solely based on your personal opinion that Dr. Reynolds would never miss a subdural hematoma?"

"That's partially correct. And also partially the fact that I know artifacts can occur postmortem in embalmed bodies. And I highly suspected that that was the case here."

At this point, Gasser began to challenge Dr. Conradi in a more personal way, contrasting her experience examining the exhumed bodies of infants—which was limited to one case—with the many exhumation autopsies conducted by the state's experts. Then he introduced a document he had been saving in case he needed it. It wasn't something he had wanted to use, because he suspected that it would make Patsy Habben even more enemies than she already had. (He later believed he'd been right.)

When Habben had gathered autopsy reports on every SIDS case in the state since the death of Parker Colson, she'd enlisted the help of Dr. Conradi's staff. One autopsy report had jumped out at her. The autopsy had been performed by one of Dr. Conradi's associates, who had noted the presence of an acute subarachnoid hemorrhage—bleeding under the membrane directly over the brain. Yet, the pathologist had listed the cause of death as SIDS. Gasser handed Dr. Conradi the autopsy report and showed her an article published by the American Academy of Pediatrics specifying the conditions that had to be satisfied to diagnose SIDS. An enlarged copy was on Gasser's easel, where the jury could read that head trauma or an injury to the brain would immediately rule out SIDS.

Dr. Conradi agreed that the diagnosis had been improper. When Habben had brought it to her attention, the cause and manner of death had been changed to "undetermined," she said. Gasser hammered home the point for the jury: Dr. Conradi was the supervisor of the entire department. One of her subordinates had made this mistake, and she had not caught it until Patsy Habben had brought it to her attention. The lesson he hoped the jury would draw: mistakes are sometimes made even by experienced, competent professionals—and even when, in retrospect, the mistake appears elementary.

Gasser was able to draw two more points from Dr. Conradi. Contrary to what Dr. Smialek had testified, in her view shaken-baby cases—whether fatal or not—involve no external signs of trauma. In fact, she added, if she found evidence of blunt head trauma, she would no longer refer to the case as a shaken-baby but as a blunt-trauma case. Second, if a baby was found to be blue at death (as Gail Cutro had testified that Ashlan was), Dr. Conradi would not consider it to be a SIDS case, since SIDS babies are invariably pale.

On redirect, Wes Kirkland again confined himself to a few focused questions and even borrowed one of Gasser's pet phrases. "Now, these petechial hemorrhages, let's just cut right to the chase, Dr. Conradi, they mean absolutely nothing, do they?"

"They mean hypoxia, lack of oxygen as a process of dying. Other than that, they have no significance as to cause of death."

Gasser had wrested several important admissions from the defense's penultimate witness, and he wanted to end with one more. By her own account, she'd come forward to stand up for the locals. She'd seemed to be the answer to Wes Kirkland's prayers: a witness who could bolster his medical testimony, call into question the state's impartiality, and slam the out-of-state experts. It was ironic that she'd no sooner taken the stand than she'd acknowledged that she was born and raised in New York and trained in Cincinnati. Nevertheless, she had stood up for South Carolina pathologists.

"Now, you are aware, obviously," Gasser began, "that other experts—that their opinion is those petechial hemorrhages did have significance?"

"I understand that."

"Okay. And what the jury's role, you will agree, is going to have to be is to weigh the background and experience of all of the experts on both sides that have testified, correct?"

"And the honesty of the experts, yes, sir."

"And the honesty of the experts. And their explanations with exhibits and photographs. They're going to have to weigh that, correct?"

"Correct."

"And it really doesn't matter where the experts were born or what state they possibly live in. I mean, that's really irrelevant, is it not?"

"No, I don't think that has any significance. I think of more significance is the honesty, the experience, and the background in forensic matters. . . ."

———

The final defense witness was Dr. John Pless, a forensic pathologist and a professor at the Indiana University School of Medicine. There was a professorial air about his testimony—but one quite different from the rumpled, scholarly presence of Dr. John Emery, the British pathologist who had collaborated with Dr. Enid Gilbert Barness. Dr. Pless, who was fifty-six, came across as a man at home in a lecture hall. His tone at all times was one of supreme confidence.

Describing his qualifications, Dr. Pless told the jury that he'd conducted about five thousand autopsies, about forty of them on exhumed bodies. When examining an exhumed body, Dr. Pless said it was important to examine the entire body thoroughly, rather than limiting the inquiry to specific areas. Wes Kirkland asked whether Dr. Enid Gilbert-Barness had done that. Dr. Pless said that she'd chosen to examine only the heads and eyes.

After reviewing all the evidence the defense had provided him, Dr. Pless had reached the conclusion that the children had died of SIDS. He found no evidence of trauma. He saw nothing unusual about Parker Colson's dura. There was some slight discoloration, but that was merely residual blood altered by the embalming process. Ashlan Daniel's dura had a blood clot on it, but this was clearly a postmortem artifact. He could tell when he examined the red blood cells under a microscope. The manner in which they clot before death looks quite different from the way they clot after death, he explained.

As for petechial hemorrhages in the brain, Dr. Pless, like Dr. Smialek before him, said that there weren't any. His reasoning also matched Dr. Smialek's: Congestion in the brain was sometimes confused with pinpoint hemorrhages, although in this case what the other experts believed to be hemorrhages most likely resulted from sectioning—the slicing Dr. Reynolds had done as part of his examination. Moreover, Dr. Pless wouldn't have read much into it even if there *had* been petechial hemorrhages, since they can be attributed to a multitude of causes, only one of which was asphyxia. Their presence would have been completely consistent with SIDS, since "SIDS is a form of asphyxia."

Kirkland asked about shaken baby syndrome. Dr. Pless saw no evidence that these two children had been shaken, and he agreed with previous witnesses who testified that serious cases of shaking always cause swelling of the brain, which was absent in Parker Colson and Ashlan Daniel. Shaken babies do not usually die instantaneously, he added, because it takes time for the brain to swell, and it's the swelling that causes the problems that lead to death.

Dr. Pless made one point that was potentially of enormous significance. He noted that by the time Ashlan Daniel was autopsied, livor mortis had set in on both sides of her body. Livor mortis is the settling of blood after death, and it can help a pathologist estimate when a person died. Blood settles in areas to which gravity takes it; if it remains in one area long enough, it "fixes" and the skin over the affected area takes on a purplish tint. Dr. Pless testified that it takes "at least two hours." Previous testimony had established that Ashlan slept on her stomach, and Dr. Pless noted that bodies are transported on their backs. Therefore, the purplish color on her front meant that she must have died in her crib at least two hours before she was discovered and turned over. Since the paramedics were on the scene shortly after 2:30, and it was after 1:00 when Gail returned from her son's orthodontist appointment, this would seem to be proof that Gail wasn't even home when Ashlan died.

Gasser wasted no time challenging this opinion on cross-examination. First, he read a passage from a forensic pathology textbook that said that livor mortis was usually evident a half-hour to two hours after death. Dr. Pless agreed with that statement. Yet, when asked about Ashlan Daniel, he refused to budge.

"Are you aware of any of the facts in this particular case?" Gasser asked him.

"Yes."

"Are you aware that the child was found sometime between 2:30—or right around 2:30?"

"I believe so."

"And was dropped off at the house approximately 12:00 or 12:30?"

"Yes."

"And according to the statements of the husband or the caregiver, it was not even put down for a nap until sometime between 12:45 and 1:00?"

"Yes."

"So an excess of two hours would mean that the child was—in your opinion, your idea and interpretation of livor then indicated the child died sometime before 12:30?"

For the first time, Dr. Pless allowed that there might be a whiff of uncertainty. "Certainly it could be less," he said.

Gasser turned to another subject. "Before a forensic pathologist signs his name to an autopsy report or a death certificate, how long normally does it take, in your experience, after the autopsy is performed to gather all this information . . . before you just go on and write down a cause of death of SIDS?"

"Well, it would vary with the jurisdiction."

"Give us some estimates, I mean, in general?"

"Oh, it might be as soon as a week to two weeks. It might be a month to six weeks."

Gasser was thinking about Dr. Smialek's diagnosis over a weekend. "What about forty-eight hours? Do you think one could do all of that in a forty-eight-hour span?"

"It is possible," Dr. Pless replied. Gasser tried to puncture his answer with his laundry list of investigative tasks that had to be accomplished—along with toxicology reports—but Dr. Pless remained firm. In fact, he held fast to almost every opinion he had stated on direct, with the exception of the timing of Ashlan's death.

Having failed to make much progress, Gasser decided to attempt to put Dr. Pless's opinions in perspective for the jury. Returning to Ashlan's dura, Gasser tried a hypothetical. Pless balked at first, but was more amenable to the form of the question than Dr. Smialek had been.

"Well," said Gasser, "I'm just asking your opinion as to if in fact it was a subdural—assume for argument's sake that that's a subdural hematoma that we're looking at. Does the presence of petechial hemorrhages in the brain, in certain areas of the brain, in your opinion is that a significant finding?"

"If they were in fact valid petechiae, I would consider it to be significant, yes."

"So if the jury finds that this is a pre-death subdural hematoma and that in the sections of the vital areas of the brain there are petechial hemorrhages, those findings would be significant and evidence of shaking? Assuming those points."

"Certainly, in shaking we see subdural hematomas and we can see sheering—the effect of sheering force in the brain, evidenced by hemorrhage in the brain."

"And it's your opinion that that is not a subdural hematoma and those are not petechial hemorrhages?"

"That's correct."

"And for clarification, that's where the battle lines were drawn and you're aware of that, are you not? Other experts indicated those are petechial hemorrhages and that is a subdural hematoma. You obviously are aware of that; that's why you're here."

"I understand that testimony has been given to that effect, yes."

A short time later Dr. Pless was excused, and the defense rested. It was nearly 6:30, the end of another long day and another long week. The trial was nearly over, but not quite. The prosecutor could call witnesses on "reply" to rebut new evidence introduced by the defense, which Gasser intended to do.

Before dismissing the jury for the weekend, the judge implored them not to discuss the case or read or watch reports in the media. He told them to return at 8:30 Monday morning. He was determined to send them the case that day.

The jurors filed out, but the long day was not quite over. After the jury was gone, Shuler ordered the press out of the courtroom as well, even though he intended to speak with the lawyers on the record. It was a most unusual move, and the reporters were both surprised and angered. Slowly and reluctantly they complied, even as one loudly vowed to call his attorney. The anger, however, was mutual: The judge had been furious to learn that earlier in the evening one of the television stations had broadcast the results of Gail Cutro's polygraph exam. If the leak had come from the state, this could be grounds for a mistrial.

Lisa McPherson was livid, convinced that the leak was the work of law enforcement. The timing was what made her most suspicious. Funny that it happened just as the defense rested, "when arguably the state's case is looking weaker and weaker," she observed.

"Judge," Johnny Gasser retorted, "let me make one thing clear. The prosecution and law enforcement—do you think we want to have to go through this again?" Gasser speculated that it could have been someone in one of the children's families, or one of their friends.

The defense moved for a mistrial, but Judge Shuler denied it. The judge did not believe that Gasser or anyone in his office had leaked the polygraph results. He was angry that it had happened, but the news report hadn't destroyed the trial—at least not yet. "I don't think there's any damage done," Judge Shuler said, "until the jury comes back and says somebody came to them this weekend and says, 'Did you hear this?' And when they do that," Shuler added, "then this whole trial is going out of the window."

64

The Last Word

D r. Enid Gilbert-Barness got the last word. The state's most contested forensic pathologist was the sole witness called by Gasser, who needed an
expert to deal with the new evidence introduced by the other side. As it turned
out, she was the only one of his three out-of-state experts who was available
to return. But in calling her, Gasser also hoped that she would simultaneously
banish any doubts the jury may have harbored about her previous testimony.

She had not been in court to hear the defense witnesses, but Gasser had
supplied her with a transcript. The first subject he introduced was postmortem
artifact resulting from embalming. How much experience had she had working with embalmed bodies?

"Well, way back in the dark ages when I first started practicing pathology,"
she said with a smile, "it wasn't unusual for autopsies to be done in a funeral
home. And I went to many—hundreds—of funeral homes to perform autopsies. And in those cases the autopsy was done after embalming. So I think I've
had a lot of experience in seeing what happens after embalming."

She agreed with Dr. Pless's assertion that blood clots before and after
death look quite different. She'd brought to court a handbook sold in her university's bookstore to first-year medical students, and she read the description
of a postmortem clot. Then she pointed out how it differed from what she'd
found, using a color photograph Gasser supplied. Another way she could tell
that the clot had occurred before death was that it adhered to the dura. Even
though Dr. Smialek and Dr. Pless had attached no significance to this fact,
Dr. Gilbert-Barness explained that a fundamental principle in her field was
that postmortem clots pull right off and can be washed away. But this one
didn't and couldn't.

Gasser asked her once again about petechial hemorrhages. If what she'd
identified as hemorrhages were actually artifacts that resulted from sectioning, as other experts had posited, then similar artifacts should have been visible in all the organs sectioned, Gasser suggested. Had she found them? No,

she replied, she'd only found them in the brains and the organs in which the original pathologists had found them.

Gasser picked up a forensic pathology text and asked about livor mortis. The purplish mottling of the skin can occur within a half hour, Gilbert-Barness testified, but it isn't fixed nearly that fast. If the body is shifted from the stomach to the back, the livor mortis will shift as gravity takes the blood from one side to the other.

After Gasser had finished, Wes Kirkland began his cross-examination by attacking the witness's methods and objectivity. "Doctor, do you remember testifying last week that sometimes you have to jump to conclusions?

"Well, possibly—if you remember it."

"Is that something you teach your medical students?"

"There are certain things in medicine that are not finite, and one has to anticipate the possibility of certain diagnoses in order to investigate it. And, therefore, I do teach medical students to always think ahead, think of all the possibilities, and then go back and investigate it further. That is how many diagnoses are missed."

"Dr. Barness, in this particular case here you were very focused on what you were looking for, weren't you? You were looking for some kind of trauma to the head, weren't you?"

"Well, I think everyone should be focused on what they want to look for and what they hope—not hope to find, but anticipate what might be present in order that it should not be missed." She had seemed to slip, perhaps betraying the lack of objectivity Kirkland was trying to reveal. Had she been examining the bodies as a neutral scientist, or had she been "hoping" to find evidence that would support suspicions?

With Pless's criticisms of the exhumation autopsy in mind, Kirkland continued to challenge her objectivity. "Dr. Barness, in this case you did not examine the interior of these bodies except in the skull; isn't that correct?"

"The external surface was very badly decomposed. It was covered with mold, which we did try to remove, and I looked at the external features of the body. I looked in the mouth for any evidence of trauma there, and we examined the skull and the cranial cavity. When an autopsy is done, the organs are all severed and removed. And that had been done, and I had read the autopsy reports. I had examined the microscopic sections. And I believed that that was adequate. I did not reopen the body cavity, no."

"Dr. Barness, isn't it true that when you did the second autopsy, you were focused in on trying to find some way to establish there was trauma to the heads of these children?"

"No, I never do an autopsy in that fashion. I think I have an open mind and I believe I am a person of absolute honesty and integrity."

In her autopsy report Dr. Gilbert-Barness had cited several articles supporting her findings. Kirkland questioned whether those articles actually supported her at all. Several were about shaken baby syndrome, but none mentioned petechial hemorrhages in the brain. Such hemorrhages, she replied, are associated with various forms of brain trauma and aren't specific to shaken babies, which was why they probably weren't mentioned.

Kirkland returned to the question of edema—one of the strengths of his case. He pointed out that all the articles on shaken baby syndrome to which she'd referred discussed swelling of the brain. She was willing to admit that edema was usually present, but she wouldn't agree that it always was.

Then she threw Kirkland a curve. "Can I go back to the edema issue?" she asked, before they'd even left it. "Because I think we're all missing the boat. First of all, it's not necessary to be present. It may be present and it may well be present in the majority of cases, but it's not always present.

"In addition to this, one of the main features of swelling of the brain is an increased weight of the brain. The brains of both these babies weighed well over eight hundred grams. Now, in my experience and the tables that I use, that is in excess of normal for a four-month-old baby."

"Doctor," said Kirkland, sounding both surprised and angry, "isn't that a direct contradiction of what you said here last week, that they were in the normal range?"

"I did not—"

"That's what you said—"

"I don't believe I did say they're in the normal range. As stated in the autopsy report, perhaps."

"They're in the normal range?"

"But in reviewing the tables that I am using in the book that I am publishing, those weights are slightly in excess of normal. So I think there is some degree, although not evident on the microscopic sections, there is some evidence of swelling of the brain."

"So your testimony today regarding the normal weight and size of the brain is different than it was last week?"

"It's not different. I didn't have a chance to expound on it, perhaps. And it was stated in the autopsy reports that they were normal, and I accepted that as the truth."

"Well, you never actually got to see the brains when they were removed?"

"That is correct. I did not see the brain, no. I saw the microscopic sections of the brain."

Concerned, perhaps, at the time this was taking—with closing statements and the judge's charge still to come—Kirkland left this line of questioning, which was probably his most successful of the trial, and turned once again to petechial hemorrhages. Although he had begun his cross in the same focused manner in which he had conducted himself the last day or two of the trial, he was jumping around now. He still scored points, and at times the witness seemed less than sure of herself, but near the end of his cross he seemed to be flailing while she stood firm. Gasser asked only a few quick questions to counter the attack, and it was over.

With the evidence complete, one challenge remained for Gasser and Kirkland. Each would have to sum up two weeks of testimony, dozens of exhibits, the twists and turns of a most complex case . . . in just over an hour.

65

Closing Arguments

Johnny Gasser spoke first and last, because the state shouldered the burden of proof. The trial had run eleven days. It was December 19, 1994, and he acknowledged what everyone had been thinking: it had consumed nearly the entire Christmas season.

He reminded the jury of their three options, and he even wrote them down on a sketch pad mounted on his easel. Guilty of Murder. Guilty of Homicide by Child Abuse. Not Guilty. He devoted most of his time to explaining what the first two meant, even though the judge would do that again.

Shortly before he concluded, Gasser took on one of the defense's big issues. He told the jury why he'd decided to go out and get the most-qualified and experienced pediatric pathologists he could find. No matter what the defense tried to say, it was not SLED's decision, he emphasized. It was the prosecutor's. There were three reasons. He owed it to Gail Cutro. The parents deserved it. And they—the jury—were entitled to no less. "This is not some sort of beauty contest," he told the jury, "where you pull for the hometown girl no matter about the fact that she may not be the prettiest or the most talented. This is serious business."

The opening statement by the defense was "an insult." A case created by SLED? SLED didn't need to create any cases. They had three hundred ongoing investigations. He himself had sixty-four cases piled in his office, awaiting his return.

That was all he would say for now, but he would return, he reminded them, to put the pieces of the puzzle together.

———

Wes Kirkland told the jurors that he had all the respect in the world for the parents and for the children. They were unfortunate victims of this whole situation. But he was not backing down from what he'd said the first day.

His side didn't have to prove anything. That was the state's burden. The state had been talking a lot about fairness, Kirkland told them, so he was going to start off by presenting the jurors with the best-case scenario from the state's point of view. He wasn't conceding it, just presenting it. Suppose the jury assumed that the only two cases involving petechial hemorrhages in South Carolina—in the whole world—were the two in this case. And suppose they assumed that all the evidence was premortem. And he'd even throw in a fair and impartial investigation by SLED. Had the state proven their case?

They had not.

Assume Gail Cutro read all kinds of weird books. And took pictures of lots of graves. Assume she was the weirdest person in the world and was obsessed with death and attention. Now had they proven their case?

No.

Why not? They had a circumstantial-evidence case, and they had to prove that all the circumstances pointed to Gail Cutro's guilt to the exclusion of every other reasonable hypothesis or explanation. And they hadn't.

The missing link in their house of cards—did they remember when he'd told them that the state's case was a house of cards?—was the medical evidence. Look at the state's experts. The most credible of them all was Dr.

Randy Alexander, and he was the one who'd told them that shaken babies didn't die without edema.

But that wasn't the only defect. They never proved motive. Why would a woman who worked in day care for fourteen years want to kill two kids? Where was the sense? And if she *did* want to kill two kids, why on earth would she save a third? And why would she kill the second when she knew she was under suspicion of having shaken the one who survived?

Obsession with death? There was no proof that Gail was obsessed with death or was seeking attention. Gail had gone to Linda Bass for grief counseling, and she was just following Bass's advice. The truth was that people grieved in different ways, and that was no crime. Some people visited a grave. Some people kept a stone face.

And what about Catherine Maier's history of violence? Her inconsistent statements? Her immaturity? She testified that Asher had been fine before he was hospitalized, but she told the nurse in her pediatrician's office and another nurse in the hospital that he hadn't been sleeping well. And she spoke to them before she had any idea that she would be under investigation. Could the jurors believe her testimony?

He ran through the long lineup of experts. The doctors from Iowa talked a lot about MRI and CT scans. They put these together with some testimony and said it all had to happen in precisely this way at precisely this time. But the *jurors* were the ones who would ultimately have to decide. These doctors had never even examined the child. Could they really narrow everything down to a couple of hours? "Science may be precise, but it's not that precise."

Look at where the other state experts came from. Sure, they all had glowing credentials, but notice how the prosecution found them: through this trial in Wisconsin, where they all testified for the state. Compare that to the defense experts: Dr. Smialek, Dr. Pless, and Dr. Conradi. They mostly testify for the prosecution. They were forensic pathologists—"cop doctors." And they also taught. They saw SIDS deaths and children who were victims of homicide all the time. They knew how to tell the difference.

And what about Dr. Reynolds, who was also a qualified, experienced pathologist? He was told that there was suspicion about this case, and so he was looking for trauma. And he found nothing. Then the state brought in Enid Gilbert-Barness, who said that there was a two-centimeter-by-four-centimeter hematoma adhering to the child's dura and that Dr. Reynolds had missed it. Ladies and gentlemen, you don't miss that. Dr. Reynolds, Dr. Smialek, Dr. Pless, and Dr. Conradi testified that you don't miss something like that. They are obvious.

And while he was on the subject of Enid Gilbert-Barness, he hoped that they remembered her testimony during the first week, when she said that the brains were in the normal range—before she'd changed her testimony on the stand just a short time ago. He didn't mean to be snide or disrespectful to Dr. Gilbert-Barness, but she'd said some things on the stand during this trial that were among the most frightening statements he'd ever heard in a courtroom. She said, "'Sometimes you have to jump to conclusions.'

"My goodness! This is a murder trial. This is a murder trial! We have had two children that have died and a woman is on trial for murder, and we're jumping to conclusions? That sums up the state's case.

"If you don't remember another thing when you go back to that jury room, remember what Dr. Enid Gilbert-Barness said. 'Sometimes you've got to jump to conclusions.'" She was looking for something, she was determined to find something, and she found it. Even though it contradicted everything that was seen at the original autopsies, when you had the best chance to observe the evidence.

We expect science to have all the answers, but it doesn't. This was an unusual event; he granted the state that much. Two SIDS cases in one day care was very unusual. So was dying in a plane crash. But they happened. Somebody had to be the statistic. Science couldn't save the space shuttle Challenger. There are things we can't explain and can't control. But we always want to blame somebody. That's what makes sudden infant death syndrome so frustrating. We don't know what it is, and we can't control it. But we still want to blame somebody.

"You should not go back to this jury room looking to blame. Your job is to obey the law," he reminded the jurors. And when they looked at all the evidence together, they would see that these were natural deaths.

"One thing that I haven't talked about is Gail Cutro herself, and who she is. This is a woman that's been accused of two murders. She's also been accused of shaking another child. This is a woman that's been in day care fourteen years, she has three children of her own, a woman who loved children—loved them.

"Unless I missed someone, I don't remember anybody on that stand that said she didn't. Her life was these children. She cared about them as if they were her own."

Please, he asked the jurors, don't jump to conclusions, the way so many others have in this case. And please return a verdict of not guilty.

———

Johnny Gasser asked the jurors to think about what they had just heard. How much time did Kirkland spend talking about the evidence, and how much time did he spend attacking SLED or Catherine Maier or the prosecution?

There was a reason: When you started focusing on the evidence, you started focusing on Gail Cutro. Mr. Kirkland attacked Enid Gilbert-Barness, but he didn't talk a lot about John Emery and Janice Ophoven. The defense wanted the jury to forget about them.

The defense had also thrown out some red herrings. Randy Alexander was a state's witness on the shaken-baby case; but he was a pediatrician, not a pathologist. The babies he saw were always alive. That's why he always saw swelling. In this case, when the babies died, their hearts stopped pumping, and there was no swelling. And the jury didn't have to look far for an example of what he was talking about. Asher Maier had suffered edema, but the swelling had occurred *weeks* after he was shaken.

Now, what about Asher Maier? Had they noticed that all the expert testimony on him had come from the state? The only expert from the defense was Dr. Smialek. And he had to rely on what the defense gave him. But even he admitted that there were only three possible scenarios. Catherine shook him and brought him to the Cutros'. He was shaken after he was dropped off at the Cutros' and before he was taken to the doctor. He was shaken between the time Catherine Maier picked him up and the time she arrived at the doctor's office.

There was all kinds of evidence that Asher was *not* a rag doll when he arrived at the Cutros' (though he was when he left). He was bringing his fists to his mouth, looking around, focusing his eyes—according to testimony from the Cutros' friends. And the child was *not* dehydrated when he was admitted to the hospital, so he'd been fed that morning. There was no other reasonable hypothesis: Asher Maier was shaken at the Cutros'.

When Gail Cutro filed an affidavit in the Maier divorce, she didn't know that Catherine would keep her report cards. She didn't know that the doctors would be able to tell that Asher had eaten on all the days that Gail swore in that affidavit that he hadn't. Lies. Like she lied about how many kids she was caring for.

Catherine Maier was an easy target in this case. Nowhere near Mother of the Year. But she didn't try to hide anything, either. Did they remember when Wilbur Smith, the radiologist from Iowa, testified that there had been a previous shaking, and he'd dated it back to June 9 or 10? And did they remember that in her SLED statement, which she gave all the way back in October 1993, Catherine had said that Asher woke up during the night following his third day at the Cutros'? Started having trouble sleeping? She didn't know that her October statement was going to prove that Asher's first shaking occurred after he started at the Cutros' day care. She couldn't have known that. The state didn't even hire the doctors from Iowa until the following June or July. That was corroboration. That was what he meant when he talked about real evidence—not the easy attacks.

There were many other examples of Gail Cutro's testimony bumping into hard, cold facts. She testified that Parker Colson was congested the day he died, but she never told Lindy Colson, and Lindy testified that it wasn't true. Why did Mrs. Cutro say this? Because she knew that children who are sick are at greater risk of dying from SIDS.

Another inconsistency: When Gail was asked in her deposition what activities she had with Ashlan Daniel, she said she had none. A few minutes later, when she was asked the same question about Parker Colson, she gave a very different answer. Playing, feeding, diaper changing, that sort of thing. But now, when she was on trial, she wanted the jury to believe that she had no contact with Parker at all. Why did she say this? Because it was already clear that she was alone with Ashlan before *she* died. Gail didn't want to admit that the same was true with Parker.

If this was all just horribly bad luck, if the stars were all aligned against Gail Cutro, why the inconsistencies in what she told the parents? The Daniels say their daughter never went straight to sleep once in her four months and eighteen days of life. Not once. And it just so happened that on the day she died she fell asleep in Josh Cutro's arms? Inconsistencies.

Just like the inconsistencies in the medical evidence. The defense experts said there weren't any petechial hemorrhages. But they admitted that if there had been, they would have been evidence of trauma. Now, what would the jury have to do to find that these were *not* petechial hemorrhages? They would have to believe that three different pediatric pathologists—John Emery with forty-four years of experience, Janice Ophoven with eighteen years of experience, and Enid Gilbert-Barness with forty-seven years of experience—

mischaracterized what they saw. Second, the defense doctors said that it was common to confuse blood vessels that burst during sectioning of organs with petechial hemorrhages. If that were true, why hadn't the pathologists found petechial hemorrhages in all the other organs that were sectioned?

Gasser pulled out his map of South Carolina—the one with one hundred blue dots representing all the SIDS cases with no petechial hemorrhages in the brain and two red dots for the two with petechial hemorrhages: Ashlan Daniel and Parker Colson.

"He talks about a deck of cards," Gasser said, glancing over at Kirkland. "Well, this is the ace, ladies and gentlemen. If this evidence doesn't convince you, nothing will." If it was so common, he demanded, then how come they weren't in all these other children?

"Now, you think about the odds of this. You think about the odds of one hundred and two babies dying in our state in thirty-one counties, what are the odds that the only two that would have brain trauma are in the same area of the state, the Midlands; the same county, Richland; the same town, Irmo; the same subdivision, New Friarsgate; the same road, Chadford Road; the same house, under the care and control of the same person? Two of one hundred and two— the only evidence of brain trauma staring you right in the face."

Turning to the subdural hematoma, Gasser said that he had the "utmost respect" for South Carolina pathologists. He'd worked with them day in and day out for more than seven years. But everyone makes mistakes. The defense wanted the jury to believe that the blood clot was caused by the autopsy. But did they remember John Emery from England? He was the scientist, the validator. He was the one who told Enid Gilbert-Barness, "This isn't enough." They had to validate their finding by introducing controls. He was the one who told her to take additional sections from the dura to compare. And when she did, she found no blood in the dura in the controls.

All three of the state's experts—Dr. Emery, Dr. Ophoven, and Dr. Gilbert-Barness—said that the only way you could get blood into the dura was by premortem force or trauma. All three of them said that independently. And they were the pediatric pathologists. They were the experts on children. The defense wanted the jurors to believe that that didn't make a difference. But it did. Kids are different from adults. If they weren't, why would there even *be* pediatric pathologists?

And if the jurors wanted more proof that there was a difference, they had only to look at Parker Colson's original autopsy. All the experts said that the finding of bronchopneumomia was miscalled. The original pathologist consulted a SIDS specialist, and the specialist told her that his lungs were normal. The pathologist then changed her diagnosis. Everyone at her hospital agreed with the change. All the experts agreed—except Dr. Smialek. Gasser submitted that he, too, had miscalled the lungs. Because he wasn't a pediatric pathologist, he didn't recognize that this was a normal finding.

Now Gasser attacked the credibility of the two main defense experts. In Kirkland's opening statement, he had promised that his experts would present evidence that these were SIDS deaths; his experts, however, hadn't even examined all the evidence until the second week of the trial. They couldn't have examined the duras, for example, until they arrived in South Carolina. Didn't that suggest that they were predisposed to say that this was SIDS?

Gasser wanted to say just a couple of things about motive, and then he'd be done. The state didn't have to prove motive, he reminded the jury. The law didn't require it. And he couldn't claim to be able to explain why anyone would kill a child. As far as he was concerned, there *was* no reasonable explanation for why people do such things. And at the time Gail Cutro was indicted, they didn't really understand her motive.

But then Renee Barefoot came forward. He wanted them to remember all the proof the state supplied to support her testimony. How did the defense explain that? Well, they never did. Barely cross-examined her, because they *couldn't* explain it. But he submitted to the jury now that faking a SIDS death in your home, and then having two "SIDS" deaths happen in that same home within eight months, was circumstantial evidence of homicide.

Now they, the jury, would have to decide whether visiting these graves and taking photographs of these graves and smelling the clothes and all of it was normal or not, but it was all part of the picture. The defense claimed that the Cutros took photographs of other graves. Gail Cutro's daily planner suggested that they had attended other funerals, but Elizabeth Lightfoot's obituary and photographs of the dead children's graves were the only ones found during the search. If there were others, nothing had prevented the defense from introducing them during the trial.

Gasser addressed a legal hurdle that the judge would soon explain: the state had to prove that the defendant had acted with malice in her heart.

"Can you get any more malicious?" he demanded, his voice choked with emotion. He picked up the demonstration doll he'd used during the trial. "This child could not scream for help. This child could not run away. This child could not protect itself. This child was helpless, totally dependent on someone else." He paused, and when he continued, he punctuated his words by shaking the doll in his hands five times: "And she *shook* . . . the *life* . . . *out* . . . of *this* . . . *child*.

"Go back in your jury room, join together, and do the right thing. Summon the courage to tell Gail Cutro, 'You will not get away with this.' It will never bring back Ashlan Daniel. It will never do anything about the pain and suffering that her family is going through. But maybe, just maybe, finally these children can rest in peace."

66

Deliberations

The jurors settled into Jury Room 224 for what they hoped would be the last time. After eleven days and innumerable trips in and out while the lawyers wrangled over they-knew-not-what, they were at home there now. It wasn't too bad. They could just about squeeze the twelve oak chairs with the reasonably comfortable brown cushions around the large oak table in the middle of the room. The walls were painted white; the closest thing to decoration was a fire extinguisher affixed to one of them. The yellow-green rug had been in place since the building opened in the late 1970s, and whatever nap it had then was by now a memory as faded as its color.

The jurors' first decision was whether to eat lunch before deliberating. Then they had to contend with cold Domino's pizza, but microwaves solved that problem. Once they'd finished, many jurors began wading through the small mountain of exhibits that had been brought back for them to review.

When they were ready, they turned to their youngest member: Richard Fuller, the twenty-eight-year-old high school physical education teacher they'd chosen as their foreman. Several jurors suggested that they take a quick vote to see how they stood. Fuller agreed and asked for a show of hands, even though at least one juror was uncomfortable with the idea.

The vote was nine to three for conviction.

None of the three expressed the firm belief that Gail Cutro was innocent, but neither were they convinced that she was guilty. They weren't ready to say—until they'd reviewed the evidence.

Marge Anderson was the most outspoken. Earlier in the trial Anderson, an occupational therapist's assistant, had demonstrated her integrity. After hearing Wes Kirkland's opening statement, she'd sent the judge a note informing him that she was acquainted with defense expert Dr. John Pless, whose name Kirkland had mentioned. The Indiana pathologist was a member of her father-in-law's church. She'd last seen him at her father-in-law's funeral five years earlier. Though she didn't feel that this connection would influence her decision, she felt obliged to bring it to the court's attention. When the judge read the note into the record outside the presence of the jury, Johnny Gasser said that he would have stricken her had he known about it during jury selection. Judge Shuler, however, thought that it revealed how conscientious she was, and after Gasser learned that she had no relationship with the pathologist and wouldn't even recognize him in a crowd, he agreed that there was no reason to remove her.

Had Gasser been privy to these early deliberations, he might have regretted acquiescing. The mere fact that they'd already voted bothered Anderson. Yes, they'd been cooped up a long time. Anderson understood the imposition— she'd celebrated her forty-fifth birthday during the trial. Furthermore, if they didn't agree on a verdict the first day, they would be sequestered overnight— and every succeeding night until they did. She knew this, and so did the others. That's what concerned her. She had the disquieting feeling that some or all of her fellow jurors cared more about voting and going home than about discharging their responsibilities.

The sense she got from most of the others was: "She did it, and let's get out of here." But Anderson wasn't willing to go along. "I was really getting angry. I said, 'You know, this is her life. I really want to make sure we discuss this.'"

Arlene Blaha remembered this as an important moment. At sixty, she was the jury's oldest member. Blaha taught nursing at the University of South Carolina and, like Anderson, had taken copious notes during the trial. Unlike Anderson, Blaha was convinced that Gail Cutro was guilty. But she and the others were affected by Anderson's little speech.

In those few sentences, Anderson had become the jury's conscience. Her fellow jurors responded in the variety of ways people do when their consciences are pricked: Some seemed irritated and resentful, others defensive, still others relieved. The bottom line, though, was that they went along. There would be no rush to judgment, no matter what season it was.

Early on they spoke briefly about Josh. They didn't need to say too much for the simple reason that no one believed him. The consensus was that he was probably the defense's worst witness. Even "Don Reeves" discounted his testimony. Of the four jurors interviewed, Reeves (who agreed to be interviewed only if his identity was concealed) was the most skeptical that the state had proved its case. Yet, asked to comment on Josh Cutro's performance, he shook his head and laughed. "I know it's the man's wife," Reeves said, "but why he want to take the blame if he didn't really do it?"

To Reeves and the others, Josh's attempt to cover for Gail was transparent. But they were not about to convict her on the basis of her husband's testimony. She was the one on trial, and she was the one on whom they focused.

One salient point on which most jurors agreed was that Gail did not come across as sincere. Reeves noted that she rarely expressed emotion—either on the stand or at the defense table. When she did, Reeves added, she seemed to turn it on and off. He didn't buy her line about being a victim. He was also troubled by the books found in her room—not so much the books themselves as her explanation that many belonged to her son. He didn't buy that, either.

John Baxley, a thirty-six-year-old truck driver, was also troubled by Gail's lack of emotion. Although she was supposed to be devastated by the deaths of the two children, he didn't see it on the stand. "She was cold," he said. "What really got me with her was she was not defending herself as much as she was mad at the way that the prosecution was asking her questions." He suggested that her case would have been stronger had she avoided testifying altogether.

Arlene Blaha was also puzzled by Gail's "flat" demeanor on the stand. And the nurse was flabbergasted that Gail did virtually nothing to try to save either of the two children who died. She could understand that Gail might have been paralyzed the first time. But a second emergency and then a third? Gail had proved even less effectual in dealing with Ashlan Daniel than she had with Parker Colson.

Blaha's reaction to Gail Cutro was in sharp contrast to her feelings about Catherine Maier. Maier impressed Blaha as honest and straightforward. She did not try to excuse her past behavior or plead for the jury's sympathy, and her approach earned Blaha's sympathy and respect. Gail Cutro, on the other hand, ended her testimony with a naked appeal for compassion, which had the opposite effect on the juror. Far from coming across as the caring individual she portrayed herself as being, Gail struck Blaha as "angry."

Marge Anderson was also troubled by Gail's lack of emotion. "During the trial," she said, "Gail Cutro just seemed like a sad-faced puppy. She never really gave any expression or any affect." If the things people said about Gail were said about her, Anderson observed, "I would be bursting in tears." At times Gail seemed to be crying, or at least quietly sobbing, but to Anderson the tears never appeared genuine. None of Gail's expressions of emotion did.

She thought she saw something else while Gail was on the stand. Anderson's husband of twenty-four years worked in law enforcement, and she'd picked up some of his habits. People in law enforcement are trained to be careful observers, and Anderson tried to take in everything she could while she sat in the jury box. Though she never mentioned it during deliberations, she believed that she saw Gail looking over at Josh during her testimony.

Gail was "trying to make sure that she was saying the right thing," Anderson suggested. "To me, it was like she was really trying to say, 'Okay, Josh, tell me what to say.'"

Anderson picked up on something else as she watched Gail seated at the defense table. The Colsons, the Daniels, and Catherine Maier all made eye contact with the jury from time to time. But not Gail. Anderson thought that this, too, was significant. When she considered it all together, Gail's behavior seemed evasive.

Almost as telling as what they discussed was what they did not. The jurors said virtually nothing about Sandra Conradi, the Charleston pathologist who had gone to bat for the local experts. They discounted her testimony because her personal stake in the case was clear. Despite Conradi's indignation, some jurors were impressed that the prosecution had brought in experts from around the world. And Wes Kirkland's effort to paint this act as disrespectful of local expertise failed to move Blaha, who was born and raised in Illinois, or Anderson, who was originally from Missouri.

Kirkland's portrayal of SLED as a "runaway train" never came up, either. The jurors did not believe that the case was concocted merely to make a name for the new Child Fatalities Department. As Blaha put it: "I didn't feel that that was true, because I thought that their evidence was well founded and very carefully obtained, from what we had been told." In her view the attack on SLED smacked of desperation and did less damage to the prosecution than to the defense. "I think that decreased their credibility," she said.

Little was said about motive. The jurors' reticence wasn't from lack of interest. Had the state failed to offer a plausible explanation, Blaha said, she is sure that there would have been a great deal of discussion. But the state *did* provide one, and the jury was apparently satisfied with it.

They came closest to discussing motive when they reviewed witnesses such as Renee Barefoot and Linda Bass. Though neither witness figured prominently in their deliberations, Blaha and Anderson remember that they found Barefoot's testimony credible, while they were troubled by Bass's. Both jurors voiced deep misgivings about the advice Bass offered Gail. And though neither came right out and said that they didn't believe all of the nurse's testimony, they clearly harbored doubts. During deliberations, jurors seemed particularly troubled by the testimony about the gown that Missy Daniel sent Gail but that Ashlan never wore. They could not understand why Gail thought she would derive comfort from smelling it, even if it *had* been worn by Ashlan—and why she later claimed that she did, even though it hadn't. They were also discomfited by Bass's testimony that this reaction was normal.

The jurors didn't discuss the lawyers, though when asked their opinions they were generally complimentary to both sides. Gasser was rated highest and praised for the clarity and focus of his presentation. Kirkland and McPherson were seen as having been a little diffuse at times but quite effective for the most part. Baxley said that he was impressed enough to consider hiring one of them if he ever needed a lawyer.

But the crux of the case came down to the medical evidence—as virtually all the lawyers associated with the case believed it would. For the jury it translated to: Which experts could they believe? Even though Kirkland had played up the local angle, his reliance on Dr. Smialek and Dr. Pless presented the jury with a choice between the prosecution's out-of-state experts and the defense's.

Dr. Smialek was the defense expert who made the strongest impression. Blaha, who had made a point of not telling the others that she was a nurse so as to avoid unduly influencing their opinions, was quite impressed with Dr. Smialek at first. But she remembered that Gasser "tripped him up" on cross-examination. Baxley remembered the same thing. He also remembered how reluctant the medical examiner was to concede anything. Both jurors felt that his objectivity and credibility suffered as a result.

Blaha had another reason for doubting Dr. Smialek's impartiality. The pathologist sat through several days' testimony at the defense table. There was nothing improper in his doing so; he had been hired by the defense, and he was helping Kirkland understand the terms and issues that would come up again and again during the trial. But some jurors concluded that Dr. Smialek was saying whatever the defense lawyers wanted him to say. (When this interpretation was relayed to Wes Kirkland, he said that it never crossed his mind that the jury might make such an inference.)

By contrast, most jurors were highly impressed by the state's experts—particularly Dr. John Emery and Dr. Enid Gilbert-Barness. (Dr. Janice Ophoven's testimony, which came early in the trial, was a vague memory by the end.) They were impressed by the experts' credentials, their accomplishments over their long and distinguished careers, and their ability to communicate effectively. Anderson admitted that the jurors particularly liked the rumpled, professorial Dr. Emery. His British accent made him easy and pleasant to listen to, and they admired his ability to answer questions clearly and concisely, without prattling on. They had confidence in Dr. Emery, who had insisted that Dr. Gilbert-Barness introduce controls to check her results, and they had confidence in Dr. Gilbert-Barness as well. Kirkland's furious attacks on her during his cross-examinations failed to change their opinions.

"I believed her the first time," Anderson said. As for Wes Kirkland's aggressive questions, "I think all of us believed that it was just because she was stating the facts, and the defense wanted to make us think that she did not know what she was saying there, like she didn't know her business." Yes, Kirkland rattled the pathologist at times, but that only made her more accessible. Were Anderson subjected to a similar onslaught, she said, "I would [be rattled], too." In fact, she went on to say, the defense attack was completely predictable: "They had every reason to, because she stated a lot of stuff that we believed in, that she did a very good job in explaining."

More than four hours into the jury's deliberations, Richard Fuller, the foreman, gently questioned the two jurors who were still uncertain of Gail Cutro's guilt. Anderson seemed to have joined the majority. The two remaining holdouts were far more reserved, and Fuller had to prod them to reveal the specific issues with which they were wrestling.

One concerned the alleged injuries that led to Parker Colson's and Ashlan Daniel's deaths. Several jurors remembered that Dr. Emery attributed the direct cause of death to trauma inflicted on the medulla. The undecided jurors thought it might help them to hear this testimony again, so Fuller sent a note to the judge.

All the testimony had been tape-recorded, and it took a few minutes for the court reporter to locate the section requested. The judge called in the jury, and the court reporter played it back, beginning with Gasser's question:

"Was there a specific area of the brain where you found these petechial hemorrhages that you, yourself, determined to be significant?"

"Yes, there are—I think Dr. Gilbert explained it," Dr. Emery said. "There are parts of the brain which in a sense are silent, in particular in a child, which are really not used. These are the parts of the brains, the hemispheres, the big parts of them. And then there are the parts of the brain which we call the medulla, which is the brain stem; and that is the primitive brain. And in that area you have the parts of the brain which control breathing and what you might call vital functions."

Not long after they heard this testimony, the jury took a second vote. This time eleven jurors were ready to convict. The lone holdout was Don Reeves.

He hadn't been as impressed with Catherine Maier as some of the others had, and he wanted to review Asher Maier's injury. It was the case to which they'd devoted the least amount of time, and it was the one least cluttered with obscure technical jargon. It was also the only case on which all the experts seemed to agree with the diagnosis (even if they didn't agree on who was responsible). To Reeves this unanimity was a relief. He had been overwhelmed by the testimony of "too many expert witnesses" whom he just found "confusing."

Baxley wasn't overly impressed with Catherine Maier, either, and he agreed that Asher's case was the key to their deliberations. It broke the stalemate of dueling pathologists and tied several medical strands together. And it was the case to which he could readily apply his own experience. As the father of three young children, he discounted the defense's insinuation that Catherine might have injured Asher while jogging with him on her shoulder. "I do the same thing with mine," he explained. "And I know babies are tough, I can tell you that. Because I've seen my children fall out of cribs before, you know, and we couldn't get to them before they fell on the floor. And the only thing it would do was, it kind of like startled them."

Anderson thought the defense attack on Catherine was effective until it went too far. Like Baxley, she was convinced that Asher's injury had nothing to do with jogging. And Kirkland's persistence had eventually pushed Anderson's attitude toward Catherine from skepticism to sympathy.

But more important to Anderson, Gail's story didn't add up. First, Anderson thought it should have been clear to Gail that something was dreadfully wrong with Asher. If Gail already had her suspicions about Catherine—and she'd testified that she did—why didn't she call 911? Why return him to the mother she suspected may have abused him? "Especially being a day care worker. As a day care worker keeping these children, you would want to make sure these children were healthy—that you're not accused of being the one to beat them."

Furthermore, "It's true this lady [Catherine] had a lot of problems. But I thought, 'If the baby's grandparents, as close as they were supposed to be with the baby, thought that there was a problem, then they would have already had that child out of the house.'"

But for Anderson, the Maier case was a small tile in a large mosaic. It wasn't the determining factor that it was for Reeves, and she wasn't the one who steered Reeves through it. That task fell to nurse Blaha, for whom it was also crucial.

For Blaha, Gasser and Wilson's timeline laid out the chronology of Asher's case in a clear and compelling manner, and the report cards supported their analysis. She wasn't impressed by the defense attacks on the report cards. If the Cutros' protestations about them were true and they only reflected food that was offered rather than consumed, and they frequently omitted illnesses, then the parents were being "duped." Either way, she considered the report cards devastating.

Then there was Rob Brown, the Cutros' friend who saw Asher the morning he was hospitalized. Blaha viewed him as a key witness "because of the fact that he was making an objective observation." And he proved instrumental in establishing the state's timeline.

In Blaha's eyes, no one piece of evidence proved the case. Like Anderson, she was convinced by the totality of the evidence. The Asher Maier case included some of the clearest evidence, but there was a great deal more that she found equally convincing.

For Don Reeves, however, the Asher Maier case was where it all came together. It was clear enough and concrete enough for him to understand—especially the way Blaha helped the jury review it. Once they'd looked at the possible scenarios that could explain Asher's injury, only one made sense to him. And once he was sure of that, any doubts he had about Gail Cutro's guilt dissolved.

They took another vote, and now they were unanimous.

One question remained: What was she guilty of? Was it murder, which would mean an automatic sentence of life in prison? Or homicide by child abuse, which could result in anything from twenty years to life?

They mulled their decision for about half an hour. Much of the time they reviewed the distinction the judge had made between the two charges. Had there been "malice aforethought" or just "an extreme indifference to human life?"

Once they'd discussed the judge's instructions, there was no real debate. They took a final vote, then Fuller sent a note to the judge.

67

Verdict

Word spread rapidly. The television cameramen quickly swung into position. Everyone was there: the Daniels, the Colsons, Catherine Maier, Patsy Habben, Richard Hunton, the Hallmans, Josh Cutro.

For Johnny Gasser, the Cutro case was the hardest thing he'd ever done. There was the sheer time invested. He had worked fifty-five consecutive days with only two days off—one for Thanksgiving and one for the University of South Carolina–Clemson football game. There were the nights when, after all he'd read about children dying, he'd tiptoed to his baby daughter's crib to make sure she was still breathing. It had been a hell of a case for a new parent.

Scarlett Wilson was also feeling emotional, but her emotions were mixed. The young prosecutor never had liked sentencing. And if the verdict went their way, that would be part of the package. "I think it's always sad because somebody's losing," she said. She paused. "I'm not saying it's not necessary." But it's not something that made her want to celebrate. "It's not a happy thing."

Patsy Habben was consumed by one thought: "If she gets off, I'm going to have to keep track of her for the rest of her life. Because if she gets a chance, she's going to kill another kid." There were other pressures, such as the challenge of running her department while agents grumbled about the time expended on this one case, but none of that even came close.

Catherine Maier felt like the outsider, as she had throughout the trial. It wasn't that the other parents weren't nice to her. But their lives were so different. And *her* child had lived. She felt that she had no right to put herself in the same category as the others. And she also felt guilty because she'd become the focus of the case. Had she lived a different life, she was sure that the trial wouldn't have been close. No one said anything like this to her, but she was sure that it had crossed everyone's minds. The flip side, though, was that in a way the verdict meant the most to her, because she was the one the defense had tried to put on trial.

Victims' advocate Nancy Moody sat with the Colsons, the Daniels, and Catherine Maier, as she had throughout. Her job was to help them get through it. And Missy was pregnant, so Moody had been with them for every word. But she really didn't know what was coming.

"I felt that she was guilty, because of the side I sit on," Moody remembers. "Because I had always heard our side of the whole story. When I sit in the courtroom and I hear verdicts come back, I can usually tell whether it's going to be a 'guilty' or an 'innocent.' This case, I couldn't tell.

"I had a real overwhelming sadness about the whole thing. I guess because I had not been privileged to see all the evidence, I was not overwhelmingly convinced. And I didn't know what to do with the burden, how to respond with the victims, how to hold them. I didn't know *what* to do. And I really didn't want the lady convicted if she wasn't guilty."

She decided to pray. "You know, somebody had to intervene bigger than all of us in that courtroom. 'If she's guilty, find her guilty. If she is innocent, please don't find her guilty. Don't make a mistake in this case.' It had a calming effect in me, that the right verdict would happen."

And then the jury filed in. It was 8:47 p.m., nearly six and a half hours after Judge Shuler first sent them off. Everyone who was seated rose, and some grabbed the hand of the person beside them.

Thom Neal had watched this whole thing happen for fourteen months, like a traffic accident you see in slow motion but are powerless to stop. He had been raised to believe that justice prevailed, and he refused to believe that a jury would put a decent woman in prison for life.

Wes Kirkland felt tense, nervous. He was thinking about the jury's request during their deliberations. They'd asked for a playback of Dr. Emery, and that didn't bode well. Kirkland felt the muscles in his stomach tighten—the way they do when you're expecting to be punched.

Lisa McPherson felt the emotion rise inside her even before the jury came in. She knew. She didn't need to look for classic signs like the jurors' averted eyes. Even before they read the verdict, she could feel the tears welling in her eyes.

The jury foreman handed a sheet of paper up to Judge Shuler, who read it silently and then handed it down to the clerk of the court. The clerk paused for a moment and then read it aloud:

"Indictment no. 94-gs-40–21178, the State versus Brenda Gail Cutro, the verdict is, 'We the jury find the defendant guilty of murder.'"

There was a gasp in the courtroom, then from the audience came the sound of crying. McPherson struggled to master her emotions. She held them in check long enough to request that the jury be polled. Then she, too, started to cry.

Gail didn't cry. She stood and listened with a blank expression—the expression she'd worn for most of the trial—while one by one the jurors repeated the word that sealed her fate.

Before he pronounced the sentence, Judge Shuler asked the defense for the motions he knew were coming. Though Thom Neal was in shock, he stood and, responding as if by rote, moved for a new trial and for an "arrest of judgment" based on arguments he'd made before and during the trial.

"I find your motions without merit, as I did earlier," the judge replied. "I think that the evidence was sufficient, although circumstantial. I think if you took it, certainly, in the light favorable to the state, which the jury could well do and obviously they did, that it did point conclusively to the guilt of the accused to the exclusion of every other reasonable hypothesis."

He asked if any of the lawyers wished to point out mitigating circumstances. "Obviously, there's not much I can do about it," since under South Carolina law only one sentence was available to him.

Wes Kirkland rose. "Your Honor, Mrs. Gail Cutro, as you've heard, is a mother of three children. She's got a husband. She's lived in the Columbia area for most of her life. We ask if there's any way that you could possibly give any mercy to her on this sentence, if you please would." Then he sat down.

Judge Shuler turned to Gail. "I'd be glad to hear from you or anybody in your family or anyone else." When Thom Neal started to introduce the Hallmans, Shuler hastily added: "Mr. Gasser, I know I should have heard from you first, but I'll be glad to hear from you in just a minute."

There had been a lot of ill will between the two sides during the trial, a lot of dirty looks exchanged. There was no telling what would spill out in the emotion of the moment. It began on a rather mild note with Gail's father, Harold Hallman, who looked uncomfortable as he stood for his brief moment in the spotlight.

"I hate that the people of this room and the jurors never had a chance to know my daughter," he said. "If they knew her, they could never think that this could happen. There's no doubt in my mind that she's totally innocent of the charges that's brought against her. I would think that I would be more guilty than she, and I cannot understand a justice system that will allow something to go this far."

As Hallman sat down, his volatile wife popped up. "I'm her mother," Patricia Hallman began. "I brought her into this world. I raised her. I know her nature. I know how gentle she is. I know how much she loves children. And I know even though that they have found her guilty—and I hope that they can sleep with this for the rest of their life—she loves children. She always has. She's never hurt a child. In fact, I've often asked her, 'Do you ever holler at your children?' I hollered at her when she was little. She said, 'Mama, all mothers holler at their children. But most of the time it's 'You sit in time out.'

"She is a good mother. She is a good baby-sitter. All the people loved her. I've never met anyone that's not met her that did not love her. She loves the Lord. She puts Him first in her life. She loves her children. She deserves to be with them.

"All this week and all the time that this has happened, we've been told, 'Stay quiet. Don't say anything.' We've not been able to defend our daughter or come forward and say anything. Now we've got the chance to do that.

"She's not been able to be with her children this Christmas. She don't have a tree up at her house. Friday her children thought we were going to bring her home. 'Where's Mama? The trial's over.' And I hope that Johnny Gasher—" she started to say, mispronouncing Gasser's name in the way that everyone in Gail's family did, before Thom Neal cut her off.

"Mrs. Hallman—" he said, half warning and half pleading.

"Sorry," she said, following a pause. "I didn't know I couldn't say that."

"Say anything you want to say," the judge reassured her. "I'm glad to listen."

"I just hope that he can live with what he's done and fabricated against our family and gotten the trial against my daughter. I hope he can live with that."

"Judge," Johnny Gasser began when the judge called on him, "I want the record to reflect that the state contacted approximately four to five other forensic pathologists around this country, experienced in this area. Every single forensic pathologist or pediatric pathologist that reviewed this evidence—every single one of them independently had the same conclusion, and that's that this woman murdered these children.

"Now, there's going to be no more Christmases for Parker Colson, no more Christmases for Ashlan Daniel, no more sitting on Santa Claus' lap, no more wrapping of presents, no more because of what she did.

"Every single independent pathologist, medical person that has reviewed this—some without any charge at all—have come to the same independent conclusion that these children were murdered. And it is not fair for these people right here"—Gasser glanced toward the jurors—"who have worked so hard and been so fair, to listen to this garbage. That is not fair."

"Judge," Lisa McPherson chimed in, "I will say that perhaps every forensic pathologist that Mr. Gasser and the state have approached comes to that conclusion. Certainly, there were forensic pathologists that we consulted who totally disagree with that position."

"I understand that," the judge said. "That's why we've been in trial for two weeks. That's the reason they build courthouses. That's the reason that we have the system that we have. That's the reason that we ask twelve people to make these decisions. It's not an easy decision for them. But I'm satisfied that they certainly could come to the conclusion that they came to."

"Judge, if I may," McPherson said, "while we certainly disagree with the jury's decision, I think I speak for the defense lawyers to say we respect the job that they've done. They've struggled with this. And in no way have we meant to take away from that."

"I understand that," Judge Shuler replied. "I understand that and they understand that." It was time to wrap things up. "Sentence of the court: Indictment no. 94-gs-40–21178, the defendant, Brenda Gail Cutro, is committed to the State Department of Corrections for a period of her natural life."

"Thank you, Judge," said Gasser, though he knew no discretion was involved.

Before sending the jurors home, Shuler thanked them for their service. He told them that he had no problem with their decision, and he reminded them that they were under no obligation to explain it to anyone. He complimented them on their diligence, wished them well, and sent them on their way.

When they were done, Gail Cutro didn't require prompting. Silently, without so much as a word or a wave goodbye, she strode to the door that led back to jail. A guard opened it, and she was gone.

68

Aftermath

Wes Kirkland, Thom Neal, and Lisa McPherson headed for a bar near Kirkland's home. As they left the courthouse, they couldn't help noticing the impromptu celebration clearly visible through the windows of Gasser's office. It added to the bitter taste of defeat—a taste that time would do little to assuage.

Kim Kirkland and Betsy Neal joined them, as did McPherson's ex, Jim Morton. They didn't drink much and they didn't stay long. Christmas, which was only six days away, seemed like a travesty to them now. It was impossible to catch the holiday spirit.

Yet, even as the defense lawyers sprinted toward the new year, they refused to leave the Cutro case behind. On the morning after the trial they filed a notice of appeal. There was no question that Gail Cutro would appeal and that they would handle it. Even if they had to do it for free—and, as it turned out, they did.

That same day Johnny Gasser and Dick Harpootlian met with the Daniels, the Colsons, and Catherine Maier. They discussed the charges still pending against Josh and Gail, and then Harpootlian called a news conference. Flanked by his deputy and the parents, the solicitor announced that Gail Cutro would not be tried again for the murder of Parker Colson or the assault on Asher Maier. One conviction was enough. Even if Gail were convicted twice more, she would still be serving the same life sentence.

Harpootlian added that the charge against Josh Cutro would be dropped. During the trial, the solicitor explained, it became clear that Gail acted without the knowledge or assistance of her husband. So Josh, who just the previous night had proclaimed to the press that SLED's Child Fatalities Department was the equivalent of the old Soviet KGB, was now free and clear.

Harpootlian, who had lost the election for attorney general and was just days away from leaving the solicitor's office, took the opportunity to praise Johnny Gasser for winning "one of the most difficult cases I have seen in twenty years." Harpootlian and Gasser called for uniformity in the way children's deaths were investigated and for better regulation of day care.

—————

In the memorandum that Thom Neal wrote supporting his motion requesting that Gail be released on bond pending appeal, the lawyer argued that the conviction would be reversed because the judge improperly allowed the state to introduce statistics and evidence involving Parker Colson and Asher Maier. Neal attached thirty-five supporting affidavits, which soon swelled to seventy. Most were written by Gail's friends and family, and by friends and neighbors of her parents.

The individuals most passionate in their support were the people who had supported Gail all along. Many had testified in court, including Linda Bass, April Rice, Rob and Jana Brown, Ramona Bowers, Renee Perry, and Ruthanne Robbins. Several members of Gail's family wrote angry letters to *The State* newspaper. One of the longest and most articulate was by her brother.

"I have seen many spectacular world events that have been tragic and which tear at my heart," Barry Hallman wrote. "None has been as close or particular to me or my family as the trial of my sister, Gail Cutro.

"We watched and heard testimony, facts, theories, lies, accusations and theatrics in the courtroom. The prosecutor portrayed a motive concocted by SLED, DSS and the Fifth Circuit solicitor's office—one that had to be held together by glue and string, supported by out-of-state experts, not because of what they specialize in but because pathologists in this state would not agree to a theory based on speculation and absence of facts.

"The sensationalism of the media coverage fueled speculation about a motive that was not there. The words and actions of John Gasser remind me of a 20th century Pilate putting an innocent 'Christ' on the cross. I pray that soon the truth will be known and that God will forgive all the transgressions that have been committed."

Despite these efforts, Gail was not released on bond—which was not surprising, since Gasser had never heard of a South Carolinian being granted bond following a murder conviction. Nor did the efforts of Gail Cutro's family and friends incite widespread outrage. No public-opinion surveys were conducted, but the consensus of the community at large seemed to be that justice had been done.

Her supporters continued to complain about the media coverage. Many people had heard about this strange disease—"Munchausen's" they called it—that was supposed to be evidence that the woman was guilty. They didn't realize that it was never even introduced at trial. It was that sort of thing that infuriated Gail's friends.

Barry Hallman recalled an incident that, in his mind, typified the ease with which some people condemned his sister. Hallman, who turned thirty-two during Gail's trial, bears little resemblance to his older sister. He is tall and thin and radiates a nervous intensity. He was able to attend the trial at times, since he worked nights as a chemical technician helping to build fuel assemblies for nuclear reactors. On one occasion, however, he couldn't go to court because he had to attend a lunch meeting.

Hallman and the plant manager arrived early for the meeting. His boss knew that Gail was Hallman's sister, and he inquired about the trial. As Hallman finished answering, a woman who joined them happened to catch the tail end of the conversation.

"Oh," she said, as she sat down, "you're talking about that murder trial. That woman is as guilty as anything." Hallman glanced at the plant manager, who looked uncomfortable but said nothing.

"How can you tell she's guilty?" Barry Hallman asked.

"Well, you've heard everything in the media."

"You know good and well," the manager broke in, "that things happen here that the media tries to make articles about—and they're not true."

"Yeah," she acknowledged, "but you can look in that woman's eyes and tell she's guilty."

"You can?" said Hallman. "Well, look into mine and tell me what I'm guilty of." When Hallman explained the relationship, the woman looked like she wanted to press a button and change the channel.

On the other hand, some of those who defended Gail based their conclusions on "evidence" that was equally flimsy. Some simply refused to entertain the possibility that an ostensibly respectable woman could have murdered a baby. It's not surprising that among them were those who had a special interest in the case. What *is* surprising, however, is how few of them made a serious attempt to follow the actual evidence introduced at the trial.

Charles and Phyllis Maier were not permitted to attend much of the trial, since they were witnesses for the defense. When questioned about evidence presented there—and reported in the newspaper—that Gail shook Asher, they were almost entirely unfamiliar with it. When it was described to them in detail, they couldn't have been less interested. Long before there was ever a trial they'd made up their minds that Catherine was responsible.

Dr. Selman Watson, who conducted psychological evaluations of the Cutros when they still hoped to reopen their day care, filed an affidavit with the court supporting Gail's appeal bond. "Based on my experience and clinical impressions of Gail Cutro," he wrote, "I do not believe she poses any risk of harm to herself or others." He wrote further: "There also was no indication from either Josh or Gail Cutro in their exchange with this examiner of any intent to be purposely vague, evasive or deceptive in their remarks." Yet, had he followed even the news accounts of the trial, he would have had reason to rethink this—as he later admitted in an interview. He explained that he was working long hours during that time and, since he didn't know if he was going to be called as a witness, "I wasn't sure if I'd contaminate anything if I were to make an appearance at trial, and then have to get on the witness stand."

Many others held strong opinions despite—or perhaps because of—a glaring ignorance of the evidence. Pat Reid, who wrote letters supporting Gail Cutro long before she was indicted, filed a lengthy affidavit expressing unwavering support, even though there were large gaps in what she knew about the trial.

In truth, it was a difficult trial to follow. It was one of South Carolina's longer trials, and much of the testimony was technical and esoteric. The accretion of evidence involving three separate cases created layers of complexity and confusion. And court sessions sometimes dragged into the evening, making it difficult for journalists rushing to make their deadlines to do more than hit the highlights.

Helen Ayer's response to the case mirrored that of many others. Ayer had been running a home day care for many years at the time, and she also headed the Midlands chapter of the South Carolina Home Child Care Association, which advocated on behalf of caregivers. On top of that, she had been appointed by the governor to sit on the statewide advisory committee that drafted rules and regulations for day cares based in homes, churches, and centers. She couldn't attend the trial, since she had a day care to run, but she received reports from people who did and she read the newspaper. Still, she was as confused as anyone.

She read the article in *The State* newspaper on Munchausen syndrome by proxy, struggled to understand it, and waited to learn more during the proceedings—in vain, as it turned out, since the term was never mentioned.

When the trial was over, Ayer found herself in limbo. She couldn't dismiss the allegations as utterly baseless, but she couldn't bring herself to believe them, either. Long after Gail was convicted, she was still wrestling with her feelings. Questioned about the case, she spent several minutes trying to articulate her thoughts before she stumbled on the truth. "I guess the thing is I don't want her to be guilty. That's the biggest thing."

It wasn't because Gail was a friend. Gail never joined Ayer's group, and they'd met only once. But the case exercised a profound influence on all day care providers in the community. Well before Gail was indicted, many of the women in Ayer's group stopped caring for infants. It wasn't just Gail's experience that rattled them. Suzanne Pope and another local sitter had also been devastated by SIDS deaths. In response, four months after Parker Colson died, Ayer's group invited three speakers to talk to them about SIDS. One was a pediatrician who chaired the pediatrics department of a local hospital. He was joined by Linda Bass and Beverly Daniel, the pathologist who had autopsied Parker Colson. Gail Cutro was in the audience, and it was after this event that Ayer met her.

Ayer had then organized a second meeting in response to apprehensions provoked by Gail's indictment. On this occasion she'd invited Patsy Habben to address the group's concern that additional day cares were under investigation, and Habben had brought Johnny Gasser to talk to them directly in order to ease their fears.

A few months after the trial, a third meeting devoted to the Cutro case was arranged when Pat Hallman asked if she could address the group. Hallman brought Jana Brown, the nurse who was one of Gail's biggest supporters, and the two of them explained to the gathering why they were certain that Gail was innocent. Hallman also read from letters Gail had written from prison and brought snapshots of her daughter.

At first Ayer and the others were impressed. Hallman appeared to be a caring individual who was devoted to her daughter. The longer Hallman spoke, however, the more uncomfortable Ayer grew. "It got to the point where she was almost trying to win our confidence, and that's where I felt like the line broke down. She had pictures of Gail when she was a baby, and I don't understand the significance of that. And she was, I think—I probably shouldn't say this, but it seemed to me maybe she was playing on our feelings, a mother for a daughter."

For Ayer, trying to make sense of it all was a frustrating, gut-wrenching experience that left her deeply ambivalent. "I still don't know whether Gail's guilty," she announced. "It's the most bizarre thing I think I've heard. I read a lot of whodunit books, and I've not heard anything like this before."

The mystery for many who followed the case was the residue of a trial that they'd assumed would explain all. But after it was over, they were shocked by how many questions remained.

They would have been more shocked to know it was a long way from over.

69

Second Thoughts

Some of the ways the trial affected people were impossible to predict. The individuals it changed sometimes sounded the most surprised. Ramona Bowers had sent her son to the day care and had fought to keep it open. She'd testified for Gail in court. Yet, when she was interviewed in her home two and a half years after the trial, practically the first words out of her mouth were: "I can't believe I was so stupid."

She had kept her son in the day care, Bowers explained, out of loyalty. She considered Gail a friend. Her resolve had stiffened during the investigation and prosecution. Her mistake was responding emotionally instead of rationally, she said.

She should have pulled her son. Even if the Cutros were blameless, they needed time to heal—to sort out their own emotions. "It was not the environment where my child should have been," Bowers said. She could have told

Gail that she was removing her son for his own well-being, not because she'd lost confidence in the day care.

The entire experience left Bowers shaken. As a teacher, she'd always considered herself a good judge of character. But that changed. "I question my ability to judge people now," she said.

She was sitting in the living room of her blue Cape Cod house in Irmo. Tate, who was four, had reached the age when boys seem incapable of slowing down. He and his sisters, who were 11 and 8, had eaten lunch, and the girls had been told to keep him in the bedroom. But Tate was irrepressible. He ventured out with his little cars. He composed a "letter" on a nearby computer. And, of course, he peppered his mother with innumerable questions.

Each time he bounded across the room, the tall, thin woman with the short blonde hair and ready smile patiently excused herself and listened. It was easy to imagine Bowers repeating this in her first-grade classroom, as insistent voices called, "Teacher! Teacher!" After a few words of encouragement, Tate, who had the blue eyes, straight nose and strong chin of his mother, raced off.

Then Bowers would settle back in her recliner and, as memory brought her back to the unhappy days of 1993, a troubled look returned to her eyes. She'd used a different day care for the girls, and she'd been happy with it, but the Bowers had moved and it was no longer convenient. Plus the price had gone up. The Cutros' day care was on her way to work, and it was cheaper.

After it closed, she paid the higher amount that she had been paying. "And I feel fine about paying that." She had a new appreciation for what was important. "He's in good hands," she said of her son. She paused to reflect. "You'd pay anything, or you'd quit your job before you'd put them anywhere you don't have a real feel for."

She'd thought she had a feel for Gail Cutro. Gail and Josh were members of the church Bowers and her husband attended. They'd been in a Sunday school class together. But that wasn't why she'd chosen them, Bowers explained.

Bowers had actually chosen the day care *after* Parker Colson died there. And she'd chosen it not *in spite* of the death, but *because* of it. Bowers knew something about SIDS. She remembered the death of Elizabeth Lightfoot, which had made such an impression on the entire church community. She knew that SIDS kills infants without warning, and she knew it was nobody's fault. Her heart had gone out to the Lightfoots, and when she'd learned about the death at the Cutros' home, her heart had gone out to Gail. It occurred to her that caring for Tate might help Gail recover. So Bowers asked her if she'd thought about taking more babies.

That wasn't the final twist. Bowers also knew that two months before Tate started, another child in the Cutros' day care (who turned out to be Asher Maier) had been injured. The doctors said he'd been shaken. But the prime suspect, in the eyes of Bowers and other parents, was Asher's mother. When Bowers discussed the matter with Gail, the caregiver had been livid. "How dare anybody hurt one of these babies!" she'd declared, sounding injured herself.

So Bowers sent Tate to the Cutros to show support. She trusted them. Josh, despite his size, was a teddy bear with kids. And Gail was gentle and sweet. "I remember her being so soft-spoken," Bowers recalled. "You could just sit and listen to someone like that talk all day long." And she cooked nutritious meals for the children—breakfast and lunch. They ate better, Bowers said, than they would have had their mothers stayed home.

The month before she signed up Tate, she brought him to the day care to spend a day. He was not yet five months old. He seemed fine. Just as he did during the two and a half months he attended. "I always felt he was well cared for," Bowers said. "He was real little, but you could read whether he felt happy or whether he was upset."

Then, a month after Tate started, Ashlan Daniel died. Bowers wondered how Gail could go on, but Josh insisted that they would be fine, Bowers recalled. Gail's mother volunteered to help out, and they were open the next day.

Bowers couldn't have done that if she'd been running the day care. She probably would have been in an asylum, she said. But that wasn't what she was thinking at the time. "I was thinking, 'Tate's always been well cared for, these are people who go to our church, these are people you need to be supportive of.'" When the police investigation picked up steam, Bowers dug in her heals. "We were adamantly convinced that they were innocent," she said.

As late afternoon gave way to early evening and shadows stalked Bowers' living room, she described a slow erosion of confidence. "I don't know which side I'm on anymore," she said.

There were things about Josh that bothered her. He'd told her that he was once a stockbroker, but she'd learned it wasn't true. When Gail's mother, Patricia Hallman, started working at the day care, she gave Bowers an earful about Josh. He treated his own son roughly, Hallman said, and he'd thwarted

Hallman from seeing her own daughter. The family that had seemed to Bowers so healthy had begun to strike her as a little "dysfunctional." She began to realize that she didn't know them as well as she'd thought. At the time, however, these uncertainties were overshadowed by her outrage at the way the Cutros were being railroaded.

Bowers wasn't sure why only Gail stood trial and Josh was let off. In addition to testifying for the defense, Bowers took time from work to attend several days of the trial. She was there the day Gail was convicted, and she wasn't the only one who was incredulous. Several day care parents were at least as angry and vocal as she. Gail had enjoyed substantial support in the community—especially among other day care operators and people affiliated with their church. Bowers couldn't gauge the attitude of the community at large. She'd been too close to the situation, she said, and her support of the Cutros was too well known. Dissenters probably steered clear.

A sound at the door interrupted her thoughts. It was Ramona's husband, Bob, returning from his job as food service director at a state psychiatric hospital. It was a measure of the hold the case still had on people, years after the trial, that Bob immediately chimed in. A deacon at their church, he mentioned that the Cutro family was still on the prayer list.

This reminded Ramona that the prosecutor had called Gail "evil," which had stuck in her gullet. "There's not an evil bone in her body," Ramona insisted. "I never saw evil, and I still don't." Bob Bowers also had a visceral reaction to the prosecutor. "To me the guy was egotistical," he said. Far from evil, the Cutros seemed "very appropriate" in their Sunday school class. In fact, Bob Bowers added, several people in the class were "more eccentric than they were."

The Bowers both laughed, relaxing for a moment from the intensity of the conversation. But soon enough Bob was serious again. He never thought they'd be faced with the "possible truth" that their child care provider was "a potential harmful person."

Ramona smiled at the euphemism her husband had used in place of "murderer." She nodded her head. "I still can't get out that 'm' word," she said.

70

Altered Lives

Johnny Gasser would not have been surprised to hear that some of the day care parents were unhappy with him. He knew he had his critics. While his performance on the Cutro case had been praised, some defense lawyers wondered aloud whether he went overboard.

Jim Morton was one of them. Morton, Lisa McPherson's ex-husband and close friend, worked in the solicitor's office for five years and was close to Gasser. After Morton left to join the defense bar, they remained friends even though they squared off in a highly emotional murder trial in which Morton's client was convicted. "Johnny Gasser is a great lawyer," he said. "Very smart, top ten in his class. And a very good advocate.

"I think in this case he lost sight of the forest for the trees. I think he should have been more objective, and I think it's a very dangerous thing when prosecutors act as zealously as he acted." In the defense lawyer's view, Gasser made up his mind that Gail Cutro was guilty and then cobbled together the evidence to prove it.

For her part, Lisa McPherson pronounced herself "devastated" by the verdict. "It's a hard thing for me to think about to this day," she said two years after the trial.

"I prosecuted for six and a half years. I typically got close to the victim and got emotionally involved." When she switched to defense, her allegiance to her clients could be just as strong. "And this was a lot more than a job to all of us," she said, referring to the Cutro case. "Gail was somebody that I believed in, who I cared deeply about, who was a friend."

In a larger sense, the case was deeply disillusioning to her. "I believe that when law enforcement wants you, they can get you. I mean, I don't think that happens all the time. I think there's a lot of good law enforcement, but I also saw that in this state, if they want you, and they believe they have the right person, you're in a whole lot of trouble."

McPherson was also disturbed by the impact the case had on personal relationships. "Johnny and I had been friends for years. He was a real good friend of my husband's, and I still feel that. But I never see Johnny, to this day, that it doesn't bring back that whole experience.

"I'm not trying to say his intentions weren't pure," she went on. "I believe they were. I don't believe he thinks he put an innocent person in prison." She thought for a moment. "Maybe the problem I have with Johnny any more is just that we simply have such totally different views about what the truth is."

Thom Neal was even more profoundly affected by the verdict. The shock he felt was largely attributable to two factors: He had never done criminal defense work, and he was naïve about the system.

"I grew up with the assumption that if you are charged with a crime, you are guilty. Right or wrong, that's the assumption. And I think this case showed me, more than anything else, that that's not always true." He had also grown up with an abiding faith that "the system will work and the system is right. And I found out it wasn't. That's a hard thing to learn when you're thirty-five years old." The lesson left him disillusioned and depressed. "I'm a cynic now, and I don't think I was before."

With his belief in the criminal justice system shaken, he fell back on a deeper faith. He went to an Episcopal Cursillo weekend. Participants were encouraged to examine their lives and the new directions they wanted to pursue. Neal emerged refreshed and determined to get involved in another church ministry, the Kairos program, which sends parishioners into prisons to work with inmates. It's designed to build a Christian community within the prison. Inmates are encouraged to examine the choices that landed them in prison and the ones they make each day.

If someone had told him years earlier that he'd be working with prisoners, he would have dismissed the notion as laughable. "The one assumption I had always worked under is that if you were in prison you were an animal, you were a monster, you were a criminal. And all of a sudden I realized that that may not necessarily be true.

"In law school you hear this concept of 'innocent until proven guilty.' I now believe it. I think I'm a better lawyer."

Wes Kirkland was probably the least affected. He'd worked hard. He believed in the case. He cared enough to labor on the appeal without compensation. But it didn't change him the way it did Thom Neal and Lisa McPherson. "Sometimes it sort of bothers me—maybe I should be changed a little more.

"If it changed me in any way, I think it made me just more cynical, which is not a good thing."

Kirkland didn't feel the same attachment to Gail Cutro that McPherson did. To him it was more of a job. A job about which he cared passionately, but a job nonetheless. And unlike Thom Neal, Kirkland felt comfortable in the role of criminal defense lawyer. Kirkland understood that you had to distance yourself. You couldn't get too emotionally involved with any one case or client. Win or lose, there was always another one waiting.

"I try not to let it get to me or think about it too much, because it doesn't do me a lot of good. I mean, I have to keep going. I still have to deal with Johnny, with that office, every day."

———

No lives were altered more radically than those of the parents of three children.

Immediately after the verdict, even while she sat in a courtroom filled with people, Catherine Maier was alone. The other parents embraced their families and friends and each other. Maier was "the same way I've always been in the end—alone. I was alone during a good bit of the trial and alone most of the fight." She tried to convince herself that it was best that way. "I'm glad I'm alone because it makes me stronger," she told herself, "and it makes me tough and it makes me okay with things. And I don't have to have somebody." When she arrived home, however, the brave front melted. She was lonely and confused.

There was never a thought of celebrating. "Nobody won. Two sets of parents had children that were gone totally. I was alone and couldn't even go home and hug my child. Gail's children don't have a mom who can be with them. Nobody wins in this situation at all."

After the verdict, Maier went to her sister's house and the two of them drank wine and cried. "We cried for Asher and we cried for Parker and we cried for Ashlan." She cried because two children had no future—and her own child's future was so uncertain. She knew that, as a result of his injury, Asher was "developmentally delayed," and she feared that he would suffer from learning disabilities. "I cried because I don't want him to grow up to be teased or treated badly." She wondered whether he would go to college or "be a Forrest Gump." And she worried that her husband's parents might teach him to hate her.

Her divorce from Chad had been finalized shortly before Gail's trial began. She'd briefly considered fighting the Maiers for custody, but she'd realized that she couldn't match their resources to pay for lawyers—and for the medical attention that Asher needed. Instead, she changed course. She enrolled at Midlands Technical College, where she had previously taken a few courses. The nursing and paralegal programs looked interesting. It was time she acquired skills and a career.

As they had so often in her life, her plans unraveled. The reasons were also familiar: She lacked discipline, and she lacked money. She had difficulty finding and holding a decent job, and she fell further and further behind in the child support the court had ordered her to pay the Maiers. The Maiers finally took her back into court, where Catherine was ordered to pay or face incarceration. When she couldn't pay, she was thrown in jail, where, the judge decreed, she would remain until she did. She seemed to have hit a new low. After a week in jail, she caught a break. Her aunt came forward and paid the debt.

Her next plan charted a more radical path that would take her clear out of South Carolina. It would also instill discipline and pay a regular salary from which child support would be deducted automatically. And this time she followed through. In November 1997, she joined the United States Navy. She was based in Pearl Harbor.

While Catherine Maier struggled to find direction in life, Missy and Davis Daniel worked to repair their fragile union. After the verdict they scrambled to prepare for the birth of their second child, due three months later. It was then that Davis realized that he couldn't face another infant in that same house, which was drenched in pain. Three weeks before Missy's due date, they moved to a house a few miles away.

The days after Reid was born should have been among the happiest of their lives. But Ashlan's death had changed all that. Missy, the worrier, was a nervous wreck. She'd been terrified throughout the pregnancy. Now she was paralyzed. First, she was afraid to leave the safe confines of the hospital. Then, even though she didn't believe that Ashlan died of SIDS, she asked that her son be sent home with an apnea monitor (their efficacy in preventing SIDS deaths had not yet been debunked). On top of that, Missy checked on him constantly, and for the first three or four months put him down in a rocker rather than a crib, believing that it was safer. Still, she couldn't sleep for worrying.

When Reid had cleared the six-month mark, past the greatest risk of SIDS, Missy still couldn't imagine having another child. "I know that I can't go through what I've just been through the past six months," she said. The joys of motherhood were almost completely overshadowed by fear and pain.

It was harder to talk about the pain. At times it was almost more than she could bear. She'd considered suicide, and she said that she still thought about it. But she knew that she had to be strong for her son. "But yeah, I wish I could die," she confessed, "because it's too much—this pain. You carry it with you no matter where you go. People talk. It hurts." She was always aware when people pointed at her and whispered, "She's the one. The one whose child died."

What Gail had supposedly sought, Missy abhorred. The last thing she wanted was attention. "You're treated different. They don't know what to say. And I understand that. They don't know how to talk to us, and I wouldn't know how, either. But I don't want to be different. I'm not different." For a long time she didn't want to run into anybody. She was "too scared." It wasn't until Reid was about four months old that "I've finally had the nerve to hold my head up. And whoever I run into, I just run into. And it's taken that long. It's taken two years [since Ashlan died] to be able to hold my head up and not worry, 'Who's going to be in the drugstore?'"

Part of the problem, she came to understand, was that she hadn't had a chance to grieve. After Ashlan died, first she worked with SLED as an investigator. Then she had to cope with the departure of Davis, prepare for the trial, testify, and listen to a parade of witnesses describe the death of her daughter in excruciating detail. No sooner had she weathered these assaults than Reid was born, and she was consumed by the responsibility of caring for an infant. There had been no time to grieve, and a reservoir of sorrow was dammed in her heart.

Every aspect of her life had been affected, including her relationship with her husband. "I can honestly say—and Davis knows this—that since we have gotten back together, we do not lean on each other for comfort," Missy said, about six months after Reid's birth. "There's a wall there. Davis and I, it's not the same as what it was. How could it be?"

Davis acknowledged the rift. "Sometimes we got real close. Certainly right after all this happened we got close. And it's kind of like we each went to doing our own thing. I don't know. It's hard to look at one another and see the pain because you don't feel like you can help. It's hard. I don't know if this happened to any other couples, but I've heard it did. You would think it wouldn't. You would think it would strengthen anything you had."

It did strengthen Davis's bond with his parents and two older sisters. His family had always been close, but tragedy cinched them closer. It was especially true in his relationship with his sisters. Even though Davis was the youngest, he had tried to act the part of the big brother who protected and supported them. "I've learned to let go and put your head on someone else's shoulder," he said.

Sometimes the pain sneaks up on him. "I have a hard time around little baby girls." They remind him of the one he doesn't have.

The birth of his son, on the other hand, made him feel "we're the luckiest people in the world." But it also made him "wary every day." Fear was never far from the surface. Years after Ashlan died, every time the phone rang at work Davis felt a knot in the pit of his stomach.

Along with the fear was a great deal of anger. He was angry with Gail, and Josh, and Linda Bass. "I went through a lot of anger. I was angry with God." He couldn't understand why his daughter had to die. Eventually, the associate pastor at his church helped him work through it. Davis found an answer that helped him cope. The reason Ashlan had to die was to stop Gail from killing again. His daughter died so that no other child would have to.

Ten months after the trial, Davis and Missy separated. They communicated regularly, and they both spent lots of time with Reid. But they couldn't bridge the gulf. Though neither seemed to want it, and neither could fully explain it, in June 1997 they were divorced.

Somehow Lindy and Gary Colson were able to support each other while respecting the differences in their styles of grieving. The alienation they felt from each other and from everyone else immediately after Parker died eventually gave way to an even stronger bond forged in the shadow of catastrophe. Lindy wasn't quite sure why. She knew that tragedies like hers "will break couples up as quick as it will keep them together. And I truthfully don't know why we got stronger from it."

She only knew that they did. "We are more understanding toward each other. And I think we both realize that, even though we don't do it out in the open, we lean on each other a lot. He's very considerate of my feelings and vice versa. And nobody else could be like that toward us because an outsider can't understand exactly what's going on. But we know."

They still had "bad days"—days when one or the other is depressed. They called them "Parker days," and no further explanation was necessary. They knew that their daughter, Kasey, would never replace their son—just as Davis and Missy knew that Reid would never replace Ashlan.

Gary tried to explain it. "Some people think that now that we've got

Kasey—and, don't misunderstand, that baby is our world; whether Parker was here or not, it would be equal. But some people think—"

"—that she has replaced Parker," Lindy interjected, before he could get the words out. "Parker will always be Parker. She is Kasey. She has not replaced him."

"It's not like you have a puppy," Gary continued, "and he runs away or gets hit by a car and you go buy another one to make yourself feel better. That's not the way this works, guys."

"People really do think that," Lindy explained.

"We had people say, 'Well, at least you didn't have him for twelve years,'" Gary recalled. "And [inside] you're going, 'Jesus Christ!'"

"I would have gave my *eye-teeth* to have him for twelve years—to get to watch him go to school!" said Lindy, brushing away tears.

People thought that once the case had ended and time had passed, the Colsons were fine. Lindy put their neighbors' thoughts into words: "They've healed, they're fine now. They're go-getters." What these people didn't know was that "every time you look at a little boy, it rips your heart out. It rips my heart out to see Missy and Davis with their baby.

"It rips your heart out, because you didn't get to see yours do that. And I think about it every time school starts. In three more years I would be standing out there with Parker, putting him on the bus to go to school for the first time. Seeing him do that. When he was supposed to graduate, that's going to be another day that's just going to rip my heart out. Because I'm not going to get to see him do that.

"There's not a day that goes by that I don't look up there at his picture." She glances at the photograph on the wall next to the mantel. "And I think, now that Kasey's getting bigger, 'How am I going explain to her, after all the love that she's had, that someone can actually [kill a baby]?'" Lindy knew, though, that someday she'd have to. And that promised to be another occasion—one of the most gut-wrenching—that would bring her back to *that* house and *that* day.

"This is never going to end," she said.

Once upon a time, when Lindy still believed that Parker died of SIDS, it was easier to cope. "I was thankful that it was SIDS, because he just went to sleep. He didn't suffer."

Like the Daniels, the Colsons asked for an apnea monitor when their second child was discharged from the hospital. They, too, endured the endless false alarms and the constant fear of finding their baby dead. And like Missy, Lindy believed that this child would be her last. "The stress level of all that first year, you know, watching her breathe—even after we found out what really happened to Parker—I just can't go through that again."

Back then, as the supposed parent of a SIDS victim, she was grateful for Linda Bass and the support group of people who truly knew what she was going through. Her own experience had taught her how insensitive not only friends but even professionals could be. Her first lesson, in fact, occurred right after Parker was pronounced dead at Bass's hospital, with Bass standing just a few feet away.

"The awfulest thing I thought I'd ever have to hear in my life, besides my son having died, was the next thing they had to say: 'We need to perform an autopsy, and we need your signature.'" Lindy was in shock. She and Gary had not begun to absorb the enormity of their loss. The idea that the doctors now wanted to cut her baby was more than she could handle. "I freaked," she said.

She was living proof that there was a need for people like Bass to intervene at moments like this, or to train others who would. Once Lindy was in a receptive state of mind, she was able to understand and support the need for an autopsy. But she wasn't ready to hear it right away. One benefit of Bass's support group was that she was surrounded by people who understood this. She could learn what she needed to know at her own speed. And Bass was always available to answer questions. Lindy derived "a lot of comfort" from the meetings, she said. "I didn't feel so alone." And Bass helped the Colsons channel their grief into constructive projects such as Red Nose Day and the softball game honoring Parker.

Lindy's attitude changed radically when the SIDS diagnosis turned into a murder charge. The comfort she'd felt knowing Parker hadn't suffered evaporated. "That's what's so hard," she said, her voice filled with emotion. "Because he did [suffer]. And I'm always wondering, was his last thought: 'Where's my mommy?'

"And she did that to me," Lindy said of Gail. "And I have to wake up every day with that thought. 'Did he think I let him down?'" Gail Cutro took more than their son, Lindy said. She took their peace of mind.

By the trial's end, Lindy's feelings about Linda Bass had also been transformed. She believed that Bass had overstepped the bounds of a SIDS counselor when she told Lindy that Asher Maier had been injured by his mother, and that Gail deserved support. Had Bass not gone to bat for Gail, Lindy speculated, more people might have been suspicious, and Ashlan might not have died. "She was counseling me at that time and counseling Gail. I'm the mother. I should have been her first concern. Not the damn baby-sitter."

These were the very tensions that had convinced Bass to run separate support groups for parents and baby-sitters. Bass said that after the Cutro case she dropped the group for sitters specifically to avoid "a conflict of interest."

71

Not Over

When Lindy Colson said that for her the Cutro case would never end, she echoed the sentiments of many of those involved. But they thought they were speaking figuratively.

In August 1998, after Gail Cutro had been in prison for four years, the South Carolina Supreme Court reversed her conviction. She had to scramble to raise the $300,000 bond, but her parents reportedly mortgaged their home and in early November she was released.

There were restrictions placed on her. The judge who had set the bond imposed two conditions: She had to wear an electronic monitor, and she was not allowed to live in the "immediate community where the victims or their families reside." (Johnny Gasser told the local newspaper that there was one more that was not part of the judge's order. Gail Cutro still had an agreement with the state DSS that she would not seek to open a home day care.)

The Daniels and the Colsons were as furious as Gail's family and friends were ecstatic, but it was not the end of the story. Gail Cutro's conviction had been overturned, but the Supreme Court had not dismissed the case. She was required to post bond because she was still charged with a crime. It was now up to the Solicitor's Office to drop the charges or try her again.

No one who knew Johnny Gasser or had followed the first trial could have been surprised when he and his boss, Solicitor Barney Giese, announced their decision. The second trial was scheduled for May 1999.

The appeal had hinged on Judge Shuler's decision to allow the state to present evidence involving all three children when Gail was tried for the murder of just one. Writing for the majority in a three-two decision, Justice James Moore argued that Judge Shuler had erred in admitting into evidence crimes against Parker Colson and Asher Maier because the state had not presented clear and convincing evidence that Gail was responsible. Catherine Maier and Josh Cutro each had access to Asher during the period he was most likely injured, and Josh also had contact with Parker Colson the day he died. Following a path many had privately trod before him, Justice Moore particularly emphasized the possibility that Josh Cutro was the perpetrator.

In a stinging dissent that was nearly three times as long as the majority opinion, Justice Jean Toal (who would later become the court's first female chief justice) opined that Gail's lawyers had never even presented the argument the majority had based its decision on, and thus the court was procedurally barred from considering it. In point of fact, she argued, her three colleagues had raised this issue themselves. Even if she ignored this problem, Justice Toal went on, the record did not support the majority's opinion. The trial judge had ample grounds to find that the state had presented clear and convincing evidence that Gail had killed Parker and injured Asher.

So, once again the Cutro case had proved its power to divide the community. Most South Carolina Supreme Court decisions were unanimous or contained a lone dissent. Three-two splits were rare, and rarer still was the vehement language the justices addressed not just to the issues but to each other.

If anyone had wondered whether passions on this subject still ran high, all doubt should have been banished a full year earlier, when the Supreme Court heard oral arguments from the two sides. The emotion in the courtroom that day was unmistakable, but it was quickly overshadowed by the scene that followed outside.

After the proceeding, local television crews conducted separate interviews in the building's lobby with Johnny Gasser and Josh Cutro. As Gasser started to leave the building, Josh quickly followed to ask the prosecutor a few questions he'd been saving. After listening to what amounted to a harangue, Gasser suggested that there was no point in continuing the conversation and turned to descend the stairs to the street.

"That's it, walk away from the truth," Josh spat. "That's what you've been doing all along." Standing under the huge marble columns in front of the building, Josh paused for a moment as Gasser continued down the stairs.

"Hey, Johnny!" Josh shouted as Gasser reached the sidewalk. "I'll be around downtown. Keep an eye out for me. And you better have at least ten people with you!"

It looked and sounded like a scene stolen from an old Western movie. And not surprisingly, Josh's implied threat led the coverage on the tube that night and in the next morning's paper. For a time it appeared that he might even be arrested, although Josh did call the newspaper thirty minutes after his outburst to explain that he was frustrated and had no intention of harming the Deputy Solicitor. In any case, Gasser never sought to press charges.

———

The second Cutro murder trial featured a new judge, new issues, and several surprises. Gasser was the lone holdover among the lawyers. He was assisted by Stacey Haynes, who essentially handled the same topics and witnesses that Scarlet Wilson had in the first trial.

For Gasser, the most important issue, by far, was trying the cases together. Since the Supreme Court's decision forced him to alter his approach, he returned to his original plan and resolved to join the charges. Even though it was still more difficult to do so in South Carolina than in most states, he was able to cite several encouraging precedents. And he bolstered his position by bringing back another strategy he'd planned for the first trial but discarded. He introduced expert testimony on Munchausen syndrome by proxy to demonstrate a pattern and motive that spanned the three cases.

MSBP usually involves a caregiver who fabricates, exaggerates, or induces an injury in a child and then rushes the child to doctors for treatment, often repeating the process while soaking up the attention of the medical staff. The state sought to apply the syndrome to a somewhat different pattern: a caregiver injuring a series of children rather than one child serially, and seeking attention from a variety of sources, not primarily medical personnel.

Gail's new lawyers bitterly opposed this effort to join the cases, arguing that the state was trying to circumvent the Supreme Court's decision by sneaking in the back door what the court had rejected at the front. Furthermore, the new evidence contemplated would merely repeat the motive the prosecutors had introduced in the first trial, only this time they would call an expert and attach a name. If permitted, the state would get everything it had in the first trial and more, even though the defendant had prevailed on appeal.

Judge Jimmy Williams, who presided over the retrial, granted the state's motions on MSBP and joinder. Though the defense was disappointed with his rulings, they could not complain about his allocation of resources. He'd allowed Gail Cutro to claim indigence and had appointed three attorneys from the Legal Aid Society to represent her.

The lead defense lawyer was Doug Strickler; he was assisted by Lee Coggiola, the chief public defender, and Beattie Butler. Williams permitted Gail to add, also at the court's expense, a private lawyer from Arizona, Tom Ryan, who was something of a specialist in medical evidence—particularly MSBP. Furthermore, the judge authorized Gail's attorneys to hire as many experts as they wished, which came to five from out of state and two from within.

Dr. Randy Alexander, the Iowa pediatrician who testified at the first trial about shaken baby syndrome, was the expert the state relied on to discuss MSBP, which he'd also written and lectured about extensively. Dr. Alexander testified that there was a pattern of abuse in this case. He based his opinion on the records he'd reviewed: medical records of Gail, Josh, and their children, and of Parker Colson, Ashlan Daniel, and Asher Maier; notes about Gail's therapy; and Gail's own writing in Linda Bass's support group. The pattern, he said, involved a fake SIDS death, the death of two infants initially thought to be SIDS victims, and the injury of a third infant caused by shaking. He also included the Cutros' own two daughters, who were sent home from the hospital as newborns with apnea monitors, and Gail's long-term fascination with SIDS. He noted a pattern of deception and Gail's desire for attention and community support.

Gail's new lawyers did their best to challenge Dr. Alexander's premises and conclusions, pointing out the ways in which the pattern he'd described differed from the more common Munchausen scenario, and arguing that Dr. Alexander's bias was apparent in his attempt to make the square facts fit into a round diagnostic hole.

Other than the new focus on psychology, the state's case did not pack many surprises. Most of the witnesses made return appearances. Having been through it before, Gasser was able to avoid or smooth over some of the problems he'd encountered during the first trial. The issue of edema, for example, virtually disappeared during the second trial.

But one returning witness divulged startling information. Suzanne Pope ran the day care where Elizabeth Lightfoot died of SIDS, and she belonged to Riverland Hills Baptist Church, from which she'd received much support during that difficult time. Pope had been a minor witness in the first trial, but she testified at greater length about her relationship with Gail Cutro during the sequel. The most dramatic moment was when she repeated a conversation they'd had the day after Parker Colson died.

In attempting to console Gail, Suzanne Pope referred to Elizabeth Lightfoot's death and that of her own son, who died of leukemia. Gail replied that she, too, had lost a child of her own—due to a heart condition. Pope had never thought to mention this to anyone, she testified, because she'd never had reason to doubt it. She'd only learned that it wasn't true ten days earlier, after the second trial had begun. It was another alleged deception that Dr. Alexander, the prosecution's MSBP witness, could now add to his list.

Gail's new lawyers, with the advantage of hindsight, delivered a more muscular defense than their predecessors had. Led by Doug Strickler, they conceded little, challenging even small points and minor witnesses. And they introduced several new witnesses who testified effectively. Gail Cutro's father and younger daughter testified, and Harold Hallman and Lara Cutro, by their very appearance on the stand, humanized Gail in a way that she hadn't been during the first trial. The defense also called a grief counselor with no ties to Gail to bolster Linda Bass's testimony and to reduce the defense's dependence on her.

The defense lawyers were also prudent in choosing whom *not* to call. They didn't bring back pathologists John Pless from Indiana or Charleston's Sandra Conradi, who wanted to defend South Carolina's experts in the first trial. To no one's surprise, the defense did not call Josh Cutro. Maryland pathologist Dr. John Smialek returned, and the defense brought in another forensic pathologist from South Carolina, Dr. Joel Sexton, who felt at least as strongly about the case as Dr. Conradi had.

Gail testified, and again she'd lost a lot of weight. But the biggest difference was in her demeanor. She rarely showed any emotion at the defense table, where she spent most of her time writing on yellow legal pads; but on the stand she smiled a great deal, especially when her lawyer showed her photographs of the day care children, which he did regularly. At other times she seemed to choke back tears. She also addressed both lawyers as "sir," presenting herself as a much more deferential witness than she had the first time.

On the last day of testimony the defense called Dr. Ronald Uscinski, a neurologist from Maryland, who provided the closest thing to a bombshell the trial produced. When the gist of his testimony was later repeated to Lisa McPherson, she pronounced herself "shocked."

Dr. Uscinski testified that Asher Maier was never shaken. In fact, Dr.

Uscinski didn't believe that there was such a thing as shaken baby syndrome. Asher was suffering from the aftereffects of a "birth injury," he testified. He'd noticed on the hospital's discharge summary that Asher was diagnosed with "periorbital ecchymosis"—a blackening around the eyes. The hospital doctors had viewed the injury as inconsequential, but Dr. Uscinski testified that it meant that "there's been a fracture somewhere." Dr. Uscinski asserted that Asher's brain scans after he was taken from the Cutro home showed one hematoma that wasn't days or weeks but "months old," and more recent blood that he believed wasn't a new injury but a "rebleed" of the original hematoma. This rebleed could have been caused, he said, by "skipping a child through a mall," "putting a child down for a nap," or "putting a child in a car seat."

Though Gasser did not ask Dr. Uscinski about the trial of British nanny Louise Woodward, in which Uscinski had also testified for the defense and propounded a similar theory, he did refer to that case and disparaged the neurologist's theory as "a courtroom diagnosis." Gasser pulled out an open letter published in a medical journal and signed by more than seventy doctors attacking the defense's medical evidence in the Woodward trial. He challenged Dr. Uscinski to produce anything at all from the medical literature to support his testimony. "There's no point in arguing the literature," Dr. Uscinski countered. "The literature says all kinds of things."

The verbal sparring may have been overshadowed by the visuals. The neurologist dramatized his testimony by showing the jurors a videotape of an operation he'd performed on the brain of an adult while he explained how it demonstrated the rebleeding he'd described.

Gasser seemed to be caught off guard by Dr. Uscinski's testimony and was not as well prepared as he'd been for the other defense witnesses. He considered calling the doctors who cared for Asher during his first weeks of life to rebut this new theory but decided not to dignify Dr. Uscinski's testimony with such a response.

The change Dr. Uscinsky's testimony had wrought on the defense's case was underscored the next morning when Doug Strickler, who had earlier hammered away at Catherine Maier, said in his closing statement that now— since Dr. Uscinski had made the shaking disappear—he owed Catherine Maier an apology. Both sides concluded with powerful, eloquent statements before the judge gave the case to the jury.

The first sign of trouble arrived four hours later, when the jury sent Judge Williams a note informing him that they were hopelessly deadlocked. The judge instructed them to try again; they did so until after 9:00 that evening, when he sent them home. The jurors returned the next morning and deliberated another six hours—for a total of more than eleven—after which their note told the judge that they'd been close but simply couldn't agree. Judge Williams acknowledged that the jury was hung and declared a mistrial.

Two days later a juror quoted in *The State* newspaper revealed that the jury's last vote was eleven to one for conviction. Commenting on Gail's testimony, the juror added: "She was the least credible of the whole shebang. She was evasive."

The next day the solicitor's office announced that Gail Cutro would be tried for a third time the following year.

———

The third trial—which Gasser promised would be the last—opened in June 2000. Most of the key players, including Judge Williams, were back. Two new lawyers sat beside Gasser at the state's table: Don Sorenson, who was Gasser's law clerk during the first trial, and Christine Sloan. Defense lawyers Doug Strickler and Beattie Butler were joined this time by April Sampson rather than Lee Coggiola.

There were two notable changes in the state's strategy: instead of calling the parents early, Gasser saved them for the end. And he was determined to counter Dr. Uscinski more effectively than he had the previous trial. He began early, eliciting from his expert witnesses testimony designed to rebut what Dr. Uscinski had offered at the last trial.

Most of the state's witnesses returned, with one exception. Dr. John Emery had died in a fire the month before the trial. But the jury still heard from him: The state introduced his taped testimony from Court TV's coverage of the second trial. Another surprise was Catherine Maier's announcement from the witness stand that she was the mother of a five-month-old baby boy named Jack. She was still in the Navy, and Asher was living with his father, who had custody.

The most dramatic change came from the defense. Gail Cutro had not impressed the first two juries, and her lawyers convinced her not to take the stand this time. This strategy carried its own risks, of course. Though jurors are instructed not to draw inferences from a defendant's decision not to testify, that doesn't mean they never do. Jurors can be left with a nagging question: What does she have to hide?

Defense attorney Doug Strickler, who had been effective during the previous trial, was even better this time. In the past, Gasser's knowledge of the case was a distinct advantage; now, for the first time, he was up against a lawyer whose knowledge and preparation rivaled his own.

During cross-examinations, Strickler continued to contest everything. This time, however, he countered Gasser's photographs, diagrams, and charts with plenty of his own. When he cross-examined the pathologist who performed the autopsy of Parker Colson, for example, he showed her a large photograph of a subdural hematoma and asked if she was sure she hadn't missed one in Parker. "They stand out like a sore thumb," he suggested and she agreed.

Later, when the defense called its expert pathologist, Dr. Joel Sexton, defense lawyer Beattie Butler handed him dozens of autopsy photographs of SIDS victims. These illustrated what the state had called petechial hemorrhages in brains, Dr. Sexton said, but he claimed they were merely examples of blood escaping from vessels during dissection.

Then Butler displayed a chart that, like Gasser's, depicted South Carolina dotted with red and blue circles. Only this one, based on Dr. Sexton's testimony, had *lots* of red dots. The defense, it appeared, had finally found a way to neutralize the state's most powerful exhibit.

Some of the best defense work took aim at the state's Munchausen syndrome by proxy evidence. Not only did Strickler and Butler (who handled much of the MSBP testimony) aggressively cross-examine every witness who raised the subject, later they introduced effective witnesses of their own. One was Dr. Matthew Koval, a psychiatrist and psychiatry professor in Charleston. Though Dr. Koval had never published or lectured on Munchausen syndrome by proxy or testified in court before, Butler led him through a cogent analysis in which he explained why the diagnosis didn't fit the facts of the case. There was no repeated pattern of injury to Parker Colson or to Ashlan Daniel, Dr. Koval pointed out, and Gail did not seem to seek attention from medical personnel.

Of the returning defense experts, Dr. Smialek again proved one of the most formidable. This time he was not even willing to admit that Asher had been shaken, testifying that he was now aware of an alternate diagnosis. When Gasser suggested he had conveniently edited his opinions to conform to Dr. Uscinski's, the pathologist steadfastly denied it.

When it was Dr. Uscinski's turn, he testified in considerably more detail than he had during the previous trial about Asher's medical condition. He'd uncovered evidence in the hospital charts, he testified, that showed Asher may have suffered a skull fracture during delivery and a seizure shortly after—perhaps more than one.

On cross, Gasser challenged Dr. Uscinski and then waited, sometimes more patiently than other times, while the neurologist turned his answers into long, argumentative disquisitions. Asked about shaken baby syndrome, Dr. Uscinski explained at great length why he didn't believe in the diagnosis. When Gasser protested that cases of confessed shakings have been repeatedly documented, Dr. Uscinski rejoined: "Not to my satisfaction."

Asked to present evidence from the medical literature to support his theory about the case, Dr. Uscinski, who declined to do so the previous year, responded this time by reading passages from five books. Together, he argued, they suggested that a subdural hematoma may result from an apparently normal birth, that sometimes such an injury may rebleed spontaneously, and that symptoms of such injuries are sometimes delayed by hours or even a month.

Gasser challenged these conclusions by reading the letter he'd read during the second trial, signed by the doctors who took issue with the defense's medical evidence in the Woodward trial. Dr. Uscinski dismissed the letter as the product of advocates. Referring to the books from which he'd constructed his own evidence, he added: "They didn't read their own textbooks."

The last evidence the defense presented was the 911 tape in which Gail sobbed as she told the dispatcher that Ashlan had stopped breathing. It was the only time the jury heard her voice, and it was an effective way to humanize her.

This time, Gasser called two witnesses to rebut Dr. Uscinski. The first was the neonatologist who attended Asher Maier in the hospital immediately following his birth. In the doctor's opinion, Asher never had a skull fracture or any other serious problems. He didn't believe that Asher had a true seizure in the hospital. He had some mild difficulty breathing, but it was not significant, the doctor testified.

The trial's final witness was pediatric ophthalmologist Dr. Linda Christmann, who had diagnosed hemorrhages behind Asher's eyes when he was hospitalized. Dr. Uscinski had suggested that these also resulted from rebleeding, but Dr. Christmann countered that the type of hemorrhage Asher suffered is caused by shaking and not by intercranial bleeding. Distinct characteristics make it easy for someone with her training to distinguish them, she testified.

The case went to the jury on Saturday, July 1, 2000. After little more than three hours, the jurors sent the judge a note saying they were unable to reach a verdict.

"You've heard almost three weeks of testimony," Judge Williams wrote back. "You've only been deliberating three and a half hours. Please keep trying." Later in the evening, the jury sent another note saying that they were deadlocked nine to three for conviction. The forewoman added that the three were immovable and one refused to discuss the matter further. Doug Strickler submitted that the judge shouldn't force them to continue deliberating when a mistrial appeared inevitable. Judge Williams sent them home for the night and asked them to resume in the morning.

The next day was Sunday, but the jurors continued their work. They deliberated all morning. A lunch break was called, then they were back at it in the afternoon. Finally, shortly before 3:00, they sent the judge a note. Following 12 hours of deliberations, they'd reached a verdict.

When everyone was back in the courtroom, they waited in stony silence. More than five years earlier the first trial had been held in this same room. The prosecutor had said this third trial would be the last. It had all come down to this.

Judge Williams asked the jury if they'd reached a verdict. They had. The jury had found Gail Cutro guilty of homicide by child abuse in the death of Parker Colson, and guilty of homicide by child abuse in the death of Ashlan Daniel. They found her not guilty of assaulting Asher Maier.

The verdict gave the judge wide discretion in sentencing. He could give Gail Cutro twenty years or he could sentence her to life. After hearing aggravating and mitigating circumstances from Johnny Gasser, Davis Daniel, Gary Colson, and Doug Strickler, Judge Williams sentenced Gail Cutro to life in prison for each conviction. She was returned to prison immediately; she would be eligible for parole after 10 years.

But still, it wasn't quite over. The next day a juror named Charles Miller contacted the defense lawyers with second thoughts. He'd been one of the three initial holdouts and had compromised, he said, only because he'd felt pressure to resolve the case and had believed a homicide by child abuse conviction would carry a light punishment. He pronounced himself "totally shocked by the sentence" and wished to help her lawyers secure Gail another trial.

He filed a sworn statement complaining of the pressure the judge placed on the jury, among other grievances. Courts rarely overturn convictions based on jurors' post-trial statements, however, and after seven years of trials and tribulation, South Carolina courts were not about to make an exception.

The defense, of course, appealed the conviction, so there was one more decision to await. The defendant's main argument was that by allowing the state to join the three cases against her and denying the defense request that she be tried separately for each, the judge had improperly stacked the deck.

The Supreme Court's decision came in August 2005. It was still a split decsion, but this time it was four–one. The court found that the cases were properly joined. The majority found a common scheme or plan in that "all three offenses are similar in kind, place, and character—each involves Shaken Baby Syndrome inflicted on an infant in the Cutros' daycare."

A decade after she was first convicted, Gail Cutro's long battle was finally over. Her conviction had been affirmed by South Carolina's highest court. She would spend the rest of her life in prison—unless and until a parole board decided otherwise.

In Whose Hands?

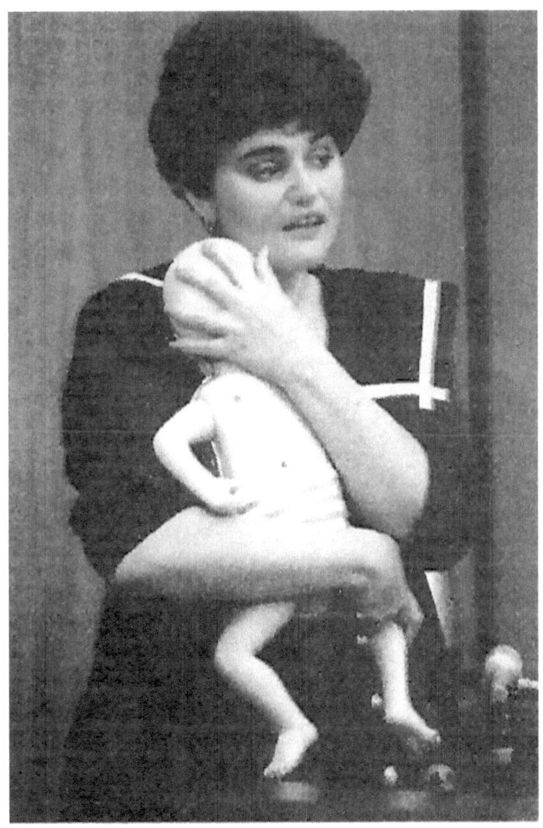

Gail Cutro holding a demonstration doll while she testifies during her trial in 1994. Courtesy of *The State*, Columbia, South Carolina.

72

—

Visiting Day

Gail Cutro was seated in the prison visiting room, which looked something like a high school cafeteria, with neat rows of Formica tables and plastic chairs. She was talking about the commingling of her marriage and business. It was February 1997, a little longer than two years after her first trial.

She was happy when Josh began working at the day care, she said. Even with the two of them together all day in confined quarters, she never felt claustrophobic. "We didn't need to be alone," she explained. Most couples reunite at the end of their respective days and feel disconnected, Gail pointed out. She and Josh didn't have that problem. Nor was there a sense of competition between them. Gesturing across the table toward her husband, Gail said simply: "He's the boss."

In person, Gail Cutro looked quite different from the woman whose image had dominated local television news during her trial. She wore no makeup, of course (it was against prison rules), and the weight she'd put on since her trial was not concealed even by the loose fitting khaki pants and top she wore. These looked vaguely military: the shirt had breast pockets and SCDC (for South Carolina Department of Corrections) was printed on the back. Her brown hair was no longer carefully styled. It was short, curly, and shapeless again.

On the other hand, during more than fifty hours of visits that stretched over six months, Gail was usually much more animated than she ever was in court. She revealed a pleasant, companionable side. She was often able to joke and laugh, demonstrating a good sense of humor. When she recounted painful events, her eyes often welled with tears, though she never actually cried.

Josh Cutro was always with her on visiting days. And even here, she deferred to him in deeds as well as words. When a visitor offered to buy her some cupcakes, she declined. Offered her choice from the vending machine instead, she finally settled on low-fat ginger snaps, which she didn't even eat. She preferred to feed cup cakes to Josh, literally holding them up to his mouth for bites. She did the same with the ginger snaps, then gave him the rest to take home.

Prison had toughened her, Gail observed. Before she had a cell to herself, she'd never lived alone and had never wanted to. But she'd learned in prison that she could survive.

Josh's world, on the other hand, seemed to have shrunk. He had no real friends, and his devotion to Gail sometimes bordered on desperation. He never missed a visit, even when he probably should have. On one visiting day he discovered a cyst near his tailbone. There was no opportunity to see a doctor, so he lanced it himself with a knife, then cleaned it in the shower. There was a lot of blood, but he stanched it with tissues that he stuffed in his shorts, and he was there when the prison doors opened.

As Josh told this story, Gail smiled proudly from across the table, raising her eyebrows and nodding her head. Her expression said: "This is one committed guy!"

Once in a while, though, Josh went a little too far—even for Gail. At one point Gail mentioned that she loves to write and diligently sends thank you notes whenever she receives gifts. Josh quickly jumped in, enthusiastically confirming Gail's prolific output. In fact, he added, she'd always been his "secretary."

Gail smiled a different smile this time. Josh continued, oblivious of his wife's expression, which seemed to say, "Give me a break!" When asked what she was thinking, however, Gail froze like a child caught muttering an obscenity under her breath. After a long silence she said in a meek tone, "Secretary?"

When Gail talked about the deprivations of prison, high on her list were family trips. She reminisced about her favorite roller coasters at Carowinds, a theme park near Charlotte, North Carolina, and at Six Flags in Atlanta. The Cutros visited those places often. Some couples take vacations to flee their children; she and Josh never went anywhere without them. During their entire marriage they never took a vacation or even a weekend trip alone. And during all that time Gail voluntarily spent a night away from Josh only once: Easter weekend 1994, when she accompanied an aunt who was visiting a daughter in

Washington, D.C. Gail felt deeply ambivalent and vacillated endlessly before she concluded that her family could manage for two days without her. The trip was wonderful, she acknowledged. Three years later she was able to describe virtually everything she did, every meal she ate.

It wasn't just the big things that evoked nostalgia. She missed movies they used to watch—favorites like *E.T.*, *Home Alone*, and *Raising Arizona*. She missed restaurants they frequented and stores where she shopped, particularly her favorite crafts store. She even had a friend send her a card purchased there, knowing that the smell would transport her back.

Most of all, Gail missed her beloved cats. Her cousin sent her clumps of their fur as a souvenir. She admired their independence, their swagger, their rebellious spirit. She liked the insouciant way they put themselves above their so-called masters, leaping onto the forbidden kitchen counter and dancing off before they could be caught—laughing in the face of authority.

———

When the subject turned from the Cutros' business relationship to the personal side of their marriage, Gail brought up another pattern. She fixed and Josh defended. That's how she says their marriage worked. When there was a problem within the family, Gail was the conciliator who solved it. She smoothed over squabbles between the kids or, at least as often, between Josh and the kids. A big part of her job, in fact, was keeping Josh happy. And often this was best accomplished by, to use Josh's own word, "spoiling" him.

When a problem from the outside world came knocking, Josh handled it. Whether it was a neighbor, a day care parent, or the police, his role was to act as the protector. He was the human shield who defended his wife from the individuals or forces that he believed were threatening her.

Though they tried to focus on the successes of this arrangement, over time they were unable to avoid the gaping failures. Gail, for instance, was never able to "fix" the tension between her husband and her mother. The subject came up often in these conversations.

And Josh? For him, every trip to see his wife was a fresh reminder of failure. It ate at him, like rust on iron. He talked incessantly about the day when Gail would come home. He vowed to have her back—even if he had to break her out.

Over many visits, which sometimes included family members, more patterns emerged. These went back to the beginning of Josh and Gail's relationship, and even earlier. They covered ground the trials never touched. And combined with other conversations, they raised questions—and provided answers—that the trials never could.

73

——

Backstory

One myth about a criminal trial is that it reveals the true character of the defendant. In reality, a defendant often appears in court in at least three distinct versions: one constructed by the prosecution, another by the defense, and one on which the jury settles—which may reflect one, both, or neither of the above. But no matter how long the trial, a great deal about the person is left out.

Though lawyers may put on a good show for the jury, privately they often see the defendant in terms less stark than the way they attempt to portray her in court. In the Cutro case, however, the contrast seemed as sincere as it was extreme. The defense saw Gail as a dedicated, caring woman who, even in prison, was more concerned about others than she was about herself. To the state she was a profoundly selfish person who managed to conceal her self-aggrandizing and murderous impulses beneath a veneer of respectability.

What is Gail Cutro really like? And how about Josh? (It doesn't seem possible to answer the first question without the second.)

At the time they were arrested, they looked very different from the two people pictured in their wedding album. The newlyweds in the photographs, who were sixteen years younger, were attractive and slender (even though Gail was nearly six months pregnant). Their hair was longer then: Josh's light brown locks spilled onto the shoulders of his tan wedding suit; Gail's pretty, brown hair flowed down the front of a floral-pattern dress, splashed with pink and green, that gathered discretely above her waist. He was eighteen, she was seventeen. It was the first relationship for each of them, and they'd only dated for fifteen months.

They started going out in April of their sophomore year at Airport High

School in West Columbia. Gail Hallman turned 16 that month; Josh Cutro had turned 17 in December. Even though Josh was a year older, he and Gail were in the same class—Josh claimed that his father simply enrolled him a year late. (Josh and Gail refused a request to release their school records.) Gail had had a serious crush on Josh beginning in the seventh grade, but he hadn't seemed to notice. He might never have noticed had it not been for Gail's brother Barry. When Barry Hallman was thirteen, he signed up for an after-school basketball program, and Josh, who was four years older and a pretty fair intramural player, was his team's coach. This coincidence gave Gail an opportunity to "bump into" Josh, who finally awoke from his slumber and saw a cute girl with a sweet smile who was almost as shy as he.

Gail's parents had separated, and her father, Harold Hallman, had moved out of the family's home. Barry took it especially hard. Even before Harold left, Barry could be a handful (as he was the first to admit). So he was the child most likely to test his mother's fortitude. Gail, on the other hand, had never been a problem. But she was the one who presented the unexpected challenge.

It seemed as though one day Gail had never been out with a boy, and the next she was spending all her time with one. Josh had his driver's license and access to a family car, and he seemed to be coming over all the time. Pat Hallman thought it was too much too soon.

Though the Hallmans were separated, they still spoke regularly, and they agreed that they needed to establish dating rules for their daughter. It was left to Pat to deliver the news to Josh. They could only date twice a week, she told him. If he wanted to go out with Gail on Friday and Saturday nights, all right. But during the week Gail needed to concentrate on her schoolwork.

Josh did not take it well. His own mother and father had been separated since he was ten, and neither had been much of a parent. Joe Cutro owned a restaurant in Columbia and had never spent much time at home. His wife, Frances, had been a waitress at the restaurant. She often left Josh with *her* mother, who also took care of a number of his cousins. As a result, Josh had had little experience with parental guidance—or, for that matter, adult supervision. He bristled at Pat Hallman's attempt to establish rules at this late date.

He did everything he could to circumvent her authority. And he was clever. Gail had been riding to school on the bus; Josh offered to drive her in his car. When he dropped her off in the afternoon, lots of times he hung around. He'd shoot baskets with Barry, or he'd just stay and chat. "When he was there, we tried to be polite to him," Pat remembered. "Sometimes we'd ask him to stay for a meal or something." But she recognized that he was taking advantage of her, bending the rules to suit himself. When she reminded him of her policy, he quickly grew defensive. "You don't think I'm good enough for her," he challenged. Pat insisted that it wasn't true. "That never entered my mind," she said. "I really didn't know anything." Her last remark referred to Josh's background, but she was also unaware that the relationship had grown serious.

When it dawned on Pat Hallman that Josh and Gail were making long-term plans, she quickly redoubled her efforts. "We did feel like that they were getting too serious and that he was seeing too much of Gail, and we wanted it to slow down," she explained. "We wanted her to go and finish school, and we wanted her to go on to college. You know, I got married when I was sixteen, and I thought I was grown, and I thought I just knew everything."

The end of the school year brought increased tension. The ostensible reason for Pat Hallman's policy (Gail's schoolwork) was gone, but she was even more eager to limit her daughter's dating. The Hallmans had recently bought a vacation cottage at Lake Wateree, about 60 miles from West Columbia. Despite their separation, Pat and Harold spent time there on weekends with the children. But Josh felt it was just another ploy to keep him from Gail.

Even the Hallmans' overtures of friendship left Josh suspecting ulterior motives. Harold had arranged a summer job for Josh at Anchor Continental, the factory where Harold was a manager. Josh only worked there a few weeks, but he wondered whether this, too, was designed to keep him occupied.

The simmering conflict finally boiled over one day when Josh took Gail to his grandmother's house. Josh's cousins were there, and what happened when Harold Hallman arrived to retrieve his daughter left a lasting impression. Harold knocked on the door, and a minute later Josh was on the porch arguing with him. It got loud, and the others came out to see what the commotion was. When Harold quietly told Gail to get in the car, Josh exploded. As was his custom by this time, he never used profanity. But cursing couldn't have sounded worse. Josh challenged his future father-in-law, asserting his right to see Gail whenever he wanted, regardless of her parents' wishes. Josh's own recollection parallels his cousins' but goes further. He recalls questioning Harold's manhood and daring him to throw the first punch. After Josh finished his tirade, Gail got in the car and left with her father.

When the summer ended and the couple began their junior year, nothing had been resolved. It seemed just a matter of time until the next confrontation. The only questions were where and when. The answers found their way into a criminal complaint. It turned out to be Pat Hallman's last stand against her future son-in-law.

Pat was home on November 19, 1976, when Josh arrived and asked to see Gail. She told him he couldn't see her. Josh refused to take no for an answer, and the conversation quickly escalated into more than an argument. Pat locked the door. Josh said he heard Gail screaming. "So I proceeded to tear the door to pieces," he said. "Gail's mother is standing there, you know, just shocked. And I grabbed Gail and said, 'Come on, let's go.'"

He drove a circuitous route (in case the cops were after him) and abandoned the car on a dirt road off the main highway. They walked back to Josh's mother's house, where the reception might have been warmer if the getaway vehicle they'd ditched hadn't been his mother's.

Meanwhile, Pat Hallman had indeed called the police. The couple avoided detection by shuttling back and forth between the homes of Josh's grandmother and one of his cousins. Eventually, though, they were caught, and Pat Hallman pressed charges. Josh was locked up in the county jail. A detective convinced Pat Hallman that unless she adopted drastic measures, her daughter would probably run away again, so she had Gail placed in a barracks-like facility for female delinquents located just behind the jail. Josh pleaded to the misdemeanor of "malicious destruction of property," paid a $100 fine, and was released, while Gail languished in detention.

At this point Josh's memory of what happened diverged from the Hallmans'. He remembered that he was determined to break Gail out, so he got word to her that he'd be outside in the early morning hours of December 11, which happened to be his eighteenth birthday. He met her at a window, which was unlocked, and he was able to raise it high enough for Gail to jump out. They celebrated Josh's birthday on a bus to Chicago, where Josh had relatives.

Pat Hallman remembered that Josh did, indeed, break Gail out of the facility, but they didn't leave for Chicago the same day. The couple went on the lam again, she said, until Josh's mother called Pat Hallman one night and told her she could come pick up Gail at her house. When the teens left for Chicago, it wasn't quite so dramatic in Hallman's version. Gail left for school that morning, but apparently never went in. She and Josh went to the bus station instead.

Eventually Gail called to let her mother know where she was. As soon as Pat Hallman knew how to contact her daughter, she began negotiating her child's return. It took six months, but in time the couple had reasons to be receptive: Josh had been arrested for shoplifting, and Gail was pregnant.

Besides, Pat Hallman had capitulated. Not only wouldn't she oppose the marriage, she promised to host the ceremony and reception at her house. Josh and Gail flew back to South Carolina in June 1977 and were married in the Hallmans' home on July 2. Afterward, Pat even drove them back to Chicago to pick up the possessions they'd left behind.

That drive was the first time Pat Hallman had ever been out of state, or farther from home than Charleston, and she was thrilled by the thought of seeing Lake Michigan. Yet, there was also the now-predictable conflict with her brand new son-in-law. They left South Carolina at night and drove straight through. Pat took the first leg of the long drive, and Josh was supposed to spell her. But when it came time to switch, Pat recounted with more than a trace of bitterness, Josh complained that he was too tired.

Two patterns were established from these earliest days of Josh and Gail's relationship. Number one: Josh was the protector. When Gail was in a bind, his job was to shepherd her to safety. It was just as they'd described it during visiting days in the prison. But in the eyes of some people who knew them well (or at least thought they did), there was a corollary to this rule. Josh was also the reason Gail was in danger in the first place. Some people came to believe that Josh was, in fact, the source of nearly all the serious trouble Gail experienced during her adult life.

The second pattern was the endless clash between Josh Cutro and Pat Hallman for control of Gail. The battles ebbed and flowed. Sometimes the ill will seemed to abate, but it never really did—it was just lurking beneath the surface.

74

Who Is Gail Cutro?

In preparing for the trials, the investigators and lawyers learned a good deal about Gail Cutro that was never introduced into evidence. Some of it, like the polygraph results, might have influenced the jury had they heard it. In fact, the polygraph examination was inadmissible precisely because the test is not considered scientifically reliable, and there is such a high probability that it would sway opinions.

Other evidence could have been introduced but was held back for strategic reasons. The defense didn't want to call any of the therapists who spent time with Gail because they didn't want to give the state the opportunity to paint her as mentally or emotionally disturbed. The prosecution's Munchausen evidence forced their hands to some extent in the second and third trials, but the defense lawyers did their best to use the witnesses they called economically, almost surgically—to lance the state's thesis and move on.

Yet, several therapists had a great deal of information about the personality of Gail Cutro. The therapist who spent the most time with her, by far, was Eve Powell, who from May 1993 until December 1994 spent more than thirty-five hours assessing Gail's mental health and providing therapy.

Powell declined to discuss these sessions or anything else about her client, even when Gail Cutro waived confidentiality and granted her permission. But Powell's notes and related documents revealed the drift of their conversations and provided a sense of their relationship over these tumultuous months.

Gail was initially evaluated at the Columbia Area Mental Health Center on April 29, 1993, having been referred by her physician. She complained that she'd been depressed since Parker Colson's death in January, adding that she visited his grave every day. Her lengthy list of reported symptoms included flashbacks, anxiety, and confusion. She said she cried frequently, had lost twenty pounds, had trouble sleeping, and, when she did manage to sleep, suffered from frequent nightmares.

The "social history" she provided afforded a glimpse of her past, although Powell apparently never explored this area with her. Gail's father left the family home—she didn't specify for how long—when she was fifteen. Her parents later reconciled. She referred to them as "very strict." She and her younger brother were close, she said. A quick inventory of her "mental status" revealed a depressed, tearful woman who was neat and generally well oriented, although subject to periods of confusion. She was of average intelligence, her insight was rated "fair," and she reported no hallucinations, delusions, or thoughts of homicide or suicide. The "diagnostic impression" was "major depression;" her strengths, a supportive family and a job; her needs, medication and therapy.

Gail also filled out a "Fee Discount Application" on which she listed total monthly expenses of $1,101. Under "Gross Family Monthly Income" she entered $1,000 for herself and nothing for her spouse, though the day care parents' sworn statements suggested it was easily more than twice that amount. Nonetheless, Gail qualified for the 99 percent fee discount, which meant that her cost for thirty minutes of individual therapy was $2.

She was assigned a psychiatrist, Dr. Robert Bank, for medication and evaluation. (Arrangements such as this are very common: A psychiatrist meets periodically with a patient to evaluate her progress and prescribe medication, while most of the treatment is provided by a therapist who is not an M.D., and usually cannot prescribe medicine.) Dr. Bank prescribed Elavil, an antidepressant Gail had taken a decade earlier when she was depressed after the birth of her third child, and asked her to return for further evaluation.

One week later Dr. Bank's notes described a woman transformed: "Feeling much better. Amazed at her progress. Sleeping well, feeling refreshed in AM. Another babysitter, on 4th mo. anniversary of [patient's] loss (5/4), suffered a SIDS death among the children she was caring for. [Patient] was able to respond helpfully, [with] comfort & info. to this friend. This altruistic gesture afforded comfort & hopefulness to her. She is now less despairing, feels she is able to 'make a difference.'"

Four days later Gail began her therapy with Eve Powell. The burst of sunshine from the previous session, however, was nowhere to be found in Powell's (uncorrected) notes: "Many feelings around SIDS death of child in her home. Much difficulty. Suicidal in March. Is connected to two other SIDS caregivers. Much [post-traumatic stress disorder] around seeing baby. Is afraid of letting go of the pain. Started babysitters support [group] for SIDS death children. Wanted to deal with those of feelings guilt of not being the one who fed him that morning. Describes the feeling of puzzle dreams to put pieces together & make child's life come back."

The following week they homed in on Gail's grief, the topic that would dominate the vast majority of their sessions. Gail reported she was still struggling with the death of Parker Colson five months earlier. "She was unable to grieve loss of baby (closed casket)," Powell wrote. "Was not able to be close to him the last day he was alive. Many issues of anger around situation, over which she had no control occurring. [Work] done to help client say things she needs to say to child."

During the next session Gail voiced her fear of causing the Colsons pain. She was also finding it difficult to return Parker's possessions to his parents. "Babies are a part of her identity," Powell went on. "Is taking on a new child.

Has associations entire belief system being invalid since a child could be lost in her care."

In mid-June, Gail was "working to develop 'trust in babies' again." She was "now aware she cannot stop SIDS process." She was also troubled by the feeling that some people were avoiding her.

Then Asher Maier was hospitalized. Powell's notes indicated that she counseled Gail during a lengthy telephone call four days later and again, briefly, the following day. They also suggest that Gail had quickly assigned blame for Asher's injury. "Has had new situation recently," Powell wrote eight days after Asher was taken to the emergency room. "Is having an easier time dealing with old [situation]." Gail was suffering again from post-traumatic stress disorder, Powell continued, "after discovering that a child she had been keeping 3 [weeks] had shaken baby syndrome from abuse by mother who previously had a child removed from custody."

When Dr. Bank saw her in July, Gail seemed to be progressing well. But in August the psychiatrist wrote: "[Patient] struggling with anniversary of child's death. . . . [S]till sleeping poorly and have [nightmares] with death as theme." Later in the month came the automobile accident in which Josh's sister was killed. And then, on September 9, Ashlan Daniel died.

"Issue of distress around SIDS death in her home," Powell wrote the next day. "Family was visited in their home to help them in their crisis. Client distressed & in shock. Spouse upset. Work done to help debrief & stabilize."

One week later Powell noted: "Client is very distressed over how some people are responding." The following week Dr. Bank added: "Much self doubt and blame. Some passive suicidal thoughts. Very anxious about investigation."

The tone of the therapy sessions began to change in October. The focus increasingly shifted to the investigation, and Powell emerged not just as a therapist but as one of Gail's defenders. "Family suffering from chronicity of investigation," she wrote on October 1, making the inquiry sound like an ailment.

In another note that seemed to be from the same period (although the date is illegible), Powell said that she consulted Dr. Bank "about client's harassment by police to answer more questions." (She went back and squeezed in "alleged" before "harassment.") Powell then "consoled" Gail by phone. Her choice of words here seemed particularly revealing. Earlier she'd counseled; now she consoled.

A week before the day care was shut down, Powell found her client more assertive. "She is resolved that she is in the right & that her innocence will come through." Three weeks later both Powell and Dr. Bank found Gail doing remarkably well. "Client much improved," wrote Powell. "Not as depressed. Feels more in control. [Medication] is controlling symptoms. She has resolved a number of problems since last visit."

This was Powell's last entry before SLED subpoenaed the file. Her final word was her January 1995 affidavit supporting Gail's bond appeal, when she wrote in part:

> [Gail Cutro's] responses and reactions both with me and with her family during intensive interactive therapy have indicated the antithesis, or opposite, of a profile of a woman who would harm a child. She was observed to be gentle in nature, and parented her own children well, supporting them in their involvement in appropriate community activities
>
> Her reactions in therapy were spontaneous and transparent and were clearly not the reactions, responses and dialogue of a perpetrator.

———

Another therapist who had contact with Gail Cutro was defense attorney Thom Neal's friend Dr. Selman Watson, who evaluated Josh and Gail when they hoped to reopen the day care. (Trained as a psychologist, Dr. Watson has a Ph.D., not a medical degree.) Dr. Watson saw Gail for several hours on only one occasion, during which he administered a series of tests and interviewed her. The Cutros waived confidentiality and gave him permission to discuss his conclusions.

When Dr. Watson sat down in August 1997 to review his sessions with the Cutros three years earlier, he was in the process of moving into a small office across the street from the courthouse in downtown Columbia. He hadn't managed to unpack many possessions. In addition to the desk, bookshelves, couch, and chairs, there were only five framed diplomas on a wall, a telephone with an answering machine, and a solitary book on a shelf titled Clinical Assessment of Malingering and Deception.

Watson was a trim man with short brown hair and a mustache. Though he was only forty-six at the time of the trial, there was a no-nonsense look in his blue eyes that suggested a man who had seen a lot of things he would have preferred not to.

It wasn't hard to understand why. He had spent fifteen years as a forensic psychologist at a state psychiatric hospital. His job was to examine patients admitted to the hospital with signs of acute mental illness and to report to the probate court whether they should be released or retained. In this capacity he had examined thousands of individuals from all walks of life.

"When you get 220 admissions a month to a psychiatric inpatient facility," he said, "you see the whole gamut of people and the tricks they try to employ to be deceptive. I mean, I've seen it all."

In his private practice he frequently testified in family court, often hired by DSS to examine parties involved in domestic cases that included custody disputes. When Thom Neal was appointed to represent a child, he would sometimes call in Dr. Watson to evaluate his client. That was how they became acquainted.

Dr. Watson said that when he interviewed and tested Josh and Gail Cutro, he was viewing them "from a pretty naïve position"—that is, he didn't know much about them. He knew that there had been two SIDS deaths in their home within nine months, and that in itself struck him as suspicious. He knew that there was a criminal investigation into those deaths. And he knew that Thom Neal believed in his clients.

In his report, the psychologist concluded that Josh and Gail had been truthful and that neither had the "capacity or sophistication necessary to construct 'alibis' that match so well. No contradictions in their remarks were ever noted or even mild discrepancies that one might pursue."

One reason he was convinced, he said, was that Gail impressed him as straightforward and sincere. "When I interviewed this lady, she had very good eye contact with me. All of her nonverbal behaviors seemed very genuine to me. She didn't look away, she didn't look down."

There were other compelling reasons to believe her. "When Gail Cutro was talking about these deaths, she had a huge reaction to this experience. She told me that it was almost impossible for her to go to the grocery store afterwards, and leave the children, because she had these thoughts that maybe one of them might die while she was gone.

"Anxiety is not only reflected in the way a person feels. Anxiety can be reflected in the quality of your thoughts, as well. And I can still see the way she was appearing in my office. Lots of tears, very shaken by this. I don't think you can fabricate that."

Dr. Watson's impressions of Josh were quite different. "I was just struck by the difference in their presentations. I mean, Josh seemed remorseful to me. There were some tears. But his eye contact was poor, looking at the ground.

"I said, 'How do you think this could have happened, Josh?' And he says, 'Well, maybe the devil did it.' I just wasn't as impressed with his presentation as I was with Gail Cutro's. . . . I think for years he was emotionally dependent on Gail. I would have thought, or predicted, he would have a very difficult time functioning without Gail, and I think initially he did. I think he really struggled there for a while, and he probably continues to struggle to some degree, because I think he was very bonded to her.

"But they're both sort of passive creatures, maybe a little schizoid, sort of socially detached. Neither one are imbued with a wealth of social skills. Neither one of them seem to have a lot of real strong friendships. Sort of withdrawn, socially withdrawn. Not crazy, not psychotic, not neurotic, no obvious personality disorders other than the dependency."

Dr. Watson had based his conclusions in part on the consistency of the Cutros' accounts. As the conversation progressed, however, it became clear that he was unfamiliar with much of the evidence presented during the first trial (the second and third were yet to come). And some of that evidence—along with other information not introduced during the trial—contradicted what the Cutros had told him.

For example, during the trial both Josh and Gail testified that the first one to notice that Parker wasn't breathing was Josh. But Dr. Watson said, and wrote in his report, that it was Gail who made the discovery. Nor was he alone; pathologist Beverly Daniel wrote the same thing in her autopsy report.

There were other contradictions. If Gail was as traumatized by these deaths as she appeared to be, and as anxious when caring for subsequent infants as she said she was, Dr. Watson wondered why she didn't limit her service to toddlers. There was also a reaction he'd expected to find but hadn't. "You know what was missing? And I've never shared this with anybody. One thing missing from both of these individuals in regards to their exterior is any sense of anger or outrage of being implicated in these deaths."

Still, in his mind Gail and the alleged crimes were incompatible. "Gail Cutro, if I had her in the hospital, I would probably give her a dysthymic disorder diagnosis. It's not major depression. Dysthymic disorder is sort of a low-grade depressive neurosis. It's what you see in the mill villages in the South. You know, these people that just have kind of a flat affect, don't look excited about too much, just seem kind of a low-grade depression that stays with them all the time because of their bare existence."

How did he think she'd acquired this condition? "I don't know, unless it was the marriage. . . . But she just gives me the impression—when I saw her, and when I saw her picture in the paper associated with the trial—that she's been kind of dysthymic most of her adult life, as if her existence has been very staid, very monotonous.

"It just makes you wonder, then: 'How can I inject some excitement into my life? How can I shake things up a bit?'"

Dr. Watson was conscious of neither the irony nor the grim pun in his last remark. Nor did he believe that Gail "shook things up" by her own doing. In fact, as he listened to descriptions of some of the evidence, he began directing his gaze elsewhere. Sometimes he did so obliquely, almost demurely. "There were two adults in the home," he said at one point. Eventually, however, he spelled out his suspicions.

During his evaluations Dr. Watson had, to a large extent, taken Josh and Gail at face value. His opinion of Gail was not drastically altered by a recitation of the evidence that convinced the jury to convict her. But new information about Josh drew a swift response. Josh had claimed that he'd graduated from high school when he hadn't, and he'd claimed that he didn't have a criminal record when he did. But a larger issue, of which Watson was also apparently unaware, was the falsified tax return.

"I'm becoming real suspicious," he said when he heard about that testimony. It was another "red flag" he associated with Josh, along with breaking down the Hallmans' door and breaking Gail out of the Youth Detention facility.

Comparing Josh and Gail, Dr. Watson said: "He has a history of violence. I mean, he broke down a door. She doesn't have a history of violence, that we know of. I mean, there are a couple of red flags in his background and none in hers. So, that's a basis for comparison, anyway."

Furthermore, he pointed out that Josh had demonstrated a propensity to act impulsively, especially when he was angry—as when he spirited Gail away from her mother's home. And the act of shaking a baby such as Asher Maier—if, in fact, Asher was shaken in their home—suggested to Dr. Watson an impulsive act by an angry person.

As for Josh's taking the stand and claiming in a manner that strained credulity that Gail never touched either Parker Colson or Ashlan Daniel on the days that they died, and that if anyone had killed them, he was the logical one to have done so, Dr. Watson offered a surprising interpretation. Although the psychologist had previously argued in his report and in the interview that neither Josh nor Gail was sophisticated enough to concoct a story and present it consistently and convincingly, now he suggested that perhaps Josh was sharper than he'd acknowledged. Perhaps Josh was using reverse psychology on the stand and only made it appear that he was desperately trying to save his wife when his real intention was to deflect suspicion from himself.

If that scenario sounds strained, Dr. Watson was not the only person whose questions about Gail led to deeper ones about Josh. He was not even the only person who suggested that Josh Cutro had an ulterior motive in testifying as he did. A one-time neighbor of the Cutros would later propound the same theory—and offer cogent reasons for believing it.

75

What About Josh?

One night after Dr. Selman Watson offered his theories, "John" and "Judy Mason" sat at their kitchen table and talked about the woman who was once their good friend. It was August 1997. They were confused and ambivalent—both about Gail and about speaking publicly. (They requested that their names be changed for the protection of their family.)

Judy's feelings were especially complicated. Her family had lived across the street from the Cutros. Judy and Gail both had an interest in crafts, and on several occasions they shared a booth at a crafts show. Judy had considered Gail her closest friend for the better part of four years.

What made the situation even more emotional is that Judy had started a family day care business before Gail and had encouraged her friend to do likewise. She'd urged Gail to register with the state and wrote a glowing letter as one of Gail's three references. Over the years Judy referred parents to Gail, recommended her as a substitute when she herself was away, and even left her own children with the Cutros during a week-long business trip.

John worked long hours in the medical profession and didn't have nearly as much contact with the Cutros. Still, he considered them good neighbors and friends. They were the kinds of neighbors who, he felt, would have done anything he asked of them. Like his wife, he isn't a particularly suspicious person. If someone had told him in advance that Gail Cutro would be *charged* with murder, much less convicted, he would have laughed at the very idea.

The Masons spent a great deal of time before, during, and after the trial puzzling over the entire affair, struggling to reconcile their image of the woman they knew with their image of a killer. It was one of the most profoundly disturbing experiences of their lives. Judy, a deeply emotional person, needed to understand with her heart; John, more of a rationalist, needed to understand with his mind.

Despite the difference in their levels of education, the Cutros and the Masons had a good deal in common. John and Judy were a year older than Josh and Gail, respectively. They first met when they all lived in the downstairs units of duplexes in a neighborhood just across Interstate 26 from downtown Irmo. The Masons arrived first, in the summer of 1986. They found one feature of their new neighborhood disappointing: There were few kids. Their daughter, "Cheryl," was seven, and there was no one for her to play with. The arrival of the Cutros, who moved into a unit across the street a few months later, fixed that. Though the Cutros' oldest child, Joshua, was two years older than Cheryl, they hit it off immediately. Joshua was a shy, sweet beanpole of a boy, and the two became fast friends. Cheryl was soon a fixture in the Cutro home, and it was this relationship that first brought the families together.

Though Cheryl wasn't capable of processing all that she saw at that time, after Gail was indicted she and her parents scoured their collective memories for clues. She was eighteen on the night her parents sat down to discuss the Cutros publicly for the first time, and they invited her to join them to add her perspective.

Over the course of an intense, lengthy interview that ran into the early morning hours, the Masons described the anguish they felt as they wrestled with the sometimes conflicting demands of loyalty, civic responsibility, and personal integrity. And they explained the reasoning that led to their tentative conclusions.

The first time John and Judy suspected something was amiss at the Cutros' day care was after Asher Maier was injured. Parker Colson's death had been a shock, but it did not strike them as suspicious. Judy's sister-in-law had had a baby die of SIDS in *her* family day care several years earlier, so she knew that such things happened. After Parker died, in fact, Gail asked Judy how long it had taken her sister-in-law to "get over it." Judy wasn't able to answer because her sister-in-law refused to discuss the experience—and never reopened her day care.

But Asher Maier's injury was different. It wasn't the injury per se that suggested to the Masons that something was wrong. When Gail told them about Catherine Maier's background, they were inclined to accept her as the presumed perpetrator. It was the rest of Gail's explanation that raised their suspicions.

It rang false. More than four years later, it was difficult for the Masons to remember details. They recalled Gail telling them that she'd had to speak forcefully before Catherine agreed to take Asher to the doctor. This struck them as unlike Gail, who in their view was too deferential to do this. "Now, she might have said that the baby seemed odd," John explained. "But to insist somebody do some course of action? That's not Gail."

What stood out most clearly in their minds wasn't the details but the delivery. First, Gail and Josh came over to their house. That in itself was highly unusual. By this time the families were living several miles apart. Judy and Gail still spoke on the phone occasionally, but they rarely saw each other. Gail seemed to have made a special trip to discuss the matter. And the story she told struck both John and Judy as "reconstructed" and "rehearsed."

"Gail pretty much spoke off the top of her head, always," John said. "I mean, that was my impression, was that she never considered what she might say. She just said what came to her mind. And this was the first time that what she said struck me like she might look at Josh and say, 'Did I get that right?'"

Further heightening the Masons' sense of artificiality, Gail repeated the story two or three times. John remembered that she was "fumbling with her hands"—reminiscent of what the polygraph operator described after Gail failed the test—and there was a vacant look in her eyes, as though she were staring at something a half-mile away.

"It just struck me as strange," John continued. "I had no suspicion of anything going on in her family, no idea of abuse. It wouldn't have occurred to me to think, you know, maybe she shook the baby, or maybe Josh shook the baby. It just struck me like, that's strange, the way she said that, and all that she just said. What was *that* all about?"

Judy had already heard the story over the phone, and although she couldn't pinpoint the differences four years later, she remembered thinking that details had been altered. "That's what struck me. It just wasn't quite the same. Gail had gone into victim mode by then." In Judy's view, Gail's "victim mode" was not the same at this point as it had been after Parker Colson died. With Parker, "it was, 'Oh, my goodness, how am I going to get past this?' With Asher, it was directing the focus away from herself"—and toward Catherine Maier. "It was a real contrast there."

The death of Ashlan Daniel changed everything. SIDS was rare, but there was no reason to suspect foul play in Parker's death. The second death, however, was another matter. Though he never tried to calculate the precise odds, John believed that this was more than a coincidence. His background in science told him so. "What I thought was, something is going on there. That's not random. It's beyond the point where—you know, wow, what [bad] luck!"

Judy's reaction to the news had nothing to do with statistics. Again, it was all about the way it was delivered. Judy was shopping in a crafts store when Gail walked up to her and announced, "It happened again."

"*What* happened again?"

"Another baby died."

The rest of the story came out in a jumble, right there in the store. Judy asked what she'd done, and Gail said she'd panicked.

"What did Josh do?"

"He wasn't there." Gail went on to describe how Josh administered CPR while she called 911. Judy wasn't sure how or when Josh suddenly appeared, but the way Gail narrated the story was as disturbing to Judy as the details.

"There was something about her that was completely different," Judy said, choosing her words deliberately. "She looked really frightened. There was agitation in the look, too, that I had never seen before." Judy found the whole experience highly unsettling. She didn't want to have this conversation with this person in this place. And at that moment "Gail did something that she'd never done to me before. She was like in my face, you know? In my personal space." Remembering that Gail's mother had been with her when she'd first approached, Judy began backing up and glancing around the store, saying, "Where did your mother go?"

Though she extricated herself from the store, Judy did not abandon her friend. She called later to offer advice. Sounding more frightened than ever, Gail predicted: "They're going to think I did this." Judy tried to support her friend by issuing a call to action. "Gail, why don't you be aggressive and see what happened? You know, you've got cats in the house. Were the cats in the crib with the babies? If your area has a higher ratio of SIDS, find out why. Get on the ball and find out what's going on."

But the defense the Cutros offered during the trial was riddled with lies, according to the Masons. They knew that Gail had gotten into the day care business shortly after Judy, not fourteen years earlier. They knew that "time out" was *not* the sole means of discipline in the Cutro home. And they'd heard Gail give different accounts of the events concerning all three children.

Worse in some ways than the lies and deceptions were the unanswered questions. How could Gail see Ashlan Daniel lying there, not breathing, and do nothing? That was something Judy just couldn't comprehend.

"I just began to feel like, I don't know this person anymore," said Judy, shaking her head, pain etched in her face. "And I felt about this big"—she spread her thumb and forefinger a quarter of an inch. "I mean, I felt like a traitor, because this is my friend. I was probably her closest friend for, you know, at least four years. I ought to be there for her, but I don't know *how* to be there for her.

"And I felt like I was finding out things that I never knew, that I was having a really hard time digesting and understanding." She paused, struggling with her emotions. "I feel like somebody I know—and loved very much—died. I really do."

As much as John and Judy learned about Gail before and during the trial, they learned at least as much about Josh—and a good deal of it came from their own daughter. Convinced that the Cutros were trying to cover something up, John was by no means persuaded that they were covering for Gail. When he tallied what he knew about Josh and what he knew about Gail, he found many reasons to advance a theory similar to Dr. Selman Watson's.

Gail had always impressed the Masons as gentle, shy, and lacking in self-esteem. None of them can recall *ever* seeing her angry. In fact, they can't remember hearing her say something negative about anybody. As far as lashing out at children, Gail couldn't even discipline her own. "I never saw Gail discipline her children," said Judy. "It was always, 'Wait till your father gets home.'"

Though her children often ignored Gail's threats, they responded when she invoked Josh's name. "Gail told me that the children were afraid of their father," Judy reported. Her daughter Cheryl said she'd seen it herself.

One time Joshua made a "smart" remark in front of his father, Cheryl recalled. It was a stupid comment but, in her view, fairly innocuous. But Josh grabbed the youngster with one meaty hand and pinned him up against the wall by his throat. "I mean, he literally had Joshua by the throat up in the corner, on the wall, and I'm—you know, my jaw dropped to the floor, because had my parents ever done that to me, I would have had a heart attack right then and there."

Josh's preferred method of discipline, Cheryl continued, was the heavy leather belt he sometimes wore. Though Cheryl never saw him use it, she'd seen him take it off, and the fear in the children's eyes when he brandished it told her that it was more than an idle threat. "There's only so many times you can threaten and not act before it loses its power," she said.

Around adults, her mother noted, Josh was often remote. Judy's first memory of him was sitting in his La-Z-Boy, glued to the tube. Right from the start, well before Judy was a regular visitor from across the street, Josh barely acknowledged her existence. Only a handful of times did he deign to interact. At best, she felt, he "tolerated" her. That was why Judy was surprised that he came over with Gail to talk about Asher's injury.

John thought of Josh as someone who was as aggressive as Gail was meek. "I'm not somebody who's intimidated by people. But he struck me as somebody who intimidates people. I don't mean just because he's big, and he can be an intimidating sort of presence, but the way he would make eye contact was very, almost aggressive.

"But he never was aggressive toward me," John hastened to add. "Never in the least bit hostile toward me. So, I mean, it's just an impression."

Josh could also be extremely defensive, John observed. At times he seemed to have a chip on his shoulder, as if he were daring John—or anyone—to try to pull rank on the basis of, say, a superior education. He liked to challenge people, and he wouldn't back down when challenged himself.

Yet, these very qualities seemed to make him a valuable ally. As John put it: "He was the kind of guy you want on your side." John and Judy also thought of Josh as "protective"—especially around children. That was one reason they felt comfortable leaving Cheryl and her sister with the Cutros when they went on their trip.

Ironically, Judy discovered Josh's protective side when he actually hurt one of her children. He was throwing a ball around with Joshua and Cheryl when he and Cheryl, who was then eight, collided. Cheryl's collarbone was broken. "And he was really upset that Cheryl got hurt," Judy recalled. "I mean he, like, ate concrete. His face was really torn up from trying to take the brunt of the fall, so that he didn't land on her. And I just remember looking at him, and I thought, 'Well, you look like you caught the rough end of it.'"

When Josh extended himself, he could also be fun to socialize with, John said. Not that the couples ever went out together. As far as John could tell, Josh and Gail had few friends and rarely went anywhere without their children. But when John and Judy visited and were chatting, Josh could be quite entertaining. He was especially adept, John said, at telling funny stories that featured his conflicts with people.

Having said all that, John was still convinced that two children were killed in the Cutros' day care. And the only explanation that made sense to him was that Josh was responsible. "We were convinced that Gail was too gentle a person to—unless there was some real dark side of her that showed no evidence—"

"And that she never knew," Judy threw in.

John settled back in his chair and proceeded to explain his theory slowly and rationally. "My take on the whole thing is that she did a fine job with day care. Was compassionate to her own kids. Compassionate to the kids that we saw her with. We referred kids over to them. We allowed our children to stay with them. I mean, she had every evidence of being a loving and kind person.

"When Josh comes into the picture in day care, suddenly a child dies of 'SIDS.' Another one is shaken. A second one dies of—'SIDS.' Some adult or child deliberately took the lives of two kids. I can't see it any other way, from what I know of the pathology reports and the testimony of experts. Which I took with a grain of salt and, you know, I was skeptical. But I don't think any of that could have been fabricated.

"And believing that Gail couldn't do those things, and knowing that Josh was a very controlling, very intimidating person, my take would have been that Gail didn't have anything to do with it, that she did what he said. If he said, 'Go call the pediatrician,' that's when she went to call the pediatrician. If he said, 'Go call 911 now,' that's when she called 911.

"If the baby's screaming and fussing, and he's in the room with the baby, and then the baby shuts up, he says, 'The baby's sleeping fine and is breathing fine, and I'm going to the school now. Make sure you get the child out of the bed in seventeen minutes.' I envision her in there in seventeen minutes, finding the dead baby.

"I never heard any testimony that would suggest that Josh wasn't there when the baby fell asleep. What keeps coming up was that Josh wasn't there when it failed to wake up.

"And then this cockamamie story he makes up about, you know, 'You should be looking at me, because I was the only one who touched the child that day.' I mean, I think that's Josh in more control. He's doing this protector role.

"But who's he fooling?" John asked, gesturing with his hands and then placing them carefully on the table. "He's a smart man. He knows darn well that the absurdity of the positions he took completely discredited what he said, and everybody knew that what he was saying was a lie. I saw it on TV. I could tell it was a lie."

"He drove away the possibility that it was him," his daughter Cheryl interjected, "just because he tried so blatantly to say that it was him, and was obviously lying. Everyone knew he was lying. The people he was trying to lie to knew it was all a lie. So he knew he wasn't fooling anyone."

"And it would strike him as kind of a funny joke," added her father, speaking more slowly as he relished the irony of what he was saying, "that he would actually be telling the truth. That's his little twist that he's got in: that he'd be telling the truth when he says, 'No, you should be looking at me.'"

76

The Barfields and the Cutros

The Masons and Dr. Selman Watson were not the only people who wondered if the jury convicted the wrong person. The same thought occurred to a number of Gail's supporters, several of whom were familiar with Josh's temper. But neither the supporters, nor Dr. Watson, nor the Masons knew much about his background. Few people did.

Among those few were two of Josh's first cousins and his stepbrother. And they wondered about Josh's role themselves.

Josh Cutro's mother, Frances Barfield Cutro, was the youngest of five children. At the time of her daughter-in-law's first trial, she was fifty-eight and the only one of the siblings still alive. And like her two sisters and two brothers before her, Frances was an alcoholic, according to Josh's stepbrother, Jody Barfield, and his cousins, sisters "Jane" and "Suzanne" (who asked that their names be changed). Frances and her siblings, they said, were troubled people who bred more of the same. For example, Josh's uncle, Charlie Barfield, was imprisoned for manslaughter. The details are sketchy. Jody Barfield heard that his uncle killed a Black man who supposedly spit on him. Josh heard he shot one of his customers while tending bar in Chicago. Charlie might have been convicted of murder but for the efforts of his lawyers, and one of them, according to Josh, was Henry Kirkland (Wes Kirkland's father).

The woman who raised Frances, Charlie, and the other siblings (including Jane and Suzanne's mother) was Josh's grandmother, Trannie Barfield, who was supposedly named for the train that was noisily passing by the house as a midwife ushered her into the world. Trannie's life, like the lives of several of her progeny, was scarred by violence—most notably when she witnessed the death of her father. As Jane and Suzanne heard it, in 1919 sixteen-year-old Trannie and her ten brothers and sisters were eating breakfast in the family dining room. Her father began walking around the table, bidding his children goodbye. Nobody understood what he was doing until he put a gun to his head and blew his brains out. The children were convulsed in shock, but their mother insisted that they finish their breakfast. So they sat at the table and ate while their father's blood drained onto the floor. Trannie herself told her granddaughters this story, which became part of the lore of a monumentally dysfunctional family.

Trannie was in her mid-to-late twenties when she married Joe Barfield. She told Jane and Suzanne that it was a happy match. The couple had five children, including twins, in rapid succession. Then, one night Joe and some buddies went out drinking and their car skidded off the road and hit a telephone pole. Joe, who wasn't driving, was the only one killed. He was thirty-four.

In that second violent moment, Trannie's life was again altered forever. She never remarried. In the wake of her grief came the realization that she was now saddled with the responsibility of raising five young children alone. She had no choice but to work in the same cotton mill where Joe had worked.

She was a single parent in need of day care before an industry had grown to supply it. (In the United States, child care only began to be institutionalized during World War II, when many women went to work to support the war effort.) Trannie had few options. While she was at work, the children were left to fend for themselves. The disastrous results could have been a case study demonstrating the vital importance of reliable day care.

Trannie's one stroke of good fortune was that a friend literally gave her a house to live in. It was in this house that her children grew up—insofar as they grew up at all. Later, quite a few of her grandchildren ended up living there as well. Neglected as children, Trannie's brood turned into neglectful, and sometimes abusive, parents. Trannie's reward—or penance—for her first round of parenthood was a second opportunity. She raised several of her grandchildren, including Jane, Suzanne, and Josh.

Jane considered Trannie her only parent and referred to her as "Mama." Jane's father abandoned the family before Jane was one, and her mother was never around. Where was her mother living at that time? "I haven't a clue," Jane confessed. "I know she would come and get me every now and then, and she'd take me maybe once't a month to go and have my hair done with her when I was a little girl. I loved her like a aunt. My grandmother was my mother."

Jane's mother made an attempt to raise only one of her children—a son she had by another man many years after Jane was born. But she never stopped having children. In addition to Jane, Suzanne, and their half-brother, she had six more babies that she literally gave away. Jane and Suzanne, who is five years older, recall hearing many discussions about the children over the years, though they have no idea what became of them.

Eventually, Jane and Suzanne's mother left the Columbia area and moved north to Greenville, where, Jane says, she "supposedly remarried" and had the son she raised. She met a mysterious and possibly violent end at forty-three. She reportedly died in her sleep of natural causes, but when Suzanne talked to the local coroner, he told her "she looked like somebody had beat the hell out of her." When Suzanne questioned the man with whom her mother had been living, he said, "No, she died of a brain hemorrhage." Though Suzanne took this to be a denial of the coroner's statement, it was actually nothing of the kind. In any event, the cause of death was never determined. The case was closed without an autopsy or an investigation.

In their early years, Jane, Suzanne, and their brother were often left alone (as their parents had been) while Trannie went to work. But Trannie retired on disability in her early sixties, after working in the mill for some thirty years, and thereafter stayed home.

Trannie's awareness of her earlier shortcomings as a parent led to an altered approach the second time around. "Mama was a good woman," Jane said of her grandmother, who died in 1982. "Very strict. Not trusting at all. She tried to raise my sister and my brother and I different, I think, than she did her own five because all five of them seemed to turn out so bad." She established rules and sometimes administered an old-fashioned whipping when the children disobeyed. "Which nowadays would be, I guess, child abuse," Jane said, "but I see now by the things I did I deserved it."

The children who turned out the best were the ones who spent the most time with Trannie. The ones who landed in trouble spent more time under their mothers' supervision—which usually meant no supervision at all. Several from this second generation grew to be productive citizens, including Jane. Though she married when she was young, and many predicted a quick divorce, at the time of Gail's first trial Jane had been married for more than thirty years and had a good relationship with her husband and children. She had also held down jobs in various fields. She gave much of the credit for her stability to her grandmother and her husband.

Josh's mother, Frances, was not the absent parent Jane's mother had been. But she wasn't the most attentive one either, as Josh himself was quick to agree. Josh, it turned out, was actually her third child. Her first was Leon ("Jody") Barfield, born three years before Josh, when Frances was nineteen. Jody said that his father was a married man with whom Frances had had an affair. A year or so after Jody was born, Frances married a jockey. But that marriage ended even before Frances gave birth to the child it produced. Following the pattern of her older sister, she gave the baby away. Suzanne and Jane recalled that Henry Kirkland arranged for this child's placement and actually came to the house with his secretary and picked her up. (Through his son Wes, Henry Kirkland acknowledged that he had represented Frances Barfield, but he declined to comment on questions involving adoptions, citing his duty to maintain confidentiality. He also acknowledged that he represented Josh's uncle, Charlie Barfield, but denied that he defended him in a murder trial.)

Not long afterward, Frances met Salvatore ("Joe") Cutro. Information about Joe Cutro's background is also full of gaps. He was born in Italy in 1910, and he apparently grew up in Sicily. When he emigrated, he moved first to New Jersey and then to South Carolina. Along the way he acquired a wife and two daughters, but his wife reportedly died in a fire—when and where isn't clear. By the time he began seeing Frances Barfield, who worked as a waitress in his restaurant, he was forty-eight and she was twenty-two. Jane remembers sitting at the supper table in Trannie's house one evening when she was eight. Frances and Joe barged in to make an announcement.

"Grandma," Joe told Trannie, "We're going to get married." Trannie, who was only seven years older than Joe, looked at the couple in disbelief. "Have you lost your mind?" she said at last. "You're an old man. What are you doing marrying her?"

They were an odd couple in every respect. Frances was several inches taller with fair skin and auburn hair. Joe Cutro was short, stocky, and bald, and always had a cigarette hanging out of his mouth. He was also both fun-loving and industrious. His restaurant in Columbia, Joe's Italian Kitchen, was close to the university and wildly popular with the college crowd. For the first time in her life, Frances would know how it felt to have money. And if that weren't incentive enough to accept his proposal, she was pregnant.

They were married in 1958. Joseph ("Josh") Cutro was born in December of that year, two days after his mother turned twenty-three. Later, she would confess to various family members that she couldn't be sure whether Josh belonged to Joe or to another man with whom she was having an affair. But Joe seemed to take to the boy—at least as much as he took to any of his children.

"Spaghetti Joe" didn't have much time for children. He was too busy working hard—and playing hard. He put in long hours at the restaurant. Jane remembers watching him stir spaghetti sauce in a huge pot, oblivious to the ashes dropping from the ubiquitous cigarette dangling from his lips. "I still to this day have not ate spaghetti that good. Ashes or no ashes, it was still good." She also recalled the stories of his gambling trips to Las Vegas and his liaisons with prostitutes.

After she married Joe, Frances helped run the restaurant. So for her, Trannie's house was a home day care. She dropped Josh and his half-brother Jody off in the morning and picked them up at night. And she paid Trannie for the service.

Suzanne and Jane remembered those days, though Suzanne's memories were more detailed, since she was thirteen years older than Josh and sometimes baby-sat him. Suzanne remembered hearing that one time, when Josh was two or three, his mother picked him up at Trannie's house and brought him to the restaurant. She deposited him outside in a swing for toddlers and went in to work. A few minutes later a rainstorm blew in. Not until several concerned customers asked about the poor drenched child did Frances remember where she'd left her son.

In most of his cousins' memories, Josh was rarely so passive. Just a few years later he was quite a handful. Although at the time of Gail's trial Josh never used profanity (at least in public), beginning when he was about six, Jane said, "he cursed like a sailor." And he soon learned how to talk himself out of trouble at Trannie's.

"Josh was always a mama's boy," Jane continued. Anytime his grandmother threatened him with the switch, Josh would quickly respond: "I'm going to call my mommy!" He'd get on the phone and she'd send a taxi to pick him up. Suzanne remembered that when he was older, some cab drivers refused to transport him because they found his language and manner obnoxious.

His cousins thought that his parents' coddling spoiled Josh. But they were quick to add that the boy was smart, and not just because he knew how to manipulate his way out of unpleasant circumstances. His intelligence became apparent as he spent time in the restaurant and, from an early age, was able to contribute. Josh remembered bussing and waiting on tables and ringing up the cash register when he was five and six. Jane and Suzanne laughed when this recollection was repeated to them. He might have thought he was accomplishing something at those ages, they allowed, but it was a few more years before he was capable of real work.

Josh's relationship with his father consisted mainly of their interactions in the restaurant, since he rarely saw his father anywhere else. Josh and Jody always slept in the family's big house in Columbia near the highway to Irmo, but their father spent precious little time there.

When his father was there in the late 1960s, Josh remembers a great deal of tension between Joe and Frances. Josh attributes this situation to his mother's jealousy and to the age difference between them. The cousins think that it had to do with Joe's philandering, especially with prostitutes. Another factor, undoubtedly, was their growing family. By the decade's end, three more children had joined the stormy household. Sal was born in 1960, Bennie a year later, and Rose Marie arrived in 1969.

Everything fell apart a year after Rose was born. The building that housed the restaurant was sold and then razed to make way for the Town House Hotel. Joe, who was sixty, decided he'd had enough. He auctioned off the equipment and retired from the restaurant business. He bought a large trailer and moved his family to a trailer park in Cayce (pronounced Casey), just across the Congaree River from downtown Columbia.

It wasn't long before it became abundantly clear that the restaurant had been the only thing keeping Frances and Joe together. Frances packed up and moved the kids into a house a few miles west in the town of South Congaree, just south of the Columbia airport. It was a fateful move in at least one respect: it meant that a few years later Josh would attend Airport High School, where he would meet Gail Hallman.

After the restaurant folded, Frances worked a variety of jobs. She put in a lengthy stint at the convenience store of the Knights Inn motel. She continued to leave Josh at her mother's house, and Josh continued to act like a kid who was used to having his way. But there was a change: He was no longer the little one. As he and his siblings got older, Trannie's house began to fill with yet another generation—great-grandchildren.

Tammie Williams was one of the younger ones. She remembers that she was scared of Josh, who seemed to pick on her "every chance he got." The child of one of Josh's cousins, she was ten years his junior and one of his favorite targets. Beginning when she was three or four, Josh would sometimes lock Tammie and another cousin in a closet or hoist her in the air and hang her by her belt loop on a nail in the wall. Sometimes Josh lifted her up, she says, and body-slammed her on his knee.

Josh's brother Jody Barfield not only confirmed Tammie Williams's account, he ruefully admitted that he hung her from a nail and locked her in a closet himself. He didn't realize it was abuse at the time, but he does now, he said. And he also saw a pattern. Joe Cutro used to beat and verbally abuse Jody—because Jody reminded Joe of his wife's affair, Barfield said. And Barfield took out his pain on Tammie.

"When you get older," he said, "you realize why you do things. But while you're doing it, you don't realize it's just history repeating itself."

Tammie Williams also looked back at those days with a pained perspective. "I guess it was torture that children get to go through when they're smaller than the other ones," she reflected. "Because I was mean to my little cousins, too, when I was growing up. I had three of them that I used to babysit and be around all the time. And they trusted me with them because I was older." What she did was "nothing drastic," she said, but she knows it was cruel. "They would ask me to spin them around, and I'd spin them around, and then I'd just let them go, you know, so they could fly through the air and everything." After considering for a moment, she added: "But they'd always come back for more, you know, so they must have liked it."

She'd been rough with them, but not nearly as rough as Josh had been with her. Even after he was married and had a child of his own, Josh continued to intimidate her. Tammie recalled spending the night at Josh and Gail's when she was about twelve. During her stay Josh led her to a converted garage, laced on a pair of boxing gloves, and used her as a punching bag. "And he was out there hitting me around, you know, for quite some time." To Josh it seemed to be a game; to Tammie it was what she'd come to expect. "I didn't get really, really hurt," she added, but more than fifteen years later, it is still a vivid memory.

The one member of Josh's family to whom Tammie Williams felt close when she was growing up was Josh's kid sister, Rose, who was six months younger than she. Asked what she and Rose used to do as young teens, Tammie responded: "Children things. What normally thirteen-year-olds do." Pressed for details, she continued: "I don't know. Get into trouble, skip school, start fires, chase boys." Tammie laughed at her own bravado, but her answer was no joke. As young teens looking for fun, she and Rose and four other girls stole a car from the parking lot of Airport High School. Rose was locked up in a juvenile facility for a few months; the others were treated more leniently.

After a moment, Tammie thought of something else she did with her cousin around this time: "Go to the store with her mom and shoplift." Police records confirm that Frances and Rose had records for shoplifting, and Tammie acknowledged that she was caught, too. "Every time me and Rose went to the grocery store, her mom would pile her purse up with, you know, meats and everything. And she's still doing it today, I'm sure."

Tammie wasn't the only family member who saw Frances Barfield in action; Suzanne was also a witness. "I had went to the store with her one Sunday, and she was putting meat in her pocketbook. It boggles the mind. And I was scared to death." After Frances paid for some small items and headed for the door, employees detained her and called the police.

When she was arrested, Suzanne said, Frances used an old trick to dodge trouble: She gave the name of her sister. It seemed to work on at least some occasions, but even so, Frances was convicted of shoplifting at least three times in the early 1980s.

And Josh? Suzanne said that he, too, was a shoplifter. She first became aware of this shortly after Josh broke Gail out of the reformatory. While the couple was on the lam, they spent a good deal of time hiding out in Suzanne's house. Suzanne remembered that Gail used her skill with a needle and thread to sew large pockets into the couple's jackets. The rest was easy for the still-slender youths. "They would go around to stores and just steal, all the time. That's all they would do. And I would keep telling them they were going to get caught. And Gail said, 'No, we won't, 'cause we're too smart.'"

Apparently, they weren't caught—in South Carolina. But Suzanne said they resumed the practice after they moved to Chicago, and that's where Josh's luck ran out. "The police caught Josh. But Gail, she ran. She got away." Although Josh claimed that he was never arrested in Chicago, a police report confirmed that he was arrested in February 1977 for "retail theft." Jody Barfield, who was living in Chicago at the time, also confirmed the arrest. Josh and Gail returned to South Carolina a few months later, and Josh apparently skipped out on his court date.

He never returned to answer the charge, and his record was unblemished by another shoplifting allegation until twenty years later—two and a half years after Gail was sent to prison. That time he was picked up in a Winn Dixie parking lot after stealing $365 worth of over-the-counter pain pills. His alleged accomplice was his mother, who was again using the alias of her dead sister. Three months later he pled no contest and received a slap on the wrist. Three months after that he was arrested at a Kroger supermarket attempting to steal $370 worth of medicine. He pled no contest again and paid a $125 fine.

Shoplifting and driving under the influence were the offenses that landed Josh's mother and siblings in trouble most often, but they were not the only crimes they committed, according to Tammie Williams. Rose became a heavy drug user, Tammie said, and she and her friends began burglarizing homes. Once when Tammie went to visit Rose in Frances's trailer, she found that her cousin and great-aunt had developed a sideline. "They had, like, thousands of these X-rated videos where they knocked over this video store. And they had them sitting in the bedroom, you know, waiting for it to cool off and everything. They was always doing something."

During the last two years of her life Rose actually started a business, though it wasn't the kind to make most mothers proud. Jane remembers when Josh broke the news.

"Oh, have you heard about Rosie?" he asked with a smirk. "She's an *entrepreneur!*"

"Do *what?*" said Jane, who confessed with a laugh that she didn't know what that meant.

"She owns her own business."

"You're kidding. What is she doing?"

"She's running an escort service."

It was called AAA Escorts, and it was listed in the Southern Bell Yellow Pages for 1992–1993 and 1993–1994. Generally, Rose lined up the girls and arranged the assignations; but sometimes, when she was shorthanded, she also turned tricks. Once, Jane and Suzanne recalled, when Rose was alone and a couple of clients beseeched her, she was forced to call on her mother for assistance—though only to drive her to and from her "date."

Rose died at age twenty-four. She was alone when she drove her car off a road that was well known to locals. "I used to live out there on that road that she was on," said Tammie, "and that's where you buy drugs at, is on that road." Tammie used to buy drugs there regularly, she acknowledged. Though she doesn't know what caused her cousin's accident, Tammie assumed that it had something to do with drugs and reckless driving. Rose was always a fast driver, her cousin said. It was a haunting repetition of the death of Joe Barfield, Trannie's husband—the grandfather Rose never knew.

———

Josh Cutro's family background does not prove, of course, that he harmed Parker Colson, Asher Maier, or Ashlan Daniel. Had he come from a family of murderers—or been one himself—that still wouldn't prove that he harmed these children. Interestingly enough, though, in an effort to argue that he was a much more viable murder suspect than his wife, it was Josh who volunteered in an interview that his own family background included his Uncle Charlie's manslaughter conviction. He later added that his cousin, Travis Barfield, was serving a life sentence for murder.

To say that his background doesn't prove anything, however, is not to say that it's irrelevant. It was certainly of great interest to Dr. Selman Watson. When a few details were provided to the psychologist, Dr. Watson saw a man with a history of violence and impulsive behavior—the kind of person he believes is most likely to shake a baby.

He might have been even more suspicious if Dr. Watson had known about Tammie Williams's and Cheryl Mason's revelations about the way Josh sometimes treated children. Or if he'd known that Josh's older daughter, Kira, was temporarily removed from his custody eleven months after his wife's first trial, when the thirteen-year-old complained that her father had physically abused her.

There was more that Dr. Watson didn't know. In June 1996, Josh was arrested for allegedly grabbing a neighbor's thirteen-year-old son by the throat. (He claimed that he was defending his daughters, and the charge was later dismissed.) And he certainly didn't know that Josh's cousin Jane and her husband Danny once visited Josh and watched in amazement as he casually brutalized one of the day care toddlers.

The child, who Jane estimated was about three or four, was "hollering." Josh told him to shut up. When the child failed to comply, Josh shoved him hard enough to send him slamming into the wall. "Stupid punk!" he yelled at the child, who was by this time hysterical. Though Josh didn't appear the least bit self-conscious, Jane and Danny decided they'd seen enough.

"These people are crazy," Danny said as they walked to their car. He was talking about Josh and Gail, but Jane was focused on the parents of the children. "If they only knew," she thought.

77

The Hallmans' Story

Gail Cutros's family and background bore little resemblance to Josh's. For one thing, the Hallmans had no recorded run-ins with the law. Pat Hallman referred to the differences between the families when she tried to explain why her relationship with Josh has been so strained. "I think he was raised different than all of us was raised. And his ideals and things are different." This became apparent to her, Hallman said, the first time Josh came to her family's Christmas Eve dinner party. "Everybody would bring food and different things, and we'd just enjoy each other's company," she said. "He told my mom that he didn't know that families did things like that without fighting and fussing and drinking and cussing."

The Hallmans were answering questions two years after the first trial in their immaculately kept home near the Columbia airport. Pat, who was fifty-five at the time, was seated at her dining-room table, where she held forth on her childhood, her children, and her marriage. Like her daughter, Pat had put on weight over the years, but her hair, though gray, had lost none of its child-hood curls. Her brown eyes sparkled through large-frame glasses, though on some occasions, when she felt she'd been challenged, they quickly turned hard and cold. Seated to her right was her grandson, Joshua, who had been living with the Hallmans for a year, Pat said, because his father couldn't handle three children alone. Joshua Cutro was still as thin as a teenager in the throes of his first growth spurt. His closely cropped brown hair and wispy mustache had the unintended effect of making him look younger than his twenty years. During several hours' conversation, he volunteered a comment only once.

Though there was still room at the table, Harold Hallman sat by the window several feet behind his wife—as though he were watching her back. He observed the proceedings warily from behind large, wire-rimmed bifocals. Harold, fifty-seven, was still trim and retained a full head of wavy, silver-streaked black hair, which he combed straight back. His thick black eyebrows and salt-and-pepper mustache made him look distinguished, like an aging gentleman on a daytime soap opera. His other visible concession to age was a stiff gait—a product of arthritic knees. As taciturn as his wife was loquacious, Harold practiced the advice he'd frequently preached to his children: "It's better to be thought a fool and keep your mouth shut than open your mouth and remove all doubt." When Harold did choose to speak, his wife sometimes spoke right over him.

Pat and Harold Hallman were high school sweethearts who grew up in the West Columbia area (about eleven miles southeast of Irmo), as their parents had before them. They began dating when Harold was a senior, and they married the summer after he graduated. Though Pat still had two years to go and wanted to graduate, her plans changed when she learned that she was pregnant. Gail was born the following April, and Barry arrived two and a half years later. Pat wanted a large family—she was one of eight siblings—and she was disappointed to learn that she couldn't have more children.

On the surface, the Hallmans appeared rock solid. Harold started as a machine operator at Anchor Continental, a company that manufactures ad-hesive tapes. It was a good job, and he advanced steadily, rising to supervisor, then superintendent and, finally, to division manager. Having grown up in a traditional family in which the mother stayed at home, Harold would have preferred that his wife do the same. Instead, Pat worked at a variety of jobs, many of them as an office temp. She eventually reached a compromise with her husband by keeping children in her home while she watched her own.

As a mother, Pat described herself as "overprotective." She attributed this quality to two incidents from her own childhood. When Pat was about two, with big brown eyes and curly blonde hair, strangers would stop her mother on the street to admire the pretty toddler. Once a couple stopped and asked if they could hold the child for a moment. Pat's mother obliged, and the couple suddenly bolted with her. Pat's father chased them for eight blocks before the strangers tired and put the youngster down.

Pat had no direct memory of this event, but she did remember the second incident, which occurred when she was four. She was playing in the yard when a car stopped and a man tried to lure her into it. When her mother came around from the other side of the house, the car quickly sped away. The man in the car, like the couple two years earlier, was never apprehended. Although Pat escaped harm, these experiences—and her family's repeated discussions of them—stayed with her. They made her "very, very suspicious" of people, she said, and they influenced the way she raised her children.

The early years, when the children were young, sounded idyllic. "Gail always loved animals and babies," Pat remembered. She had a hamster, a cat, and a dog. The first baby Gail loved was her brother, whom she insisted on calling "my baby." From her earliest years she was extremely protective of him. "If you bought something for Gail," her mother recalled, "you had to buy something for Barry. 'If you can't buy for Barry,' [Gail would announce,] 'don't buy for me.'"

When Pat went to work, the children were enrolled in a family day care run by a neighborhood woman. One day Barry came home with marks on his legs. The woman had disciplined him with a switch, and Gail was outraged. So were her parents, who never sent them back. After this incident, Harold insisted that his wife stay home, and Pat began "keeping" a neighborhood child.

Though the episode reinforced Pat's overprotective impulses, her children appeared unaffected. Gail was a happy, obedient child, said Pat, but Barry was a handful, complete with scars, broken bones, and countless stories of the Cain he raised—whether it was "spray painting" the living room with a garden hose or burning a piece of furniture at his grandparents' house.

Gail was a source of concern to her parents only in regard to her health. When she was three or four, her doctor said there was a problem with her kidneys. He sent her to a specialist and to a hospital for tests. There was never a clear diagnosis, Pat said, but Gail emerged from the experience with a profound distaste for doctors, hospitals, and particularly needles. Though Pat recalled that one doctor suggested Gail's condition might severely shorten her life, she apparently outgrew whatever ailed her.

In other respects, her mother continued, Gail was a normal child. She enjoyed the same things as other girls her age. She loved her Barbie dolls. She learned to cook when she was quite young, and she made cookies for her brother. Pat and Harold had always liked working with their hands, and they passed this passion on to their children. Pat taught Gail to knit and sew, and Harold taught Barry carpentry, among other skills.

As the children grew older, the Hallmans took them hiking and camping. They also purchased a membership at a riding stable north of Columbia. Gail, in particular, loved horses. When she was a young teen, riding became a big part of her life. She had few friends when she was growing up, and her love of animals may have helped fill a void. Horses were also the bond that connected her with one of her friends.

When Gail was thirteen, she met "Sally," who lived nearby. If Gail was fond of horses, Sally was besotted. She owned a horse that she rode and exhibited at shows, to which Gail sometimes accompanied her. As the girls grew closer, they slept over at each other's houses, played with Barbie dolls, and listened to Elton John and Bee Gees records. Sally once joined the Cutros on an overnight camping excursion, and her family reciprocated by inviting Gail to spend several days with them at Myrtle Beach.

In a separate interview, Sally remembered Gail as a cute girl with an olive complexion and curly brown hair that hung to her shoulders. The words she used to describe her were "sweet," "innocent," and "shy." The girl *she* knew seemed incapable of harming *anyone*. Gail's gentle nature was not a quality Sally took for granted, either—especially at that age, when peer pressure fostered adolescent cruelty. "A lot of people back then, you know, if you're friends, they turn on you," Sally said. "But she was real nice." Other girls were often "hateful" and showed off by smoking cigarettes and acting tough. Gail "never did anything like that," Sally said. She couldn't recall one instance when Gail was nasty or even angry.

But all was not smooth sailing in the Hallman household. Pat tried to put the best face on the situation, but she acknowledged several problems. In an earlier conversation, she'd said that Barry had transferred from Airport to Brookland-Cayce (or B.C.) High School, because "there was a subject that Barry wanted to take over there that he could not get at Airport." This time, however, she acknowledged that Barry was expelled from Airport—but explained that it was all her fault. "I really got him threw out of school," she confessed, laughing in embarrassment. The Hallmans' house was not on the bus route, so Pat drove him to school on her way to her temp job. Barry had been late on several occasions and was told he'd have to stay for detention. Pat thought this unfair.

"I told them that I'd had trouble with my distributor cap, that the car wouldn't start, and that's why Barry was late." She thought that would take care of the problem and was incensed when it didn't. "The man told me, he said, 'We've got this rule: If kids are late three times, they have to stay in detention.' And I said, 'Well, they're stupid!'" That ended Barry's career at Airport. But, Pat quickly added, Barry told her that he was glad that she did what she did, because going to B.C. "was the best move that he ever made."

An earlier move had proved much more wrenching for the family. When Gail was fourteen or fifteen, Harold moved out of their home and didn't return for two years. He was working long hours at the plant, Pat said, and they kept getting longer: sixty, seventy, sometimes eighty hours, seven days a week. "He was tired, and I didn't handle it very well. Because with him working like that, we were not having time for family. We didn't have any quality time at all, because all Harold was doing was coming home, and sometimes he would eat, and sometimes he was too tired to eat. And he was mostly just sleeping there. And I would pack his lunch, and sometimes he would eat a meal with us, but most of the times he would be late coming in, and we would be already eating whenever he would come home. And it got where he was so tired that I just couldn't talk to him."

After about a year of this, they decided it couldn't go on. "We just come to the conclusion that none of us was happy anymore. It had gone on for too long, and everybody in the house was becoming unhappy. And so he said, 'I think I'll move and stay with Mom for a while.'"

During the two years Harold stayed with his mother, Pat hastened to add, "we still spent a lot of time together. A lot of people didn't know we were separated because of the way he had been working and he was gone so much. During the time we were separated, we bought our lake house together." They spent a good portion of their summers and holidays in the house on Lake Wateree, northeast of Columbia. Harold would commute the fifty-five miles to and from work. Their neighbors at the lake weren't even aware that they'd separated, Pat added.

After a pause, Harold said: "We make mistakes."

"But you know what?" Pat continued without missing a beat. "We learn from it. I think that God sometimes allows things to happen to us, like I was fussing about the quality time, and even though he was coming home every night, I felt like that me and the children were missing out on something. But then when he moved out and stayed with his mom, I realized that at least he was coming home every night. That we had that. And I think as we worked through this and spent time together, he and I realized what we had together to start with but that we had let a gap come in there with his job and me not handling it real good. And as we bought our lake house and worked together . . . we realized that what we had was worth saving."

What effect did the separation have on their children? In separate interviews, several perspectives emerged. According to Josh Cutro, "The whole separation thing basically had no effect on Gail because around the time that occurred and all, I was basically taking care of Gail. We were going out to eat together every day. I was buying clothes for Gail. . . . I had already basically taken over responsibilities of a husband. Except we were not living together at that time."

Gail agreed. Sitting next to Josh in the prison visiting room, she suggested that her father's absence had a much more profound effect on her mother than on her. By the time she and Josh left for Chicago, Gail said, she was convinced that her mother's marriage was all but over, and that her mother actually envied her own relationship with Josh.

Gail's brother had a different view. Barry Hallman was deeply affected by his father's departure. He eventually understood that Harold felt caught in the squeeze between his responsibilities at home and work. When his father broke the news to Barry, Harold had said: "I can't take the pressure." But the explanation didn't make it any easier for his son. "Even looking back and knowing what I do now," Barry said, "it was not easy at that time for me. We had such a relationship—why did he want to leave? Was it my fault?" He saw his father on weekends and during the summer at the lake house. In time Barry adjusted; he had no choice. But he never stopped asking, "Do you think you're ready to come home yet?" The reply was always, "I've still got some personal things to work out."

"It led to a lot more mischief that I got into," Barry said. "You know, I got into drinking. And it probably pushed me more into that, because, you know, when you don't have the associations that you want, you look for associations in other places. And I probably got into more trouble that way later on. But also, I believe I gained a lot more maturity and understanding for certain situations and have grown more compassionate because of the situations that I went through." Asked if he believed that Gail was affected, Barry responded: "As close a family as we was, I really don't see how she could *not* have been."

There were some matters that the Hallmans did not bring up. When questioned about these, they addressed some willingly, some reluctantly, and others not at all. The first was Pat Hallman's supposed psychic powers. As Missy Daniel had learned during her meeting with Gail and her mother at the Winn Dixie, Pat Hallman believed that she had a special gift. Asked to describe her psychic powers, Pat was startled by the question, but answered without hesitation, "I don't have psychic powers." Then she added: "I'm very psychic." Eventually she clarified the distinction. She'd had about ten "visions" over the years, but she hadn't willed them and can't control them. She believed that they were "gifts from God" and that to invoke or provoke a vision was beyond her power.

The first sign of her "gift," Pat said, was at her birth. "My mom said when I was born, I was born with a veil over my face." A doctor and a midwife delivered her, and her mother's cousin was also present. "Well, I've delivered a lot of babies," the doctor told Pat's mother, "but this is the first time I've seen anything like this." Years later the doctor told Pat that the "veil" was "a membrane" (a pediatrician interviewed suggested that it was most likely a piece of the amniotic sack), but the cousin contradicted him and said it was a piece of lace. When the midwife removed it, she told Pat's mother, "You're going to have a very special little girl here. She'll know things sometimes or sense things."

Pat said her first such experience occurred when she was eight. "I saw an angel," she told her mother, who only then informed her of the veil and the midwife's prediction. She said she saw another angel when she was eleven. She did not communicate with the angels, but in each case she remembered feeling "very safe." She also saw "some people that had died" and "some ghosts," she remembered.

She had visions of some of her grandchildren before they were born, she went on. "I did not know it with Joshua, and I don't know it all the time," Pat explained. But when Gail was pregnant with Kira and asked her mother if she knew what the baby would be, this time she knew. "I felt that Gail was going to have a little girl," she said, "and she was going to be blonde and fair." When

Gail was pregnant with Lara and asked again, her mother's first answer was that she didn't know. "And one day I was just washing dishes and this picture came into my mind. And I called her up and I said, 'You're going to have another little girl, but she's going to look like you and she's going to be petite.' And she is."

Her husband didn't believe in her powers. "I believe in God," said Harold Hallman.

"I believe in God, too," his wife responded. "But I think God gives some people gifts."

She had never had any visions concerning Gail's criminal case, she said, nor have either of her children ever had similar experiences, as far as she knew. She didn't consider her experiences indicative of any real power. "I think that people all have a little bit of psychic in them, and that in some people it's just stronger than others."

Pat's daughter told a different story when she was interviewed six months later, however. Gail said that her mother claimed to be "a witch" and had the power to "cast spells." Josh, Lara, and Kira, who were with her in the prison visiting room, all confirmed this claim. Moreover, they said that they believed that she really was a witch. Asked whether she agreed, Gail hesitated. "I think she believes that she's a witch," she said at last.

But what did Gail think? She answered with an anecdote. Pat had been upset with a guard at the prison and had cast a spell on her. A short time later the guard tripped and hurt herself. Gail said that she believed that her mother had intimidated the guard. In that sense, her mother does wield power, but Gail attributed most of it to psychology. Would she characterize her mother, then, as psychologically manipulative? Maybe at times, she granted. Wasn't it hard growing up in a household with a woman like this? "Well, it wasn't really that hard, because I was a good girl. I didn't do bad things. And I was sickly, also. So it wasn't that big a problem for me."

The second matter about which the Hallmans were reluctant to talk concerned their son. According to Josh's cousin Jane, Barry Hallman spent time in a local mental hospital. Jane wasn't sure precisely when, why, or for how long. She was only sure of the name of the facility: Charter Rivers in West Columbia. Josh and Gail confirmed this information, but Gail refused to say anything about it, and Josh's information was as sketchy as Jane's. Charter Rivers wasn't founded until 1982, so Barry was at least nineteen at the time he was there. He seemed to have stayed a month or longer, and then he ran away.

It was unclear whether he ever returned. In the late 1990s the hospital's full name was Charter Rivers Behavioral Health System, and its advertisement stated: "Treating emotional, behavioral, alcohol & drug problems." Neither Pat, Harold, nor Barry Hallman himself was willing to discuss this subject.

The third topic was the mental health of Harold Hallman. Harold apparently went though a period during which he became obsessed with Abraham Lincoln. He grew a beard like Lincoln's and told people either that he was Lincoln or that he was the reincarnation of Lincoln. This information, too, came from Jane, who said that she heard it from Josh and Gail and also from someone she knew who worked with Harold. Josh's brother Jody Barfield confirmed that Josh and Gail told him the same thing. Jane believed that this situation occurred during the time Pat and Harold were separated. She had no idea whether he ever sought treatment.

When Josh was asked if he remembered a time when Harold Hallman told people he was Abraham Lincoln, he seemed caught off guard. "No," he said after a moment, and then he laughed. Asked if he was sure he didn't remember anything like that, he was uncharacteristically silent. Prodded a third time, he finally produced an answer: "I remember—well, when he was young, he had that beard like that. Before, when he used to play softball for Anchor down at the park from my grandmother's, that me and my brothers always went and played at—and I don't think it was an obsession with him being Abraham Lincoln or anything. Everybody else was obsessed with— 'Oh, yeah. That man looks like Abraham Lincoln.' That's what everybody would say."

When Gail was asked the same question later the same day, she was seated in the prison visiting room next to Josh (who only permitted these interviews in his presence). Surprised by the question, Gail was also at a loss for words. Before she could answer, Josh quickly cut in. "You remember," Josh prompted, followed by his story about fans commenting on Harold's appearance at the softball games.

When Harold, Pat, and Barry Hallman were asked about this matter, they all declined to comment. In addition to anything else this enigmatic anecdote might say about Harold Hallman, it is worth remembering that Abraham Lincoln was, and is, hardly the revered statesman for many South Carolina residents that he is in other parts of the country.

78

A Third Opinion

"We learn much about who we are, and what is normal, by our early childhood experiences. And many people grow up in very dysfunctional families, thinking that what they're experiencing is what other children are experiencing. And that's, of course, often not the case."

The speaker was Dr. Geoffrey McKee, who was explaining why it is crucial to try to understand a person's family if you want to understand the individual fully. Seated in his cluttered office, the fifty-three-year-old forensic psychologist with thinning blonde hair looked like a college professor. But the office was a little too institutional-Spartan to pass as a college professor's chamber; it lacked a carpet, a couch, and an overstuffed chair.

Dr. McKee was chief of forensic psychology at the William S. Hall Psychiatric Institute in Columbia. In this capacity he was frequently asked by the state to evaluate people accused of crimes. Sometimes his evaluations were ordered by a court, which was the case when he examined Susan Smith, the South Carolina woman who drowned her two children. In his private practice, however, he was often hired by defense lawyers. In the late 1990s he also devoted a good deal of time to publishing his research—so he *was* something of an academic, after all.

Dr. McKee was the third psychology professional who saw Gail Cutro, after Eve Powell and Dr. Selman Watson. He was hired by Wes Kirkland to help the defense prepare for the expected Munchausen testimony. Kirkland asked Dr. McKee to evaluate Gail's competency to stand trial and to offer his diagnosis of her mental condition. He also asked whether, in Dr. McKee's opinion, she fit the profile of a woman suffering from MSBP. After Dr. McKee had completed his work, the prosecution decided not to try to introduce this evidence in the first trial, so he didn't testify. He almost testified in the second trial, but the results of the tests he administered to Gail had not been turned over to the prosecution, so he was excluded. He finally testified in the third trial, at which he explained why he didn't believe the diagnosis fit.

Two and a half years after Dr. McKee saw her, Gail Cutro agreed to waive confidentiality and allow the psychologist to discuss his evaluation. Like Dr. Watson, Dr. McKee saw Gail only once—four days before her first trial. His evaluation included a clinical interview, which lasted about two hours, followed by a battery of tests. He also reviewed numerous documents, including Gail's medical records. Unlike Dr. Watson, Dr. McKee did not evaluate Josh Cutro and was not asked to write a report, although he did file an affidavit that the defense used in support of Gail's appeal bond.

Though he has worked for both prosecutors and defense lawyers, the best indication of his objectivity, Dr. McKee said, is the frequency with which he *does not* testify for the side that hires him. "If you don't testify for the party that retains you," he explained, "it's most likely that you don't have information that will be helpful to their case." (In other words, you're not simply a hired gun who will say whatever the person paying wants.) McKee figured that he testifies for the defense about half the time when he's hired by that side and for the state about a fifth of the time when he's retained by the prosecution.

Asked whether he would consider the mental health of Gail's parents and brother important in understanding who she is, Dr. McKee was emphatic: "Very much so. We often learn how to relate to other people by how our parents treated us. And so their personalities and their interpersonal styles become our first significant influence to our own.

"Certainly, if there is a history of mental illness in a patient's family, the genetic contributions of that mental illness may show up in the patient. And so, having a family psychiatric history is very important."

McKee knew nothing about Gail's family apart from the little she told him. He had heard nothing about possible mental illness, and he was not asked to comment on whether there was, in fact, such a history. Her biological family, after all, was not accused of anything. Harold and Barry Hallman were successful, dependable, and productive in their jobs. Their marriages appeared to be thriving, and they were working to be a good grandfather and father, respectively. They believed in Gail's innocence and supported her. There was no crime in any of this.

Still, exploring a possible history of mental illness seemed particularly important not just in light of Dr. McKee's comments, but also in view of Gail's own remarks to Patsy Habben shortly after she failed her polygraph. Gail said then that, in the words Habben wrote in her contemporaneous notes, "she wasn't okay mentally."

What did Dr. McKee find? In some respects his conclusions were similar to Dr. Selman Watson's. He found a woman "of average intelligence" who was depressed. "Certainly, she was acutely depressed, because she had been charged with these deaths," he said. Dr. Watson, in his report, had attributed Gail's depression entirely to the investigation. But Dr. McKee parted company with him on that point, even though McKee had more reason to draw this connection since he saw Gail just days before her trial, whereas Dr. Watson saw her before she'd even been charged with a crime.

"She is a woman that, at the time when I saw her, suffered from depression," McKee said, "and had suffered from depression for much of her life, I think." She also exhibited anxiety, along with "a strong interest in health concerns. She was a rather unhealthy child, a sickly child. She had a chronic urinary-tract infection that required treatment on a number of occasions, and she still remained quite concerned about her own physical health. Not that she was necessarily hypochondriacal, but she certainly was somatically concerned." Gail's medical records told him that she was frequently tested for conditions she complained about, and the results often came back negative. He explained that "a lot of chronically depressed people prefer to present physical ailments rather than psychological ailments and tend to define their emotional problems in terms of physical ailments that, in some ways, are more acceptable."

He saw her condition as chronic not just because it was long-standing, but because it seemed as though "it might reflect a personality style. So, for example, when someone is under stress, some people become very angry and combative and confrontive and argumentative and take it very personally in kind of a paranoid, narcissistic way. Others become quite guilt-ridden, anxious, and they withdraw and accept fault very readily, even when it is not realistic that they are at fault. And those kinds of styles can be detected on personality inventories" such as the tests he administered to Gail. Gail, he noted, had more in common with the second personality style.

McKee believed that Gail had been unhappy most of her life. "And yet, on the other hand, I think that she tends to deny a lot of her depression." She had a tendency to think: "'Yes, I am feeling sad, yes, I am depressed, but it's not that bad.' And, at times, she has even defined herself as a rather happy person, all while she's seeking treatment for depression."

Why would she deny her feelings? "Perhaps, if she really came to grips with how depressed she was, how overburdened she was, she might have to be confronted with doing something about it."

Is he suggesting that she might be suicidal? "Maybe," he said. "I'm not going to speak about her marriage, because I did not see [Josh]. But there are situations in which a couple is chronically unhappy in their marriage. They don't recognize it, or when it's pointed out, they deny it, because if they accept that they are chronically unhappy, then they might have to divorce. And that divorce may be the worse of two evils—it's more anxiety-provoking to separate than to remain in this chronically unhappy state." Having said that he isn't commenting on Gail's marriage, McKee added: "Gail is of that type."

Asked how Gail dealt with anger, McKee said, "One of the aspects of Gail, as I saw her back then, and it's characteristic of people who have this kind of cluster of anxiety and depression and somatic concern, is that they are angry, and they don't acknowledge the anger.

"One of the reasons why they don't acknowledge the anger is because if they give vent to that anger, it might create an even worse situation. People might leave. People receiving that might cut them off, might abandon them. And so, people with this style will accept a lot of stress, a lot of unhappiness, as preferential to being abandoned."

Gail, he added, was "out of touch with certain emotions that are uncomfortable for her, or unpleasant for her, principally anger."

———

The most important relationship in Gail Cutro's life was her relationship with Josh. Before she met Josh and after she met Josh: That's the way many people saw Gail's life—or lives. Certainly her parents did. Before Josh, they had a daughter; after, she was gone. Not that her mother ever gave up her claim. Nor did Gail divest herself of her mother. But with Josh, everything changed.

Marriage did nothing to reconcile these two irresistible forces in Gail's life. Neither time nor common enemies would heal the wounds or bind together Gail's mother and husband.

Why were they constantly at loggerheads? Cathy Lucas had a ready explanation. As one of Pat's six sisters—five of them younger—Lucas was thirteen years younger than Pat and less than five years older than Gail. Cathy spent a lot of time with her sister's family while she and Gail were growing up, and she had many opportunities to observe Pat Hallman and Josh Cutro in close quarters.

"They're both domineering," Cathy Lucas said. "When you get two domineering people, they're not always going to see eye to eye." In this instance, it was an understatement. Pat and Josh rarely agreed on anything—especially on matters pertaining to Gail.

There was nothing unique, of course, about a husband jostling with his mother-in-law. But the duration and degree were, to say the least, unusual. The struggle they waged for longer than twenty years—up to, during, and after Gail's trials—resembled a custody dispute during a particularly acrimonious divorce.

Some of the more remarkable moments in this long-playing drama occurred just before and just after Gail's first trial. After Josh and Gail were indicted, they moved out of 1101 Chadford Road and in with the Hallmans in Pelion. Ironically, the time when Josh found the Hallmans' behavior most egregious was also the time when they appeared to be most generous. Not only were they willing to share their home, but the Hallmans—who, according to Barry Hallman, would eventually pay $75,000 for Gail's defense—also bought a double-wide trailer and moved it onto their land for Josh, Gail, and the kids to live in. While the Hallmans were fixing up the trailer (among other things, Harold built a deck for it), there was a good deal of tension in the overcrowded house. Gail was about to stand trial, Josh was commuting to Columbia to work at Burger King, and Pat and Josh were living under one roof.

When Josh spoke sharply to Gail about the shoes she'd forgotten to pack for him, Pat Hallman had heard enough. As Josh remembered it, his mother-in-law stormed into the room.

"I'm sick and tired of you yelling at my daughter. I want you out of my house. I want you away from Gail forever."

"We'll be glad to leave," yelled Josh. "If you don't want us here, we're gone."

"No. I want Gail to stay here, and the kids can stay if they want to."

"I've got news for you," said Josh. "We're married."

"Gail's not yours," Pat Hallman spat back. "Gail is mine. I had her, and she is mine. I want you all to get a divorce."

"Gail, do you hear this?" said Josh, incredulous. "This is what I've said all along, all these years."

As Josh recounted it, the scene ended with a tug-of-war. He told Gail they were leaving, and as they started to go, Pat Hallman grabbed Gail by the arm. Josh grabbed her other wrist and yanked Gail out of her mother's grasp.

A day later, Harold Hallman met with Josh to patch things up. He succeeded—for a time. During and immediately after the trial Gail was incarcerated. Joshua stayed in the house with his grandparents, and Josh and the girls lived in the trailer. About two weeks after the conviction, when Josh said he was at his "weakest," Pat accused him of molesting his daughters.

Josh blew up. He threatened his in-laws, and he said he came very close to harming them. Pat didn't report these allegations to the police or the Department of Social Services. Instead, she asked a minister she and Josh both knew to "investigate." The minister (who agreed to an interview, then changed his mind) met with Josh. Then he and a woman Josh says was a counselor met with his daughters. They apparently concluded that the charge was baseless.

Josh emphatically denied ever molesting his daughters. He did acknowledge that he and the girls slept in the same bed right after the verdict, but he said that was understandable and innocent. "Right after the verdict and all, Kira, Lara, and myself were totally upset. They didn't want to sleep in their rooms by themselves. And, you know, they slept in the bed with me, each of us basically crying ourselves to sleep. And that's it."

Josh was so angry and so vocal about his feelings toward the Hallmans that they went to court to have him evicted. They told the magistrate he had threatened their lives. Questioned on this subject, Josh didn't deny it. "I was ready to kill them," he almost bragged. "And it was only by the grace of God that I didn't go right over there and just rip them to pieces." It was this side of Josh Cutro that led many of those who knew him to conclude that if anyone was murdered at 1101 Chadford Road, he was responsible.

There was another school of thought, however, that suggested the real source of danger wasn't the loud, angry guy who trumpeted his feelings transparently. It was the shy, quiet one who didn't even know how she felt—and was out of touch with her anger.

79

The Quiet One

Josh never had a problem expressing anger, but Gail was a different story. The first time she was interviewed in prison, in February 1997, she was asked to think of instances when she was angry. Sitting at a square Formica table in the visiting room, Gail considered for a while before she gave up.

She couldn't think of any. Perhaps, under the circumstances, with an appeal pending, she was afraid of what she might reveal. But few people who knew her, including close friends, could think of examples, either.

Asked what she did when she got mad, Gail said she generally read a book. She looked a little uncertain, as if she wasn't sure this was the correct answer. If she were really angry, she amended a moment later, she would cry—and then read a book.

During the tug-of-war between Pat and Josh in which Gail was the rope, she cried. After her mother accused her husband of sexually abusing her daughters, Gail took her parents' names off her visiting list, and they weren't allowed in the next time they came to the prison.

This was the kind of behavior Dr. McKee said he would expect from Gail. Caught between two controlling personalities, he would expect someone like her to respond with "depression, dependency, discomfort in expressing their wishes and wants, and a general lack of assertiveness." There would be a lot of unexpressed anger "and a lot of self-damaging, self-punitive kinds of stuff. The kind of self-talk that we do: 'Oh, I should have done this, I should have done that. Why am I such a wimp?'

"People with these results on the personality tests that I administer are often described as chronically angry people, who express their anger in indirect ways," Dr. McKee explained. "It would be my impression that she would likely express the anger in more passive-aggressive ways, that she would just forget to do things that people want her to do. It's not entirely intentional, it's not entirely conscious, but that would be a way in which she could frustrate someone else and express her anger that way."

A number of people offered observations about Gail that, in light of Dr. McKee's analysis, seemed to underscore how distant she was not just from her anger, but from all her emotions. For example, after Parker Colson died, Gail called her aunt, Cathy Lucas, for advice. Lucas, who was unable to have children, had miscarried years earlier.

"You know what it's like to lose a baby," Gail told her. "And I don't know how to react. What emotions am I supposed to feel?"

Another woman who saw a good deal of Gail under emotional circumstances was Gloria Hogan. Her daughter Rachel was the three-year-old who stayed with the Cutros during the investigation, even after the day care was officially closed. Gloria was surprised, even then, by the obvious disparity between Josh's reactions to the police investigation and Gail's. Josh was angry, and Gloria, who had great confidence in the Cutros and was grateful to them for keeping Rachel, sympathized. She would be "furious," Gloria said, if *she* were being harassed by the police. But Gail seemed, at most, "peeved."

"It was like she didn't really have any feelings of her own," Gloria said. "Josh had the feelings." Now that she thought about it, Gloria added, it wasn't just anger. It was all emotion. You could always tell what Josh was feeling, but not Gail. "Her affect was pretty flat most of the time," said Gloria, who was once a nurse. Gloria always felt more comfortable communicating with Josh; it was clear to her that "he was the one that was in charge." He answered the phone when she called. When she first arranged to drive to the day care, Gail couldn't give her directions; she had to hand the phone to Josh. And over time it seemed that she was always deferring to him—on decisions and on emotions.

Gail's friend Judy Mason saw her every day when they lived across the street from one another, but never saw her mad. Never? "Never," Judy answered without hesitation. She couldn't even recall hearing Gail say one derogatory word about anyone. "It certainly was not her nature to say negative things about people," Judy said. Asked if she could think of anyone else with whom she'd spent so much time without ever once observing the person in a state of anger, Judy laughed. The question had never occurred to her, but the answer was "no."

Josh's cousin Jane was the only person interviewed who has actually seen Gail express anger—or at least was the only one willing to admit it. But she had to work through tumultuous family dynamics herself before she talked about that.

Jane's relationship with Josh and Gail ran hot and cold over the years. At times they were close, at other times Jane "fell out" with one or both. When Gail went to prison, they were on good terms. Jane had attended her trial and lent her support. She visited Gail in prison, and Gail wrote her warm letters. For a time Jane took care of Lara and Kira in her own home from Thursdays through Sundays so that Josh could work weekends at a Winn Dixie. Then Kira actually moved in with Jane and her husband Danny and stayed for two weeks. It was after Pat Hallman accused Josh of molesting his daughters, and Josh moved into a motel near the airport. Josh and Kira had a dispute that was so heated that Josh dropped Kira off at a convenience store where his mother worked and told the twelve-year-old not to return home. Josh's mother called Jane, who came and picked her up.

When two weeks passed and Josh failed to call for or even contact Kira, Jane got in touch with his lawyer, Lisa McPherson. "I want you to tell me what I need to do to get legal guardianship of Kira," Jane told her. She and Danny loved Kira and were willing to raise her, Jane went on, and Kira had said that she wanted to stay with them, as long as Jane agreed to take her to see her mother. McPherson said she'd have to check with Gail. When Jane called back, the lawyer said that Gail was willing to sign. "The only thing that I ask of Josh—I don't want any support from him for Kira at all—just pay her school fees," Jane told McPherson. "Just for the books that she has to have."

Jane thought they had an agreement, but a few days later Josh called and told Kira to pack her clothes—he was coming to get her. Kira was distraught, and Danny tried to dissuade Josh, but the big man was angry and determined. As Josh left with his daughter, Danny told him that anyone who would throw out his own twelve-year-old daughter wasn't welcome in his home.

That was one of the more emphatic ruptures in Jane and Danny's relationship with Josh and Gail. They were still estranged when Jane agreed to be interviewed, but Jane didn't volunteer with an ax to grind. In fact, she didn't volunteer for an interview at all. She was one of a number of sources Pat Hallman recommended as people who knew her daughter well. Hallman took it upon herself to call these people and suggest that they agree to interviews. Hallman herself had had disputes with Jane, but she clearly believed that Jane was not the kind of person to hold a grudge. Hallman did take the precaution of telling Jane not to say anything bad about the family and to confine her remarks to "what a wonderful person Gail always was to you."

At first, Jane was not sure that she wished to be interviewed. Soon after she agreed, in March 1997, her children expressed dismay that they would be identified through her, and Jane asked that her name be changed. Like John and Judy Mason, Josh and Gail's former friends who lived across the street, Jane was well aware that insiders would recognize who she is.

In her opinion, Jane said early on, the jury erred: Gail couldn't have harmed the children. After numerous conversations that extended over six months, and following much reflection, Jane's opinions changed—and changed again. In the process she dredged up memories that she hadn't thought about for years, and she ultimately resolved to reveal all that she knew.

Jane first met Gail when Josh started dating her. "I always thought she was real good-hearted," Jane recalled. "And she seemed to be sweet." Unlike so many members of Jane's own family, Gail seemed to be a giver rather than a taker. In those days "she was young and slim. I thought she was a real pretty little girl."

Years later, when Jane had to go to the hospital to have her gall bladder removed and her husband Danny was out of town, Josh and Gail drove her. "And when Gail walked me into the hospital," Jane remembered, "she cried and cried." Another time, when Danny was in the hospital, Josh and Gail visited him every night.

"Gail was just so kind-hearted. She seemed to love babies. That's the thing I couldn't get over. It hurts to even think that somebody that sweet could be capable of something like that."

Jane particularly enjoyed socializing with Gail when Josh wasn't around. "She was such a different person when she wasn't around him," Jane observed. Alone, Gail could be outgoing and fun. Her reserve melted in the company of Jane, an extrovert who enjoyed, in her own words, "cutting the fool."

Once, Jane recalled, Gail invited her to a concert in which various church choirs performed—including the choir in which Josh sang. After sitting through quite a few songs, Jane announced that she was bored.

"You want to go?" asked Gail, who was equally bored.

"Won't Josh know that we've gone?"

"Well, we won't tell him. We'll just sneak out." They went to the mall for a yogurt, returning when the concert was over.

It was a glimpse of the adventurous, rebellious streak that Gail generally kept bottled up. Gail acknowledged this side of her personality in an April 7, 1995 letter to Jane in which she praised the music of the alternative-rock group The Cranberries. "It gets to my Bohemian side," she wrote. It was the same spirit she admired in cats, and it was no coincidence, perhaps, that she named one of hers Freedom.

Most of the time, however, there wasn't much room in her life for independence. Once Josh began working in the day care, they were rarely apart. Jane could understand a relationship between "homebodies." She and Danny didn't roam far, either. What Jane couldn't understand was why Gail "waited on Josh hand and foot" and tolerated a husband who yelled at her "all the time." An example that Jane heard regularly was: "Gail, get your big butt in here and fix me something to eat!"

"You're crazy to put up with that," Jane told her. "I wouldn't put up with that five seconds." Yet, Jane never heard Gail talk back. "I don't know how she could of stood it. I'd of knocked the crap out of him."

What was in some ways even odder was that Gail didn't seem to get angry about it. "She never showed her emotions that way. The only emotion she ever showed was her good emotion. Always trying to help somebody." The most Jane saw her do was mime a kind of cartoon version of frustration. Jane demonstrated by clenching her hands into fists, raising them in front of her face, and shaking her head as she "growled" in frustration. It came across as cute rather than angry.

Gail had a whole repertoire of such mannerisms. If she saw some morsel of food that she particularly liked—say, cherries that she was buying for dinner—she would shake her head in the same way and say, "MmmmMMMMMM mmmmmm! It's so good! I just love it!" It was the same innocent charm that had appealed to Sally, her horseback-riding friend, years before. But with Jane, who was flamboyant herself, Gail was much less reserved and much more exuberant.

That wasn't the way she was with Josh. Jane says that Gail was "scared to death of him." Once, when they were talking about a spate of robberies in the area, Jane offered her cousin advice. "If somebody ever tries to rob you, you just let them take your purse."

"Oh, no," said Gail. "I'm not letting them have my purse."

"Gail, it's not worth your life."

"Well, if I come home without my purse, and I let them take the money, Josh would kill me. So I'd rather go ahead and let *them* kill me and get it over with."

It sounded like one of Gail's deadpan jokes, but "she was serious," Jane said.

Jane suspected that Gail's fear was rooted in her husband's violent temper. Once when the couple was visiting, Jane witnessed an argument punctuated by Josh's shoving Gail around the room and then raising his hand as if to slap her. Before he did, Gail retreated into the bathroom and locked the door. Danny ordered Josh to back off. "Don't ever do that in my house again," Danny commanded. Even though Josh was three times Danny's size, he complied.

Jane had, of course, watched Josh vent many times over the years. As for Gail, Jane recalled witnessing only two outbursts of emotion that struck her as strong and genuine. One was anger and one was sorrow.

The first occurred in 1977, shortly after Josh and Gail's first child was born. It started with an obscene phone call. It was directed at Jane, who immediately recognized the voice, she said: it was Gail's brother, Barry Hallman. When she called Josh and Gail to complain, Josh told her that Barry, who was in high school at the time, hadn't gone to school that day. Jane said that she never understood what had set Barry off, but the biggest surprise was yet to come. While Jane was on the phone with Josh, Gail picked up the extension and jumped into the conversation. "You're full of shit!" she spat. "Barry ain't did nothing. It was probably one of your men friends."

"It was such a shock to me when she said that," Jane continued, "because I had never heard her talk like that before. *Me* saying that, you know—you'd think nothing of it. But when I heard *her* say it, I almost passed out. It was so out of character for her, because I always thought she was so sweet and innocent.

"It was like some other person had stepped into the body of this person I knew."

Gail wasn't through. She threatened to come over to Jane's apartment and beat some sense into her. She completed her tirade by calling Jane "an old cow." Jane's riposte included the two words Josh often threatened to slap on Gail's back when she was moving too slow: "At least I'm not a wide load like you."

When asked about this incident, Josh offered a very different account. He contended that Jane was the one who liked to make phony phone calls, and she was harassing Pat Hallman with a barrage of them. Barry was merely defending his mother, Josh claimed. Jane acknowledged that she used to disguise her voice on the phone, but she insisted that it was always in fun and never malicious.

What was more remarkable than this eruption was how long Gail's bitterness endured. After the phone call, Gail would periodically drive by Jane's apartment and holler: "White trash!"

Once, when Jane was at her grandmother Trannie's house, Gail drove up with one of Jane's young nieces. The girl jumped out of the car, gave Jane and Danny the finger, and shouted "Go fuck yourself!" Then she rejoined Gail in the car, and off they roared.

The rift lasted for nearly five years. It ended only when Trannie died, and Josh and Gail came knocking on Jane's door. Once they were back in each other's good graces, Jane says, she bore no grudge. "I don't hold it. When we got back on friendly terms again, I never thought about her saying that."

Gail's second display of deep emotion—this time sorrow—did not come after Trannie died, or after Josh's sister Rose died, either. It was after the death of Parker Colson. Josh and Gail came over to Jane's house, and Gail collapsed in Jane's kitchen. "She was sitting on my kitchen floor, just screaming and crying and going on. She was just having a fit, saying: 'Oh, my God! Oh, my God! I can't stand it!' And I remember I got on the floor, and I was trying to hold her, to comfort her."

Even though Gail's behavior seemed out of character, Jane is convinced that it was not an act. "She was sincere. She was hurting. I had never seen her like that." It was more in keeping with the way she herself would have reacted, Jane said. Gail was much more inhibited. "If she was going to grieve or anything, she's the type of person that would just sort of hang her head and sit down, you know?"

Jane attributed Gail's behavior to the depth of her feelings for Parker. Though she'd only cared for him for three months, Parker was her favorite. "She went on about him all the time," said Jane, who recalled Gail enthusing: "I wish I could keep him. I wish he was my baby."

When Jane thought back on this scene during Gail's first trial, it seemed to prove that Gail couldn't have harmed Parker. Jane could much more easily imagine Parker Colson crying and Josh shutting him up—permanently. But after she'd talked through all that she'd seen and heard, she was struck by the disparity in Gail's reaction to Ashlan's death.

Jane didn't learn of the second death until two weeks after it occurred. It was at a gathering in Jane's home following the death of Josh's sister Rose. Josh's brother Jody Barfield and his wife had flown in from Arizona, and they were all sitting in Jane's living room, talking about the previous year's presidential election. Jody had voted for George Herbert Walker Bush, Josh and Gail for Bill Clinton.

"Clinton's a baby killer," Jody challenged. "He believes in abortion." If Jody had tried, he couldn't have picked two subjects that packed a greater emotional wallop for Gail. She was at that very moment under investigation as a possible baby killer. Furthermore, she herself had had two abortions, in 1978 and 1979.

Jane did not recall any specific response from Gail or any change in her demeanor. Nor was there an argument or discussion.

Later that day Gail and Jane were sitting next to each other on a love seat. Gail turned to Jane, apropos of nothing, and said, "We had another baby that died in our house." If this remark was triggered by Jody's comments, the connection escaped Jane.

"What?" said Jane, who remembered an item in the paper two weeks earlier about a four-month-old baby that had died in New Friarsgate. But the address the article included had been the Daniels', and there'd been no mention of the Cutros.

"What? Another baby died?"

"Mmmmm hmmmmmm," Gail said slowly, nodding her head. There appeared to be a trace of a smile on her lips.

"What happened?"

"I don't know," Gail said, calmly. "I went in there to check on her and something just told me to look at her, and I couldn't see that she was breathing." Jane was struck not only by Gail's words but also by her expression. She was so calm and nonchalant, with that faint Mona Lisa smile and a distant, almost vacant look in her eyes. It wasn't the look of someone who was feeling emotional about what she was describing. It was blank, matter-of-fact. "It was like a person in shock would look," Jane said.

"I read about a baby dying in New Friarsgate in the paper," Jane told Gail, "but I had no idea that the baby died in your care." This bit of news seemed to awaken something in Gail, who was suddenly more animated.

"Josh! Josh!" Gail called to her husband. "She read about it in the paper! She already read about it!" Asked what emotion propelled this remark, Jane said she didn't know. What struck her at the time was that Gail's response was "weird." Asked whether there was pride in Gail's voice—as Jane's imitation of it seemed to convey—Jane said that the thought never occurred to her. Perhaps there was, she allowed. What was most salient to Jane was the marked contrast between Gail's cool demeanor this time and her earlier hysteria in the kitchen. "I thought it was awfully strange," Jane said.

Jane didn't tell Gail what Danny's immediate reaction was when she informed him of this new death: "Knowing Josh, he's got insurance on those kids." It was black humor. At the time, there was no reason to suspect foul play. But Danny's immediate reaction was to think of Josh—and money.

Jane mulled it over. She couldn't believe that the two dead babies were a coincidence. "I thought Josh had did something. I never thought her. She had a good heart."

Over time, however, Jane was invaded by doubts. She'd never even heard about the shaken-baby case until Josh and Gail were indicted and she read about it in the newspaper. That was hard to understand. Then there was the conversation they had about Gail's experience in jail before her family posted bond. Gail confided to Jane that she'd "cried every night."

"I know," Jane sympathized. "I would have went crazy too, worrying about my kids."

"No," Gail corrected. "I was worrying about Wolfie and Sebastian"—her cats. "It just drove me crazy knowing that nobody was feeding them or anything. I knew the kids were being taken care of."

Jane thought this reaction bizarre. "But that was Gail with a pet," she said. "Because Gail used to say she'd run off the road and kill herself before she'd run over a dog. And I used to think that was so strange. I'd say, 'You are weird. I'm not going to run my car off the road to avoid a dog or something and kill myself.' And she said, 'I'm not going to run over no animal. I couldn't live with that on my conscience.'"

For Jane, the most disturbing conversation of all was one they'd had on the subject of conscience. She thought about it a lot when she was sitting in the courtroom during the first trial. Not that she wanted to. In fact, she tried hard to dismiss it from her mind.

The conversation occurred in 1982, shortly after Trannie died and Jane and the Cutros were back in touch. They lived in the same condominium complex, and Jane and Gail were hanging out one day when Jane confessed, "I have the worst conscience. I could never run around on Danny. I eat a pork chop that's bigger than my husband's, and I feel guilty. I'd drive myself crazy. Are you like that?"

"No," Gail said, "I've never been like that."

"What do you mean?" asked Jane.

"I can block it out. I just tell myself it didn't happen, and it goes away."

"Do *what?*"

"It just goes away."

"Wait a minute. Explain to me how you do it," Jane demanded.

"I just put it completely out of my mind. And it didn't happen. And that way, I never think about it again. I've always been able to do that."

80

Simple and Calm

A number of people who knew Gail thought of her as a calm and relatively simple person. Beneath the surface, however, her life was nothing of the sort.

Nowhere was this clearer than in her relationship with her mother. On the surface, Gail's loyalties were clear. During Josh's innumerable clashes with Pat Hallman, Gail invariably sided with her husband. She called him "the boss," while she, Josh, and their children commonly referred to Pat Hallman—out of her presence—as "the witch."

Gail expressed anger at her mother even more clearly—though no more directly—in a letter she wrote to Jane from prison in April 1995. Reacting to her mother's suggestion that Josh had molested their daughters, she wrote: "Has Josh told you all the crap my mother has been doing? She's hurt me beyond repair. I can't believe she would go this far. It's too much for me to bear. I'm so thankful Josh and the kids have ya'll and that you're there for Josh. . . ."

Near the end of the letter she mentioned her mother once more: "Hopefully I'll soon be home. I'll be glad to get away from these terminal PMS sufferers. Talk about hateful mean women. My mother might be at home here."

Yet, Gail was not the type to confront her mother—or anyone else—directly. The punishment Gail exacted, according to Josh, was to strike her parents from her prison visiting list. In classic passive-aggressive style, she didn't bother to inform them; they discovered it only when they were refused admittance. The Hallmans were restored to the list, Josh added, when he decided to forgive them for the ordeal Pat Hallman had put him through.

In the prison visiting room Gail was asked if it made her uncomfortable to be caught in the crossfire between her mother and her husband. At first she refused to admit that she was caught: "I always know where my loyalties are. And they're with Josh, not with my mother." She also said, more than once: "I am my own person."

Her assertion of independence, however, failed to take into account the many ways in which Gail identified with, imitated, and depended on her mother. Like Pat Hallman, Gail dropped out of high school and got married. Both said they wanted to complete their schooling, but they soon had children and never went back. Like her mother, Gail intended to have a large family, but settled for fewer children than she told people she wanted. And like her mother, she worked a succession of temporary jobs until she settled on day care, which allowed her both to work and to stay home with her kids, as her husband desired. Over the years the once-slender child even came to resemble her mother in physique.

Gail's dependence on her mother continued long after she was married to Josh. Unable or unwilling to discipline her children, Gail sometimes asked her mother to help. When there was a crisis in her life, Gail inevitably called her mother. When her credit rating made it difficult to finance a car, the Hallmans bought one for her and let her make payments to them. When she found herself without a home, she and her family moved in with the Hallmans. After Ashlan Daniel died, her mother drove from Pelion each day to help run the day care. When Gail received letters from Missy Daniel, it was Pat Hallman who wrote back; and when Gail agreed to a meeting, Pat accompanied her and did much of the talking. When Gail was indicted and ordered to stand trial, the Hallmans bailed her out and paid for her defense.

Unlike Pat, Gail was never separated from her husband. But even in this respect she managed to imitate her mother. In a conversation that foreshadowed the fabricated SIDS death she described to Renee Barefoot six years later, Gail told a nurse in 1986 that she and her husband were separated—even though it wasn't true. Could this have been a simple misunderstanding? If it was, it was a strange one. After recording this "fact," the nurse went back and crossed Josh's name off the previous page, where household members were listed, and noted that Gail "hopes for reconciliation." Six months later the same nurse recorded Gail's assertion that she and her husband were "reconciled."

So, while Gail sided with Josh against Pat, she certainly hadn't shed the influence of her mother. When this was suggested to her, she again attempted to demur. But she had to agree that her mother did help her run the day care after Ashlan Daniel died.

At this point Josh, who was sitting across the table from Gail, suggested that he worked in the day care only because Gail needed him. And then, when the children died, he had to shoulder the responsibility. "I have to do everything," he complained. "It's always me."

"It's my fault that I was depressed?" she shot back, looking stung as tension suddenly crackled across the table. A moment later her voice rose and her eyes began to well, although no tears coursed down her cheeks.

"I had to go with Joshua and do this orthodontic procedure, and I didn't know how long it was going to take, and my bladder was killing me," she began. "And I needed medication, and I had to call the doctor to see if I could get medicine. And it was their lunch hour. When am I supposed to get time to, like, kill Ashlan all of a sudden, when I've got all this other stuff I have to deal with?"

While Gail is completing this thought, her daughter Lara, who is sitting to her left, attempts to interrupt. "Can I say something?" she asked. In the silence that followed Gail's statement, Lara repeated her question twice. No one seemed to notice. Finally, when a visitor gave her permission to speak, she launched into a description of a Flintstones cartoon of which she'd apparently been reminded by the talk about Pat Hallman. Comparing her mother to Wilma and her father to Fred, she recalled that the cartoon centered on a visit from Wilma's mother during which Fred was on his best behavior while his mother-in-law, who wouldn't leave, was on her worst.

Lara's interjection diverted her parents' attention for a few minutes, but it did nothing to alter the mood. A short time later, Josh returned to the control that Pat Hallman exercised over her daughter's life. If only he and Gail had refused Pat Hallman's demands that they leave Chicago, Josh said, they would have avoided all the trouble that followed.

"What am I supposed to do?" Gail demanded, her voice rising. "Call her up on the phone right now and just cuss her out?"

"Yeah," Josh shot back. Then, because he doesn't subscribe to profanity, he added: "Just get someone else to do the cussing."

"What do you think I can do?" Gail asked, sounding suddenly weary of an argument they've been over too many times. "Just tell her to go away and leave me alone for the rest of my life?"

"Yeah," said Josh, enjoying the opportunity to slam his nemesis. "Do that."

It was several minutes before Gail overcame her distaste for the subject to respond once more. "Well, Josh," she said in a tone of resignation, "you just want it to be us and nobody else, and you just want to keep everyone else out." It was the first and last time she spoke of how possessive Josh was. And Josh, for once, had nothing to say.

But other people who knew the couple also brought it up. Cathy Lucas,

Gail's aunt, also had the sense well before Josh and Gail were married that Josh needed to be in control. "It's not that I dislike him or anything like that," she said. "I just think he's a controlling person and doesn't give Gail an opportunity to be Gail." This behavior seemed to peak after Gail was sent to prison. When Lucas visited, she had no opportunity to speak to Gail privately because Josh was always by her side. Even when Lucas was leaving, and Gail walked her to the exit, Josh insisted on tagging along. "And sometimes you just want to discuss women things, you know?" Lucas said.

Josh's cousin Jane complained of a similar experience when she visited Gail. Worse than attaching himself to every conversation, Josh kept shooting her dirty looks, as if he resented sharing Gail. "He was serving me cold coffee," Jane said.

How far did Josh go to control Gail's life? He never missed prison visiting hours, so no one saw Gail alone. He explained to some people that prison rules were involved, but the prison's officials denied that. Most remarkable of all, Josh decreed himself a kind of warden of Gail's postal service. He insisted that Gail forward to him all the mail she received in prison—unopened. He then reviewed the letters and decided which to pass along intact, which to summarize for her, and which to discard. Jane said that she heard this from both Josh and Pat Hallman. Hallman also told Jane how she'd circumvented Josh's rules—twenty years after he'd enraged her by defeating her dating rules. Wishing to communicate directly, Gail's mother sent her a postcard. Along with the message she wished to convey, Pat Hallman included an unflattering remark Gail had made about Josh—knowing that her daughter wouldn't dare send it to him.

Was Josh's tight grip on the flow of information proof of his own guilt? Did he stay glued to Gail's side because she knew the truth, and he couldn't take a chance that, intentionally or not, she'd let something slip?

Whatever this said about Josh, it seemed to speak volumes about Gail and her marriage. Josh and Gail were not the easygoing couple many people in the community thought they were. Gail's life was not simple or calm, as Dr. Selman Watson, for example, seemed to think. And the twenty years she spent trying to navigate a course between her mother and her husband—her personal rock and hard place—did not leave her in the best mental or emotional health.

81

Odd Logic

Pat Hallman had theories about Parker Colson, Asher Maier, and Ashlan Daniel. Parker died from the DPT (diphtheria-pertussis-tetanus) vaccine he was given five weeks before his death, she said. Asher was injured by his mother. Catherine Maier never fought to get Asher back from the custody of his grandparents, Hallman asserted, because she was afraid she'd shake him again, and then everyone would know the truth. And Ashlan died of SIDS, plain and simple. She'd had a cold. At her parents' request she was sleeping on her stomach. Both were risk factors.

Why was Gail targeted? In Hallman's view, nobody wanted to believe the truth. They were more interested in finding someone to blame. "It's so much easier for Gary Colson to be angry with Gail than to be angry with God," she said. The police and the prosecutor recognized opportunities for career advancement. A big case was more important to them than an innocent woman. And if Patsy Habben and Johnny Gasser were nagged by second thoughts after they convinced the parents that their babies had been killed, it was too late to express them. They were in too deep.

Hallman was equally convinced that Gasser and Habben knew nothing about the real Gail. The portrait that she and Gail's other supporters drew is that of a shy, sweet woman who consistently maintained her innocence, was supported even by her fellow inmates, and was a model prisoner. The implicit argument of Gail's defenders boiled down to questions that they considered rhetorical. How could Gail Cutro be a good mother and wife, a lover of children and animals, and a baby killer? Where was the evidence that she had the capacity for such behavior? The answers were clear to them: She couldn't be all those things, and the evidence didn't exist.

In the prison visiting room Gail seemed willing to discuss any subject, even when her children were present. Her parents' presence, on the other hand—particularly her mother's—certainly influenced the discussion. Gail herself acknowledged that her mother "dominates" conversations, and all comments about her parents—by Gail and by others—invariably occurred in their absence. But the person who exercised the greatest influence on what Gail said was Josh.

Occasionally he answered questions for her. When asked to back off, however, Josh usually complied. At other times he threw her hints, reminding her of answers. Sometimes these occurred when her answers veered from ones he'd given out of her presence, sometimes when she hesitated a beat too long. These exchanges, along with Gail's explicit acknowledgment of Josh's influence on her, created the impression that they were doing their best to tell one story. This did not necessarily mean that the story was invented. It just seemed more important to them to remember the same account than to remember the events themselves.

Yet, Gail also asserted several times, "I am my own person." A few minutes after her first such declaration, however, she acknowledged that her parents had always sheltered her and that she'd gone from being entirely dependent on her mother to being entirely dependent on her husband. Later, when asked what she would change about herself if she could, she offered revealing answers. She wished that she weren't so gullible, so that people wouldn't "walk all over me" and "take advantage." Prompted to reflect further on her "sins" or "imperfections," she continued: "Being too slow. I should be able to get more accomplished in a day." After a moment's reflection, she who had proclaimed her independence added: "I'm happy with my time management, but that's what he would say." She gestured toward Josh. "And I'd like to do it for him."

When Gail was asked direct questions about her trial, her responses were usually articulate, and she almost always locked eyes with her visitor. No question was forbidden, but Gail didn't answer every one.

Those she declined to address were never directly about the murder charges. One example was a question about a book she'd read. An avid reader well before her conviction, in prison Gail read voraciously. One book, which must have tickled her bohemian side, was If I'd Killed Him When I Met Him, an offbeat and funny mystery by Sharyn McCrumb. Filled with strange subplots, including a torrid love affair between a woman and a dolphin, the book was basically about two wives, separated by a century, who were charged with killing their husbands. Their trials created a stir like the one that surrounded Gail's. Queried about comparisons she may have drawn between these trials and her own, Gail changed the subject. Perhaps she felt she'd been burned enough by her reading habits.

Over the course of these many conversations, two patterns emerged. Most immediately, it was easy to see the Gail her supporters tout. The shy, deferential, selfless Gail was unmistakable from the first meeting. The little-girl charm and mannerisms were often on display, and her enthusiasm could be contagious. But another impression grew over time. Some of her answers came across as contrived or deceptive. Others seemed to reveal something different from what she intended. Several comments on the allegations struck a particularly discordant note—a note to which she and her family seemed tone deaf.

"I didn't have time for that in my life," Gail announced at one point, speaking of murder as though it were a piano lesson. "Dance, karate. We didn't have time to fit this in my schedule," she continued, glancing around the table at her visitors, who included her parents, son, and husband. "Did they think I sat down and made time to murder a child? How did they think that was going to make my life any better? Besides the fact that I would never hurt a child, I wouldn't benefit from that." Gail's mother and father nodded in silent assent. Only an outsider seemed to think that this reasoning sounded strange.

Josh chimed in with his own brand of logic: "We saw how much those kids meant to Missy and Davis and Lindy and Gary. Other parents' kids didn't mean so much to them. Out of all the children we kept, Parker and Ashlan are the two we would definitely not have done something to because those kids are in the forefront of those parents' lives."

If Parker and Ashlan were the two children Josh and Gail "would definitely not have done something to," does this mean that they would—or did—"do something" to the others? Gail made a similarly jarring remark. Speaking of the murder of which she was convicted, she said: "I would never do this to my family. My family means everything to me." Her argument, like Josh's, was striking as much for what she didn't say as for what she did. The implication was that she may have wanted to commit murder, but her desire to protect her family outweighed the urge. This logic would have made sense to most people if Gail had been explaining why she'd rebuffed the romantic overtures of Brad Pitt. But murdering a baby?

Perhaps it's a mistake to read too much into the extemporaneous comments of two people unused to analyzing their words. Their arguments may say less about their ethics than about their conversational skills. Perhaps it would also be unfair to make too much of the chilly behavior of Gail's parents during a visit. But it may be worth noting that Harold Hallman borrowed a deck of cards from the prison guards, as several other prisoners' visitors did to help pass the time. But Hallman, unlike the others, played solitaire. After two hours he announced that he was ready to leave.

In response to his announcement, Pat Hallman added that they might as well be going, since it was "such a pretty day." Gail began sobbing—whether as a result of her mother's insensitivity to her own confinement or her parents' abrupt departure when she was only allowed visitors two weekends a month, it was impossible to say. In any case, a minute later Gail whispered to her mother that she wanted her father to stay. "She wants me to stay?" he responded when his wife relayed the message. "Okay," he shrugged. "We'll stay a little longer."

There was less room for ambiguity in a comment Pat Hallman had made to Gail earlier in the day. "You always wanted to take care of children," she said. This statement would have been unremarkable were it not for a conversation that Hallman had had about a month earlier with Anna Soza.

Anna Soza was Gail's fifth-grade teacher, and Hallman had called her while lining up character witnesses from Gail's past who would have positive things to say about her if they were interviewed. Soza remembered Gail as a sweet, quiet child who tried to please. Hallman and Soza chatted for a few minutes, and Soza later repeated two of Hallman's comments that struck her as important. The first referred to a conversation Hallman had had with her daughter early in Gail's day care career, before any children were injured.

"Gail had told her," Soza said, "that something might happen to one of those children in her care, and she would get the blame for it. Why would [Gail] say it if the thought was not there?"

The second revealed Gail's motivation for starting her business, and it wasn't because she loved children so much. "She did mention that the only reason that [Gail] started with the day care—I believe Josh had lost his job, and she was taking the children as a supplement for income," Soza said.

The state of the Cutros' finances was itself a murky subject. The couple gave the general impression that they were doing well, but SLED's investigation raised serious doubts. Josh's cousin Jane had often wondered how they managed to shop in stores that she couldn't afford. She remembered accompanying Gail to an upscale department store and finding, to her amazement, that the clerks knew Gail by name. Richard Hunton learned during his investigation, however, that the Cutros often neglected to pay their bills. The evidence, he said, was in their trash, where he found bills discarded in unopened envelopes, past-due statements, torn up letters from collection agencies, and letters threatening legal action.

When SLED searched their home, Hunton was surprised to find bottles of unopened perfume—more perfume than a woman could possibly use. There were clothes on hangers with the tags still on them. It was puzzling. On the one hand, they were living a lavish lifestyle that was apparently beyond their means. On the other, they were acquiring and hoarding products for which they seemed to have little use. To Hunton, it was "one more indication that they were being deceptive."

Deceptive words and deceptive deeds: Time and again Gail's evasions damaged her credibility. If she was truly innocent, why did she insist on repeating in prison that she and Josh believed that they were each permitted to care for six day care children—a total of twelve? And why did she feel compelled to add that her former neighbor, Judy Mason, who had much more child care experience than she, had told her so? Mason said that she warned Gail more than once that she was taking care of more children than the regulations allowed.

So did Pat Reid, who inspected Gail's home for the food program she was running and wrote supportive letters when Gail was fighting to keep her day care open. And so did Suzanne Pope, who had been Elizabeth Lightfoot's baby-sitter and talked regularly to Gail after Parker Colson died. All three women were supportive of Gail and did not want to believe ill of her. Yet, all three flatly contradicted her.

In prison, Gail denied telling anyone that Catherine Maier lost custody of her daughter because she abused the child. In fact, Catherine was never accused of abusing her daughter. But Linda Bass said that her description of Catherine as "a known abuser" was based on information she received from Gail. And Pat Reid distinctly remembers Gail saying that Catherine Maier's daughter had been removed from her custody after she shook the child. Asked what her reaction would be if she learned that it wasn't true, Reid said, "I would be really shocked to think that Gail would, you know, be lying and misrepresenting a story. But I don't know if she had all the facts. I would be surprised and disheartened, like I was disheartened about finding out that they had more [than six] children in their home."

When Gail was asked about some of the ostensibly damning statements that sources attributed to her, she often said that she couldn't recall. She couldn't recall telling Patsy Habben that she knew she "wasn't mentally right"—but if she did, she said a little later, she must have meant that she was not in the proper frame of mind to take a polygraph examination. She didn't remember telling Missy Daniel that she'd take the polygraph and kill herself. But if she did, she must have meant that her therapist had warned her that submitting to the test could send her over the edge. She didn't remember meeting Renee Barefoot or talking to anyone in 1992 about a SIDS death in her home. And this time she didn't offer any explanation.

82

The Protector

From the beginning, Josh was Gail's rescuer. Even before they were acquainted, in Gail's mind he was her hero. She and Josh sat near each other in seventh grade, and that was when she developed a crush on him. But it was a dream that clinched it, Gail said. She was surrounded by fire—helpless, desperate, doomed. At just that moment Josh arrived, breaking through the wall of flames and sweeping her up in his powerful arms, movie-style. When she awakened, her infatuation was complete.

It took Josh some time to catch on, and longer to act. But even before they got together, Josh adopted the role of Gail's protector. And he was always aggressive about it. Any time he saw a boy bothering Gail or directing what he construed to be unwanted advances her way, Josh would step in.

Later, of course, he "rescued" Gail from her parents and then from the youth detention facility. Sometimes his efforts were an imposition. Gail wasn't happy to be "saved" from relatives or friends with whom Josh didn't want to share time, and she almost certainly didn't appreciate being "protected" from her own mail.

There was another sense in which Josh was the protector. Any time Gail was in trouble, Josh was the shield. When DSS investigator Gary Kirkbride investigated the 1991 injury of the seven-month-old who had the bruise on his back, Josh did the talking. When caseworkers came to check the Cutros' numbers, Josh sent them away. When rumors swirled around Gail, Josh called the police and told them to back off.

His performance in court during his wife's trial was his most public and dramatic rescue effort. When it was suggested to Gail that Josh's testimony was another attempt to save her, Gail protested. He'd been trying to explain why he felt guilty, since he was the one in charge of the children. No, she was told. He was telling the jury: "If you want someone, take me." Josh listened to this exchange with his head bowed. Uncharacteristically, he said nothing.

Josh continued his efforts even there, in prison. At times, however, the results fell just as flat as they had in court. Gail mentioned that she and Josh handed Asher Maier back and forth throughout the morning on the day he was hospitalized. Neither of them was ever alone, so they couldn't have hurt him. A short time later Josh offered a different version: "Gail took Asher, and then I took Asher, and then I had him pretty much." It was such a blatant discrepancy that Gail quickly amended: "Well, we passed him back and forth."

"Well, we—well, at a certain point, I took him," Josh sputtered, recognizing his mistake, "and then I'm the one who handed him over at the end of the day."

There were at least two other children never mentioned during the trials whose lives hung in the balance under the Cutros' care. The first was in 1985, when Lara was three weeks old, and Gail noticed that she'd stopped breathing—had actually turned cyanotic, or blue, from lack of oxygen. Panicking, Gail shouted for Josh, who rushed in and revived the baby. They drove her to the hospital, where the doctors admitted her for observation.

Lara's older sister, Kira, had suffered what were diagnosed as apnea spells and seizure activity while still in the hospital immediately after birth, and the doctors suspected that Lara might be experiencing something similar. A sleep study led them to diagnose central sleep apnea—a periodic failure of the child's automatic breathing. The results were sufficiently equivocal, however, to lead Dr. Donna Rosenberg, a pediatrician and child abuse expert who was consulted by the prosecution before Gail's trial, to doubt the diagnosis. After a week the hospital staff taught Josh and Gail CPR, and Lara was sent home with a machine that monitored her breathing during sleep.

About three months later Lara had another apparent cyanotic spell. This one occurred during the day, and the child never lost consciousness. Gail phoned her pediatrician and told him that Lara's lips had turned blue. The doctor was not overly concerned; he told her to call back if the problem persisted. After about an hour Lara's lips were normal, and Gail never reported any recurrences.

More than likely, nobody would have given these episodes a second thought had it not been for the events eight years later. After Ashlan Daniel's death, however, investigators were looking for patterns. And in Lara they thought they saw a precursor. Gail was alone with a baby. Gail noticed that the baby had stopped breathing. She panicked and called for Josh, who did what he could to revive the child. Was this the first example of the pattern?

Josh and Gail had described Lara's initial "spell" many times to doctors, police investigators, psychologists, and lawyers. In this version, Gail was alone when she made the discovery. She said she was about to turn in for the night and went to check on the baby one last time. She screamed for Josh, who ran in to help.

In prison, however, she changed an important detail. She said she was not alone with the baby when she noticed her condition. The baby, Josh, the other kids, and she were all in the same room. Most were watching TV. Even her grandmother was there. And they were all in the room when she walked over to the crib.

This new detail was hard to credit. It would have a mother putting down her baby for the night in a family room where a TV was blaring and people were talking. And the mother was about to retire herself before her two-year-old (Kira's age at the time). Even more difficult to reconcile, this version contradicted what Josh described, under oath, when he was deposed on April 29, 1994—long before Gail was indicted.

"Well, Gail called out to me and when I come in there," Josh testified, "[Lara] was laying in the crib and she was blue." It is clear from this sentence alone that Josh was in another room. There was no mention of a television or kids crowding around the crib. His wife, Josh added, was "scared to death" and "in shock." Josh was the one who resuscitated Lara, while Gail stood by, paralyzed.

If Lara is added to the list, the authorities knew of four children who experienced life-threatening events in the Cutros' home: Lara Cutro, Parker Colson, Asher Maier, and Ashlan Daniel. (Kira Cutro's only known event occurred in the hospital.) In each instance, according to the Cutros, Josh took charge and either personally attempted to save the child or directed the rescue effort.

But there was also a fifth child that the authorities never knew about. Rachel Hogan was the three-year-old who was the only day care child who stayed on with the Cutros after the day care was officially closed. According to her mother, Gloria, when Rachel was two and a half—before Asher was hurt and before Ashlan died—Gloria received a phone call around lunchtime. It was Josh Cutro, who told her to rush right over and get Rachel: Her lips were blue. Rachel was conscious and alert, Josh assured her, but he wanted Gloria to have her checked by a doctor.

Gloria immediately called her pediatrician and arranged to bring Rachel in during the lunch hour. Then she and her husband, Sam—who wasn't working while undergoing treatment for cancer—raced to the Cutros' house. When they drove up fifteen minutes later, Josh was waiting at the door with Rachel. Gloria, a nurse, could still see signs of cyanosis around Rachel's mouth and under her fingernails, but they were faint. By the time they arrived at the doctor's office, about ten minutes later, Rachel looked perfectly normal.

When Josh was asked about this incident while driving to visit Gail in prison, he said that he had no recollection of it. "The things I remember most about her," he said of Rachel, "is the aggravation from her two messed-up parents. I don't remember Rachel ever being blue or anything like that." Told that Gloria and Sam had independently recalled driving to pick her up and take her to the doctor, Josh retorted: "Well, that right there is something they wouldn't do. They didn't live together. They were always apart. You never could get a hold of them." He then launched into a long diatribe about the Hogans and their failings as individuals and as parents.

Not long after making these comments, Josh arrived at the prison to find Gail extremely upset. Precisely why was unclear—Josh later offered conflicting explanations—but she soon stormed away from the table where they were talking, rising so abruptly that she knocked over her chair. When she returned a few minutes later, Josh threatened to leave and never come back if she repeated this performance. The couple then talked privately for several minutes.

Later, after the storm had apparently blown over, Gail was asked whether Gloria and Sam Hogan ever came to her house to pick up Rachel and take her to the doctor because she'd turned blue. Gail laughed: "Gloria and Sam came together?"

What was most remarkable about her reaction wasn't that Gail responded to the messengers before she responded to the message; it was that she never responded to the message at all. About the real question—Did Rachel turn blue in your care?—Gail expressed nothing: no surprise, no indignation, no horror, not even curiosity about when and under what circumstances it was supposed to have happened. She simply parried with the same defense her husband had used. Only when she was pressed did she answer the question: She said that she remembered no such event, then added her own unflattering reflections on the Hogans.

As for the Hogans, Gloria readily acknowledged she was later hospitalized for emotional problems. That was one of the reasons the Cutros kept her daughter overnight. The Hogans eventually divorced, and there were times when they were separated before then. But they said that they were living together the day Rachel was taken to the pediatrician.

The Hogans didn't remember the exact date, though each of them believed that it was some time between the deaths of Parker Colson and Ashlan Daniel. Rachel's medical records proved them right: She was taken to the office of Dr. LaRue Penny Jr. on June 4, 1993, five months to the day after Parker Colson died.

Four years later Dr. Penny agreed to read what he'd written on Rachel's chart that day. He'd noted a temperature of 101.4 and "fever started last night." Then: "Day care personnel felt she looked 'blue around the lips.'"

The rest of his notes indicated that he could find nothing wrong with Rachel besides the fever and a red throat, a culture of which came back negative. Though he sometimes noted "duskiness" in patients with a fever, he saw no cyanosis himself that day and could offer no explanation of a possible cause.

It isn't hard to understand why Josh and Gail attacked the Hogans. Well before Gloria disclosed this episode, she had revealed information that had cast the Cutros in a negative light. When Patsy Habben and Richard Hunton were interviewing all the parents who had used the Cutro day care, they interviewed Gloria Hogan on the evening of April 5, 1994. The next day Gloria contacted Patsy Habben and said she wanted to correct a false assertion. In her initial session she had lauded and defended the Cutros. She had sworn that Rachel had not stayed with them after they closed their day care. On April 6, she sat for a second interview to set the record straight.

"Last night," she told the agents, "I wasn't expecting the question concerning the Cutros' care of Rachel after closure, I didn't use good judgment when I answered the question, my loyalties were torn, and I knew that as soon as I answered the way that I did that I was wrong. . . ."

Gloria proceeded to tell the investigators what they already knew: Rachel continued staying with the Cutros past the October closing and into January—despite the fact that Gail had testified in her deposition that she didn't recall keeping any children overnight and only baby-sat Rachel, whom she falsely called her godchild, "between two and five" times after the day care closed. Despite the Hogans' canceled checks, Gail claimed that she never charged for the service.

During her second SLED interview, Gloria also confided that after she'd moved her daughter to another day care, she'd attempted to visit the Cutros with Rachel a half-dozen times. Each time, the child refused to go. "As soon as I told her we were going to visit, Rachel would scream, 'No, I don't want to go there; I don't want to see Gail.'"

Furthermore, Gloria said, during the time she attended the day care Rachel began forcefully throwing her dolls, something she hadn't done before. And when Gloria or Sam came to pick her up at the end of the day, she couldn't wait to leave. By contrast, "at her new day care . . . I have to almost chase her to get her to go home, and she seems much happier. . . ."

When the Cutros read Gloria's second statement, they were furious. What they didn't know was that Gloria still believed in their innocence and still felt loyal to them. Her conscience and her fear that she would be caught had convinced her to correct her false statement, but she remained deeply grateful to the Cutros for having cared for Rachel during those months when she couldn't herself. And deep down, she didn't want to believe that she'd left her child in the care of a murderer any more than Davis Daniel wanted to.

When Gloria met with the SLED agents, she didn't mention the cyanosis because it never entered her mind that abuse might be involved. The first time the possibility occurred to her was after she asked about the evidence introduced at Gail's trial. Gloria then thought of something else she'd never told SLED: Around the time Rachel began staying overnight with the Cutros, she suddenly developed a fear of water. She'd never had a problem bathing before, but for the next three years she hated baths and was deathly afraid of water on her head. Though Gloria didn't know it, Rachel's phobia began around the time that a neighbor reported hearing a child's scream coming from the Cutros' home, the incident Josh and Gail explained to a caseworker as Lara screaming when they brushed her hair.

Gloria never learned the origin of Rachel's phobia. When she and Sam discussed it at length, aside from Rachel's experiences at the Cutros', only one other possibility occurred to them. Gloria's son by a previous marriage had given Rachel a bath. Sam was inclined to believe that the boy inadvertently did something that scared her, but Gloria didn't accept that explanation. Her son was eighteen and extremely responsible, she said. He assured her that the bath he administered was unremarkable. And he and Rachel adored each other before and after the bath.

In the prison visiting room, while the Cutros were discussing the Hogans, Gail weighed in with her own version of Rachel's phobia before she or Josh could be asked about it—as though she anticipated another accusation. Rachel had always been scared of water during her stay with them, Gail said. In fact, she added, sometimes the only way she could get Rachel to bathe was to put her in the tub with Lara, which seemed to calm her.

The Hogans and Catherine Maier were not the only people Josh and Gail attacked while defending themselves. Years earlier the Cutros had demonstrated a willingness to impugn anyone who suggested that their child care methods might be flawed. The most notable example was "Dr. Smith," who examined the boy whose mother discovered a bruise on his back. Dr. Smith wasn't sure what or who caused the bruise, but he reported it to DSS and Gary Kirkbride investigated. Josh and Gail immediately countered by informing the mother that Dr. Smith was "a quack" and urging her to stop using him—even though Dr. Smith's partner was the Cutros' own pediatrician, and the doctors regularly covered for each other.

In the visiting room, Josh and Gail continued to attack those they blamed for their circumstances. The group included Johnny Gasser, Patsy Habben, Richard Hunton, and Irmo police officer Tim Stephenson. Less obvious targets of their wrath included the parents of Catherine Maier's former husband, Charles and Phyllis Maier, for not warning them about Catherine; their former church friend Rose Bozard, whom Gail called "a little off"; and Missy and Davis Daniel, for persuading Gail to take the polygraph exam. Even Linda Bass, one of Gail's staunchest supporters and strongest witnesses, was not exempt. They blamed her for not telling them that Missy Daniel feared that Ashlan had apnea—which, in any case, Missy denied. Finally, they blamed their lawyers for a variety of perceived offenses, foremost for losing. These were the lawyers who, in addition to their efforts during the first trial, charged nothing for handling Gail's first appeal—the same appeal that ultimately gave her two more chances to be acquitted.

83

Attention

Some of the more poignant moments in the visiting room were occasions when Gail was flanked by her two young daughters. Even as the girls literally hung on her arms, Gail seemed strangely detached, an impression underscored by her children's habit of addressing her as "Gail." Gail generally faced them when they talked about something they'd done, but she rarely commented or altered her expression. Kira was often silent; it appeared hard for her to compete. At one point she announced, as much to herself as to the others, "No one listens to me." Afterward, she stopped talking.

Lara, on the other hand, talked compulsively, especially during the early stages of a visit. When she sensed that no one was listening, she tried harder. She made faces: cute ones, dramatic ones—anything to garner attention. When her father grew weary, he told her, "Quit running your mouth, Lara." So she directed her efforts exclusively on Gail, who stared blankly in her direction, then looked right past her. "Listen. Listen. Listen. Listen." Lara tugged on Gail's sleeve, and slowly, reluctantly, Gail's eyes returned to her. Whether Lara was seeking praise or a laugh or just an acknowledgment that what she said was important, she was rarely rewarded.

At moments like this it was easy to imagine Gail as a child—a child who looked almost exactly like Lara. A child who bubbled with enthusiasm, with the playful innocence she still exhibited at times. And it was easy to imagine her trying to secure her parents' attention, which was so often trained on Barry and the trouble he created—when it wasn't fixed on Pat, who dominated all conversations. Gail said that when she talked to her mother, she "couldn't get a word in edgewise." Or, as Josh put it: "If you called Pat Hallman to tell her her house was on fire, she'd burn up before you could get the words in." It was easy to imagine Gail tugging on her mother's sleeve, saying, "Listen. Listen. Listen. Listen."

Josh said that Gail's mother and brother, Pat and Barry Hallman, are "always seeking attention. They're not happy unless they're the attention of everybody. But as far as Gail and Gail's father, they don't want any attention. And if you don't know they're even around, they're happy."

Josh may have believed this, but was that why Harold Hallman left the family—because he was happy to recede into the woodwork? Was that why Gail ran away with Josh?

———

Was Gail aiming for anonymity, or was she clamoring for sympathy and attention, as the prosecutor insisted? Many details, only some of which would have been admissible at trial, support the prosecution theory.

She had few friends when she was growing up. As an adult, she seemed almost as isolated. The people to whom she felt closest were relatives, and Josh did his best to distance her from them. Though Gail was rarely physically apart from her husband and children, she was emotionally distant.

Early in her marriage, Gail's job was raising her children. Yet, according to "Dr. Lambert," the pediatrician she used for six of those years, she was not equal to the task. From the beginning Gail was "anxious, nervous, and insecure," the doctor said. Of course, many, if not all, new parents feel anxious and unprepared. The trouble was that six years later Gail was still overmatched. "She had no control over her children," Dr. Lambert said. They were "running wild," while Gail struggled "like somebody who just can't cope with reality, with what God has given her. I mean, she was not the kind of person that should have children. She was not an effective parent in any way."

Reviewing his records during an interview after the first trial, the pediatrician discovered a host of injuries that, in retrospect, he found troubling. At age four Kira suffered a laceration above the ear—a neighbor reported Gail hit her with a stick. Kira was treated in the emergency room, and the injury was reported to DSS. DSS determined she was hit by her brother. Another notation revealed that when Joshua was seven, his mother threw a shampoo bottle that hit him in the eye. Dr. Lambert never learned the background. "I don't know why I didn't report her at that time," he said. A year later Joshua was back with a laceration of his scalp. Again, no explanation. He found similar entries disturbing. And he can't fathom why Lara turned blue while Gail was playing with her.

Looking back, Dr. Lambert wished that he'd been more vigilant in seeking explanations. In his view, the Cutro children suffered an inordinate number of injuries. And the injuries themselves were troubling. They don't suggest to him an abusive home, but one in which there was "just lack of supervision. It was like, who's paying attention?"

The Cutros stopped paying their doctor bills and, in 1987, stopped using Dr. Lambert. Their final balance due, the doctor said, was $50.00 (which they never paid).

Gail was not officially in the day care business then, and Dr. Lambert only learned of that venture when Gail was arrested. To say the news surprised him would be an understatement: "She was not the kind of person that should run a day care. She had trouble taking care of her own children. I can't imagine her taking care of anybody else's." Although he didn't follow her first trial closely, he wasn't surprised by the result. "I mean, I could see this woman snapping. This woman had a screw loose."

These early years must have been particularly stressful for Gail, who struggled to manage her children while her husband and mother continually clashed. Later, as the children grew, Josh's discipline took hold. He ordered them around, and they soon learned the consequences of flouting his will. "The Cutro children seemed to me to be too well behaved and too quiet," said Gloria Hogan in her first SLED statement. She went on: "Josh seemed to be stern with his own children. I observed that Joshua and Kira would never interact with Josh, almost like they wouldn't question him; they appeared to have a look on their faces as though they were afraid to say anything to Josh."

Gail still took care of the kids, but (as Gail would later put it) Josh was "the boss." Once the children were all in school, Gail had time on her hands. She loved her crafts work; it was the one part of her life that truly belonged to her and her alone. But she could never make enough money at it to satisfy Josh, even before he lost his job. Once he did, she needed to work. And she wanted to work. Virtually all the women she knew had jobs. Her mother suggested child care, and her closest friend was already running a day care. As a high school dropout, Gail didn't have many options, and day care sure beat What-a-Burger, which was one of the first places she worked.

She'd taken care of kids who were referred by her friend and neighbor Judy Mason, and she'd substituted for Mason when her friend was away. One of the children Judy took care of was autistic, and extremely difficult to connect with. Judy wasn't sure how Gail would do with this child, but when Judy returned the child's mother couldn't say enough about Gail.

So Gail took the plunge. She registered with DSS. Three friends, including Mason, wrote glowing references. Gail filed the paperwork, and that was that. She was in business.

Many of the early parents seemed quite satisfied. Given the needs of the community and her ties to Riverland Hills Baptist Church, through which she received many referrals, Gail was in the right place at the right time. Her business took off. It was probably the most impressive accomplishment of her life.

But then came the change. It had been Gail's creation and achievement, but once it had the earmarks of success, Josh stepped in. The place was soon transformed. Josh answered the phone. Josh answered the questions. The pattern that had begun with Josh and Gail's relationship had now extended to their family and business. Gail supplied the idea and the impetus, and Josh eventually took over. It wasn't a hostile takeover because Gail, the overtaken, was passive. But the result was that Josh owned nearly all of her life. He even encroached on the one area where he couldn't supplant her: He began helping with her crafts. What was left that was uniquely hers?

Among other things, her needs. Another day care provider was one of the first to glimpse them—though she didn't know it at the time. Suzanne Pope was the woman who took care of Elizabeth Lightfoot, the baby who died of SIDS well before Parker Colson died. Pope was forty-two when Elizabeth Lightfoot died, and she'd been in the child care field for twenty years. Her reaction to the death was so intense that she checked herself into a mental hospital. Without the help of an exceptional therapist, she said in an interview after Gail's first trial, she doesn't think she could have survived—much less resumed caring for children.

Pope was released after a week of treatment. When she went to church the following Sunday, the outpouring of sympathy at Riverland Hills was overwhelming. She was aware of it, but she was too depressed to respond. She spent most of the time crying and looking down to avoid eye contact. After the service had ended and most people had left, Pope noticed someone watching her from the center aisle. She glanced down the pew and saw Gail Cutro staring at her. When their eyes met, Gail smiled, then turned and walked away.

"Oh Lord," Pope thought, "she's probably afraid something like this is going to happen to her." But that wasn't what drew Gail, and that wasn't why she smiled. What Suzanne Pope had seen was closer to a look of envy than one of fear.

Pope knew Gail casually because Lara Cutro was in the Sunday school class that Suzanne and her husband taught. The next encounter Pope remembered was the day after Parker Colson died. Someone from Riverland Hills had called her about it, and she wanted to offer Gail a modicum of the support she herself had experienced in her hour of greatest need, but she couldn't face a visit until the next day. "It was very hard," she recalled. "It brought back zillions of memories."

When she stopped by, Pope talked to Gail about Elizabeth Lightfoot's death and the death of her own son from leukemia soon after. And that's when Gail responded by saying that she, too, had lost a child—as Pope would first reveal during her testimony at Gail's second trial. This announcement elicited even more sympathy from Pope, who had no reason to doubt Gail.

Apparently the sympathy Gail was soaking up after Parker Colson died had not been enough. So she'd made up this story, and suddenly her own experience more perfectly matched Suzanne Pope's. It echoed what Gail had done months earlier, after Elizabeth Lightfoot's death, when she'd invented a SIDS death in her own home and elicited the sympathy of Renee Barefoot.

No, it wasn't Gail's fear that she would experience the same things that led her to stare at Suzanne Pope in church; it was her need to experience those things.

Suzanne Pope and Gail Cutro were in touch regularly after the condolence call. Did they become friends? "Well," Pope said, "'friend' sometimes is used loosely. Yeah, I guess I could say that I thought we were becoming friends. I mean, we never really did anything together." What they did, basically, was talk about SIDS. Pope found their conversations extremely valuable because, though she'd been in therapy, she'd never had an opportunity to talk with someone who had been through what she had. Gail had the Sitters' Support Group that Linda Bass counseled, but Pope hadn't been able to join until several months later—and she only attended two or three meetings, because she couldn't handle "living it over and over." Pope's first "support group," and the enduring one, was Gail.

When Ashlan Daniel died, Pope rushed to Gail's side shortly after hearing the news. Gail didn't seem upset, she said. But the death hit Pope hard. "It could have been me," she kept thinking. It wasn't mere empathy. The first person Davis and Missy Daniel had approached about day care was Suzanne Pope, who told them that she hadn't cared for infants since Elizabeth's death and still wasn't ready. The Maiers had also approached Suzanne Pope about caring for Asher before they asked Gail. The convergence of these events—and Pope's realization of what they meant—overwhelmed her again. Knowing how deeply she herself was affected, she tried to talk Gail into taking time off. But Gail saw it differently: "To her, the best answer was to go on, because she loved her kids. What might work for one person might not necessarily work for the other person. So it was not for me to judge right or wrong on how someone responds to a tragedy."

Not long after, the Cutro day care was closed, and the question was moot. But the larger issue didn't disappear for Pope, any more than it did for Gail. When the Cutros were arrested, it hit Pope with a vengeance. In truth, she'd never gotten over Elizabeth's death. She'd always wondered what people really thought, and she lived in dread of the day when the police would come for her. "When Gail was arrested, I totally freaked out," she said. If Gail was innocent, it could just as well have been Pope under arrest. If Gail was guilty, Pope could have saved those children if only she'd told the parents "yes."

The first scenario was the one she dwelled on. "I really felt sorry for Gail," she said. And she wondered: "Why can't people see there's a problem with SIDS?" She knew then that she couldn't continue caring for children of any age. The morning after Gail's arrest, Pope gave all the parents two weeks' notice. A fortnight later she was out of the day care business, and she vowed never to go back.

The only time anyone from law enforcement spoke to her was when Patsy Habben and Johnny Gasser paid a call before the first trial. They wanted to compare Gail's behavior to that of a day care operator confronted by a legitimate SIDS death. Though the Lightfoot case had occurred long before the Child Fatalities Department even existed, Habben had checked out the circumstances and told Pope during the visit that they were convinced it was SIDS. That was precisely what Pope needed to hear, and it was instrumental in her recovery. It was also the very point that Linda Bass had been arguing for so long. In Bass's view, there should have been a formal procedure to exonerate the Lightfoots, Pope, and all other caregivers touched by SIDS. But there was no such procedure then, and nothing had changed.

As for the case against Gail, Pope felt too close to pass judgment—before and after Gail was prosecuted. When Gasser sat Pope down and described the evidence, she thought, "Something's not right here." It made her wonder, "How can you know someone that long and not know them?" Another part of her retorted: "You've been there. You know you're innocent." That meant that

Gail might be, too. "Honestly, I cannot say that I've made up my mind one way or the other," she emphasized. "It's too touchy for me."

She never expressed any doubts to Gail, however. Gail was her friend. Suzanne Pope was one of several friends Gail met through their involvement with SIDS. Though Gail's interest in Pope predated the Lightfoot child's death, it was only after Parker Colson died that they grew friendly. It was death that drew them together.

In fact, SIDS became a large part of Gail's life. Before Parker died, Gail seemed to be a lonely woman who had little she could claim as her own. Afterward, she had quite a bit. She had friends such as Suzanne Pope, Lindy Colson, Missy Daniel, Linda Bass, and therapist Eve Powell. While the last two were professionals who worked with her, they both behaved as though the relationship was more than business. Bass and Gail frequently chatted on the phone, and, after the day care was closed, Bass hired Gail to clean her house. Powell counseled Gail above and beyond their scheduled appointments and visited her regularly for the first six months of her prison term. Both were vocal defenders who wrote letters proclaiming Gail's innocence.

The attention and support did not stop there. Through Bass, Gail became a leader. She organized the Sitters' Support Group, which offered each participant attention, sympathy, and friendship. Bass also encouraged Gail to express her feelings in writing, which she did in "SIDS—A Babysitters Story." It was an account of her grieving in diary form. It began on her thirty-third birthday, nearly four months after Parker Colson died, and ended shortly after what would have been Parker's first birthday, about four months later. Bass was so taken with it that she edited it—changing the form, correcting a few grammatical and spelling errors, and cutting some of the more mawkish passages. Then she typed it and made copies to distribute. Suddenly Gail was, in effect, a published author. Not bad for a high school dropout.

Working with the Colsons to help produce "Red Nose Day" afforded Gail even greater recognition. But the most attention she ever received in her life, prior to her arrest, has to have been her appearance on local television, when she and Lindy Colson were interviewed about SIDS. It was an opportunity to be seen by the entire community—as a victim and also as a kind of SIDS expert. This must have been heady stuff for a woman whose husband claimed that she never wanted attention and was happy to be ignored.

SIDS, and Parker Colson's death, had become a central focus of her life. The story she wrote for Bass said so again and again. One of the more restrained passages read: "You left us 7 months ago, and it still hasn't gotten any easier. Missing you still crowds out each day, each one filled with thoughts of you."

How much did SIDS and death dominate her days after Parker died? Her Monthly Planner for 1993 answered the question. Everything listed for January was related to Parker's death. She also began numbering the weekly anniversaries of his death, which she continued not just through that month but for the entire year. In June, Gail began noting not just the weekly but also the monthly anniversaries of Parker's death. The first time she did this—June 4—happened to be the day Rachel Hogan turned blue in the Cutros' home. When Ashlan Daniel died in September, Gail began noting the weekly anniversaries of *her* death as well.

During the year she also noted in her Monthly Planner her children's field trips and doctors' appointments. But nearly every other entry—and there were dozens—was directly related to what she and others were calling SIDS.

84

A Theory

How do the pieces fit together? Here is one last theory—this time the author's.

It began with an empty space—a void—inside a deeply troubled young woman. In her writing for Linda Bass, Gail Cutro asked: "Why is there such an empty hole some where in my being?" That hole, she claimed, was the absence of Parker Colson. Parker: the child she took care of, along with thirteen other children (not counting her own), for a period of about three months. But the public reaction to Parker's death, and then to Ashlan Daniel's, seemed to fill that hole with an entirely new "family."

Her new network of caring people didn't focus on her mother or her children or Josh—they focused on her. Never in her life had she had this many friends: Linda Bass, Eve Powell, Suzanne Pope, the people in her support group, the therapists at the mental health center. And she shared special bonds with Lindy Colson and Missy Daniel.

In the story she wrote for Bass, Gail recalled an intimate moment with Lindy Colson at Parker's visitation. "She was so gentle and loving the way she talked to me and caressed my face," Gail wrote. "I knew then that one of my fears was unfounded. She didn't blame me." Gail left the funeral home a few minutes later with her parents, who urged her to rest and try to eat. "How could we eat how could we rest when they were going to bury our baby the next day?" Here, yet again, she referred to Parker with the first-person possessive. But the proximity she thought was her due was publicly denied her at the funeral. "We sat in the crowd not near the family," she complained. "I remember feeling the need to be with the family, sharing the grief, not just among all of the strangers."

Referring to one of her psychiatrists, she wrote: "Dr. Bedenbaugh seems to think I hold on to the pain because I'm afraid that once I let go of that there will be nothing left. No Parker, No memories, Nothing."

Is it possible that Gail Cutro killed Parker Colson for the same reason—to fill the void? Not the void that followed Parker Colson's death, but the one that preceded it. The void that was her life.

Perhaps Gail Cutro sensed the "empty hole" in her core long before Parker entered the scene. By the time her daughter Kira was born, she was already overwhelmed by the pressure of living in a crossfire. Buffeted by mounting bills and the unbearable tension between her husband and mother, it was all she could do to get through the day. Perhaps the complications surrounding Kira's birth afforded a brief respite. For a time it was not clear how serious the baby's condition was or whether she would survive. Suddenly, Gail and the baby were the center of attention. The other problems dissolved. Maybe the danger and the attention were like a massive shot of adrenaline. Was it exhilarating that for once she could feel something?

The apnea monitor with which Kira was sent home prolonged the attention by reminding Gail's friends, acquaintances, and family of the danger. False alarms are common with these devices, and for all the supposed anguish they caused her, Gail was undoubtedly rewarded with an outpouring of sympathy that affirmed her special status as the mother of an endangered child.

When Kira rapidly outgrew her condition, and the monitor was returned, did Gail miss the attention? Did she secretly hope for a reprise?

Lara was healthy at birth. No apnea monitor was required, even though the prevailing medical opinion, which wouldn't be refuted convincingly until the late 1990s, was that apnea, like SIDS, ran in families. Was Gail disappointed? Did her knowledge of apnea and SIDS, gleaned from the literature given to her after Kira's experience, suggest a way to get what she wanted?

Four months later Gail told her internist that she was "very depressed." She made it clear that this wasn't merely postpartum depression when she added that she'd been depressed, off and on, for several years. It had been getting worse, she said, since Lara was born.

Suppose, in her desperation, Gail decided to fake an "apnea spell," confident that she wouldn't be caught because everyone knew that apnea ran in families. And who would suspect her, anyway? She wouldn't do anything that struck her as too dangerous—just cover Lara's nose and mouth for a minute and call Josh. Wouldn't it be intoxicating to realize that she, Gail Cutro, high school dropout, managed to fool an entire hospital? On top of that, there would be something even more seductive. She would feel the ultimate power—the power of life and death—literally in her hands.

After Lara turned blue in her crib and was hospitalized, she was sent home with an apnea monitor. Again and again Gail told the dramatic story of how Lara nearly died. But in time this, too, faded. The monitor was taken away, and Gail was still depressed. But this time she wasn't going to have another child. She was stuck with her dead-end life—unless she found another means of escape.

Gail didn't possess the imagination or the insight to have created Lara's condition—or to understand how it would make her feel—if chance hadn't presented Kira. But it did. And after that fulfilling experience, which swept her up in a secret excitement, she wanted nothing more than to repeat that high. And she knew how to get it.

Perhaps it worked the same way with SIDS.

Fate presented the death of Elizabeth Lightfoot. Gail watched from the wings as Suzanne Pope was suddenly the center of attention, showered with sympathy. It reminded Gail of her experience with her daughters, only on a much grander scale. Did she long for people to regard her the same way they did Suzanne Pope?

In time, of course, people did. It began with a little experiment. She simply passed the word to Rose Bozard that what happened to Pope had happened to her. Then there was the interview with Renee Barefoot, when Gail described the SIDS death that never happened. Was that Gail's dress rehearsal for murder? Or perhaps it was an audition, to see if she could play the part, to see how it made her feel. To Barefoot, Gail appeared shattered. "She just had this look in her eyes like she wasn't all there," Barefoot remembered. It was a vacant, unfocused look. When Barefoot's description of that look was repeated to Josh's cousin Jane, Jane said that it sounded like what she saw when Gail told her about Ashlan Daniel's death. To Gail's one-time friend Judy Mason, it sounded like Gail's "victim mode"—the way she looked when she came over to talk about Asher Maier's injury, or when she cornered Mason in the craft store to talk about Ashlan Daniel.

Then came the death of Parker Colson, Gail's professed favorite. David Caldwell, SLED's criminal profiler, theorized during the investigation that Gail killed Parker and Ashlan because she wanted them for herself. She wanted to own them, to possess them, and murder was the ultimate form of possession. It was also the ultimate assertion of power by a woman who often felt impotent.

If Gail was guilty, were these the kinds of angry, impulsive acts often associated with the suffocation and shaking of babies? Experts agree that many of these acts are committed by exasperated and self-absorbed parents or baby-sitters who lash out to silence a baby's screams. Dr. McKee suggested that Gail harbored a deep reservoir of unexpressed anger. Was this the lethal combination?

Perhaps. But this view does not account for Gail's fascination with Suzanne Pope, or her "rehearsal" with Renee Barefoot, or the glazed look in her eyes that Barefoot described. When Barefoot's description of Gail's behavior was repeated to Dr. McKee, he said that it sounded like someone dissociating—that is, mentally and emotionally stepping outside herself. In a state of dissociation, a person may view her actions as though she were observing another. Was that what happened to Gail? Was that why she told Patsy Habben that she knew she wasn't "mentally right"? Was that why she described both deaths as unreal?

In her "Babysitters Story" Gail wrote of Parker Colson: "I thought that because we were trained in CPR and I had called 911 everything would be ok. We had brought Lara back. We could do it again. At this point all events are fuzzy. I can't remember things that happened. It was as if things weren't really happening, it wasn't real."

Her description of finding Ashlan Daniel was even more striking. On the witness stand at her first trial, Gail testified (as previously described) that she was about to awaken the child to feed and change her. As she bent down over the crib, something looked wrong. The child was too pale.

"Something's definitely wrong," Gail testified, recalling her thoughts, "but I don't want to admit it."

"What do you mean you don't want to admit it?" asked Lisa McPherson.

"I don't want to believe it," Gail corrected herself, leaving one to wonder whether "admit" was tantamount to a confession.

"Did you touch her at that point?" McPherson asked.

"No, I did not." Instead of checking for a pulse or administering CPR, she ran from the house looking for Josh, who was picking up Lara at school.

"If I touched her," Gail explained, "it would make it real."

"It would what?" asked McPherson, in what sounded like a double-take.

"It would have made it real."

Was Gail fleeing—physically *and* psychologically—not just from a death but from a murder? And was this why she didn't need to check on the child: because she already knew that Ashlan was dead, and by her own hands?

If murder was Gail's method of jump-starting her moribund emotions and filling her void, SIDS was a perfect cover. SIDS parents and other care-givers invariably blamed themselves; Suzanne Pope was a classic example. A murderer, therefore, would not even have to conceal feelings of guilt. She could confess to such feelings with impunity. She could openly collect mementos from her victims, like the "trophies" serial killers often take. And each time she went home, she would surreptitiously reinforce the oldest stereotype about murderers: that they return to the scene of the crime. When Jane asked her how she could stand to stay in that house, Gail said that she found it "comforting."

If Gail was, indeed, guilty of suffocating the children, one sentence in her "Babysitters Story" almost sounded as though she was flaunting her crime: "The pain is so raw, so stifling, it feels as if it will suffocate you, close off the airway."

To paraphrase one of the questions Gail asked in the prison visiting room, What could she gain by killing these babies? How about: power, sympathy, and attention—and new relationships through which they could be channeled.

The first of these relationships was with the dead children. She could not "own" them by giving birth, but she could take them by inflicting death. It was the only way she could forge a continuing relationship. In her mind, the deaths united them forever. She may have considered the other day care children in some sense "hers," but that could only be temporary. Eventually, they would all leave her. Not only that, as infants grew to toddlers they passed from Gail to Josh. Parker Colson and Ashlan Daniel would never change and never stray. She could create a shrine to Parker in her living room, where his photograph and footprints were framed. She could idealize him in her writing. She could visit him daily in the graveyard and bathe him in her grief.

Gail's ownership of Parker and Ashlan bought her Lindy Colson, Missy Daniel, Eve Powell, Linda Bass, and the rest. These new relationships must have felt deeper than the superficial acquaintances that passed for her social life. And when the conversation flagged, she could always talk about the deaths.

On that score, she rarely required prompting. The extent to which Gail was consumed by these deaths, and passed her obsession on to her children, can be gauged by the comments of her daughters' teachers. "Kira was having a great deal of trouble concentrating in class and would cry very easily," her fifth-grade teacher told the Irmo Police Department in 1994. "I became very concerned and sent a note to her mother" about two months after Parker died. "Mrs. Cutro called me back at school and explained that Kira had been very upset because one of [Mrs. Cutro's] babies had died. At the time, I did not know that Mrs. Cutro kept children in her home. Mrs. Cutro was very emotional over the phone and kept talking about the baby that had died, and I assumed that it was one of her own children. She told me that she and Kira would go to the cemetery to visit the baby, and that this helped both of them deal with the situation." Thoughts of the dead baby continued to haunt Kira for the rest of the year, the teacher added.

When Gail met with a Special Education teacher to review Lara's progress, she again rambled compulsively about Parker, the teacher told SLED. Gail cried as she confessed the guilt she felt for failing to save Parker. What convinced her that she could have done so, Gail explained, was her earlier rescue of Lara, which she also described in detail.

When the teacher tried to focus on the subject of their meeting, according to the SLED report, "Gail kept bringing the conversation back to the death of Parker." The teacher was "surprised that Gail would be seeking attention or [having] such a personal conversation with a stranger such as herself because Gail barely knew" her. If sympathy was what Gail sought, she missed the mark. The teacher left the meeting suspecting that Gail had induced Lara's apnea, resulting in the reading disability that had required the teacher's intervention.

Still, Gail succeeded often enough in eliciting the reactions she desired. But even if this was her aim, it doesn't explain why she chose this particular method to achieve it. Three towering questions remain: Why would she kill a baby? Why more than one? And why not her own?

Only one person knows the answers—and it's likely that even she doesn't know them all. In any case, she maintains her innocence. Any attempt to answer these questions must be speculative. With that caveat, Dr. Joel Dvoskin was willing to offer general information about crimes of this type that might shed light on Gail Cutro.

Dr. Dvoskin was a forensic psychologist who had written widely, and testified frequently in civil and criminal courts, about mental illness and violent crime. He also consulted with a wide array of government and corporate clients and taught at both the University of Arizona's College of Law and its College of Medicine. (Earlier he was in charge of all mental health services in New York State prisons and for five months ran the New York State Office of Mental Health, the largest agency of its kind in the country.)

Dr. Dvoskin was careful to acknowledge that he had never met or communicated with Gail Cutro. He based his responses on information about the case and the principal participants that he was given, which included Dr. McKee's notes and test results.

Most of the cases of women who killed children with which Dr. Dvoskin was familiar—indeed, with which anyone in his field would be familiar—involved women like Susan Smith and Waneta Hoyt, who killed their own. Only a few were serial killers who killed outside their families. Florida baby-sitter Christine Falling confessed to killing three children in her care and later admitted that she actually killed five, two of whom were initially diagnosed as SIDS victims. Manuela Marshal, another Florida baby-sitter, confessed to killing two children and leaving two more brain-damaged. Genene Jones was a pediatric nurse in Texas who was convicted of killing one infant, though she almost certainly killed more than a dozen of her patients and injured still more.

Undoubtedly there are many others, but they aren't nearly as common as women who kill one child—especially mothers who kill their own. Furthermore, not much is known about them; no one has collected data on them. Even in cases where the women confessed, their statements aren't necessarily enlightening. Christine Falling, for example, offered a vague guess that she was angry at the children for screaming.

Still, Dr. Dvoskin was convinced that conclusions can be drawn about most women who kill children. "If you're not psychotic or so distraught that you aren't thinking clearly, and you choose to work out your pain by killing a child, it certainly would be my generalization that the level of narcissism that that takes is very high. And I would say that's very likely to be a commonality in all these cases, whether it's your own kids or somebody else's.

"It's as though they are saying, 'It's about me,'" Dr. Dvoskin continued, defining the kind of narcissism he was talking about. "And 'it' is everything— *everything's* about me. So in the Susan Smith case, the kids were an impediment to what she wanted in her immediate future and had no independent value or meaning or rights. To kill any kid, you would have to be able to think that way."

People suffering from attachment disorders—and Gail Cutro sounded to him like such a person—are unable to treat others as whole human beings, with their own needs, desires, and rights. Dvoskin described how they process relationships: "I only respond to the part of you that meets a need of mine. And you almost literally don't exist when you're not meeting my need."

Usually, individuals who think this way have failed to bond properly with their own parents and carry into adulthood that same inability to connect with people. At least, that is the theory, Dr. Dvoskin said. "And that would explain why some people care a great deal more for animals than they do for people." Animals don't object to being treated as less than human. "Your cat really doesn't need for you to care about it, other than feed it so it stays alive. When you pet me, you pet me; when you don't, I'm on my own. Dogs give you unconditional love. You don't have to feel guilty if you ignore them.

"Babies are less convenient for most of us." Being a parent, he added, is "the best thing I ever did in my life. But no one would ever describe parenting as convenient."

Dr. Dvoskin was not a big fan of diagnostic labels. They can be pejorative, and they tend to lump together people who don't always share the most important characteristics associated with a diagnosis. But sometimes, he acknowledged, they can be helpful in pulling together a constellation of behaviors that one wouldn't otherwise link.

"Certainly, a lot of people would call Gail a case of borderline personality disorder," Dr. Dvoskin said. People with this diagnosis exhibit attachment difficulties and typically have trouble regulating and expressing emotion. "They exaggerate their responses. They don't ever have little disappointments. Everything's either elation or just a horrible end of the world.

"They tend to be especially sensitive to a feeling of abandonment. They have exaggerated fears of abandonment. They'll scream 'You've abandoned me!' because they want you to go to the store with them and you've got another commitment. Literally as if you had left them in the desert with no water. You just think, 'Where is this coming from?'"

As Dr. Dvoskin's comment suggested, borderlines can express intense anger that is not just inappropriate but may appear inexplicable. When Manuela Marshall confessed to Florida law enforcement agents that, as a nineteen-year-old baby-sitter, she killed two children and left two more brain-damaged, she provided a remarkable window into this kind of thinking. Near the conclusion of a long interrogation, Marshall described what happened when she killed two-year-old Kathy Ricks.

> She climbed into my lap, and I was right there. And I got mad that she left, that she didn't want to stay in my lap anymore. And I said, "Damn, I love you!" And you, you don't want to stay with me. I was loving her. I was being nice to her, and she didn't want to stay with me. . . .
>
> I went into the room to play with her, but she really didn't want to play either. And when I tried to play what she wanted to play, she didn't want me to play, and it just kept making me mad inside. Then she crawled on the bed to put her baby [doll] in bed, and I just said, "Well, wait a minute. Why don't you put her here?" And she just looked at me and said, "No." And I said, "You don't want to do anything with me, do you?"
>
> And I went up and grabbed her and started—I just [got] real mad inside and I said, "Fine, if you're wanting to be on the bed, you can be on the bed." [But] she didn't want to stay on the bed. . . . It made me so mad. She had a quilt thing, so I put the quilt over her and held the quilt down and that didn't hold her still. She was still trying to get out. So I just laid across her. I was so angry inside. I, I couldn't stop myself. It just made me mad. I was loving her and she left me and she didn't want me to play with her. She didn't want me to do anything with her. And I'd never done anything to hurt her before.
>
> I think at one point she said, "Get off of me," but it was like, "No, we're going to lay here because I want you to, and you didn't want to do anything with me. So now you're going do what I want you to do." And the next thing I knew, she wasn't breathing.

Whether or not this confession helps explain the deaths of Parker Colson and Ashlan Daniel, it does seem to explain Gail's behavior in the prison visiting room. There were two instances (previously described) when Gail responded to visitors' remarks with uncharacteristically strong emotion. The first occurred after Harold Hallman announced that it was time to go. Immediately after the second, Josh threatened to leave and never return—possibly repeating a threat that provoked Gail's outburst. In the first case Gail began sobbing. In the second she rose so abruptly from her chair that she knocked it over as she stalked from the table.

Both can be decoded with the help of Dr. Dvoskin's comments. In each case Gail's response was anger. The second expression was fairly straightforward. Her sobbing in the first looked like something else, until you remember Gail's statement that when she's angry, typically she cries. In each case the response seemed inappropriate and inexplicable—especially since any threat from Josh was clearly hollow, coming from the man who never missed a visiting day. Her reactions make sense only when you realize that the triggering event was threatened abandonment, and that for borderlines (which Manuela Marshall and Gail Cutro appear to be), abandonment is the omnipresent fear.

Gail's inability to express her anger in a socially appropriate manner is common among borderlines, according to a therapist who wrote a book on treating the disorder. "The problem for many Borderline patients," says Marsha M. Linehan in *Cognitive-Behavioral Treatment of Borderline Personality Disorder* (1993), "is not the overexperience and expression of anger, but rather the underexpression of it; that is, they are anger-phobic. . . . Many patients are afraid that if they do get angry, they will lose control and possibly react violently. They also fear that if they engage in hostile behavior, overtly or covertly, they will be rejected."

What could have motivated Gail Cutro to kill a child? "The behavioral principle is this," said Dr. Dvoskin, "if you want to know the reason for the behavior, look to its consequences." Rage sometimes builds for years in a passive person who doesn't know how to express anger, he said. When such people "snap" or commit an act of violence, they discover an effective way of dealing with it. "They now have a way of blowing out that rage that's worked for them—maybe for the first time in their life. This is somebody who's been eating rage as a passive victim of other people's meanness for literally her whole life. Who finally finds a way to feel powerful. Think of the times you've been mad, and maybe it was your boss and you couldn't do anything about it. It doesn't feel good. In fact, it feels horrible. I don't know where this quote comes from, but I use it over and over again: 'I wanted to throw stones at the temples. But I had no stones. And there were no temples.' It can feel very good to finally blow up, if you're not a person who's used to that."

Why did she target infants? A pop-psychology view, Dr. Dvoskin said, is that she saw herself in the babies and, by killing them, spared them the pain she herself was forced to endure. Dvoskin thinks that explanation unlikely and suggested an alternative: "What else can she control?" Babies were readily available to her, and no matter how much anger Gail expressed, they could never complain. "You take the anger out on somebody where it's safe to do so." It was the one area in her life where she could exercise such complete control that she could allow herself to relinquish control of her anger. And perhaps she blamed the babies for abandoning her or rejecting her love in the same narcissistic, irrational way that Manuela Marshall did.

The Renee Barefoot incident suggested a degree of planning and premeditation that's rare in child homicides. Dr. Dvoskin wasn't convinced, however, that the psychology behind the acts was as calculated as one might infer. He doubted that Gail Cutro sat down and decided one day that she would attempt to replicate the experience of Suzanne Pope. More likely, the image of Pope being treated the way Gail wanted to be treated created a lasting impression. "And then, one day you're sort of at wit's end," Dvoskin speculated. "You're angry and lonely and disconnected, and *boom*! I'm not even sure it's a cognitive process. It's sort of a memory of an emotional picture."

The powerful sensations of the moment would have been reinforced by the secondary gains. And during the initial stage, these would have extended well beyond mere attention. "Not only didn't she get caught," Dr. Dvoskin pointed out, "she got praised and was made to feel connected. And she was nurtured." In other words, she received the emotional support so sorely lacking in the rest of her life.

If Gail was beset by these impulses, why didn't she kill one of her own children? Again, the experience with Kira might have awakened her to excitement and possibilities that hadn't existed before. Gail wouldn't have realized she missed the stimulation until after Kira had outgrown her condition.

If this was the case, then Lara would have presented another opportunity. And Lara's life *was* in danger. She did turn blue in her crib. If Gail was responsible for that, perhaps she spared Lara because she feared that Josh would blame her. Or maybe she was experimenting, unsure how long one had to block the airway. It's also possible that Gail lost her nerve, or that Lara survived out of sheer luck.

In any event, Gail decided not to have more children and terminated two pregnancies, even though she claimed she'd always wanted a larger family. She has explained that she couldn't stand the stress of the baby monitors. Perhaps there was another reason. Maybe she knew that the next baby wouldn't be so lucky.

And, in fact, assuming Gail committed these crimes, there was a strong chronic component. Once wasn't enough. Had it been, it's almost certain that she never would have been caught. It was the perfect crime. Parker Colson's death had been ruled SIDS. No one was investigating, and no one was complaining. She'd acquired many secondary gains long before Asher Maier was hurt. Why didn't she stop?

"This is a palliative, rather than a curative, in terms of the rage," Dr. Dvoskin explained. "It makes it better for a while, but what's wrong is still wrong." He knows this from the reports of women who have committed similar crimes. Afterward, "people describe a stunning sense of relief, and calm, and peace. Although they also often report that it may not last so long."

He suspected that Gail's "crazed look" that Renee Barefoot and others described was, as Dr. McKee suggested, dissociation. But he considered it at least as likely that Gail dissociated not to commit crimes but to deal with "the aftermath of guilt." Gail's old friend Judy Mason and Josh's cousin Jane observed "the look" during conversations with Gail long after the events she was describing. Barefoot may have witnessed Gail's reaction to her own lie—and perhaps Gail knew, even then, where it would lead.

Dissociation, however, was no more than a brief respite. It might temporarily relieve the guilt, but the guilt always returned. If Gail fell into the pattern of many serial killers, Dr. Dvoskin said, then killing blew out the rage and left her temporarily calmer. But knowledge of her crime later brought shame, remorse, and ever deeper depression. These, in turn, would have refueled her rage—until the cycle repeated.

85

Denial

At the conclusion of their first interview, the Masons, the Cutros' former neighbors, seemed convinced that children were, indeed, hurt at the Cutros' day care—but that Gail wasn't responsible. Judy Mason didn't want to believe that someone she loved was capable of behavior that violated everything she held sacred. "And I recommended children to go to her day care," she added. "That is not an easy thing to live with."

Other people had their own reasons for wanting to believe that Gail was innocent. Helen Ayer, who headed a division of the South Carolina Home Child Care Association, didn't want to believe that anyone who shared her calling—and whom she actually knew—could do such a thing. And like many other day care providers, Ayer was afraid that she would be tarred with the same brush.

Some parents stood firm after the first trial. "Carol" simply saw no evidence that either Josh or Gail could ever harm a child. Gail spent months tending to the special needs of Carol's son, who had pneumonia and then repeated bouts of bronchitis. Gail made sure he always received his proper medication, which had to be administered as many as four times a day. Thinking about the crime Gail was convicted of, Carol asked: "How can someone that gave that care to the sick child do the other?"

There were also parents like Ramona Bowers, who were once staunch supporters but later reconsidered. During the investigation Bowers sent angry letters to politicians. She once told Patsy Habben that she would remove her son from the Cutros' day care "only if you stand in front of the door and prevent me from going in."

Bowers later thought a lot about the powerful effect of denial. "When you want in your heart to believe that this person's innocent, you look at everything and try to justify it in your brain. You don't want to accept that you could have put your child in harm's way."

John and Judy Mason, who had long avoided grappling with emotional issues such as loyalty and denial, and then had struggled with them through that lengthy first interview, wrestled with them again afterward. During a follow-up interview held before Gail's conviction was overturned and she was retried, they said that they'd discussed the evidence and theories raised during the first interview and arrived at some painful truths that changed their minds.

"I think Gail killed those two children," Judy said. "I think that she probably would have killed Asher if something hadn't intervened. And I had come to that conclusion at the time of the trial, too." As she worked through the information, old and new, she dredged up thoughts and feelings from that time. What emerged were discrepancies between Gail's statements to Judy and the testimony of multiple witnesses.

One that stood out involved Asher Maier. "I had been told by her that she had not held him that day," Judy remembered. "And then, in the trial, I heard someone say that [Gail] greeted them at the door that morning holding him. And, you know, it was a lot of things like that that really just kind of started piling up. And it made me realize that she had not been honest with me about things that had taken place."

Judy couldn't remember the other discrepancies, but some of her recollections suggested possibilities. Gail told her that she and Josh eventually received a group-home license that allowed them to care for twelve children. During the trial, however, it was clear that they hadn't. Gail had also confided to Judy that Ashlan Daniel did not go down quickly or easily for a nap. The Daniels testified to that effect during the trial, but the Cutros contradicted them.

"There was a discrepancy in what I was told by her, and what came out in court, on every one" of the three children, Judy said. These discrepancies had convinced her that Gail was guilty, but she hadn't been ready to confront that knowledge. "I think I was just trying to delude myself," she said. As in Ramona Bowers's case, emotion trumped logic. In the end, she said, she "had to be honest with myself."

As a scientist, Judy's husband John had long since decided that the babies' deaths could not have been natural, and he was convinced that Gail's account of Asher's injury was "reconstructed." He just considered Josh the more likely culprit.

"But up to that point," he explained, referring to the first interview, "I could not fathom Gail doing it. And so, the lens that I was viewing it all through, the paradigm I was holding onto was: She couldn't have. And so why would she make up stories? Was she frightened that, if she told the truth, it would sound incriminating? Or did she think that if she said it this way and then a different way, that she could make it seem better for Josh, if he was the one?"

It was much easier for John to entertain the possibility that Josh did it, and that was the theory he propounded at the first interview. But it didn't take into account all the evidence. There was a lot he'd never known. By the end of that long night, he wasn't as sure as he'd been at the start. There were too many threads that didn't fit. The more he thought about them, the more they seemed to point to Gail. It was the only logical conclusion.

Josh's cousin Jane experienced something similar. Like Judy, Jane couldn't believe that Gail was capable of murder. Yet, during the trial she, too, had had second thoughts. She kept replaying Gail's remark that had so disturbed her, the one that suggested an absence of conscience: "I just tell myself it didn't happen, and it goes away." It was, of course, the very definition of denial, and during Gail's trial Jane was eager to put it into practice herself by banishing all doubts about Gail from her mind. After all, Jane was there to demonstrate her support. This was no time to dwell on misgivings.

A few years later, however, when Jane was asked to resolve her knowledge of Gail with evidence that emerged from the trial, her doubts intensified. When she reviewed events, new interpretations occurred to her. She'd been puzzled, for example, by Gail's reaction to Parker's death—when she literally collapsed on Jane's kitchen floor. Jane had attributed this outburst to the depth of Gail's feelings about Parker. Later, another explanation seemed more plausible: "I think she realized what she did. Because she did it, you know? I think it hit her. I think it must have hit her, what she had did to him. Maybe she couldn't block it out then or whatever." And maybe that explained why she later failed the polygraph.

Previously Jane had asserted that Gail couldn't have murdered these children. What changed her mind? "I just used my common sense, and not my emotions. How many times can two babies die in one place, the same age, another baby's got brain damage, you know? I mean, it's just too unbelievable.

"And it's like everybody I talked to, they'd say, 'Wouldn't you have quit watching those babies when the first one died?' My God, I would have, because I would have went completely crazy. I mean, there's no way I could have ever kept another baby. There's just no way in Hades. And they just kept right on like it was nothing."

Jane considered for a moment before she continued. "But still, I will have to say this. If I'd been on that jury, I don't know if I could have convicted her. It would have been hard, because to me it wasn't proven that she really did it. It was just the circumstance that all those babies died there."

Before she finished, Jane revealed one more tidbit that was a fitting final twist. One of Gail's favorite movies, she said, was *Serial Mom*. Released the year Gail stood trial, this black comedy, directed by John Waters, starred Kathleen Turner as Beverly Sutphin—the quintessential suburban housewife. Or so she appeared to be, until we learn that beneath her perfectly presentable exterior hid an explosive temper. When it was triggered—invariably by utterly innocuous comments or situations—she killed the person who had offended her, often in an extremely gory fashion. Yet, no one can believe that she, of all people, was actually a serial killer—least of all her family. When even they can no longer deny the truth, they do their best to conceal it and keep her from killing again. Eventually, however, she's apprehended and tried for murder.

In the movie the cops find a stack of books on murder in the Sutphins' trash. They confront Beverly's husband, who counters: "I'm sure those are my son Chip's books." But the detectives know better; they've already traced the books to his wife. Discussing the Cutro parallel, Jane said that Gail was always an avid reader, whereas Joshua had never been a particularly good student—much less a bookworm who read in his spare time.

Near the film's end, another character defended Beverly using the precise terms that Gail Cutro would later adopt. Beverly, the character declared, is "a normal housewife trapped in a nightmare of circumstantial evidence!"

———

What about Josh? If he didn't injure the children himself, wasn't he still involved? Didn't he have to know? These questions lingered in the minds of many. The authorities had once believed that Josh was involved. After all, they indicted him—and they didn't drop the charge until Gail was convicted.

Understanding Josh can be as difficult and speculative as deciphering Gail. Various theories have been floated, and the solicitor's office wasn't alone in offering more than one. This final theory is, again, the author's.

Josh, of course, always maintained that his wife was innocent. On the other hand, according to his stepbrother Jody Barfield and his cousins Jane and Suzanne, Josh had always had a fair-weather relationship with the truth. Jody said that Josh lied regularly. Jane called him "a compulsive liar," and Suzanne agreed that "he's a bullshitter."

SLED uncovered documents that supported these assertions. In addition to his falsified tax returns, several résumés Josh sent to prospective employers were seized from his home. In one he said that he'd graduated from Gage Park High School in Chicago, a claim he repeated on various employment applications. In another he asserted that he'd graduated from Midlands Technical College in Columbia. By his own admission, both claims were false: In an interview, Josh acknowledged that he'd never graduated from high school or college.

From his trial testimony to his deposition to the various jobs he'd told parents he'd quit in order to work with Gail, it was transparently clear that Josh was willing to play fast and loose with the facts. It was equally obvious to the Masons that he and Gail sometimes "reconstructed" events when they felt threatened. All of this would seem to suggest guilty knowledge.

For another man, this would be strong circumstantial evidence that he knew how the children died. But not necessarily for Josh—precisely *because* he ignored the truth so often. Josh's form of denial seemed to include a denial of reality, when reality proved inconvenient. It wasn't the denial of a psychotic, who breaks with reality; it was the denial of a narcissist who preferred to live by his own rules. He was, in other words, a master of rationalization. Once, when asked about his imperfections, Josh said that he needs to work on his temper. Yet, a few minutes later he defended—even exalted—his anger: "When Jesus went into a temple area and seen that gambling was going on, all sorts of things that were wrong, that was disgracing the temple, He got angry and He did something about it. I do the same thing. It doesn't mean I'm committing a sin—as Jesus was not committing a sin just because He was angry. He knew what the Lord wanted, and that's what He did. And that's what I do."

And this was a man talking about his *imperfections*. The level of narcissism inherent in these comments was typical of Josh. His propensities for blaming others and for indulging in breathtaking grandiosity were as much a part of him as his massive frame and pale blue eyes.

By his own description, Josh was a neglected child who had little opportunity to bond with his parents. His subsequent relationships reflected that. Jane and Suzanne said that Josh was never very good at making and keeping friends. Asked why not, Suzanne had a ready answer: "Because he thought he was a big shot and everybody was little."

"He always wanted to order everybody, and tell everybody what to do," added Jane, who first saw the pattern in their childhood games. "Just like when we'd play baseball on the side of the house. And as soon as I would strike him out, and it was my time to go in to hit the ball, he would quit. And then the next day, he'd say, 'All right, I won't do it this time. I'll let you go to bat first.' And I'd go to bat first and get struck out. And he'd go back in, and then, just as soon as I'd struck him out: 'I quit! I quit!'"

Jane laughed at the memory. "I mean, that's just the way he was. If he couldn't win, he didn't want to play. And if he couldn't have his way, he didn't want to do it." Of course, all children go through a phase of development during which they behave this way. The problem, according to Jane, was that Josh never really outgrew it. "Josh looks out for number one," she said. And it isn't a style conducive to making friends.

Even in the prison visiting room, playing cards with his wife and daughter, Josh insisted on winning. When the cards weren't falling, he simply cheated. He wasn't subtle, either. "Do you think we're stupid?" Gail said at one point. "We see what you're doing." Josh smiled in response, but he didn't stop. Jane wasn't surprised to hear this story. "He's going to get what he wants," she said, "any way he can."

On a later visit Josh told Gail about a recent trip to Myrtle Beach during which he and Jody Barfield arm-wrestled. Josh won easily, and this gave him the idea of setting up a booth where contestants bet twenty dollars for a chance to win fifty if they beat Josh. They never did it, but when Gail heard this, she immediately pointed out that gambling was illegal. That hadn't occurred to him, Josh replied.

"You never think about laws," Gail spat. "You just do what you want to do." It was an interesting exchange, coming from a prisoner to her visitor.

Josh's me-first philosophy separated him from would-be friends. For example, when asked whom he felt close to besides Gail and his children, the only name Josh mentioned was Barfield's. But Barfield didn't put much stock in this. "He couldn't possibly respect me or care anything about me," Barfield said, "to lie to me the way he does."

When Gail was in trouble, Josh's response was automatic. An attack on Gail was an attack on him. He grew up in a family of criminals. He may have had fewer run-ins with the law than the rest, but he undoubtedly learned how to handle himself at his mother's knee—just as he'd learned to shoplift. The first rule, of course, was: Don't get caught. When there was a problem, get your story straight, deny everything, and cast blame elsewhere. And don't rely on anyone to back you, because most of your so-called friends and family will be too busy looking out for themselves.

His young cousin Tammie Williams knew the drill. Her childhood had a lot in common with Josh's. Unlike Josh, though, she had no qualms talking about it. She told the truth because there was no one she was trying to protect.

For those who still wondered if Josh was the one who harmed the children, the division of labor that so many day care parents described was only the most obvious reason to reject that theory. It wasn't just that Gail took care of the babies and Josh cared for the toddlers. Once the babies died, Gail was consumed by them. The shrine she constructed for Parker Colson, the notations she entered in her Monthly Planner, the article she wrote for Linda Bass—these were not the kinds of things that would have occurred to Josh. The children's deaths became the core of Gail Cutro's life. She couldn't stop talking about them long enough to have a conference with her daughter's teacher. Josh's life, on the other hand, revolved around them only to the extent that external forces—the police and prosecutors—dictated.

Did Josh know what Gail was up to? Probably not before Parker died. But then she began lying and collapsed on Jane's kitchen floor. It's hard to believe that Josh noticed nothing, but it's easy to believe that he ignored what he saw. He was never going to turn her in, no matter what she did. He'd fought too long and hard to possess her.

There were also secondary benefits for Josh. He was the one who was so possessive, so obviously dependent on his wife. And he was the one who had endangered them both by introducing crimes like shoplifting and tax fraud into their lives. Gail's crimes represented a dramatic reversal. Suddenly, she was the guilty one who had jeopardized their lives, and she was the weak one who was dependent on him. For a man who demanded control, that must have felt like enormous leverage.

When Gail became a suspect, so did Josh. They were both asked questions, and it was almost second nature for him to coordinate their answers. Going to the Masons' house after Asher Maier was hurt was probably a practice session to work out the kinks. Gail needed the practice more than Josh did. He'd been doing this sort of thing his whole life. He could rationalize to the point of convincing himself he was telling the truth. Perhaps that's why he was able to pass the polygraph while Gail, despite what she told Jane about her ability to make unpleasant experiences disappear, couldn't.

Gail had learned a lot about denial at the foot of the master. But Josh was in a class all his own. And in this case, all he had to do was avert his eyes.

86

Thinking Like an Investigator

Two years after Gail Cutros' first trial, *The State* newspaper ran a two-part series called "Who's Watching Day Care?" It was written by Clif LeBlanc, who had covered the trial for the newspaper, and he used the case as a hook to examine the larger issues. Of the many statistics he cited, one neatly encapsulated the problem. The state's Day Care Licensing division had eighteen full-time regulators to oversee an industry comprising four thousand registered or licensed day cares that served 123,000 children. And, again, these numbers did not even include the vast majority of day cares, which were not licensed or registered.

LeBlanc reviewed the many flaws in the investigations of the Cutro day care—especially before SLED's Child Fatalities Department stepped in—and outlined corrective measures that the various agencies had already adopted or would adopt shortly after his articles appeared. The most important message for parents, however, was sprinkled between the lines and then delivered at the very end. It boiled down to this: You can't count on government to protect children in day care. Though this may seem to absolve government of responsibility, it was only stating the undeniable reality of the situation.

Time hasn't changed that. In 2013 the *Minneapolis Star Tribune* won a Pulitzer Prize in journalism for a series on day care safety. The articles found that 51 children in Minnesota died in day care during the previous five years—48 of them in home day cares. Government regulators hadn't even noticed the statistical spike until the newspaper uncovered it. The articles also found that

Minnesota was not making as much information available online about problem facilities—especially family day cares—as other states. And it sometimes took years for regulators to close unsafe operations.

In addition to identifying the many flaws in the state's tattered safety net, the newspaper also noted that there is not even a national database to quantify the number of children who die in day care each year. A dozen states don't even require child care facilities to report deaths to their states' licensing agencies.

Another big problem the series identified involved the attitude of parents. "Parents sometimes turn a blind eye to problems," the paper found, "and often direct their anger at regulators, not the provider, when a day care is shut down." The newspaper's conclusion? "Loyalty blinded parents to serious problems."

Indeed, misdirected loyalty may be one of the greatest dangers to children in day care. As Ramona Bowers can attest, parents who bond with caregivers may unwittingly endanger those who need and deserve their attention most: their children.

What can parents be expected to do? First, no matter how thoroughly they check out a day care for quality and safety before enrolling a child, the job doesn't end there. In a sense, that's when the real work begins. Parents can never learn as much about a facility and the people who run it when they're shopping for a day care as they can after they make the choice. It's only when the child is enrolled that they have regular access to the operation and can observe it in action.

They should take advantage of that opportunity to monitor their children's care. Parents would do well to think of themselves as investigators. They can be subtle about it; they don't have to pretend they're with the FBI. But it behooves them to keep their eyes and ears open, and to drop in unannounced from time to time. They should ask questions, talk to other parents, and listen to their own instincts. When their gut warns them that something's wrong, they should be ready to make a change.

They don't have to learn everything there is to know about the caregivers and the service they're providing. Obviously parents who use a day care can't be expected to learn what the police did during a seven-month investigation of Josh and Gail Cutro. Learning to think like an investigator doesn't require conducting surveillance and searching through the caregiver's garbage.

Thinking like an investigator means that you ask questions, and you don't assume that you already know the answers. And you ask them in a way that's designed to elicit information. Not all questions are. For example: "Everything's fine, right?" isn't a question. It's a plea for reassurance.

There were issues at the Cutro day care that raised red flags for some parents. When there's a personnel change, parents need to pay attention—especially when the new caregiver changes important rules and seems to be running the show. When telephone calls aren't answered or returned, and no explanation is offered; when doors are locked and shades are drawn, and parents are kept waiting outside, the caregivers have effectively barred unannounced visits. That should probably be a deal-breaker.

When Lt. Patsy Habben from SLED's Child Fatality Department sent her son to kindergarten, she chose the same school that her daughter happily attended, which made it convenient. But she didn't assume that he'd be safe. The first thing she did was thoroughly inspect the premises. She asked the staff if they used Clorox to disinfect, and she asked where they kept it. When she saw a container that hadn't been secured, she said, "This won't do."

She asked the teachers lots of questions, and she showed up unannounced. And not just in the beginning. She continued to do so periodically. She also tested the staff. Not pop quizzes in math or spelling—these tests were more important. She sent some of her daughter's medicine to school with her son. It was medicine virtually identical to the correct medicine her son was taking, so if the teachers hadn't noticed, no harm would have been done. But Habben was glad to see that they didn't administer it. They sent it home with a note that included the relevant health regulation prohibiting them from doing so.

Needless to say, Habben did not make herself popular with the kindergarten staff. But her job wasn't to make friends; it was to ensure that the teachers were taking good care of her son.

This approach runs counter to the social conventions many parents are used to. Checking up on a caregiver, and asking lots of questions, may be viewed by some as impolite, unneighborly, or downright disloyal. Not that parents spend much time thinking about it. They're more likely to avoid such behavior instinctively.

Other factors may play a role. Obviously cost and convenience are relevant. Expenses mount swiftly with multiple children, and many parents endure long commutes even before they add a day care shuttle. Sometimes there's only one affordable choice within range. And the decision to change providers may require taking time off from work to restart the selection process. This alone may pose real challenges.

In addition to the physical and financial tests, most of us are not used to firing someone in such a direct way. When we're dissatisfied with a plumber's work, we can simply call another one next time. But making a change in child care is different. It's much more personal. Issues of race and class can make the prospect almost impossible for some people. A mother in suburban New York employed a nanny to care for her children. The mother worked in the city and rarely had an opportunity to observe her employee with her children. But the mother's friends reported that the nanny was often inattentive at the playground and rarely interacted with her young charges—and when she did, she was frequently cross. The mother was disappointed but not shocked. She was an intelligent woman who had recognized her employee's limitations. But she was well-off and white, and she made it clear to her friends that there was no way she was going to fire her poor, Black nanny. In essence, it was simply too politically incorrect.

In the broader context, it's easy to understand why parents focus on relationships with caregivers—and try to avoid friction. Day care is the glue that holds family life and work life together. But when parents become invested in "bonding" with day care employees, they can lose sight of the children to whom they *really* owe allegiance. That blindness is dangerous.

Maybe it takes a case like Gail Cutro's to hammer the point home. It certainly had an impact on one state. "The citizens of South Carolina were profoundly affected by this case," declared Sherry Driggers, the day care licensing director, nearly three-and-a-half years after Gail's first trial. Driggers knew because she fielded so many calls. Many were from average citizens worried about the quality of care their children were receiving. "And we did have a lot of calls from media, wanting us to come in and talk about what parents needed to do," she added.

Everyone seemed to want answers to the same question: "What is quality child care?" The questions didn't cease when Driggers left work, either. People would approach her with questions in the grocery store.

If the Cutro case grabs people's attention and helps explode complacency about day care—and forces parents to confront their vulnerability—perhaps that would be an appropriate legacy. It's the one that helped Davis Daniel learn to live with his daughter's death. Ashlan Daniel died, her father came to believe, so that other children wouldn't have to.

Afterword

At this writing (February 2023), Gail Cutro has applied for parole five times, and five times she has been denied. She first sought parole in September 2004, even before her final appeal had been decided. The second time was in 2013 followed by parole hearings in 2015, 2017, and 2019.

The hearings were not elaborate affairs. They lasted around ten minutes. The prisoner appeared before the seven-person parole board—which sits in a conference room in Columbia—through a video linkup. Gail was allowed to invite up to five people to join her at the prison to participate in her presentation: three supporters along with a lawyer and minister. In 2013, she was accompanied by her daughter and son, Lara and Joshua. Two years later, Joshua and his girlfriend attended. Each year Gail answered questions posed by the board chairman, and her children told the board that they missed their mother and needed her back in their lives. At the two most recent hearings, she was alone.

After the prisoner finished answering questions, members of the community were ushered into the conference room to give their own presentations to the board. Typically, the people who appear are the victims and/or their families. Lindy and Gary Colson, who had by then divorced, and Davis Daniel were accompanied by relatives at the hearings. In voices filled with emotion, the speakers took turns urging the board to deny the parole request. Most poignantly, Kasey Colson—Parker's little sister—spoke in 2019 about the brother she never got to meet, and the fear she has felt as a mother with a son of her own. In the last three hearings, Johnny Gasser made an appearance to underscore what the case meant to the community, even though by then he was a partner at a defense firm he had cofounded.

When the speakers concluded, they filed out of the conference room and the parole board made its decision. Seated around a table, all the members had electronic switches that illuminated a red light or a green light on the table before them. When they voted, they could see the result immediately. If it isn't unanimous, a discussion ensues. None was apparently needed to decide Gail Cutro's fate.

The most dramatic moment in the hearings occurred in 2013. After Gail described how she had prepared herself for parole (she'd earned her high school equivalency degree and had joined prison groups to improve herself) and what she intended to do once she got out (attend to her elderly parents, who had agreed to pay her a salary), the board chairman asked, "What was going on that made you commit this crime?"

Gail paused before answering. She had probably decided in advance that protesting her innocence was not a winning strategy. "I got caught up with some things that my husband was doing," she began. "And"—she hesitated for a moment here—"I don't know exactly how far he was involved in this, but, um, I have serious doubts of his innocence."

That was her complete answer, and it was the last thing she said at the hearing. It was the first time on record that she did not proclaim her innocence. In the three hearings since, she has not denied her guilt.

It was far from the first time, of course, that a finger had been pointed at Josh. In 2013, however, it was highly unlikely that it was part of a strategy devised by the man himself. Josh and Gail had divorced years earlier, and it had been a long time since they'd seen each other. For much of that interval, Josh had been in prison himself.

Nearly all the crimes for which Josh Cutro was convicted were related to drugs. They began, as previously noted, with his arrest in 1997 for shoplifting over-the-counter pain pills. But for several years the punishment was almost laughable. The change came in 2002, when his life seemed to spin out of control. In August he was arrested at a bar for threatening to kill a man with a loaded gun. The following month he was arrested again on charges of selling Ecstasy to a narcotics officer.

It all came crashing down in July 2003. He asked a female police officer posing as a prostitute in a motel parking lot to sell cocaine for him. When she attempted to arrest him, he drove off. The officer called for backup, and the chase was on.

Before Josh was apprehended, he hit two police cars, ran over an officer's foot, and was shot in the leg as he sped off. When he finally wrecked his car after several more high-speed maneuvers, he emerged with a knife and threatened officers. This time he was shot in the arm before he was taken into custody. He'd hoped the police would "shoot me in the head," Josh told a reporter the next day. "I felt it was time for me to move on."

Two things about this arrest particularly upset him, Josh continued in that interview. He was not in the motel parking lot to solicit prostitutes. "I've got plenty of girlfriends," he insisted. And the initial police report had said that he was selling crack. "That was no crack," Josh said with characteristic bravado. "That was just the best cocaine around."

In July 2004, he pled guilty to assault and battery with intent to kill, vehicular assault, and selling drugs. And he seemed contrite. "I'd like to apologize to the court for all my wrongdoings, and I accept responsibility," he declared. He was sentenced to twelve years in prison (and was required to serve at least ten).

If he'd intended to make a fresh start once he got out, it didn't take long before his resolution was derailed. In May 2014, he was arrested after a hit-and-run auto accident. Once again he pled guilty. He was sentenced to six months.

In the wake of these developments, perhaps there will be more questions about who the real villain was in the Cutro day care. And in truth, it's easy now to see why Josh Cutro was never a suitable caregiver. But if the Cutro case has anything to teach, it's that we also need to recognize that danger may be draped in a deferential personality and a shy smile.

Appendix

Interviews with Two Experts

Each of these women offered practical advice about how to keep children in day care safe. The second pointed out that her comments are just as germane to the care of a host of other vulnerable individuals with whom she has worked, including the elderly, people with disabilities, and patients in hospitals or rehab facilities. Neither of these experts was shown the manuscript of *In Good Hands* in order to ensure that their answers were independent and based entirely on their own knowledge and experience.

Flora Colao was interviewed on October 10, 2015.

Colao, who was sixty-two at the time of this interview, is a therapist who works with children and adults on detecting, stopping, and treating abuse and other trauma. She is also a consultant and teaches personal safety and crime avoidance. She earned a master's in social work from Adelphi University in 1976, and went on to found two programs in New York City: a rape crisis center at St. Vincent Hospital and the Children's Safety Project at Greenwich House. As a pioneer in working with child abuse victims, the only training available in the 1970s, she says, was workshops. When her daughter was born in 1976, Colao brought her to work for her first eighteen months. That decision not only solved her own child care problem at the time, it proved to be a canny career move. When St. Vincent colleagues saw all the toys in Colao's office, "I was getting referrals because people assumed I worked with kids before I actually did." She still spends about a week every month in New York, but she's now based in San Francisco.

Q: Have you had experience dealing with safety in day care—both home-based day care and day care centers?

A: Yes. I've worked with children who were victimized in those settings. I've also had parents who were terrified of putting their kids in day care, or who were terrified that something happened because they saw a change in their child, and they didn't know what it meant. So a lot of the calls I got from parents were, "I don't know, should I be concerned?" I have a number of parents with child abuse histories who installed cameras in their homes. They had home-based care of their children, and they wanted to make sure that their kids were safe. And they had monitors that they could check to see what was going on.

Q: Did you find that having a monitor was useful?

A: For a lot of parents, it gave them a sense of security. For other parents, it created all kinds of anxiety. One woman discovered her babysitter—if the baby took a nap, she would leave. Sometimes a half an hour, and [the mother] didn't know where she went. And that was very disturbing. And then it was, "How do I confront her on this? What do I do?" Another woman discovered the babysitter was spitting on her floor. It was: "I don't even know why this is happening, but it just grosses me out. She's really doing a good job taking care of my child, but she's spitting on the floor."

Q: So they got information, and sometimes they didn't know how to process it.

A: Yes.

Q: Did you ever advise parents that perhaps they ought to install some sort of monitoring device?

A: I had a mother whose kid had bruises. And she was like: "She said he fell." And I said, "You can either fire her immediately, take a few days off, and find someone new. Or, how does your kid seem? What's going on? Have you thought about some sort of monitor?" I always bring it up as a question, not as a suggestion, because I think that parents are already frightened. And for the family that can afford it, then it becomes: "I'm a bad mother if I *don't* do it."

Q: I have certainly read about home day cares where the providers have cameras and make available to the parents the ability to stream what's happening with their children from their own computers at home or work. Have you had experience dealing with parents on this issue?

A: Oh yeah. And a lot of parents find it very reassuring. For a lot of parents that means: "I know my kid is safe." It's like being in the other room, and I can look in the window and see what's going on. But I don't have to let my kids see me to get upset that we're separated. A lot of parents find that very reassuring.

Q: Do you think it's a reliable indicator about how things are going there?

A: I think it can be. I mean look, if people are going to be deceptive, they're going to be deceptive. But I do think it makes staff think differently. If you know people are watching, you behave differently. I think that's the nature of humans.

Q: Have you offered parents advice on how to choose a child care facility or caregivers?

A: Absolutely. The first thing I tell them is they should check in with everyone they know whose judgments they trust. Find out where they sent their kids. What they liked, what they didn't like. What was the quality of the care their kids got? How did their kids do? How are their kids now? Ask their kids—if they remember it—how do they remember it? Because the kid's assessment is probably your best assessment. If the child is articulate enough to tell you, you're going to get a much clearer understanding of what it was like. Kids will be very precise in their detail of what they like and don't like. And they'll tell you if there were mean teachers. They'll tell you if it's not fun. Because you want your kids to have fun. You want them to thrive. You want them to learn, if it's a preschool setting. Mostly you want them to be in a loving environment that's safe.

Q: At what age are children able to process what's happening to them and therefore, whether it's at the time or later, tell you what really happened?

A: I think the information is going to vary. By the time the kid is three or four, they can give you the emotional information. Why a kid particularly likes or dislikes someone varies. I can tell you my own experience with my grandson. We worked very hard to find him a good preschool. And we did. Highly recommended, highly regarded. He initially seemed to be thriving and liking it. Then he wasn't. He wanted to stay home. Now his not liking it coincided with his baby sister being born. Was it jealousy? You go back and forth. You question yourself, you doubt yourself. It was a place that had all the qualities. You could drop in any time. There were windows you could look in. The caregivers seemed genuinely loving. But he was increasingly miserable. He was like, "They don't like me. They say I'm bad." And really, what we later discovered was he had a teacher who just had a hard time with active boys.

There was one point where I decided to pick him up early, and four boys were in the office at pick-up time. Four four-year-olds were sitting in the office, and I walked in and I was like, "What happened?" And one of the kids said, "Oh, he was bad, too." And then I realized, "You know what? This is the wrong place." We went from there to a pure play-based place. He didn't learn a lot, and when he started school, he was completely unprepared. So he had to make up a lot, which he did. But he had a blast. He felt accepted. He felt loved. What's your favorite thing about school? "Dirt mountain." He would be outside playing in the dirt. Now he had four loving [parents and grandparents] around him all the time, but he was still in a situation that was not good for him.

Q: Now you described a situation where he had this new sister and all these other collateral issues. And you've got separation anxiety. So if a young child resists going to a new day care, is this a red flag? How can a parent tell what's a real red flag, and what may be masquerading as a red flag but is not?

A: You have to look at it from the whole child point of view. This kid is clearly having a hard time with something. If parents haven't dealt with their own history, then for them, it's "Oh my God, she's being abused." I have a young mother I work with. She's constantly convinced her kids are being abused. Because of her own history. It's like the constant terrorized call. "He had a stomach ache when it was time to go to school." And I was like, "Yup. Four-year-olds who don't feel like going to school sometimes have a stomach ache. Let's see. Let's play detective a little bit. Let's ask him what's going on." And it's really walking her through how to talk to her child. What is it about school? "Do you know what you were supposed to do today?" And then it turned out that there was some anticipation about a project they were doing that he didn't want to do. And that's really what the stomach ache was. So you have to ground yourself as a parent, take several deep breaths, and be curious and not make assumptions. Because if you're curious, the kid can eventually get to what it is.

My granddaughter switched classes in her preschool. She's four. We went through this tremendous separation. "I don't want you to go. I'd rather be with you." And then I was like, "Well what is it? I'm trying to understand. You used to love school. And now you're so unhappy." Then it was just, "It's a new classroom. You can't do a project unless they ask you. And you have to pick a project, and I don't know what to pick." It was just: "This is overwhelming for me because the system is different." Now, if I was a nervous parent or grandparent with my own history to project onto it, I would be like, "Oh my God, somebody in this class is being awful to her." And I would start looking—because as humans we look for patterns—I would start looking for what's different about this classroom. Oh, the other one has the door open and this one has the curtain on the door. You'd start looking for wrong things. You have to be open and curious, and try to figure it out from the kid's point of view.

Q: How important is it for parents to learn to play detective when they're dealing with day care?

A: I think it's important when you're dealing with anything. The truth is you have to be able to know what's really going on, and the more curious you are, the clearer an understanding you'll have. It has to be part of your thinking, and not necessarily always assuming something is sinister. I always ask the kids, "What was the best thing that happened today? What was the worst thing that happened today? Was there anything that made you angry? Was there anything that made you laugh?" In just those four questions you get a wealth of information. They'll tell you what's going on, because that's how they remember. "I didn't like it when Ella wouldn't share with me. I really liked doing that project. It really made me laugh when so-and-so said 'fart' to the teacher."

Q: Of course what we're assuming here is verbal skills that make it a lot easier for a parent to keep track of what's going on. It's got to be a lot more challenging with preverbal children. And a lot of them are these days, with two working parents being so common. So for parents who have preverbal children, what are some of the red flags they should be concerned about and try to explore?

A: It's very tricky with infants. It's very tricky with nonverbal toddlers. You have to know what's normal for your kid. If it's normal for your kid to initially cry at separation, I wouldn't worry. But if you have a kid who normally cries for a minute but by the time you walk out the door they've stopped, who is now clinging onto you—I remember working with a father whose son was abused in a day care center. And he said, "I look back and I remember being angry that he was wrinkling my shirt, that he was clinging so hard that he was crumpling my shirt. And now I feel so guilty. I was worried about my shirt, and here was my beautiful boy going through this, and I didn't realize it." Part of it is getting to know what's normal for your child in different situations. How does your child react to relatives they don't know, friends of yours they don't know versus people that they know but are not necessarily family? That's a good gauge. Also, you want to look at eating patterns and sleeping patterns. Has that changed significantly? The problem is with different stages it changes. But if you're seeing something that's really different, that's certainly something to look at and think about. How their play changes, if they stop playing. If you have a kid who's normally happy and now is not so happy, you would be concerned about that.

Q: What are some of the positive characteristics parents should be looking for in the facility and the caregivers that will provide them with reassurance that this is the kind of environment that will be good?

A: Is it warm and loving and does it seem to be responsive to kids? Do they have age-appropriate toys? Do the other kids seem happy to be there, or is everybody crying or sleeping? I'm always concerned if they're all sleeping. I've heard of situations where kids were drugged, because that made life easy for everybody. Does it seem physically safe? Does it seem baby-proofed and child-proofed? Does the caregiver seem to have an individual understanding of your child?

There's one of the best home day cares right in my neighborhood. I see them in the park all the time. They're limited to six children because the director puts her own kids in. And one of her things is she takes kids out every day, no matter what the weather. She tells parents, "I believe very strongly they need to be outside. No matter what age they are, they get at least a half-hour outside every day. We go across the street to the park." I've seen her with kids in the rain, splashing in puddles. In the sun, playing in the sand box. I see her all the time. One of the things that's really wonderful is that she genuinely adores all of her kids. But she's also very clear on their individual personalities. So she'll say, "This one's a shy one, so back off; don't rush her. He's really active. I've got to watch him. He's going to climb." She knows all the kids very quickly. And so does her staff. She knows who has allergies. "Put extra sunscreen on her. That one will never keep a hat on her head." You want to look for: Do they have an individual sense of who they work with?

Q: Suppose a parent does some research, checks some references, goes to meet with the caregivers at this facility that's highly recommended, is able to observe and feels pretty good, and then she notices that there's an outlet that's uncovered. Is that a deal-breaker?

A: I think you bring it to their attention. "Hey, wow. I'm really liking everything, but I see that outlet's uncovered." Sometimes there's a very simple explanation: "I totally forgot. I was plugging this in. Thank you for bringing it to my attention." Then it's sort of like, we all do it. We all make those quick errors. But I would also be more watchful. I would come back unannounced a couple of times to see what's going on.

Q: What if the caregivers don't like the disruption of having people come unannounced?

A: I would want to know the rationale for it. And I would want to let them know. The couple of moms I know who had their issues, one of them was just really upfront with the day care center. "I know you're perfectly fine. I have heard only good things about you. I really have this terrible anxiety. If you tell me I can't come, I can't leave him here." The woman was like, "Oh, I'm so sorry that happened to you. Yes, of course." Once she heard that, she only needed to drop by once or twice and she was fine. The other thing you can do, and I have had parents do this, is say okay. And then say, "Oh, I have to pick him up early today." And show up to pick him up early. I think there are ways to do it. "Oh, I'm sorry, I'm running late." And show up late to see what it's like when other kids are there.

Q: Do you think visiting unannounced or unexpected periodically is a really important part of playing detective?

A: Yeah, I think it is. It's an important thing to be able to do, and it's important to know. But I think the bulk of the information you get in regard to quality child care is from other families and particularly other kids. And you see kids who thrive and you see kids who don't. I got a call recently from a grandmother, and she said her daughter is in a single-parent situation. Has to work. Works full-time. She's got him in a day care. He's sick all the time, but what she finds really distressing is he's so aggressive. I heard this and I thought, "This may be this kid. But I wonder, is he somehow having to fight for attention? Is he not getting attention unless he's fighting?" When you see that kind of behavior, what else is going on?

Q: How important is it for parents to talk to other parents?

A: I think it's crucial. And not just one other parent, but several other parents. And finding out what their experience is, what works. For millennia, children were raised in communities. That's not happening anymore.

Q: We're talking about after they select the day care. When their kids are in day care, they don't just assume everything is going okay. They need to keep talking to other parents. What is going to come from those conversations?

A: I'll use my grandson's example. He was miserable. He was one of four children with a time-out in the office at four years old. At his birthday party, my daughter casually said to one of the other parents, "I don't know what I'm going to do. He just hates school." It set off this groundswell. The other mother said, "So does mine." We found out that all the boys hated school. This was not an individual child's problem. This was a systemic problem. So talking to other parents: "How's he doing? How's she doing? Does she like school? She really hates the art class." It's all information that's helpful.

Q: What about the relationship of parent to caregiver. Let's assume we're dealing with a mother who is the primary contact and a female caregiver. I'm aware of situations where there was a real closeness and a bond formed between the mother and the caregiver. And that seemed very important to the mother. Is that an important factor—positive or negative—in the day care equation?

A: Oh I think it can be a very important factor. Look, there's positives and negatives in everything. But I think that if you feel close to the people taking care of your kids, you do feel like you can rely on them and you're going to get the feedback you need when something's up. The negative side is that it's always hard for us to see flaws in people we care about.

Q: What about the way that relationship can affect a parent's willingness not only to see problems, but to act on them?

A: Then you need sort of a sounding board. If it wasn't somebody you knew, what would you do? Or if someone came to you, what would you do? I do that with kids sometimes. Would you want your best friend to go to this school? "No!" Okay, why? "Oh, she'd hate it." That always gives you a clue of what's going on.

Q: How difficult can it be for parents to decide they need to make a change in day care? What are the factors that can make it difficult?

A: It is very difficult. Because it is starting the process all over again, having had a negative experience and wanting to avoid that. So in some ways you're having to reassess how you made your first decision and trying to figure out your next decision. And all the more reason you'll need to rely on parents. And you'll need to be able to articulate what went wrong the first time around, and what you're really needing this time around. My grandson being the perfect example: We knew that the second place was not the ideal place for him, but we knew it was the right place as a stopgap.

Q: Have you counseled parents who were in the process of deciding to fire one day care and hire another one?

A: I have. And it's hard. Sometimes it's really clear why they're leaving. Sometimes it's just not the right fit. It's not the right fit for my child's temperament. And it becomes an issue of knowing your child and knowing what works for your child.

Q: Have you found sometimes that the parents have a hard time accepting the role of being the employer firing an employee, and feeling that they need to have justification that they can articulate in order to feel that they can do so?

A: Yeah. It's funny you should say that. One mother was like, "My kid is miserable, but there's no real reason." And I was like, "That's a reason. Your kid is miserable. For whatever reason, this is not a fit for your child." The kid would say, "She's boring." And it was really that you just had someone who didn't play with kids, and he really needed to be engaged. She was keeping the kid clean and fed and taking the kid to the park, but she wasn't engaging and the kid was unhappy. That's a reason. Being unhappy is a reason. Sorry, it isn't about you. It's the way your personalities are. But that was a reason. I think we all feel like we have to give—I had one mother who said, "Well I'm just telling her I'm moving." Because she was going to move in a few months. She said, "I'll just tell her I want to get the new person on board before the move, because I don't want to hurt her feelings."

Q: That's a big deal, isn't it? The hurt feelings issue.
A: Exactly.

Q: And was that okay?
A: Look, whatever it takes to get it done. Whatever your reason, it doesn't matter. You want your kid in another setting because this one isn't working.

Q: Is it okay to make things up?
A: Why not? I always tell people, "Lying is an important social skill that we rarely teach our children except by example." Now obviously you want to be honest on the important things, but there are times that it just makes things easier to say this is what's going on because it's pragmatic. What I always try to do with people is, "Okay, what is it about owning this that's so hard for you?" You usually have someone that's spent their lives pleasing others, so they would rather lie because it's too uncomfortable for them. I do try to get them to work on that. "Why is that so uncomfortable? Aren't you entitled to all your feelings the same way your child is? It's interesting to me that you're saying your child's feelings are important, and that's why you want to make the change, but your feelings are not important enough. We should maybe work on that. But do whatever's easiest to get this done." That's the other piece of it. Otherwise people, while they're working on themselves, don't get what needs to get done for their kids, and their kids have to be the priority.

Q: How can parents know what's going on in their children's day care? What you've told me so far is: They can talk to other parents. They can talk to their children, if their children are verbal. They can . . .

A: Observe when they're there, observe other kids.

Q: Observe in the park, if it's a facility that takes kids out, as the one you described. Some have camera capability—they can monitor remotely. Are there other ways that we haven't talked about that parents can find out what's going on in their children's day care?

A: If you can find someone that's already been through that program, you want to talk to them before you enroll your kid. I would also talk to the teachers. They let you know some of what's going on. Both the positive and the negative. "What do you like about working there? How long have you been there? I have a colleague whose daughter is thinking of going into this [field]. Would this be a good place?" They'll tell you. I had one teacher from a day care center say, "Well, we haven't had a raise in four years. Everybody's getting frustrated. It's not easy work." That's an interesting thing, because if you have unhappy employees, it makes it harder for them to be patient and loving with your kids.

Q: You're thinking of larger set-ups where there are multiple employees.

A: It's harder with home-based day care, when there's a lot of infants. I'm a great fan of volunteer something if you can. I'll do a story telling sometimes or a story reading. I've done crafts projects at different centers. Because I think it does give you a sense of what's going on and how they interact.

Q: There's one thing we haven't talked about. What about the government? Does the government help to keep day care safe?

A: Well there are all kinds of regulations and accreditations. So you definitely want to have a place that's accredited, that meets all the guidelines. And that does mean fingerprinting staff, that does mean doing background checks, all of that.

Q: In some places at some levels. Home day care does not necessarily require what you just described.

A: In California it does. Everybody has to be fingerprinted and go through a background check before they can set up a legal home day care. There are illegal ones all over the place, but to be a legal home day care you have to. It's not hard to set it up. It's time-consuming.

Q: Would you have confidence that a day care center that did all that was required would then qualify to be called safe?

A: Well I certainly think it's safer. It's much safer. And then you want to look at what it's like in terms of child friendly—then all those other things need to be looked at.

Q: Based on your knowledge and experience, whatever state someone lives in, how much can you count on the government monitoring safety in day care in the United States in 2015?

A: It's probably cursory. I think people get licensed. Once they're licensed, not a lot is looked at. There aren't repeated checks. But all new employees, at least in California, are supposed to go through the checks. It's safer, but you still have your own work to do. Let's put it that way.

Q: It sounds to me from our conversation so far that there aren't a lot of bright lines that allow you to tell parents, "If you see this, do this."

A: No there aren't.

Q: There are a lot of gray areas. But are there *any* bright lines? Not even something that you set out in advance. But just looking back on your experience, have there been behaviors that have been described to you where you say, "If it were me, I'd be gone tomorrow"? Bright lines in child care.

A: I think the father, when he was saying his kid was clinging onto him. When you have a kid who's pleading with you, "Please don't leave me there." That's pretty right there. There's something wrong. The bright line is really: Know your child and know what's really out of character for your child. No matter what their age, you know it. And the more tuned in you are to your child, the clearer it's going to be when something's wrong.

Q: From the little research that's been done in this area, it appears that home day cares, small home day cares, are the most dangerous for children. Does this correspond to your experience and your view?

A: Well, you know, I've had a few people who went to home day cares where something went really wrong. I think home day cares—I would have to check the research, but there are a lot more accidents in home day care. And I think the situations where there have been outright abuses, they happen everywhere because it's dealing with a troubled person or troubled people. And that's a different kind of situation. But accidents, the less monitoring and the less—Sometimes it's just lack of information. People don't understand why something would be dangerous until a terrible accident happens. So it makes sense to me that home day cares may be more dangerous, but I suspect this might be more about accidents than abuses. But I don't know.

Q: Two of the explanations I've heard from another expert who has studied this—and there's a lot of speculation, because as I said, there isn't a lot of research—but one is that when you have a single individual in a home, it's common that they take care of more children than they're supposed to. The legal number is often six, and that includes your own children under the age of twelve.

A: Right.

Q: And many of the women who are doing this have young children, but many take more than six in addition to their own. And the more children you have, the less supervision they're getting.

A: Right.

Q: Second, in a day care center or a preschool like the kind you've been discussing, where you have three or four employees, there are not only parents watching, there are other employees watching . . .

A: Coworkers watching, right.

Q: When you have one person working alone, there's less of that kind of scrutiny that you talked about earlier. And that may lead people to behave in ways that aren't safe.

A: Yeah, I think that's true.

Q: Now I want to go back and look at some of the things you've said, and maybe you can expand on them. What would make day care safer in this country? If you were the day care czar—if we had a day care czar, and you were she—and you could wave your wand and say, "By my decree, tomorrow all of these things will be true of every day care in the country," what would you do?

A: First of all, you do need whoever is providing day care to have child development information and training. And that's something that should be publicly available, or very low cost. Caregivers need the information, they need to understand what children are like at different stages of development, what their basic needs are, how you are enhancing their development by things that you do. That has to be part of it. It does need to be a situation where there are regulations that make sense and they're uniform. Because at this point I don't think they are. So there needs to be training, there needs to be education, there needs to be accreditation. There need to be safe environments.

Q: When you say caregivers need an education in child development, it's possible that some people are thinking, "Well, they've been parents themselves and they've raised a kid up to age fifteen, and now they're running a home day care. They obviously have their education in child development through the experience of raising a child."

A: Right. And they have it for children of the temperament of the children they've raised. They don't necessarily have it for the temperament of other children. And I'm not saying they have to go back and get a degree. But I think workshops on child development, workshops particularly on zero to three.

Q: So there's a lot to learn beyond simply your own experience as a parent.

A: Exactly.

Q: Are there other things you'd like to see widely adopted in child care?

A: Work-based day care. That's the other thing. Families do better in the places where there's a day care center at the workplace, so parents can go and visit their kids on lunch hour and see that they're doing okay. That's something that's really helpful.

Q: So if more companies made a larger commitment to making day care part of the benefit package—

A: Then you'd have happier employees, fewer absences. There would be so many things that would work well with that set-up. And in terms of technology, that's all part of it. I think it's reassuring to parents to check up on how their kid is doing. I know one mom: "Oh, I just keep the little screen on my computer at work. And then I just periodically say, 'Oh, what's he doing? Oh, he's fine.'"

Q: There's no reason why there couldn't be that little window on every parent's computer, if there were a commitment—if the government offered funding. Or maybe it should be the parents who decide—the equipment isn't that expensive—"We're willing to go in on this." Or maybe the providers should charge a little more money and install the equipment themselves. Is this important?

A: I think it depends on—You know, some people see it as invasive. You kind of have to figure out what works for you and what does not.

Q: Any final thoughts?

A: When you visit a program or a place or someone's home, look around and say, "Is this someplace where I would want to be?" My granddaughter's day care center, you walk in and you see places to climb, places to flop down. There's a fish tank. There's art all over the walls. It looks like a fun place to hang out. So you also want to get that feeling: What does it feel like to be here?

———

Nora Baladerian was interviewed on October 11, 2015.

Baladerian, who was seventy at the time of this interview, is a psychologist who is best known for her work with children and adults with disabilities—especially those who have been victims of trauma or abuse. Based in Los Angeles, Baladerian earned her Ph.D. in psychology at Sierra University in 1985. She currently directs the West Los Angeles Trauma and Crime Victim Center, and is a prolific author and frequent guest speaker at professional conferences. She also has experience working with the elderly. The focus of her work these days, she explains, is reducing the risk of abuse. And a big part of that is convincing the primary caregivers of individuals who are enrolled in programs that abuse can and does happen everywhere. To illustrate, she described a special school for children with disabilities where eight children with autism who were all under the age of ten were beaten daily and subjected to verbal and emotional abuse. Their parents noted the children's bruises and their drastically altered behavior, and asked the teachers for explanations. "Here's the interesting thing," Baladerian says. Even though the parents did not believe the "stock answers" they were given about children "playing rough" and falling down, "there is a universal denial that the school staff could be the source of their children's problems."

Q: I don't know if you've had enough experience with day care settings, such as the kind I've been looking at, but the parents you've worked with have a certain relationship with the teacher, a certain respect for the teacher's role, and when they're told by the teacher, "This is what's going on," they have a tendency to accept that. I'm wondering how that might correspond to the head of a day care, whether it's a larger center or the kind I'm looking at, a home-based day care.

A: What I'm looking at is a loyalty to the teacher or the program director. They really, really trust this person.

Q: Why?

A: Ah. Well, I think one aspect with my kids—but I think it's true of any kids—the individual who is the care provider has a reputation. And so they trust that. Oh, they've been here for a year or two years. And they have let's say a day care license. And we know that when people are licensed they have met X criteria. And they would not want to lose their license, because this is their livelihood. And look at how wonderful they are, because they're dealing with kids all day. And that's a hard job. That's a really hard job to deal with ten, twelve, eight kids or whatever. So there's enormous trust without reflection. They're not asking questions. They're not insisting on dropping in. Which is part of my Ten Tips [on my website].

Q: And that's the next thing I was going to ask. You mentioned that the school you were looking at didn't allow unannounced visits. Some parents get around that by picking up a child early or late. Is that something that parents were able to do to allow them to get insight into what was going on?

A: They didn't tend to do that because they didn't suspect the school.

Q: What about peering through windows? Was that even a possibility at that facility?

A: It didn't occur to anybody that I've talked to so far, which is a lot of people. You peek through a window if you suspect something. But they weren't suspecting the school. They would talk to their partners—their husbands and wives: "What in the heck could be going on?" And they would even dance around it. "Well, do you think it could be at the school?" "No. It couldn't be."

Q: I'm wondering whether—not in this place, because you've already spelled out the limitations of the inquires—but there are plenty of examples of technology being used to help parents monitor all kinds of facilities. The nannycam, if you have an au pair. You've got home-based facilities where there's a camera in a room that's often used for the children's care. Is any of that being used these days, in your experience, to give parents of these children an opportunity to see how things are going?

A: No. There's been quite a bit of discussion about that. The petitions that have arisen asking for some kind of electronic monitoring have universally been denied because the recording would involve other children. This is a public school—or it may be a private school funded by the county. And so it would violate privacy rules. So no, you can't do that. In Texas in August or September 2015, they finally got legislation passed that allows videos in special ed classrooms only. But that's the only state where that's happened. Now parents have put recording devices—audio recording devices—sewn them into their kids' clothes. Interesting, huh?

Q: Surreptitiously.

A: Oh yes. Because they're not allowed to record anything. So they sew it into their kids' jackets and things like this. I love those. And then they have listened later. None of the parents that I've worked with directly have done that, but I do a weekly news feed. I read news articles on abuse and people with disabilities across the nation every week. So I kind of keep up with that.

Q: Wow.

A: Parents who have done the recording surreptitiously and then listened to it later have heard horrible goings-on, and usually that's their [kid's] last day at that school. And then the next day they may confront the school or they call the police or something. But those are the only parents that have gotten through that barrier, the invisible brain barrier that says, "It couldn't be at the day program. It's got to be something else."

That's why I wrote the Ten Tips. That was for a woman who was seventy and finally said, "I cannot adequately care anymore for my thirty-six-old child with autism. I just can't do it." And so very reluctantly she put her child into an independent living program with caregivers in his apartment—three staff—who would be caring for him. He started to have bruises when she visited him once a week. And she asked, "What's going on with the bruises?" And the staff said, "Oh, you know, he falls a lot." So after many weeks of that, she hid a nannycam in his room. And after a week she came home to watch it, and what she saw was her naked son on the floor of his bedroom being kicked and beaten by two of the male staff while the female staff watched from the doorway.

Q: Awful.

A: And that was pretty much daily. So then she knew what happened. And after two weeks of this—he's continuing to get beaten—she went back and confronted the staff, which is not the recommended thing to do. But nonetheless, that's what she did. And their immediate action was to do what? Run to the bedroom and find the nannycam currently running and destroy the evidence.

Q: That's right in your Ten Tips: why not to [confront abusive caregivers].

A: It's ten tips to become aware that abuse exists period. And that there isn't any one locale—school, or a day program, or a residence—that's going to be safe. Just know that. It's basically for [parents] to have a wakeup call. Abuse exists. It occurs anywhere you are not with your kids. If you see signs of anything that is weird, odd, off, let that be a wakeup call to you to heighten your awareness, and then to start doing something different. Dropping in, asking for supervisors, changing staff, putting in a nannycam. And when they feel sure that their child is being abused, remove the kid and call the authorities. And document what they're doing. But the first thing that has to happen is awareness that abuse can and does happen in places where you've been promised it will never happen.

Q: Let me ask this. You've written that you are not a suspicious person. You expect that people will behave properly.

A: [Laughing] How dare you! How dare you!

Q: And you recognize that sometimes this doesn't serve you so well. And you have to make adjustments. And you can try to train yourself to be more suspicious. But you choose not to try to change your personality, just adjust as you must. I said that not to try to contradict what you were just saying, but to ask you this. Do you recommend that parents, when their child is in a day care or a facility like the one you were describing, should their attitude be one of suspicion? Or what kind of attitude do you recommend they enter with?

A: Oh, um . . . I don't know exactly how to characterize it. That's a great question, and I feel like I'm caught with my pants down. On the other hand, this is a very specific kind of situation. If I have a kid that needs care, I'm in a different situation. Or if I have a parent [who needs care]. It could be anybody. But if I am responsible for another human being, and I have to deliver that human being to X location, I think it's good to know a couple of things. One, anybody can be abused anywhere. You don't have to have a disability. I was just working with a person who was a hospital patient sexually assaulted right after a procedure while she was in the twilight zone. She was definitely disabled in that moment, but she's not a person who has a disability. But I would say, in answer to your question, because children are so vulnerable, that's a reason to say, "I wonder what precautions I should be taking." It's knowing that my special person is more likely to be a victim of abuse than others. That would be an important piece of information to have. If I have that piece of information, then I might be more alert to changes that signal abuse.

Q: Changes in a child's behavior, you mean.

A: I do trust people, and I have gotten into very bad situations because I do trust people. I just do. But in this, I'm talking about the importance of being alerted to possible danger. It would be a great help in not necessarily avoiding but maybe shortening the time when somebody is under an abusive situation. I mean if my kid came home with bruises all of a sudden one time, and I was told, "Oh, well, they were falling on the playground," I might buy that. But I wouldn't buy it every day if I were made aware that abuse happens, and it happens by responsible adults in responsible agencies. That's the difference. The Ten Tips works just as well with seniors as it does with children or adults with disabilities.

Q: I'm glad you brought that up. And we'll talk about seniors again before we're finished. But I want to focus on the kind of balance you might try and strike between creating in the parent's mind the possibility that something bad could happen and scaring the bejesus out of them when they're already nervous—especially in the early stages of sending a very young child, an infant or a toddler, to day care, which is not even necessarily a choice.

A: To me, it's sort of like saying, "Never cross the street." There's the possibility if you cross the street you're going to get squooshed like a bug, right? It's a kind of balance. I don't know if you remember this: Trust and verify. It's all trust and verify and monitoring for me. And so that's why in my book on risk reduction, I promote the idea of getting to know the people that are going to be caring for your kid. But not only getting to know them, verify what you've learned. So, for example, if they come to see me as a therapist, and I see their child alone in a room behind two locked doors—the one to the office and the one from the main reception area— how do they know I'm not abusing their kids? They don't. But a precaution might be to look me up and see if I'm really licensed. And a precaution might be to inquire about me to other people that they may know, or sit in the room with me. Or what I do is I invite them to do this. I leave my doors unlocked between the hallways and my office, and I invite parents to pop in for no reason from time to time, so that the kid gets the picture, "Oh, my parents could pop in anytime." It's a safety factor and a model.

Q: Is that really important for day cares, that they are open, accessible, available?

A: Oh yes. People should be invited to pop in anytime. And if they're not, if they're told, "No, you can only come at X hours" or "You have to have an appointment"—Actually, in several of the cases that I have been working on, they have been told, "You can come visit anytime you like, but you have to have an appointment." Some parents figured that out when they were seeing these vast changes in their kids, and just decided to go without an appointment, and have seen—Let's see, who was that? One had the aide who was kicking the child—and that's when there were bruises—and another was where her kid was put in the cage all day. And when she would go for visits to the classroom before, she had to say what time. The office would call the teacher and say, "Sally is coming," which gave them enough time to get the kid out of the cage. So she never knew.

Q: Is that a deal-breaker: You can't visit unannounced without an appointment?
A: Yeah. Absolutely.

Q: That's a red flag that says, "I'm not using this facility."
A: Absolutely. And the same thing for a nursing home. I used to work with the elderly. That's an absolute red flag.

Q: Are there others that you feel as strongly about?
A: Here's another thing that I'm very unhappy about: background checks. The fact of the matter is you can do background checks initially, which is usually done. Often in day care, because they're tight for getting staff in, they don't complete the background check before employment begins. But even so, the background check depends upon how extensive you do it. You could do one that's just for your county, or you could do one that's just for your state, but it doesn't address certain things. If he's moved into the state from another place where he's been in prison, for example, it's not going to show up. I had a client who was sexually assaulted by her Medicaid-paid transportation provider. In the aftermath—after she reported it and it was being investigated—the law enforcement officer went to the transportation provider's office and said, "You have hired this person. Did you do a background check?" "Sure did." And the officer said, "Can I see it?" And the provider reached into his desk and pulled out an unopened envelope. So the officer said, "Let's open it." And they found that he was a convicted murderer on early release.

And that's why my client and others were sexually assaulted by this guy, who actually left her in the forest to fend for herself, and she got up and ran after him and said, "You have to take me home. My mom's going to be really mad that I'm late." Which is very typical of people with developmental disabilities. However, this guy is out now. And he can go to any state not contiguous to Oregon and work without that being found out. He can work in elder care. That's easy. He can work in day care. He can work in anything, and it's not going to be found out unless they do a more extensive national data background.

Q: Is there a national database?
A: No.

Q: Is that something you advocate—that there should be some big national database for caregivers?

A: Of course. Absolutely. Can you imagine if in the day care programs you're working with they have convicted murders out on release, having paid their debt to society? So that's why I say, "Parents, do your own."

Q: Now home-based day cares are a little different in that they're really small. The provider is usually a parent, usually a woman who often has young kids of her own. Many times they're not registered. They may charge less money. They may have good word-of-mouth in the community. And those who are registered—in South Carolina, to register a home day care, you just have to fill out a piece of paper and get three people to write recommendations for you and voila! That's it. So there isn't any real check.

A: But the parent can do their own check. They can do their own background check and they can Google them, for goodness sake. "Mary Jo Smith arrest." "Mary Jo Smith abuse." And you can do your own background check. You can pay for it yourself. I think it's worth $15 or $30 [which some online services charge]. It's your kid's life. So if the state doesn't do it, then fine, the parents should do it. If their kid needs a shot, they're going to pay for it. If they need a child car seat, they're going to buy it. So why not buy some knowledge about the person? And it's not just the woman. Who else is in the house? That's when we get into real trouble. It's the boarder, it's the uncle, it's the grandpa that could be abusive, a drug addict, somebody who's not doing too well so they're staying at mom's house, or grandma, or auntie, or whatever she is. They're making a little money mowing the lawn, and might not have such a great background, and you wouldn't necessarily want your kid with that person.

Q: And the other thing about the home-based day care situation is most states have a rule that says you can only care for six children, and that includes your own children under the age of twelve. And I think it's extremely common for that rule to be ignored—by both the caregiver and the parents, who obviously see different numbers than what they ought to know is the requirement.

A: In the home, if those people were asked, "You know, I'd really like to have a nannycam in here. Is that okay with you?" Would most say yes or would most say no?

Q: Good question. I don't know.

A: I think it's a test. I think if they say no, I might choose somebody else. Because why wouldn't they be open to having the day care available remotely? Now we're in an age of knowing. When my kid was young, my kid went to day care of course, and I never was alerted to any of these things. But I remember I did take her out of one after a week. And I can't remember exactly what all the circumstances were, but I had a bad experience or a bad feeling. I didn't see anything bad happening, but it just was not good. And I removed her. I was innocent in those days to this as a problem. And I actually got very good day care most of the—all of the time.

Q: The most vulnerable population is young, preverbal children—infants and toddlers—who can't communicate in words, can't come home and complain by speaking sentences. . . . You're dealing with a population where the communication difficulties can be common for years, maybe a lifetime. And that has to create a real vulnerability. How do you and the parents deal with that?

A: I wrote a book called "A Risk Reduction Workbook for Parents and Service Providers: Practices to Reduce the Risk of Abuse, Including Sexual Violence, Against People with Intellectual and Developmental Disabilities." I couldn't think of a longer title. It's a complex rubric which I think you'll be able to grasp pretty quickly. Before, during, and after. You like that?

Q: I get it.

A: Yeah. And the analogy is some natural disaster: floods, hurricanes, tornados, earthquakes, whatever. We don't want it to happen, but it could. And a lot of people prepare—like if they know a hurricane is coming, they leave. They drive away. Or if it's an earthquake, a lot of us in California have earthquake separation kits or disaster kits or whatever you call them. So we're sort of ready in case that disaster happens. We should do the same with abuse. We should have our disaster preparedness kit, which includes informing the children that sometimes people do bad things to us. It's just part of life, like crossing the street. You don't want to get squooshed like a bug. You tell them about getting squooshed like a bug. Not to scare them. Just to say, "This could happen. We don't want this to happen to you, so we take these measures." And this is all the "before" [stage].

Now kids who don't have language, you can't do this. But for elders who may be aphasic and may not be able to speak anymore, for them they have icons that they can point to, or cards that are like icons that they can put in a sequence to indicate that someone has been hitting them or sexually abusing them or starving them or something. So you teach them. Because they're taught all sorts of things, you know, "I need to go to the toilet." Or "I want a sandwich." Or "I want my iPad." Their emergency is not having their iPad. They're able to communicate that in one way or another. Lunging for the iPad. Or lunging for the fridge. Or trying to get water. So parents know how kids communicate whatever it is that they are able to communicate. And then you build on it. So in my book, for example, I have a communication workbook. I just took stuff off the Internet that shows a speech and language teacher, a neighbor, a bus driver, a custodian. So you want them to be able to communicate if something bad happens—which we don't want, but it could. Who done it? So they can point to the custodian.

Then there's the "during." And during "during," parents can't do anything because they're not there. But then "after" is essential. It's absolutely essential. It's when they can use that communication book and then reenact what happened at school.

Q: Are you talking about doing this routinely, or only when you know there's been a problem?

A: When you know there's something very wrong. When he comes home with bruises. They shouldn't come home from school like that. That's when you do your "after."

Q: I'm of an age, not so different than yours, where I dealt with aging parents. So we find ourselves again playing parent, finding caregivers, doing the same kinds of things that my wife and I did many years ago with our two young boys. In your experience, is this process pretty similar?

A: I would say so. I would put in nannycams once parents are at home, and you have caregivers coming into the home. I would certainly put up nannycams, and I would do the background check, and all the things we've talked about. Pop in frequently. I would check weight, and health, and blood pressure, and the indicators for aging people. I would check the meds. Do the meds seem to be disappearing at the rate they should be?

Or are the pills gone—being sold somewhere? Are they losing weight? Gaining weight? Sleeping all day? So it's basically the same stuff. It's trust but verify. And it's monitoring, monitoring, monitoring. If I could put it in three words, it would be: "trust, verify, monitor."

Q: Those are good ones.

A: If there were another one, it would be "awareness." Be aware that abuse can happen to your loved one. They are vulnerable. So it's assisted living. It's an acute care hospital, where I've had several clients who were sexually abused. One was a woman with an intellectual disability and a broken arm who was sexually assaulted by the nurse's aide. And she reported this to the charge nurse, and the charge nurse said, "Oh, my gosh. Don't tell anybody. Don't tell anybody else. We'll take care of it." And she reported it again to another nurse, and then all the nurses got mad at her. And then they had the HR person finally come down, who told her, "Don't tell anybody." Nice, huh?

Q: Yeah.

A: So a few weeks later she told her mom, but by then all the evidence was gone. She was in there for a broken arm. It could be anywhere.

Q: We all have occasions when, if we are not permanently disabled, we are temporarily disabled. And I was thinking about sexual assaults on campus and how frequently alcohol is involved. It's like you are disabling yourself.

A: Oh yeah. A self-induced temporary disability. There's a lot of drunkenness around these parts. Yeah, we do that to ourselves, and it's sort of acceptable. But I think that abuse at any level of any person who's vulnerable at any time [is unacceptable]. Sometimes people say, "Oh, the MOST VULNERABLE PEOPLE ARE blah blah blah." I go to these conferences all the time, and it says, "Most Vulnerable Population" and then it names some teenagers or whatever. And I'm thinking, "What about the three-week infant that's being sexually assaulted by the dad? That's pretty vulnerable." I don't want to make comparisons, but how many thousands of infants at their six-week check-up have syphilis and gonorrhea? But you can't really say, "I don't like comparing, though my people are THE MOST whatever."

Q: I think most people in this country don't understand that, or want to understand that. They don't want to even contemplate it.

A: Yeah. And they don't want to contemplate abuse of children. And they don't want to contemplate abuse of children and adults with disabilities. Even elder abuse has finally, over the last twenty years, gotten some play. And still we don't have general knowledge of abuse of people with disabilities. And I don't know how much is really accepted about abuse in day care. Do you?

Q: No.

A: Is it a high awareness or a low awareness?

Q: I think it's a pretty low awareness because people, when they select a day care, they get really emotionally invested in believing a) they made the right choice; and b) this person loves my child as much as I do. My child is in as good hands as he or she would be with me. A lot of people have a need to believe that because they feel guilty, and because they really, really *want* to believe it. Flora Colao, who I interviewed yesterday, was talking about playing detective—you have to play detective sometimes. It seems to me you're saying the same thing.

A: Yes. An investigator is investigating something. There's a belief that something may be wrong or may go wrong. Whereas the others are not thinking that something may go wrong. They're thinking, "Thank God I found someplace for my child to be safe!" And even though there's these screaming signs that he's not okay there, they don't take the next step to say, "Maybe it's the place he's at all day." I don't know how to get through that, except keep saying, "It happens everywhere. It can happen to anyone." I was doing a lecture on abuse and special ed. And [afterward] a couple of teachers came up to me and said, "You know, I've been a special ed teacher for forty years, and I've never had a kid abused that I've ever taught." And I said, "Then you just didn't know about them." They said, "No one would abuse a special ed kid." So I learned from that that this must be a pervasive belief: They're so vulnerable, that no one would ever do that. And so special ed teachers hang on to [that belief] for dear life.

And then I get those kids.

Notes on Sources

When people are quoted in this book, unless otherwise indicated, I interviewed them myself. Most of the interviews with the day care parents, the lawyers, and the Cutros and their families occurred after Gail Cutro was convicted in her first trial and before her conviction was overturned on appeal. Some sources were interviewed multiple times over many months, but the majority took place in South Carolina in 1997, as noted in the text.

Two experts who were quoted were also interviewed more than once, but later. Forensic psychologist Dr. Joel Dvoskin was interviewed in 1999, and sociologist Dr. Julia Wrigley was interviewed in 2005.

Several sources were parents who asked that their names be changed to protect the privacy of their children. Virtually all of these individuals knew full well that their identities would be readily apparent to insiders within their community. The first time a pseudonym is introduced, it appears in quotation marks. These are the only names that have been changed.

The account of Gail Cutro's first trial was based on tape recordings of the trial and the complete transcript. In some instances I also interviewed the lawyers about particular moments in the trial, and I referred to these while recounting the testimony.

I attended the second and third trials, and my descriptions of these came from my own reporting. I also attended the oral arguments on the first appeal, and I witnessed the confrontation between Josh Cutro and Johnny Gasser immediately after.

I had access to a vast collection of documents related to the Cutros. In addition to the array introduced into evidence in the trials, I was able to obtain many that were not part of that collection but were invaluable in affording me insight into the operations of the day care. These materials included the statements that all parents who had used the day care gave the police. I was also able to review case notes recorded by the investigators from SLED's Child Fatality Department; the prosecutor's notes; the notes taken by various employees of the two Departments of Social Services that investigated; the public health records from the mental health professionals who had treated Gail Cutro as well as her medical records. As discussed in the text, Gail Cutro also allowed me to interview Dr. Selman Watson and Dr. Geoffrey McKee, and to read Dr. Watson's evaluation and Dr. McKee's test results.

Other documents in the text appeared verbatim. Missy Daniel's letters to Gail Cutro, for example, and Pat Hallman's letter back, were reproduced complete and unchanged. In these cases, as with Gail Cutro's "Babysitters Story," I did not alter the grammar or spelling. They were quoted exactly as they were written.

Several audio recordings were also quoted from extensively. Most of these were recorded by SLED, and they included Missy Daniel's meeting with Gail Cutro and Pat Hallman, and the message Missy later left on Gail's answering machine. I also obtained audio recordings of Gail Cutro's parole hearings.

The books and newspaper articles listed below provided valuable information. Some of them were mentioned in the text, but some that were not contained essential background material from which I drew. I particularly want to acknowledge *Irmo and the Dutch Fork Legacy: A Centennial Celebration,* a rich and absorbing history of the area.

Selected Bibliography

Able, Gene (editor and chief writer), *Irmo and the Dutch Fork Legacy: A Centennial Celebration* (Irmo, S.C.: The Independent News for the Irmo Centennial Commission, 1990).

Bell, Nicole, "Husband of Convicted Child Killer Pleads Guilty to Variety of Charges," wistv.com, January 16, 2004.

Brundrett, Rick, "Cutro Trial Juror Admits He 'Caved In'" *The State* (Columbia, S.C.), July 6, 2000 (following the verdict after the third trial).

Brundrett, Rick, "Cutro Says He Was Hoping to Commit 'Suicide by Cop,'" *The State* (Columbia, S.C.), July 4, 2003.

ChildCare Aware of America, "Child Care in America: 2014 State Fact Sheets" (www.childcareaware.org).

Cutro, Gail, Parole Hearings of January 30, 2013; January 27, 2015; January 25, 2017; April 24, 2019.

Egginton, Joyce, *From Cradle to Grave: The Short Lives and Strange Deaths of Mary Beth Tinning's Nine Children* (New York: William Morrow and Company, 1989).

Egginton, Joyce, *Circle of Fire: Murder and Betrayal in the 'Swiss Nanny' Case* (New York: William Morrow and Company, 1994).

Emery, John; Gilbert, Enid; Zugibe, Frederick, "Three Crib Deaths, a Babyminder and Probable Infanticide," *Medicine, Science and the Law*, 1988; 28(3):205–11 (about the Pankow case in Wisconsin).

Firstman, Richard; Talan, Jamie, *The Death of Innocents: A True Story of Murder, Medicine, and High-Stakes Science* (New York: Bantam Books, 1997).

Howatt, Glenn; Olson, Jeremy; Schrade, Brad, "The Day Care Threat," Minneapolis *Star Tribune*, May-December 2012. (Winner of the 2013 Pulitzer Prize in Journalism for local reporting.)

Koenig, Sarah (host and chief writer), "Serial," podcast produced by WBEZ Chicago, October-December 2014.

LeBlanc, Clif, "Who's Watching Day Care?" *The State* (Columbia, S.C.), January 21–22, 1996.

LeBlanc, Clif, "'Guilty' Was One Vote Away," *The State* (Columbia, S.C.), June 15, 1999 (following the hung jury after the second trial).

LeBlanc, Clif, "Cutro Faces Charge of Shoplifting," *The State*, September 26, 1997.

LeBlanc, Clif, "Cutro's Husband Sentenced to 12 Years," *The State*, January 17, 2004.

Lundstrom, Marjie; Sharpe, Rochelle, "Getting Away with Murder," Gannett News Service, December 12, 1990. (Winner of the 1991 Pulitzer Prize in Journalism for national reporting.)

Miller, Jeff; Pardue, Douglas, "Burying Our Mistakes," *The State* (Columbia, S.C.), May 22–25, 1994.

Santelli, Josephine J., *The Daycare Rating Book: How to Find, Select and Evaluate High Quality Childcare—and Keep It Once You've Found It* (South Burlington, Vermont: Up Spirit Press, 2004).

Siegel, Barry, *A Death in White Bear Lake: The True Chronicle of an All-American Town* (New York: Bantam Books, 1990).

Acknowledgments

In its earliest stages, this book was supported by a Prudential Fellowship for Children and the News at Columbia University's Graduate School of Journalism. I would like to thank the Prudential Foundation and Columbia professors Dr. Nicholas Cunningham, Samuel Freedman, LynNell Hancock, Michele Ingrassia, David Klatell, and Steven Ross for their help during my fellowship year.

My debt to my many sources in South Carolina is huge and obvious. Without all of them, this would have been a very different book. Their contributions redoubled my determination to see this project through. I am profoundly grateful to them all.

Many others helped me behind the scenes. I would particularly like to thank Elizabeth Dearborn, Phil Dematteis, Jay Elliott, Joan Larson, Rick Layman, Bob Lescher, Gigi Mark, Dr. Donna Rosenberg, Peter Rubie, and, as always, Andrew Vachss.

Alice Vachss, my eBook publisher and editor, was extraordinary. Not only did she fuss over the details with her brilliant legal mind, she was the readers' constant advocate, always pressing for a powerful narrative, but never at the expense of clarity.

About the Author

DAVID HECHLER is a writer, editor, and a reporter who has covered the legal beat for many years. He was the Executive Editor of *Corporate Counsel* magazine, where his reporting, writing, and editing earned top awards from the two major business press associations.

A graduate of Grinnell College, Hechler went on to earn a master's in teaching from Brown University, and taught high school English for seven years. He then completed a second master's degree at Columbia University's Graduate School of Journalism.

His work at Columbia led to his first book, *The Battle and the Backlash: The Child Sexual Abuse War*, which won critical praise from publications as diverse as *The New York Times* and the *Michigan Law Review*. *In Good Hands* was also incubated at Columbia. He began working on it there as a Prudential Fellow for Children and the News.

In 2017, The American Society of Journalists and Authors awarded *In Good Hands* first prize for a book of general nonfiction.